This is an annual. That is to say, it is substantially revised each year, the new edition appearing in January of that year. Those wishing to submit additions, corrections, or suggestions for the 1990 edition should submit them prior to June 1, 1989 using the form provided in the back of this book. (Letters reaching us after that date will have to wait for the 1991 edition.)

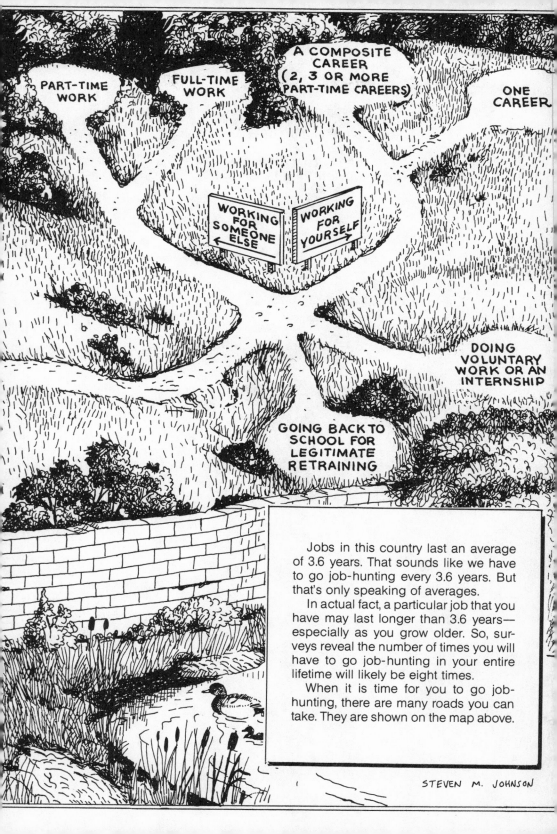

Jobs in this country last an average of 3.6 years. That sounds like we have to go job-hunting every 3.6 years. But that's only speaking of averages.

In actual fact, a particular job that you have may last longer than 3.6 years—especially as you grow older. So, surveys reveal the number of times you will have to go job-hunting in your entire lifetime will likely be eight times.

When it is time for you to go job-hunting, there are many roads you can take. They are shown on the map above.

Other Books by Richard N. Bolles

The Three Boxes of Life,
  And How To Get Out of Them

Where Do I Go From Here With My Life?
  (co-authored with John C. Crystal)

1989 Edition

What Color Is Your Parachute?

A Practical Manual
for
Job-Hunters
& Career Changers

by

Richard Nelson Bolles

Ten Speed Press

Cover art by Jeannie Winston
The map drawing on the frontispiece is by Steven M. Johnson,
author of *What The World Needs Now*

© Copyright 1981. United Features Syndicate, Inc. Used by permission.

Type set by Haru Composition, San Francisco, and The Mac Studio, San Francisco
Consolidated Printers, Inc., Berkeley, California
Printed in the United States of America

Contents

How You Can Make It Better Still: A Systematic Approach To Job-Hunting & Career Change

For Further Help:

How To Find Your Mission In Life

Miscellanea

The Preface

In Memoriam
John Crystal
1920-1988

He said:
"Be yourself. No one else is qualified."
He said:
"In order to get a job you will be happy in,
You must know what you want to do.
Asking this question is so simplistic,
It is embarrassing. But
Most people do not know what they want to do
With their lives."
He said:
"There may be central casting in Hollywood,
and personnel in the Army,
But it's not like that in real life.
Most jobs,
And particularly the better ones,
Are never listed
In the ads or agencies."
And he said:
"The biggest myth of all
Is that there are no jobs available.
Between one and two million jobs open up
Every month."

He said,
And he lived,
And he died.
September 10, 1988.

He was a brilliant man.
And **Parachute** owes much of its popularity
To him.
Without his ideas
And insights
Into the job hunt,
This book would have been
A shadow
Only
Of what it is today.
And the thousands of lives
That have been changed by these ideas
Would not have been changed
To anything like that degree.

He was a laughing man,
Who loved the irony in life.
We sat and laughed
Together
In many a city
Over many a meal,
In many an outdoor cafe
During these past twenty years.

He was a learned man,
Spoke a dozen languages
Fluently
And loved to confound the waiters
In this ethnic restaurant or that
By ordering his meal
In their language
Without a trace of accent.
Had a degree in economics,
From Columbia College
And a degree in wisdom
Which Life had bestowed on him.

He was a well-traveled man,
Having been a counterspy in Europe
During the Second World War,
And then having helped set up
The European division

Of a large well-known corporation,
In the days of peace.
He loved Italy
And Austria,
And went back there just this past June
To renew his love affair
With the hills so alive
With the sound of music.

He was a trusting man.
Too trusting, sometimes.
"A loving and beloved voice
Rings softly in my ears,"
Said he,
"My mother's,
Unfortunately long ago,
Saying over and over again,
'You are much too trusting a soul
Ever to survive
In this world.' "

And when people lied to him,
Or took advantage of him,
As they occasionally did in his life,
He was an angry man,
Yes, he could be a
Very angry man - -
Most particularly at the injustices
Done not to him
But to the innocent job-hunters
Who went forth, as he said,
Like lambs
Among wolves.
"I share passionately,"
He once wrote to me,
"Your cordial dislike for liars.
Why in God's name,
I wonder,
Are there so many of them?"

He was a gracious man.
The thank-you note
Was always forthcoming
Written in his own hand
After every act of kindness
Extended to him
By anyone.
He was always so
Gracious,
He'd preface every request with
"If you wouldn't mind . . . ."
He was always so
Grateful
To his associate Nella
Who rescued his organization
When it was floundering
And put it,
And him,
On an even keel.

And, he was a loving man:
Adored his daughter,
Barbie,
And his beloved Diane.
Spoke glowingly of his sister
Isabel,
And was a friend to me
As few friends are,
Through thick and thin,
Never failing to salute
Any talent he saw in others:
"Dick, you are one of the two
Best teachers
I have ever seen
In my life."
He said it over the years
At least two dozen times to me; but then
He was that way with everyone,
For he was always
Dipping into the well of compliments
That he carried

Please turn to page 378

*Fairy Godmother,
where were you
when I needed you?*

Cinderella

CHAPTER ONE

A Job-Hunting
We Will Go

Okay, this is it.
You've been idly thinking about it, off and on, for
some time now, wondering what it would be like.
To be earning your bread in the marketplace.
Or maybe you're already out there,
And the problem is choosing another job — or career —
The old one having run out of gas, as it were.
Anyhow, the moment of truth has arrived.
For one reason or another, you've got to get at it —
Go out, and look for a job, for the first time or the twentieth.
You've heard of course, all the horror stories.
Of ex-executives working as taxi-drivers
Of former college profs with two masters degrees
working as countermen in a delicatessen.
Of women Ph.D.s who can only get a job as a secretary.
Of laid-off auto-workers waiting for the call (back to work)
that never comes.
And you wonder what lies in store for *you*.

Of course, it may be that the problem is all solved.
Maybe some friend or relative has button-holed you
and said, "Why not come and work for me?"
So, your job-hunt ends before it begins.
Or, it may be that you came into your present
career after a full life doing something else, and
You know you're welcome back there, anytime;
Anytime, they said.
And, assuming they meant it,
no problem, right?
So long as that's what you still want to do.
Or maybe you've decided this is the time to
adopt a simpler way of living,
And, so far, it's going well.
But for the vast majority of us,
that isn't how it goes.
We have to find a job, we do,
And no one's making it any easier.
We feel like Don Quixote, mounted, lance in hand; and
the job-hunt is our windmill.

Those who have gone this way before us
   all tell us the very same thing:
      This is how we all go about it, when our job-hunting time has come:
       We procrastinate,
         That's what we do.
          Busy winding things up, we say.
           Or, just waiting until we feel a little less 'burnt-out' and
           more 'up' for the task ahead, we say.
          Actually, if the truth were known,
          we're hoping for that miracle,
          you know the one:
          that if we just sit tight a little longer,
          we won't have to go job-hunting at all, because
          the job will come hunting for us.
         Right in our front door, it will come.
        To show us we are destiny's favorites,
       Or to prove that God truly loves us.
        But, it doesn't, of course, and
         eventually, we realize, with more than a touch of franticness,
      that time and money
    are beginning to run out.

     Time to begin our job-hunt (or career change) in deadly earnest.
    And all of our familiar friends immediately
   are at our elbow, giving advice —
solicited or unsolicited, as to what it is we should do.
"Jean or Joe, I've always thought you would make a great teacher."
So we ask who they know
in the academic world,
and, armed with that name,
we go a-calling. Calling, and
  sitting, cooling our heels
   in the ante-room of the Dean's office,
    until we are ushered in, at last:
     "And what can I do for you, Mr. or Ms.?"
    We tell them, of course, that we're job-hunting.
     "And one of my friends thought that you..."
    Oops. We watch the face change,

And we (who *do* know something about body language),
    Wait to hear their words catch up with their body.
        "You feel I'm 'over-qualified'? I see.
            Two hundred applications, you say, already in hand
                For five vacancies? I see.
                    No, of course I understand."
                        Strike-out. Back to the drawingboard. More advice, from
                            well-meaning family or friends:
                            "Jean or Joe, have you tried the employment agencies?"
                            "Good thinking. Which ones should I try?
                            The ones that deal with professionals? Where are they?
                            Okay. Good. Down I'll go."
                            And down we do go.
                        Down, down, down, to those agencies.
                        The ante-room again.
                    And those other hopeful, haunted faces.
                A new twist, however: our first bout
            with The Application Form.
        "Previous jobs held.
    List in reverse chronological order."
Filling all the questions out. Followed by
That interminable wait.
 And then, at last, the interviewer,
She of the over-cheerful countenance, and mien —
She talks to us. "Now, let's see, Mr. or Ms.,
What kind of a job are you looking for?"
"Well," we say,
"What do you think I could do?"
She studies, again, the application form;
"It seems to me," she says, "that with your background
—it is a *bit* unusual—
You might do very well in sales."
    "Oh, sales," we say. "Why yes," says she, "in fact
    I think that I could place you almost immediately.
        We'll be in touch with you. Is this your phone?"
            We nod, and shake her hand, and that is the
                Last time
                    We ever hear from her.
                        Words are apparently not always to be believed;
                            Sometimes they are used just to soften rejection.
                        Strike out, number two.

Now, our original ballooning hopes that we would quickly land a job
  are running into some frigid air,
    So we decide to confess at last
      Our need of help — to some of our more successful friends
        in the business world (if we have such)
          Who *surely* know what we should do, at this point.
           The windmill is tiring us. What would they suggest
             that Don (or Donna) Quixote should do?
              "Well," say they (beaming warmly), "what kind of a job
                are you looking for?"
                  Ah, *that*, again! "Well, you know me well, what do you think
                  I can do? I'll try almost anything,"
                we say, now that it's four minutes to midnight, as it were.
            "You know, with all the *kinds* of things I've done —"
        we say; "I mean, I've done this and that, and here and there,
   It all adds up to a kind of puzzling kaleidoscope; but you see things
That I don't see, so there must be *something* you can suggest!"

"Have you tried the want-ads?" asks our friend.
"Or have you gone to see Bill, and Ed, and John, and Frances and Marty?
Ah, no? Well tell them I sent you."
So, off we go—now newly armed, with new advice.
We study the want-ads. Gad, what misery is hidden in
Those little boxes. Misery in jobs which are built
As little boxes, for the large spirits of men and women.
But, nevertheless we dutifully send our resume, such as it is,
To every box that looks as though
It might not be a box.
And wait for the avalanche of replies, from bright-eyed people
Who, seeing our resume, will surely know
Our worth; even if, at this point, our worth seems increasingly
Questionable in our own eyes.
Avalanche? Not even a rolling stone. (Sorry about that, Bob.) Not a pebble.

Well, time to go see all those people that our friend said we
ought to go see.
You know: Bill, and Ed, and John, and Frances and Marty.
They seem slightly perplexed, as to why we've come,
And in the dark about exactly
Just exactly what it is they are supposed to do for us.
We try to take them off the hook; "I thought, friend of my friend,
Your company might need—of course, my experience *has*
Been limited, but I am willing, and I thought perhaps
that you…"

The interview drags on, downhill now, all the way
As our host finishes out the courtesy debt,
Not to us but to the friend that sent us; and
then it is time for us to go.
Boy, do we go! over hill and valley and dale,
Talking to everyone who will listen,
Listening to everyone who will talk
With us; and thinking that surely there must be
Someone who knows how to crack this terribly frustrating
job-market;

This job-hunt process seems the loneliest task of our lives.
And we idly wonder: is it this difficult for other people?
Well, friend, the answer is *YES*.

Are other people *this* discouraged, and desperate
And frustrated, and so low in self-esteem after
A spell of job-hunting?
The answer, again—unhappily—is
YES.

YES.

YES.

8

*Well, yes, you do have
great big teeth; but, never mind
that. You were great to at
least grant me this interview.*

Little Red Riding Hood

CHAPTER TWO

Rejection Shock

From our youth up, we are taught to hate rejection. At least **most** of us are. I know rejection rolls off some people like water off a duck's back. It doesn't bother them at all. Or at least so it appears. And I know that others actually crave rejection and thrive on it, as ancient warriors went out to meet the dragon. Not so with me. Faced with rejection, I usually go into a corner and whimper a lot. Or jump into bed, curl into the fetal position, and turn the electric blanket up to nine. And so apparently it is with the majority of us. We hate rejection. We'll do anything to avoid it, and I mean **anything.**

But then, along comes the job-hunt. Eight times in our lifetime we have to go through this painful process. And, except at its very end, it is **nothing but** a process of rejection, even as I described in the previous chapter. My friend Tom Jackson (in his *Guerrilla Tactics in the Job Market*) has aptly captured this, in his depressingly accurate description of a typical job-hunt as:

NO NO NO NO NO NO NO NO NO NO NO NO NO NO
NO NO NO NO NO NO NO NO NO NO NO NO NO NO
NO NO NO NO NO NO NO NO NO NO NO NO NO NO
NO NO NO NO NO NO NO NO NO NO NO NO YES.

And why does the job-hunting system in this country put us through all this? Because, **the job-hunting system in this country is no system at all.** It is in fact Neanderthal. (Say it again, Sam.)

Year after year, that 'system' condemns each of us to go down the same path, face the same obstacles, make the same mistakes, and face the same rejection.

Moreover, the 'system' is such that often we are given absolutely no warning that we are about to become unemployed. All of a sudden, it is upon us.

And gradually, but only gradually, do we begin to learn what the rules are of this 'system.' And what the rules are, concerning the whole world of work. Slowly and painstakingly we piece them together, and discover finally that there are twelve of them:

1. You will get hired sometimes, for reasons which may have nothing to do with how qualified you are, or aren't. On some unconscious level, you just strike a spark.

2. You will not get hired sometimes, for reasons which may have nothing to do with how qualified you are, or aren't. On some unconscious level, you just don't strike a spark.

3. You will get promoted sometimes, for reasons which may have nothing to do with how well you are doing there.

4. You will not get promoted sometimes, for reasons which may have nothing to do with how well you are doing there.

5. Your employer may treat you well, in accordance with their stated values.

6. Your employer may treat you very badly, in total contradiction of their stated values.

7. Your employer may go on forever, and you may have a job for life, if you want it.

8. Your employer may go out of business, without warning and at a moment's notice, dumping you out on the street.

9. Your employer may stay in business, but you may be abandoned, terminated, fired or otherwise put out on the street, without warning, and at a moment's notice.

10. If you are terminated suddenly, your employer may do everything in the world to help you find other employment.

11. If you are terminated suddenly, your employer may feel that they do not owe you anything. You will feel as though you had been unceremoniously deposited on the rubbage heap.

12. Other employees may promise they will fight to save your job, but you need to be prepared for the fact that when the chips are down, they may actually do nothing to help you.

THE REACTION

Our instinctive first reaction to the fact that "this is how things are" is usually anger. Sometimes fierce anger. Sometimes just a kind of cold soul-chilling disillusionment about the workplace and how it treats its people. If we are wise, we learn to let go of that anger and get on with our lives. But many ex-workers, we know, stay locked in to that anger for the remainder of their lives. They can never forgive the world of work for being so different from what they thought it was going to be. Their anger is a burning fire within them, gradually consuming them.

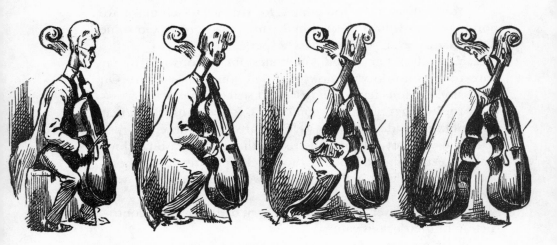

This would not be so, if it were relatively easy to find another job. The anger is perpetuated by the fact that the job-hunting system slowly and systematically strips men and women of their self-esteem, and leaves them feeling devalued and discarded by our society. When it happens to **You,** you go into personal psychological Shock, characterized by a slow or rapid erosion of your self-image, and the conviction that there is something wrong with you. This assumes, consequently, all the proportions of a major crisis in your life, where irritability, withdrawal, broken relationships, divorce, and loneliness may become your constant companions; and even suicide is not unthinkable. All because of the job-hunting system in this country, which is actually a 'non-system.'

This 'non-system' has been given a name by personnel experts. They call this non-system "The Numbers Game." That's right, the numbers game.

THE NUMBERS GAME
AND HOW TO USE IT

You can guess where the term came from. It came from the world of gambling, where if you place sufficient bets on enough different numbers, one of them is bound to pay off, for you. Ah, I see you have grasped immediately what this has to do with job-hunting. Resumes, you say? Ah yes, resumes.

If you're going to use them, you have to play them just like a numbers game: send out just as many as you possibly can. Because, according to a study some time back, only one job offer is tendered and accepted in the whole world of work, for every 1,470 resumes that are floating around out there. Sending 1,469 gets you nowhere. The 1,470th get a job. Hence, "the numbers game."

It's terrible. But you should try to understand it, in all its parts. The reason why you ought to understand it is that you may want to use some parts of it to **supplement** your main job-hunt, as outlined in chapters 4 through 6.

A study of *The Job Hunt* by Harold L. Sheppard and A. Harvey Belitsky[1] revealed that the greater the number of auxiliary avenues used by the job-hunter, the greater the job-finding success. It makes sense, therefore, to know all the avenues that are open to you, how they work and what their limitations are, so that you can choose which avenue or avenues you want to use, and how you want to use them. You will then be in the driver's seat about these matters, as you should be.

The parts of this game most commonly alluded to in books, articles, and elsewhere are:
- mailing out your resume
- answering newspaper ads
- placing newspaper ads
- going to private employment (or placement) agencies
- going to the federal/state employment agency
- contacting executive search firms
- contacting college placement firms
- using executive registers or other forms of clearinghouses
- making personal contacts through friends, personal referrals and so forth.

We will look at the virtues, and defects, of each of these now, in rapid succession; to see why they usually don't work -- and how you might get around their limitations. I will quote some statistics as I go along, in order to *illustrate* the aforementioned defects. So, on with our exciting story.

---

1. In their book, *The Job Hunt: Job-Seeking Behavior of Unemployed Workers in a Local Economy.*

ANSWERING
NEWSPAPER ADS

Experts will advise you, for the sake of thoroughness, to study the job advertisements in your newspaper **daily** and to study all of them, from A to Z -- because ads are alphabetized by job title; and there are some very strange and unpredictable job titles floating around. Then you are advised that if you see an ad for which you might qualify, even three-quarters, send off:

a) your resume, OR

b) your resume and a covering letter, OR

c) just a covering letter

NEWSPAPER ADS

Where found:
1. In the business section of the Sunday *New York Times* and the education section; also in Sunday editions of the *Chicago Tribune* and the *Los Angeles Times*.
2. In the business section (often found with the sports section) of your daily paper; also daily *Wall Street Journal* (especially Tuesday and Wednesday's editions).
3. In the classified section of your daily paper (and Sunday's, too).

Jobs advertised: Usually those which have a clear-cut title, well-defined specifications, and for which either many job-hunters can qualify, or very few.

Number of resumes received by employer as result of the ad: 20 to 1,000, commonly.

Time it takes resumes to come in: 48 to 96 hours. Third day is usually the peak day, after ad is placed.

Number of resumes **not** screened out: Only 2 to 5 out of every 100 (normally) survive. In other words, 95 to 98 out of every 100 answers *are* screened out.

In short, what they're telling you is that you're playing the Numbers Game, when you answer ads. And the odds are stacked against you just about as badly as when you send out your resume scatter-gun fashion. How badly? (Better sit down.) A study conducted in two sample cities revealed, and I quote, that "85% of the employers in San Francisco, and 75% in Salt Lake City, did not hire any employees through want ads" in a typical year. Yes, that said **any** employees, **during the whole year**.[1] Well, then why are ads run? That explanation is rather long, and beyond the scope of this book. But if you're dying to know the answer, I refer you to the chapter called "Blind Ad Man's Bluff" in David Noer's book, *How to Beat The Employment Game*.[2]

Of course, you may be one who still likes to cover all bets, and if so, you will want to know how your resume can be the one that gets through the Screening Process. (Let's be honest: answering ads has paid off, for **some** job-hunters.)

Most of the experts say, if you're going to play this game:

1. All you're trying to do, in answering the ad, is to avoid getting screened out, and to be invited in for an interview. Period. So, quote the ad's specifications, and tailor your resume or case history letter (if you prefer that to a resume) -- so that you fit their specifications as closely as possible.

2. Omit all else from your response (so there is no further excuse for Screening you out). Volunteer nothing else. Period.

3. If the ad requested salary requirements, some experts say ignore the request; others say, state a salary range (of as much as three to ten thousand dollars variation) adding the words "depending on the nature and scope of duties and responsibilities," or words to that effect. If the ad does not mention salary requirements, don't you either. Why give an excuse for getting your response Screened Out?

---

1. Olympus Research Corporation, *A Study to Test the Feasibility of Determining Whether Classified Ads in Daily Newspapers Are an Accurate Reflection of Local Labor Markets and of Significance to Employers and Job Seekers.* 1973. From: Olympus Research Corporation, 1670 East 1300 South, Salt Lake City, UT 84105.
2. Ten Speed Press, Box 7123, Berkeley, CA 94707. Or at your local library.

THINGS TO BEWARE OF
IN NEWSPAPER ADS

BLIND ADS (no company name, just a box number). These, according to some insiders, are particularly unrewarding to the job-hunter's time.

PHONE NUMBERS in ads: don't use them except to set up an appointment. Period. ("I can't talk right now. I'm calling from the office.") Beware of saying more. Avoid getting screened out prematurely over the tele-phone.

FAKE ADS (positions advertised which don't exist)— usually run by placement firms or others, in order to fatten their "resume bank" for future clout with employers.

THOSE PHRASES which need lots of translating, like: "Energetic self-starter wanted" (= You'll be working on commission)
"Good organizational skills" (= You'll be handling the filing)
"Make an investment in your future" (= This is a franchise or pyramid scheme)
"Much client contact" (= You handle the phone, or make 'cold calls' on clients)
"Planning and coordi-nating" (= You book the boss's travel arrangements)
"Opportunity of a lifetime" (= No where else will you find such a low salary and so much work)
"Management training position" (= You'll be a salesperson with a wide territory)
"Varied, interesting travel" (= You'll be a salesperson with a wide territory)

PLACING ADS YOURSELF

Sometimes job-hunters try to make their availability known, by placing ads themselves in newspapers or journals.

PLACING ADS

<u>Name of ads (commonly)</u>: Positions wanted (by the job-hunter, that is).

<u>Found in</u>: *Wall Street Journal,* professional journals and in trade association publications.

<u>Effectiveness</u>: Very effective in getting responses from employment agencies, peddlers, salesmen, and vultures who prey on job-hunters. Practically worthless in getting responses from prospective employers, who rarely read these ads. But it *has* worked for some.

<u>Recommendation</u>: If you take odds seriously, you'd better forget it. Unless, just to cover all bets, you want to place some ads in professional journals appropriate to your field. Study other people's formats first, though.

<u>Cost</u>: Varies.

ASKING PRIVATE EMPLOYMENT AGENCIES FOR HELP

The two places that every job-hunter knows instinctively to turn to when looking for a job is want ads and employment agencies. We just dealt with the first of these. Now let us look at the second. Employment agencies seem very attractive when one is "up against it." We all like to think that somewhere out there is someone who knows just exactly where all jobs are to be found. Unhappily **no one** in this country knows where all the jobs are. The best that anyone can offer to us is some clues about where it is that **some** jobs are to be found. Those places which know where some jobs are to be found are called private employment agencies. The Yellow Pages of your phone book will give you their names.

PRIVATE EMPLOYMENT AGENCIES

PRIVATE EMPLOYMENT AGENCIES

Number: Nobody knows, since new ones are born, and old ones die, every week. There are at least 8,000 private employment or placement agencies in the U.S. Maybe a lot more.

Specialization: Many specialize in executives, financial, data processing, or other specialties.

Fees: Employer or job-hunter may pay. Be sure to ask which is the case. Fees vary from state to state. Tax deductible. In New York, for example, a fee cannot exceed 60% of one month's salary, i.e., a $15,000-a-year job will cost you $750. The fee may be paid in weekly installments of 10% (e.g., $75 on a $750 total). In 80% of executives' cases, it is the employer who pays the fee.

Contract: The application form filled out by the job-hunter at the agency **is** the contract.

Exclusive handling: Don't give it, even if they ask for it. If you find a job independently of them, you may still have to pay them a fee.

Nature of business: Primarily a volume business, requiring rapid turnover of clientele, with genuine attention given only to the most-marketable job-hunters, in what one insider has called "a short-term matching game."

Effectiveness: Some time back, a spokesman for the Federal Trade Commission announced that the average placement rate for employment agencies was only 5% of

PRIVATE EMPLOYMENT
AGENCIES continued

those who walked in the door. That means a 95% failure rate, right?

<u>Loyalty</u>: Agency's loyalty in the very nature of things must lie with those who pay the bills (which in most cases is the employer), and those who represent repeat business (again, employers).

<u>Evaluation</u>: An agency, with its dependency on rapid-turnover volume business, usually has no time to deal with **any** problems (like, career-transitions). Possible exception for you to investigate: a new, or suddenly expanding agency, which needs job-hunters badly if it is ever to get employers' business.

ASKING THE FEDERAL-STATE
EMPLOYMENT SERVICE
FOR HELP

UNITED STATES EMPLOYMENT SERVICE

Number: 2,600 offices in the country. USES (often called "Job Service") has been greatly reduced in staff and budget over the years.

Services: Most state offices of USES not only serve entry level workers, but also have services for professionals. Washington, D.C. had most innovative one. Middle management (and up) job-hunters still tend to avoid it.

Nationwide network: In any city (as a rule) you can inquire about job opportunities in other states or cities, for a particular field. Also see Job Bank (page 27).

Openings: Ten years ago, a study revealed that nine million non-agricultural job vacancies were listed with USES during the year. Today, the figure is probably larger.

UNITED STATES
EMPLOYMENT SERVICE
continued

Placements: Of the 15+ million job-hunters who registered with USES ten years ago, approximately 30% were placed in jobs. Almost half of these were blue-collar jobs, and another quarter were white-collar jobs. A survey of one area raised some question about the quality of placement, moreover, when it was discovered that 57% of those placed in that geographical area by USES were not working at their jobs anymore, just 30 days later. (That would reduce the placement rate to 17%, at best; an 83% failure rate. It's probably closer to 13.7% placement, hence an 86.3% failure rate.) There is no reason to believe things have changed.

ASKING HEADHUNTERS, OTHERWISE KNOWN AS RECRUITERS OR EXECUTIVE SEARCH FIRMS FOR HELP

If you play the numbers game, and especially if you pay someone to guide you through it, you will be told to send your resume to Executive Search firms. And what, pray tell, are they? Well, they are recruiting firms that are retained by employers. The very existence of this thriving industry testifies to the fact that employers are as baffled by our country's Neanderthal job-hunting 'system' as we are. **Employers don't know how to find decent employees, any more than job-hunters know how to find decent employers.** So, what do employers want executive recruiting firms to do? They want these firms to hire away from other firms or employers, executives, salespeople, technicians, or whatever, who are already employed, and rising. (In the old days, these firms searched only for executives, hence their now-outdated title.) Anyway, you will realize these head-hunting firms are aware of, and trying to fill, known vacancies. That's

EXECUTIVE RECRUITERS

Name: Executive recruitment consultants, executive recruiters, executive search firms, executive development
specialists, management consultants, recruiters.
Nicknames: Headhunters, body snatchers, flesh peddlers,
talent scouts.
Number: Some 12,000 professionals, currently.
Volume of business: They had combined billings of more
than $2 billion a year.
Number of vacancies handled by a firm: Each staff member
can only handle six to eight searches at a time (as a
rule); so, multiply number of staff that a firm has (if
known) times six. Majority of firms are one to two staff
(hence, are handling five to ten current openings); a few

are four to five staff (twenty to twenty-five openings are
being searched for; and the largest have staffs handling
eighty to one hundred openings.

why, in any decent scatter-gun sending out of your resume, you
are advised -- by any number of experts -- to be sure and
include Recruiters. Not surprisingly, there are a number of
enterprising souls who will sell you lists of such firms.

You can get lists of such firms from:

1. *Directory of Executive Recruiters,* published by Consultant
News, Templeton Rd., Fitzwilliam, NH 03447. Published yearly.
Lists several hundred firms and the industries served.

2. *Directory of Personnel Consultants by Specialization (Industry
Grouping).* Published by the National Association of Personnel

Consultants, Round House Square, 1432 Duke St., Alexandria, VA 22314, 703-684-0810.

3. *Directory of the Members of the National Association of Executive Recruiters.* Published by the National Association of Executive Recruiters, 5881 Leesburg Pike, Suite 302, Falls Church, VA 22041, 703-998-3008.

The question is: do you **want** these lists, i.e., are they going to do you any good?

Well, let's say you decide to send recruiters your resume (unsolicited -- they didn't ask you to send it, you just sent it uninvited). The average Executive Search firm may get as many as 100 to 300 such resumes, or "broadcast letters" a week. And, as we see above, the majority of such firms may be handling 5 to 10 current openings, for which they are looking for executives who are presently employed and rising.

Well okay, that Executive Recruiter is sitting there with 100 to 300 resumes in his or her hands, at the end of that week -- yours (and mine) among them. You know what's about to happen to that stack of People-in-the-Form-of-Paper. That old Elimination, Winnowing, or Screening Process again. Your chances of surviving? Well, the first to get eliminated will be those who a) are not presently on the level being looked for, or

b) are not presently employed, or c) are not presently rising in their firm. That's why even in a good business year, many experts say to the unemployed: Forget it!

I do think it is necessary, however, to point out that things are changing in the Recruiting field. For one thing, some firms now call themselves Recruiters when yesterday they would have been called Employment Agencies. These new Recruiters do indeed represent employers; but they are hungry for the names of job-hunters, and in many cases will interview a job-hunter who comes into the office unannounced or mails them a resume. I have known so-called Recruiters who truly extended themselves on behalf of very inexperienced job-hunters. So, were I job-hunting this year, I think I would get one of the aforementioned Directories, look up the firms that specialize in my particular kind of job or field, and go take a crack at them. As long as you don't put all your eggs in that one basket, you really have nothing to lose.

ASKING COLLEGE PLACEMENT CENTERS FOR HELP

COLLEGE PLACEMENT OFFICES

Where located: Most of the 3,280 institutions of higher education in this country have some kind of placement function, however informal.

Helpfulness: Some are very good, because they understand that job-hunting will be a repetitive activity throughout the lives of their students; hence they try to teach an empowering process of self-directed job-hunting. Other offices, however, still think they have done their job if they have helped "each student find a job upon graduation," through the use of recruiters, bulletin board listings, and the like; i.e., if they help their students with this one job-hunt this one time.

Directory: A directory listing many of these offices is published, and is available for perusal in most Placement Offices. It is called the *Directory of Career Planning and Placement Offices*, and is published by the College Placement Council, Inc., Box 2263, Bethlehem, PA 18001.

"CATHY" by Cathy Guisewite

If you are not only a college graduate but also a hopeless romantic, you will have a vision of blissful cooperation existing between all of these placement offices across the country. So that if you are a graduate of an East Coast college, let us say, and subsequently you move to California, and want help with career planning, you should in theory be able to walk into the placement office on any California campus, and be helped by that office (a non-altruistic service based on the likelihood that a graduate of that California campus is, at the same moment, walking into the placement office of your East Coast college; and thus, to coin a phrase, "one hand is washing another"). Some places do do this.

But, alas and alack, dear graduate, in most cases it doesn't work like that. You will be told, sometimes with genuine regret, that by official policy, this particular placement office on this particular campus is only allowed to aid its own students and alumni. And sometimes not even its own alumni. One Slight Ray of Hope: on a number of campuses, there are career counselors who think this policy is absolutely asinine, so if you walk into the Career Planning office on that campus, **are lucky enough to get one of Those Counselors,** and you don't mention whether or not you went to that college -- the counselor will never ask, and will proceed to help you just as though you were a real person.

This restriction (to their own students and graduates) is less likely to be found at Community Colleges than it is at four-year institutions. So if you run into a dead end, do try a Community College near you.

ASKING REGISTERS
OR CLEARINGHOUSES
TO HELP YOU

These are attempts to set up "job exchanges" or a kind of bulletin board where employer and job-hunter can meet. The private clearinghouses commonly handle both employer and job-hunter listings, charging each.

REGISTERS OR CLEARING-HOUSE OPERATIONS

Types: Federal and private; general and specialized fields; listing either future projected openings, or present ones; listing employers' vacancies, or job-hunters' resumes (in brief), or both.

Cost to job-hunter: Ranges from free, to $75 or more.

Effectiveness: A register may have as many as 13,000 clients registered with it (if it is a private operation), and let us say 500 openings at one time, from employer clients. You must figure out what the odds are for you as job-hunter. Some registers will let employers know of every client who is eligible; others will pick out the few best ones. A newer register may do more for you than an older one.

The idea of registers or clearinghouses is a very popular idea, and new entrants in the field are appearing constantly. On the following cards, we list some examples:

REGISTERS ETC.
continued

General Clearinghouse Listing Present Vacancies: The State Employment Offices in 48 states, covering more than 300 separate labor market areas, have set up a computerized (in most cities) job bank to provide daily listings of job openings in that city. If every employer cooperated and listed every opening they had, each day, it would be a great concept. Unhappily, employers prefer to fill many jobs above $11,000 in more personal, informal ways. So the Job Bank remains a rather limited resource for such jobs. Can be a helpful research instrument, however. A summary of the job orders placed by employers at Job Banks during the previous month used to be published under the title of "Occupations in Demand at Job Service Offices." It is apparently no longer available.

A Clearinghouse of Newspaper Ads: The idea of someone reading on your behalf the classified sections of a lot of newspapers in this country, and publishing a summary thereof on a weekly basis (or so), is not a new idea -- but it is apparently growing increasingly popular. Problem: how old the ads may be by the time you the subscriber read them. That answer will turn out to be the sum of the following times: a) the time it took for the hometown paper, in which the ad first appeared, to be sent to the town in which the clearinghouse operates; plus b) the time the clearinghouse

REGISTERS, ETC.
continued

held on to the ad -- especially if it just missed "last week's" edition of the clearinghouse Report; plus c) the time it took, after insertion in the Report, before the Report came 'off the press'; plus d) the time it took for the clearinghouse's Report to get across the country to you (discount this last, if you live in the clearinghouse's backyard; otherwise give this Large Weight, especially if it is not sent First Class/Airmail -- or have you forgotten about our beloved Postal Service?); plus e) the time it takes to get your response from your town to the town in which the ad appeared. You'll recall from page 14 that most classified ads receive more than enough responses within 96 hours of the ad's first appearing; how likely an employer is to wait for you to send in your

response many days, or even weeks, later, is something you must evaluate for yourself -- and weigh that against the cost of the service. If you want it, there are several places offering this service. Among the most reliable: the *Wall Street Journal* publishes a weekly compilation of "career-advancement positions" from its four regional editions. Available on some newsstands, or order from: National Business Employment Weekly, 420 Lexington Ave., New York, NY 10170. 212-808-6792.

Register for Teachers: *The NESC Jobs Newsletters* are published by the National Education Service Center, 221A E. Main St., Riverton, WY 82501. 307-856-0170. Between April and August, this weekly series of newsletters lists about 58,000 job openings annually. Each week's edition contains only new listings, none repeated. The newsletters are published year 'round, with fewer listings in the months August to April. You select one or more of fourteen different job categories, and receive listings of jobs in those categories only.

Register for Government Jobs: *Federal Career Opportunities,* published biweekly by Federal Research Service, Inc., 370 Maple Ave. W., Box 1059, Vienna, VA 22180. 703-281-0200. Each issue is 64 pages, and lists 3,200+ currently available federal jobs, in both the U.S. and overseas.

Register for Nonprofit Organizations: ACCESS, 67 Winthrop St., Cambridge, MA 02138 is a new organization designed to ultimately become a clearinghouse of job opportunities for the more than 450,000 nonprofit organizations in this country. Currently, they access an impressive sampling (only) of those 450,000. To disseminate this information, they are linked already with the career planning offices in about 20 colleges across the country, and growing rapidly. But they are willing to

REGISTERS ETC.
continued

help individuals with the information on vacancies that they already have, which is constantly updated. Individuals desiring a three-month job search based on their resume and cover letter (describing their job interests, desired geographical location, and salary) can have it done for a very low fee, by writing to its director, Jim Clark. If the service fails to turn up "appropriate job listings" within the three-month period, your fee is refunded.

Registers in The Church: Intercristo is a national Christian organization that lists over 30,000 jobs, covering hundreds of vocational categories within over 1,000 Christian organizations in the U.S. or overseas. Their service is called Christian Placement Network. In 1987, 13,000 people used the Christian Placement Network;

one out of every twenty-five job-hunters who used this service found a job thereby. (That, of course, means twenty-four out of twenty-five didn't.) Their address is 19303 Fremont Ave. N., Seattle, WA 98133, and their toll-free phone number is 800-426-1342. Jeff Trautman, Executive Director.

Register for The Blind: Job Opportunities for the Blind, 1800 Johnson St., Baltimore, MD 21230. 301-659-9314, or 1-800-638-7518. Exists to inform blind applicants about positions that are open with public and private employers throughout the country. Maintains a computerized listing. Also, they have cassette instructions on everything for the blind job-seeker. Operated by the National Federation of the Blind in partnership with the U.S. Department of Labor.

OTHER REGISTERS OR CLEARINGHOUSES

Is a thing a register or not? If job listings exist all by themselves, they tend to be legitimately called "registers." If they exist within the framework of a journal or magazine which also contains other material, they tend to be called "ads." There is a list of such journals: see Feingold, S. Norman, and Hansard-Winkler, Glenda Ann, *900,000 Plus Jobs Annually: Published sources of employment listings.* Garrett Park Press, Garrett Park, MD 20896. This book lists more than 900 journals which carry employment want ads. The following list is only a sampling of the registers which exist:

For Internships and Jobs with Nonprofit Organizations: *Community Jobs,* published by the Community Careers Resource Center, 1516 P St. NW, Washington, DC 20005. Phone 202-667-0661.

For Jobs Overseas: *International Employment Hotline.* Monthly issues profile international employment opportunities. International Employment Hotline, Box 6170, McLean, VA 22106.

For Jobs in Criminal Justice: The *NELS Monthly Bulletin,* National Employment Listing Service, Criminal Justice Center, Sam Houston State Univ., Huntsville, TX 77341, 713-294-1692. A nonprofit service providing information on current job opportunities in the criminal justice and social services fields.

For Jobs with Youth or Children: The Child Care Personnel Clearinghouse, Box 548, Hampton, VA 23669, publishes a biannual list called *Help Kids.* You *must* enclose $1 for postage and handling, in order to get it, however.

For Jobs Outdoors: Environmental Opportunities, Box 670, Walpole, NH 03608, publishes a monthly listing of environmental jobs, internships and positions-wanted notices under the same name. Each issue contains twenty-four to forty full-time positions in a variety of disciplines. The Natural Science for Youth Foundation. 16 Holmes St., Mystic, CT 06355, publishes a bimonthly job-listing, called *Opportunities*. The Association for Experiential Education, CU Box 249, Boulder, CO 80309, 303-492-1547, publishes a nationwide "Jobs Clearing House" list.

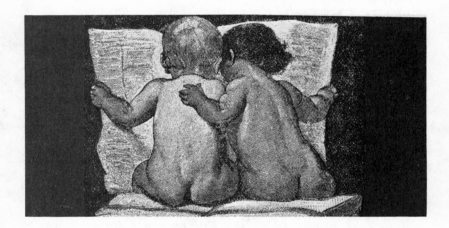

One final word about registers: the very term "register" can be misleading. The vision: one central place where you can go, and find listed every vacancy in a particular field of endeavor. **But, sorry, Virginia; there ain't no such animal.** All you'll find by going to any of these places is A Selected List of some of the vacancies. A smorgasbord, if you will.

So far as finding **jobs for people** is concerned, these clearinghouses and agencies, like employment agencies, really end up finding **people for jobs.** (Think about it!) Heart of gold though they may have, these agencies serve employers better than they serve the job-hunter.

And yet there are always ways of using such registers to gain valuable information for the job-hunter and to suggest places where you may wish to start researching your ideal job (more in chapter 5). So at the least, you *may* want to consult the Federal job bank (if there is one in your city), and perhaps a relatively inexpensive Register (if there is one in your particular field), as auxiliaries to the main thrust of your job-search.

OTHER IDEAS THAT MAY HELP YOU

OTHER IDEAS

<u>Your resume in a book</u>: Some organizations circulate small booklets which are essentially mass distribution of people's resumes in concise form. Forty-Plus Clubs do this, through their *Executive Manpower Directory*. So do some of the executive registry places. Evaluation as to its worth to you as job-hunter: well, it's a gamble, just like everything else in this Numbers Game system. A real gamble, if you are trying to start a new career. You have to boil your resume down to a very few words, normally. And then decide if you stand out. If not, forget it. If yes, well . . . maybe.

OTHER IDEAS

<u>Off-beat methods</u>: Mailing strange boxes to company presidents, with strange messages (or your resume) inside; using sandwich board signs and parading up and down in front of a company; sit-ins at a president's office, when you are simply determined to work for that company, association, or whatever. You name it, and if it's kooky, it's been tried. Sometimes it has paid off. Kookiness is generally ill-advised, however. $64,000 question every employer must weigh: if you're like this **before** you're hired, what will they have to live with **afterward?**

To summarize the effectiveness of all the preceding methods in a table (you do like tables, don't you?), we may look at the results of a survey the Bureau of the Census made. The survey, made in 1972 and published in the *Occupational Outlook Quarterly* in the winter of 1976, was of 10 million job-seekers. Unhappily, it appears today that nothing has changed; the conclusions this study reached are still totally consistent with the experience of today's job-hunters:

USE AND EFFECTIVENESS OF JOB-SEARCH METHODS

Percent Of Total Jobseekers Using the Method	Method	Effectiveness Rate*
66.0%	Applied directly to employer	47.7%
50.8	Asked friends about jobs where they work	22.1
41.8	Asked friends about jobs elsewhere	11.9
28.4	Asked relatives about jobs where they work	19.3
27.3	Asked relatives about jobs elsewhere	7.4
45.9	Answered local newspaper ads	23.9
11.7	Answered nonlocal newspaper ads	10.0
21.0	Private employment agency	24.2
33.5	State employment service	13.7
12.5	School placement office	21.4
15.3	Civil Service test	12.5
10.4	Asked teacher or professor	12.1
1.6	Placed ad in local newspaper	12.9
.5	Placed ad in nonlocal newspaper	**
4.9	Answered ads in professional or trade journals	7.3
6.0	Union hiring hall	22.2
5.6	Contacted local organization	12.7
.6	Placed ads in professional or trade journals	**
1.4	Went to place where employers come to pick up people	8.2
11.8	Other	39.7

*A percentage obtained by dividing the number of jobseekers who actually found work using the method, by the total number of jobseekers who tried to use that method, whether successfully or not.
**Base less than 75,000.

Well, anyway, Mr. or Ms. Job-Hunter, this just about covers the favorite job-hunting system of this country at its best, except for personal contacts, which we give special treatment in chapter 5.

The Numbers Game.

If it works for you, right off, great! But if it doesn't, you may be interested in the other plan -- you know, the one they had saved up for you, in case all of this didn't work? Small problem: with most of the personnel experts in our country, there is no other plan.

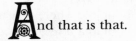nd that is that.

PRAY, as though everything
depended on God;
then work, as though everything
depended on You.

You Can Do It!

Reprinted with special permission of King Features Syndicate, Inc.

The upshot of the previous chapters is: we all start out in life thinking that if we are ever tragically thrown out of work, or quit, someone out there will come to our rescue, steer us in the right direction, and hook us up with a proper job. Voila! Our troubles will be short-lived. We are, of course, unclear about **who** that someone will be: a union, or the government, or private agencies, or newspapers -- but we believe it will be **someone.** Alas, when our time comes, and we are completely out of work, instead of someone coming to save us, there is only the sound of silence.

Many unemployed people have sat at home, waiting for God to prove that He loves them, by causing a job to just walk in the door. It does happen. But not often enough for you to ever count on it. The previous chapter surely drove home to you these common sense facts:

No one else on earth cares as much about what happens to you as you do. Therefore **it is You who must take over the management of your own job-hunt or career-change, if it is to be successful.** No one else is going to be willing to lavish so much time on it, as you will. No one else will be so persistent, as you will. No one else has so exact a picture of what kind of job you are looking for, as you do.

If your job-hunt were a movie script, and we were casting the lead, we would have to choose You, as the best qualified for the part. By a long shot.

So let us assume you are currently looking for work. You may not be. Lots of people use this book and do the exercises in chapters 4 and 5 simply in order to raise their self-esteem. They write and tell me so. "Don't let your readers think these exercises are only useful if you're job-hunting or changing careers! I found a whole new sense of well-being from doing the exercises, even though I'm in a job I love."

But, let's assume you are reading this book because you are currently looking for work. If you are, this may be due to either of two forces in your life: external or internal.

The **external forces** you are already familiar with, I'm sure: mergers, takeovers, "downsizing," restructuring, places going out of business, age discrimination, racial discrimination, sex discrimination, and heaven knows what else. But the upshot of it all is that one day you are summarily dismissed, fired, canned, terminated, "made redundant," or whatever other euphemism our society can come up with. Anyway, you are out of a job -- and in many cases, totally without warning. It may be that you gave that organization the best years of your life, and you are of course livid, angry, and depressed.

On the other hand, perhaps you are now looking for work due to **internal forces.** No one has taken your job away; you could probably still have it for the next twenty years. But the pressure to leave that job is inside of you. The internal time clock has struck midnight. You're ready to chuck this job. You're tired of it, bored, fed up, and hungry for something new, exciting, and challenging. Or, if your work has given you that in spades, you're stressed, burnt out, exhausted, and hungry for something peaceful, calm, and secure. You're ready -- in a word -- to change careers.

Either way, whether due to external or internal forces, you're looking for work. The time is now. And you want some guidance and help. Now, what can we tell you to do?

Well, we don't know what to tell you until you say how much time you're willing to put to it, and how systematic you want to be. **Many job-hunters do not want a system.** They do not want to forge through all the chapters of this book. They do not want to spend hour after hour of self-searching exercises.

They do not want to put blood, sweat, and tears into their job-hunt. Rather they want essentially to throw themselves on the river of job-hunting, and see where it carries them.

They want, well, just a few hints. And maybe a little Hope, thrown in. That's all. They figure if someone will tell them just a few things they should be aware of, or a few things they could do differently, that should be enough to get them through.

I have to say that **if it's a full-fledged career-change you're thinking about, a few hints won't be enough. You will need all of the systematic process discussed in chapters 4, 5, and 6.** But if you're just going out looking for the kind of work you've always done, and you're not in the mood to put in a lot of time and effort on your job-hunt, maybe one of the following thirty-five hints will give you a brainstorm, and be just enough to make your job-hunt work. You never know.

Okay, here they are:

THIRTY-FIVE HINTS FOR TODAY'S JOB-HUNTER

(Can be read in the time it takes to eat a burger at a fast-food outlet.)

1. You must be ready to go job-hunting *anytime,* for no matter how good a job you have been doing at your present workplace, that job may vanish - - Poof! - - tomorrow without any warning whatsoever, due to circumstances entirely beyond your control.

2. If you have been unjustly let go, your first great need is to let go of your righteous anger at how different the world of work is from what you thought it would be; otherwise, that anger will cripple your job-hunting efforts. You will reek of it to every employer you go see, even as a drunk reeks of strong drink.

3. No one owes you a job; you have to fight to win a job.

4. By and large, the major difference between successful and unsuccessful job-hunters is **the way that they go about their job-hunt** - - and **not** some factor "out there," such as a tight labor market.

5. If you want your job-hunt to succeed, make a list of what you would do if you had to make your job-hunt fail. Yes, I said fail. Put the factor that would most surely make your job-hunt fail, at the top of your list, then the next one, and so forth. (One man's surest factor was "Sit at home.") In a second column, state the opposite of each factor (for example, "Get out of the house every single day") and you will then have a list of what you must do in your job-hunt, **and** the order in which you must do it, in order to make it succeed.

6. Do not expect that you will necessarily be able to find exactly the same kind of work that you used to be doing. Be prepared to define some other lines of work that you can do, and would enjoy doing, using your same skills and experiences. Always have a plan B.

7. Take the job-label (e.g., "I am a steelworker") off yourself. You are a person who . . . .

8. The more time you spend on figuring out what makes you stand out from nineteen other people who can do what you do, the better your chances.

9. Forget "what's available out there." Go after the job you really want the most.

10. If a thing turns you on, you'll be good at it; if it doesn't, you won't. (This hint courtesy of David Maister.)

11. Figure out whether you're best with People, or with Things, or with Information. It makes a difference.

12. In trying to change careers or go into a new field (for you), don't look for the **rules** or generalizations. Look for the **exceptions** to the rules. The rule is: "In order to do this work you have to have a master's degree and ten years' experience at it." You search for the exception: "Yes, but do you know of anyone in the field who hasn't got all those credentials? And where might I find him or her?"

13. Go after organizations with twenty or less employees. That's where two-thirds of all new jobs are. You will want to see the boss, not "the personnel department." (Only 15% of all organizations, mostly large organizations, even have personnel departments anyway.)

14. Two-thirds of all job-hunters spend five hours or less a week, on their job-hunt; determine to spend six times that much. I said "six times."

15. Job-hunters visit an average of six employers a month; determine to see at least two a day.

16. The greater the number of job-hunting avenues you use, the greater the likelihood that you will find a job. That's what studies of job-hunting have revealed. As we saw in the previous chapter, page 35, there are at least nineteen different job-hunting avenues out there. The average job-hunter uses less than two of these nineteen methods. The greater the number **you** use, the greater the likelihood of your finding a job.

17. Expect that your job-hunt is going to take some time. The average job-hunt lasts between six and eighteen weeks, depending on the state of the economy. Don't count on the "six weeks"

minimum. Be prepared for the eighteen weeks or longer. Experienced outplacement people say that your job-hunt will probably take one month for every $10,000 of salary that you are seeking.

18. Look as sharp as you can **at all times** while you are out of work. Be neat, clean, well-dressed whenever you are outside your home; you never know who will see you -- and possibly recommend you to someone who is hiring.

19. Go after many different organizations, instead of just one or two.

20. Go face-to-face with employers, whenever possible, rather than sending paper, such as a resume.

21. The major issue you face with employers is not what skills you have, but **how** you use them: whether you just try to "keep busy" or try to actually solve problems, thus increasing your effectiveness and the organization's effectiveness, too.

22. Whatever you produce, be sure it is something you are proud of. A University of Michigan study found that one out of four American workers felt so ashamed of the quality of the products they were producing, that they would not buy them themselves.

23. The manner in which you do your job-hunt and the manner in which you would do the job you are seeking -- are **not** assumed by most employers to be two unrelated subjects, but one and the same. A slipshod, half-hearted job-hunt is taken as a warning that you might do a slipshod, half-hearted job, were they foolish enough to ever hire you.

24. There are not merely two things which will get you a job -- Training or Experience -- but three: Training, Experience, **or** a Demonstration of your Skills right before the employer's eyes. If there is any way that you can show an employer what you are capable of doing -- through pictures, samples of things you have made or produced, or whatever -- do it, during the interview.

25. If you and the employer really hit if off, but they cannot at that time afford to hire you, you might consider offering to do volunteer work there for a week or two, so they see firsthand how good you are at what you do. Or if you feel you're worth, say, $20,000 a year, but they can only pay $15,000 you might consider offering them three days a week of your time (15/20 = 3/5 of your week), and you can go look for other work to fill the remaining two days. (This hint courtesy of Daniel Porot.)

26. Don't be wearied by rejection. We saw Tom Jackson's model (from *Guerrilla Tactics in the Job Market*) of the typical job-hunt as NO NO NO NO NO NO etc. But remember, you only need two YESES. Two, so that you'll have at least two things to choose between. And the more NOs you get out of the way, the closer you are to those YESES.

27. If you are handicapped, don't feel that you're different from other job-hunters. Every job-hunter is handicapped. The only question is: What is the handicap, and how much does it show? If you are a job-hunter, and you think you're **not** handicapped, think again. There are probably 8,431 truly different skills that human beings possess. The average job-hunter can only do 700 of those. Believe me, you're handicapped. Sit down and put Mozart on the stereo or CD, when you're searching for some humility.

28. Treat every employer with courtesy, even if it seems certain they can offer you no job there; they may be able to refer you to someone else next week, *if* you made a good impression.

29. Don't assume **anything.** ("But I just assumed that . . . .")

30. Send short handwritten thank-you notes that very night, to everyone you talked to that day in your job-hunting activities -- secretaries, receptionists, etc. -- thanking them for seeing or helping you.

31. Be gently persistent, and be willing at least a couple of times to go back to places that interested you, to see if their "no vacancy" situation has changed.

32. Once you know what kind of work you are looking for, tell **everyone** what it is; have as many other eyes and ears out there looking on your behalf, as possible. If you happen to own a telephone answering machine, you might even consider putting it on that machine, in your opening message.

33. When calling on an employer, ask for twenty minutes only, and don't stay one minute longer unless the employer begs you to. Tell them you like to honor commitments. This will almost always make a big impression.

34. Whenever you are speaking to an employer, don't "hold forth" all by yourself for longer than two minutes, at any one time. During the entire interview, talk one-half the time, listen one-half the time.

35. Organizations only hire winners; go to that organization and to the interview as "a resource person," not as "a job beggar." (This hint courtesy of Daniel Porot.)

WHEN HINTS AREN'T ENOUGH

Now, these hints may be **all** that you need. One or two of them may strike just the right chord in you, give you just the idea that you need, in order to go out and do a smashing job on your job-hunt.

But, we can't leave it at that. If the hints work for you, fine. But what if they don't? Then, you're going to need something more. You're going to need a life preserver. You're going to need a more systematic way of getting at your job-hunt.

As I said earlier, this is particularly true if you're thinking of changing careers. You don't necessarily have to go back to college and get retrained, in order to change careers. But you do have to sit down and do some thorough homework on yourself, and some thorough research about what's going on out there in the marketplace.

Jobs in this country last an average of 3.6 years. That sounds like we have to go job-hunting every 3.6 years. But that's only speaking of averages.

"Same career, change of career, same career... change of..."

In actual fact, a particular job that you have may last longer than 3.6 years - - especially as you grow older. So, surveys reveal the number of times you will have to go job-hunting in your entire lifetime will likely be eight. When it is time for you to go job-hunting, there are many choices you can make. These are the choices you face:

(1)   Should I make a career change?
      OR
      Should I stay in the same field/career?

(2)   If I choose to stay in the same field/career:
      Should I move to a different organization, though staying in the same type of job?
      OR
      Should I stay in the same organization where I am now?

(3)   If the same organization:
      Should I stay in the very same job as I am now in?
      OR
      Should I move to a different department or a different job there?

(4)   If I make a career change:
      Should I change careers by going back to school and retraining?
      OR
      Should I change careers without going back to school?

(5)   If I change careers without further schooling:
      Should I look for a new career in which I work for someone else?
      OR
      Should I look for a new career in which I work for myself?

(6)   If I look for a new career in which I work for someone else:
      Should I seek a job at decent or even high pay?
      OR
      Should I seek for a volunteer job at first, or even an internship?

(7)   If I look for a new career in which I work for myself:
      Should I seek a career made up of just one job?
      OR

Should I seek a composite career, made up of several (two to five) different jobs/careers?

(8)   And, once I have answered all the above questions, **what** is it I should do?

No matter how you answer these questions (or even if you haven't got a clue as to how to answer them), **you have got to do some homework on yourself before you go out there pounding the pavements.** This homework always has three parts to it:

1. **WHAT.** This has to do with your skills. You need to inventory and identify what skills you have that you most enjoy using. These are called transferable skills, because they are transferable to any field/career that you choose, regardless of where you first picked them up.

2. **WHERE.** This has to do with job environments. Think of yourself as a flower. You know that a flower which blooms in the desert will not do well at 10,000 feet up -- and vice versa.

Every flower has an environment where it does best. So with you. You are like a flower. You need to decide where you want to use your skills, where you would thrive, and do your most effective work.

3. **HOW.** You need to decide how to get where you want to go. This has to do with finding out the names of the jobs you would be most interested in, **and** the names of organizations (in your preferred geographical area) which have such jobs to offer, **and** the names of the people or person there who actually has the power to hire you. **And,** how can you best approach that person to show him or her how your skills can help them with their problems. How, if you were hired there, you would not be part of the problem, but part of the solution.

Now, to be sure, these three basic questions will be approached by you in a slightly different way, depending on your goals and choices, above. If you ultimately become sure that you want to go into business for yourself, then the HOW will consist in identifying all the people who have already done something like the thing you are thinking of doing, so that you can go interview them and profit from their learnings and mistakes before you set out on your own. And the HOW may consist in identifying the potential customers or clients who would use your services or buy your product.

Or again, if you plan on staying at the same job and in the same organization where you presently are, you may find that the HOW section applies to how you move (get promoted, etc.) **within your organization,** rather than out in the job-market. And even if you plan to stay in the same job exactly, the WHAT and the WHERE questions will help you to function much better there because you will know more surely what your skills or strengths are, and where you can best use them.

(As one satisfied worker recently wrote me, "The skills inventory you have people do in chapter 4 of your book is something I do every two or three years. Each time I do it, I find out more specific things about what I do well. This information tells me what to watch for in the world - - what kind of tasks I can volunteer for and do very well at. I know more about the **kind** of thing I want to be, do, be surrounded by. I am now sensitized and ready to recognize them when they swim by.")

THE RULE:
TAKE NO SHORTCUTS

You *will* need to systematically deal with all three questions of WHAT, WHERE, and HOW. You will not want to skip over any of the three.

If you only do the homework on the WHAT, you will be like a cart without any horse to pull it. It just stands helplessly beside the road.

"WHAT" furnishes you with the cart; "WHERE" furnishes the horse to pull it; and "HOW" furnishes the road along which your cart and horse travel, to your chosen destination.

HANDICAPS AND YOUR JOB-HUNT

Most of us think that when we go job-hunting, we have some special handicap, that requires special handling. We need a book written just for job-hunters who have our handicap. Or so we think. Here is a list of some of these handicaps -- an expansion of a list originally put together by Daniel Porot.

If you check off one or more items on this list, you are a handicapped job-hunter (though that **doesn't** mean you need a special book for job-hunters with your handicap):

MY JOB-HUNTING HANDICAPS

I am Hispanic
I am Black
I am Vietnamese
I have a physical handicap
I have a mental handicap
I never graduated from high school
I never graduated from college
I am just graduating
I just graduated a year ago
I graduated too long ago
I am a self-made man
I am a self-made woman
I am too handsome
I am too beautiful
I am too ugly
I am too thin
I am too fat
I am too young
I am too old

I am too new to the job-market
I am too near retirement
I have a prison record
I have a psychiatric history
I have never held a job before
I have held too many jobs before
I have only had one employer
I am a foreigner
I have not had enough education
I have had too much education
I am too much of a generalist
I am too much of a specialist
I am a clergyperson
I am just coming out of the military
I've only worked for volunteer organizations
I have only worked for large employers
I have only worked for small employers
I am too shy
I am too assertive
I come from a very different kind
   of background
I come from another industry
I come from another planet

The true meaning of the above comprehensive list is that there are about three weeks of your life when you're employable. That is, if your handicaps could not be overcome. But of course they can be overcome. I will say this at greater length in chapter 6, but for now let me emphasize: **There are two kinds of employers (or clients or customers) out there:**

- those who **will** be put off by your handicap, and therefore **won't** hire you;
  AND
- those who will **not** be put off by your handicap, and therefore **will** hire you, if you are qualified for the job.

You are **not** interested in the former kind of employer, client, or customer, no matter how many of them there are. You are only looking for those employers who are not put off by your handicap, and therefore will hire you if you can do the job.

The most important thing for you to know is that **your best chance of bridging whatever handicap you have or think you have is careful preparation on your part.**

As Daniel Porot says, the employers, clients, customers who will not care about your handicap will be most impressed if you approach them, not as a job-beggar, but as a resource person. The secret of coming to them as A Resource Person is that you tackle chapters 4, 5, and 6 systematically and methodically.

In this sense, these three questions -- WHAT, WHERE, and HOW -- when thoughtfully and diligently answered through your own persistent homework, give you a bridge over any handicap you may have.

TRAVELS WITH FARLEY by Phil Frank (c) 1982 Field Enterprises, Inc. Courtesy of Field Newspaper Syndicate

BEWARE OF THE DESIRE FOR MAGIC

How do you go about answering the WHAT, WHERE, and HOW most effectively?

You want, of course, to hear that we are about to reveal a bunch of techniques which will inexorably guarantee you a job, if only you follow them faithfully. This desire for magic, the thirst to see unicorns, and to restore pretty maidens once sawed in half, lives on in us all. But alas! No such luck.

Any successful job-hunter or career-changer will tell you there is rarely magic. And that's because it takes three things to find a job:

a. **Techniques and Effort.** There are things others can teach you, and they **will** increase your effectiveness and improve your chances. You need to take these very seriously and really keep at them (that's the Effort). But, by themselves, these are not enough.

b. **Art.** As in the phrase: "There's a real art to the way she does that." We refer here to the special stamp that each person's individuality puts on what they do. A certain amount of the job-hunt others cannot teach you. You bring your own unique art to the job-hunt, as you do to everything else you do. It's that extra pizzazz, enthusiasm, and energy that is uniquely yours, which must be present, before you can be successful at the job-hunt. We cannot clone you. Genuine individuality always marks every successful job-hunt.

c. **Luck.** Following certain techniques faithfully, and combining them with your own individual art in the way you do it, will not in and of themselves get you the job. There is always a certain amount of luck involved in any successful job-hunt. You have to be the right person in the right place at the right time. If you are the right person in the wrong place at the wrong time, you won't find that job -- no matter how much technique, effort, and art you have put into it.

These factors have varying importance, depending on which part of the job-hunt you are dealing with.

Your own individual way of doing things, your "art," is most important during the WHAT. This is because skill identification is more of an art, than a science. We can give you the basic rules, but a lot of it you have to do in your own individual way.

Techniques become most important during the WHERE and the HOW: those parts of the job-hunt can more easily be defined.

And Luck becomes most important during the HOW part of your job-hunt.

What Can a Systematic Approach Give You? Obviously, it cannot give you good luck, or give you individuality. You must already possess that individuality, and you must have Lady Luck smile on you at least a little, for your job-hunt to succeed. But, by using the Systematic Approach in the next three chapters, the **amount** of luck you will need is greatly reduced. "Luck favors the prepared mind," as someone has observed. This Systematic Approach, if followed faithfully by you, **will** give you a thoroughly prepared mind.

The remainder of this book is therefore devoted to describing those techniques in detail, along with instructions on how you are to go about them. Chapter 4 is devoted to WHAT. Chapter 5 to WHERE. Chapter 6 to HOW. Appendix A has further helpful instructions.

RESOURCES FOR YOU TO DRAW ON

As you go through the following chapters, you will naturally want to know what or who there is to help you, as you go through your job-hunt or career-change. Here are the types of resources you can draw on:

I. *Yourself.* Doing the homework, tackling the exercises in chapters 4, 5, and 6, and reading and rereading these chapters is to be preferred above all other resources, for any number of reasons. First of all, knowledge which you gain for yourself is more ingrained than knowledge that is simply handed to you by others. Secondly, the job-hunt process rightly understood is itself a preparation for, and training in, skills you will need to exercise once you get the job; to deprive yourself of the opportunity to get valuable practice in these skills during the job-hunting process, is to make it just that much more difficult for yourself on the job. Thirdly, even if you pay money (and a whole lot of it) to one kind of professional agency or another, there is no guarantee that they will do the process any better than, or even as well as, you would do it yourself.

Miss Peach by Mell Lazarus.

M O R A L

Every investment of your money is a gamble unless you have first tried to do it on your own, know what you did find out, what you did not find out, and therefore what kind of help you now need from others.

II. *Books and other visual or audio materials.* If there's a particular place where you get bogged down, a particular technique that confuses you, a particular obstacle you want help in getting around, then check out Appendix B -- where such things are listed, by subject. I would urge you, however, to read all the way through chapters 4, 5, and 6 **first,** to get an overview. I get letters from readers which say, "I've only read part of your book so far, but I want to know what you have to say about . . ." And, of course, they refer to a subject that is covered in the chapters they haven't yet read. (Usually a second, embarrassed letter follows: "Please disregard my first letter . . .") So, do look before you leap, do read before you write. And if, after you read this book, there's something that's perplexing you, do check out the different subjects, books, and comments of mine that are to be found in Appendix B. That's why they're there.

III. *Free professional help.* When people get bogged down in their job-hunt, they often rush off to pay some career counselor to help them. Well, that's okay; counselors need to make a living too, and they are often **very** helpful. But sometimes, if you'll just stop to analyze exactly what you need at that particular moment, you might discover there is professional help for you that is available **at no cost.** Examples of where such free help is to be found:

☐ the reference librarian, at your local library or college library;

☐ career counseling offices at your nearby community college;

☐ job-clinics at your local chamber of commerce, federal/state employment agency, advertising council, and the like;

☐ local federally funded "job clubs," for specific populations, such as WIN recipients, etc. Your local federal/state employment office often knows their locations and times of meeting; funding comes, in most cases, from the Job Training Partnership Act of the Federal Government;

☐ self-directed job-support groups that meet in local churches or synagogues, in many communities.

There is a section in Appendix C at the back of this book that lists **a few of these,** only, and tells you how to find others. In some cases, the help listed there isn't totally free. But the charges are so small, that for all intents and purposes one may classify them as free.

The likelihood that such help is available in your community increases if you are from certain disadvantaged groups, such as low income, or welfare recipients, or youth, or displaced workers, or those laid off permanently. Ask around.

"Let's put it this way — if you can find a village without an idiot, you've got yourself a job."

From The Saturday Review, 8/8/77. Reprinted by special permission.

IV. *Professional help for a fee.* Now here, a lot depends on what kind of help you need or want. Is it aptitude/skills testing? The granddaddy of all such firms (I myself went to them, back in 1946) is Johnson O'Connor, nee Human Engineering Laboratory, located in some of our principal cities in the U.S.: Atlanta, Boston, Chicago, Dallas/Ft. Worth, Denver, Houston, Los Angeles, New Orleans, New York, San Francisco, Seattle, Tampa, and Washington D.C. There are other such firms around the country. Many colleges and universities will give you vocational testing, for somewhat more modest fees. You do need to ask whether it is **aptitude** testing or merely **interests** testing. The distinction is important.

If you want help with the overall process of job-hunting, Appendix C in the back of this book has a **Sampler** that lists some of the career counseling places to be found around the country. Unfortunately, it only lists a few of these, because it is only a Sampler. Your Yellow Pages will help you find a more comprehensive list of these in your area, under the headings of "Aptitude and Employment Testing," "Career Counseling," "Executive Consultants," "Management Consultants," "Personnel Consultants," and "Vocational Consultants." You will have to pick your way with great care through those woods. Just when you think you've gotten safely to grandmother's house, you may find there is a wolf there. Appendix C has an introductory section **which I would urge you read no less than three times** before you ever venture forth to press your money and your job-hunt or career-change into somebody else's hands.

Some professional groups have their own counseling centers. For example, if you are a clergyperson, you will want to look at the church career development centers which have sprung up all over the country. A list of them is to be found on page 303.

V. *Your family or friends.* I believe as a general rule -- there are exceptions -- you ought to try never to go through the job-hunt all by yourself alone. Co-opt **somebody** -- your partner or mate, a grown-up son or daughter who lives nearby, your best friend, someone you know well from your church or synagogue to be your weekly support person.

PRACTICAL EXERCISE
(SO YOU DON'T GO IT ALONE)

Choose a helper for your job-hunt -- friend rather than family, if possible. A **tough** friend. You know, taskmaster. Ask

them if they're willing to help you. Assuming they say yes, put down in both your appointment books a regular weekly date when they will guarantee to meet with you, check you out on what you've done already, and be very stern with you if you've done little or nothing since your previous week's meeting. Tell them that it is at least a 20,000 hour, $500,000 project. Or whatever. It's also responsible, concerned, committed Stewardship.

Where did we get 20,000 hours? Well, a forty-hour-a-week job, done for fifty weeks a year, adds up to 2,000 hours annually. So, how long are you going to be doing this new job or new career that you are looking for? How many years do you plan to stay in the world of work? Ten years? That means 20,000 hours. Longer than that? Even more hours. So, it's at least a 20,000-hour project.

Why $500,000? Well, figure it out for yourself. Say you hope to start this new job or new career of yours at $20,000 a year. Even if you are forty years old, you still have thirty good years of work left in you. So, let us say that over that period of thirty years you get enough raises to make your annual salary somewhere between $25,000 and $30,000. Multiply this by thirty years, and you get a total earnings of something in the neighborhood of more than half a million dollars. If you've got more years ahead of you, or a higher potential salarywise, you're talking about even more money.

So, it's at least a 20,000 hour, $500,000 project that you're working on, with this job-hunt or career-change of yours. That should get you going!

You can judge your age
by the amount of pain
you feel when you come in
contact with a new idea.
　　　　—John Nuveen

CHAPTER FOUR

The Systematic Approach To
The Job-Hunt and Career-Change:

PART I

What

Skills Do You
Most Enjoy Using?

Well, let us begin by getting motivated.

There is a vast world of work out there, where 116 million people are employed in this country alone -- many of whom are bored out of their minds. All day long. Not for nothing is their motto TGIF -- "Thank God It's Friday." They **live** for the weekends, when they can go do what they really want to do.

There are already more than enough of such poor souls. The world does not need you or me to add to their number. What the world does need is more people who feel true enthusiasm for their work. People who have taken the time to think -- and to think out what they uniquely can do, and what they uniquely have to offer to the world.

This is, of course, where you come in. If you are willing to sit down and do this task of inventorying what you most love to do, you will be on the way to giving the world what it most needs.

The world needs you to be doing work that you love to do; moreover that is your birthright, and your destiny. But, it doesn't just fall into your lap. **You have to put in some time to make it happen.** That time begins with inventorying your skills.

Is this inventorying hard work? Well, it can be.
Is it fun? Well, it can be. It all depends on your attitude.
I remind you of some words of the famed Victor Frankl:

"We who lived in concentration camps can remember the men who walked through the huts comforting others, giving away their last piece of bread. They may have been few in number, but they offer sufficient proof that everything can be taken from a man but one thing: the last of the human freedoms -- to choose one's attitude in any given set of circumstances, to choose one's own way."

And so it is, that in tackling this homework you can choose to see it as a lot of drudgery and hard work, which you would never do were it not for the difficult labor market that you face.

Or, you can choose to see it as **fun** -- an exploration of the inner world of yourself, where you unwrap your skills with the joy that children have when they unwrap their gifts at Christmastime.

You can also choose to see this process as a means of gaining the weapons to protect yourself from being manipulated by others. For, at job-hunting time you are very vulnerable, and therefore very much at risk of being thus manipulated by others, be they those who might make money off your plight, or future employers, or even well-meaning friends.

Not long ago, I overheard two college students talking, in Central Park in New York City. We'll call them Jim and Mike. In half a minute of conversation they perfectly illustrated how well-meaning friends can "do you in":

Jim: Hey, what are you majoring in?
Mike: Physics.
Jim: Physics? Man, you shouldn't major in physics. Computer science is the thing these days.
Mike: Naw, I like physics.
Jim: Man, physics doesn't pay much.
Mike: Really?
Jim: Switch to computer science.
Mike: Okay, I'll look into it tomorrow.

Well, you see my point. Upon such little conversations do huge life-decisions depend. This is why it is so important for you to do your homework, identifying your favorite and strongest skills. Settle it in your mind right now:

Before you go out to pound the pavements, **you have got to know what it is you want,** or else someone is going to sell you a bill of goods somewhere along the line that can do irreparable damage to your self-esteem, your sense of worth, and your stewardship of the talents that God gave you.

Okay, let us begin.

WHY DO YOU BEGIN WITH
YOUR SKILLS?

You begin the systematic approach -- whether you're just doing a normal job-hunt or you want this to be a full-fledged career-change -- in exactly the same way: by first of all identifying your skills. Now, many people just "freeze" when they hear the word "skills." It begins with high school job-hunters: "I haven't really got any skills," they say. It continues with college students: "I've spent four years in college. I haven't had time to pick up any skills." And it lasts through the middle years, especially when a person is thinking of changing his or her career: "I'll have to go back to college, and get retrained, because otherwise I won't have any skills in my new field." Or: "Well, if I claim any skills, I'll start at a very entry kind of level." All of this fright about the word "skills" is very common, and stems from a total misunderstanding of what the word means. A misunderstanding that is shared, we might add, by altogether too many employers, personnel departments, and other so-called "vocational experts."

By understanding the word, you will automatically put yourself way ahead of most job-hunters. And, especially if you are weighing a change of career, you can save yourself much waste of time on the (currently popular) folly called "going back to school for retraining."

So, herewith our crash course on skills:

Skills are the most basic unit -- the atoms -- of your life in the world of work. You can see this from the diagram on the next page.

If you prefer definitions to diagrams, here they are:

• A **career** is your total life in the world of work. Careers are often, in everyday conversation, spoken of as though they were synonymous with "**Fields** of knowledge" or "majors" -- so that when we mean to say "field change" we often use instead the more popular phrase "career-change." But in the end it doesn't matter which phrase we use.

• A **job** is defined by what is above it and below it. Above it is "Field," and below it are "**Tasks**" and "Skills." Thus it is that a

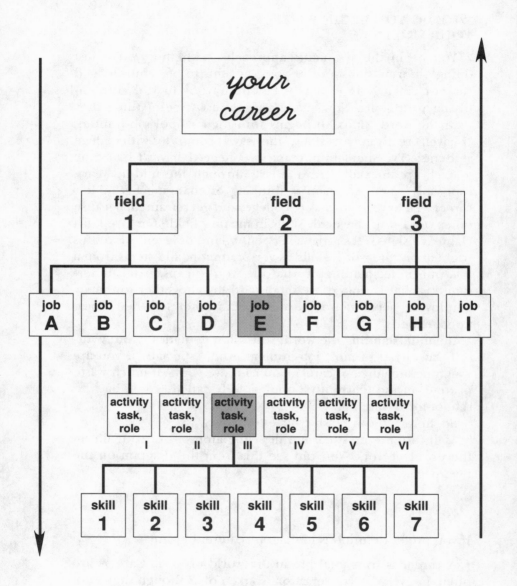

job is a particular kind of work in a particular field, where you set your hand to particular tasks using particular skills.

• As for "**Skills,**" you can of course call them by other names -- and many prefer to: your God-given talents, gifts, aptitudes, or whatever. The name does not matter. They are the essence of what you have to offer to the world, within the world of work.

According to the "Bible" of career counseling -- the fourth edition of the *Dictionary of Occupational Titles* (U.S. Government Printing Office, Washington, D.C., 1977) -- skills break down, first of all, into three groups according to whether or not they are being used with **Data (Information),** or **People,** or **Things.** Thus broken down, and arranged in a hierarchy of the less complex skills at the bottom to the more complex skills at the top, they come out looking like inverted pyramids:

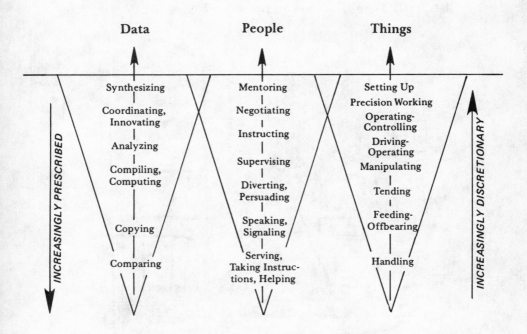

Before we end this brief crash course, let us note from this diagram:

FOUR LITTLE KNOWN FACTS
ABOUT SKILLS

1. The skills are ranked in a hierarchy, one above the other, and **each skill,** as you go up the inverted pyramids **typically includes or involves most or all of those skills which are listed below it.** We can see this clearly, by looking at the skills that are used with People (see the boxes on the following pages). This particular list of definitions, incidentally, is taken from the third edition (1965) of the *Dictionary of Occupational Titles,* Vol. II, pp. 649-50, as modified and adapted by Dr. Sidney A. Fine. Note that the list differs slightly from the one in the previous pictorial, and also from the list found in Appendix A (just checking to see if you're awake):

At your public library, in the 1977 edition of the D.O.T., as the *Dictionary of Occupational Titles* is called, you can find similar lists for Data and Things (on pp. 1369-71).

"... and give me good abstract-reasoning ability,
interpersonal skills, cultural perspective, linguistic comprehension,
and a high sociodynamic potential."

WORKING WITH PEOPLE
Increasing Levels of Skill
Beginning With
The Most Elementary Definition

TAKING INSTRUCTIONS — HELPING
Attends to the work assignment, instructions, or orders of supervisor. No immediate response or verbal exchange is required unless clarification of instruction is needed.

SERVING
Attends to the needs or requests of people or animals, or to the expressed or implicit wishes of people. Immediate response is involved.

EXCHANGING INFORMATION
Talks to, converses with, and/or signals people to convey or obtain information, or to clarify and work out details of an assignment, within the framework of well-established procedures.

COACHING
Befriends and encourages individuals on a personal, caring basis by approximating a peer- or family-type relationship either in a one-to-one or small group situation, and gives instruction, advice, and personal assistance concerning activities of daily living, the use of various institutional services, and participation in groups.

PERSUADING
Influences others in favor of a product, service, or point of view by talks or demonstrations.

DIVERTING   Amuses others.

CONSULTING
Serves as a source of technical information and gives such information or provides ideas to define, clarify, enlarge upon, or sharpen procedures, capabilities, or product specifications.

INSTRUCTING
Teaches subject matter to others, or trains others, including animals, through explanation, demonstration, practice, and test.

TREATING
Acts on or interacts with individuals or small groups of people or animals who need help (as in sickness) to carry out specialized therapeutic or adjustment procedures. Systematically observes results of treatment within the framework of total personal behavior because unique individual reactions to prescriptions (chemical, behavioral, physician's) may not fall within the range of prediction. Motivates, supports, and instructs individuals to accept or cooperate with therapeutic adjustment procedures, when necessary.

continued next page

INCREASING LEVELS OF SKILL continued

SUPERVISING
Determines and/or interprets work procedure for a group of workers, assigns specific duties to them (particularly those which are prescribed), maintains harmonious relations among them, evaluates performance (both prescribed and discretionary), and promotes efficiency and other organizational values. Makes decisions on procedural and technical levels.

NEGOTIATING
Exchanges ideas, information, and opinions with others on a formal basis to formulate policies and programs on an initiating basis (e.g., contracts) and/or arrives at resolutions of problems growing out of administration of existing policies and programs, usually after a bargaining process.

MENTORING
Deals with individuals in terms of their overall life adjustment behavior in order to advise, counsel, and/or guide them with regard to problems that may be resolved by legal, scientific, clinical, spiritual and/or other professional principles. Advises clients on implications of diagnostic or similar categories, courses of action open to deal with a problem, and merits of one strategy over another.

2. As you note the increasing complexity of the higher skills on these pyramids, you will of course -- in keeping with the modest nature for which you are doubtless widely known -- be tempted to identify your skills down near the bottom of the inverted pyramids -- "just to be on the safe side." But in fact, it is in your own best interest to claim the highest skills that you legitimately can. Because, the higher the skill that you have, the more you are given room to be creative. You will be free

to carve out the job so that it truly fits you. On the other hand, the lower the skill you claim, the more you will have to "fit in" -- following the instructions of your supervisor and doing exactly what you are told to do.

3. The higher the level of skills that you can honestly and legitimately claim for yourself, on the basis of your past performance, the less likely it is that the jobs which use such skills will be advertised through normal channels. And because they are not advertised through normal channels, you will absolutely need to use the unorthodox methods described in chapters 5 and 6 to find out about them.

4. However, the more unorthodox the methods you use to find such jobs, the less people there will be to compete with you for that job. And in fact, if you succeed in uncovering an unmet need within the organizations of your choice, there is an excellent chance that they will be willing to create for you a job that did not even exist before you walked in. (They may have been **thinking** about creating such a job, but they never got around to doing it until they saw you.) This means you will be competing with no one, since you will be the sole applicant for that newly created job.

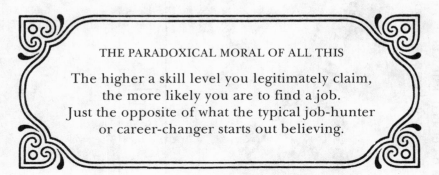

THE PARADOXICAL MORAL OF ALL THIS

The higher a skill level you legitimately claim,
the more likely you are to find a job.
Just the opposite of what the typical job-hunter
or career-changer starts out believing.

So, if you would do your job-hunt or career-change most effectively, you must identify your skills and be able to fill out this diagram completely:

If you **cannot** fill this out off the top of your head (**and 99.6% of all job-hunters can't**), then you will find detailed instructions for doing this on pages 218ff. Now or later, but before you begin your job-hunt or career-change, go there and do it!

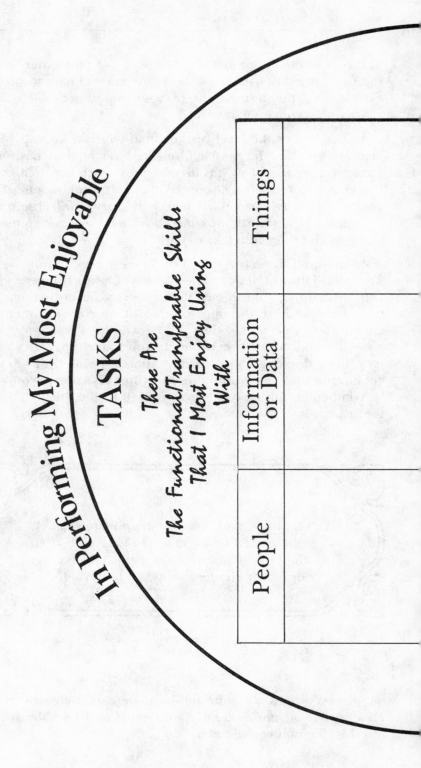

In Performing My Most Enjoyable

TASKS

These Are
The Functional/Transferable Skills
That I Most Enjoy Using
With

People	Information or Data	Things

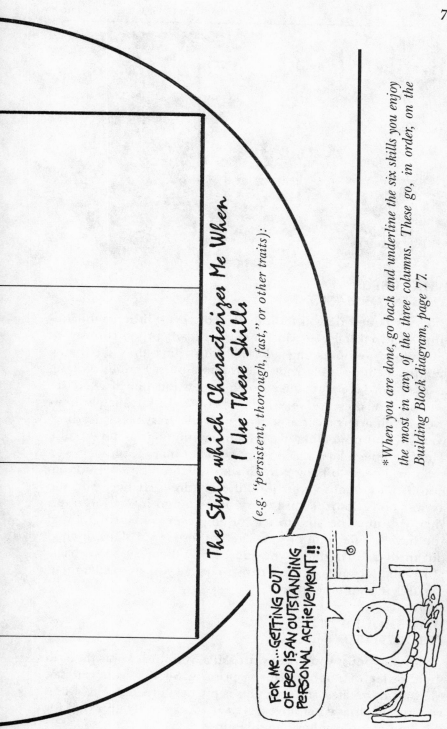

The Style which Characterizes Me When I Use These Skills

(e.g. "persistent, thorough, fast," or other traits):

*When you are done, go back and underline the six skills you enjoy the most in any of the three columns. These go, in order, on the Building Block diagram, page 77.

FOR ME...GETTING OUT OF BED IS AN OUTSTANDING PERSONAL ACHIEVEMENT!!

WHAT USE IS
THIS INFORMATION?

That's a question you should ask about **everything** in the job-hunt. And I'll tell you why. There are loads of job-counselors and other well-meaning advisors who think they are being helpful if they simply keep job-hunters busy. Period. As long as they can keep you **busy** doing paper and pencil exercises on yourself, they are very happy people. Unfortunately however, if you aren't clear as to where all this busyness is leading, you will end up feeling like a hamster running on a treadmill. The first fifteen laps may be fun, but after that . . . phooey.

So, you need to know **why** this information (or any information) is important to your job-hunt or career-change. And the answer boils down to this: every time you go into a job interview, you must be able to tell an employer convincingly what you have to offer him or her. The answer is your skills, spelled out in detail. Therefore you must know them by heart, backwards and forwards. If it is a career-change you are contemplating, this is even more true.

WHY SHOULD IT BE
PRIORITIZED?

Not only must you know your skills, you must know them in their order of importance, or priority. So that you can say, "This is my greatest strength, this is my next greatest, etc." when you approach **any** employer, even if you are only applying for the kind of job you have held before.

Moreover, every time you decide to turn your job-hunt into a full-fledged career-change, you will likely be rearranging the "building blocks" of your skills, into a new order of priority. Hence the absolute importance, once you know what your skills are, of **putting your skills in the order of priority for you,** as in the building-block diagram. If you skip over this step, you are essentially committing job-hunting suicide.

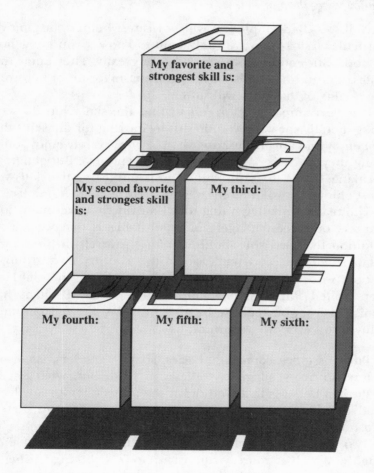

If you don't know how to prioritize your skills **(and 83.7% of all job-hunters and career-changers don't),** then you will find detailed instructions for doing this on page 213. Now or later, but before you begin your job-hunt or career-change, go there and do it!

SPECIAL PROBLEMS

In figuring out WHAT you would most enjoy doing, it will not be surprising if you run into some problems. Let us look at the more common ones:

1. "I don't see why I should look for skills I enjoy; it seems to me that employers will want to know what skills I do well, whether I enjoy using them or not."

Well, yes. **Bad** employers will not care whether you enjoy a particular task -- they will only want to know if you know how to do it. But **good** employers will care greatly. They know that unless a would-be employee has enthusiasm for his or her work, the quality of that work will suffer.

It is **very** important for you to find the skills you do well, but generally speaking you do this by looking for the skills that you enjoy and are enthusiastic about. People rarely enjoy something they do very badly (there **are** exceptions). But generally speaking, listing the skills you do well and listing the skills you most enjoy are two different ways of arriving at the same list.

The reason why Beginning with Enjoyment makes many job-hunters or career-changers uncomfortable is that we have a tradition that says you shouldn't enjoy yourself in life. It was established years and years ago in this country by a group of people who thought it actually sinful to enjoy oneself. They were called Puritans. It would be nice if the Puritans had vanished from our culture by now; but, alas, the Puritan mentality is still everywhere around us.

Puritans today come in all sizes, shapes, genders, ages, and colors. Puritans allegedly believe in God; but, what a god! A Puritan believes that God didn't intend us to enjoy anything. And that if you enjoy it, it's probably wrong for you. Let us illustrate:

Two girls do babysitting. One hates it. One enjoys it thoroughly. Which is more virtuous in God's sight? According to the Puritan, the one who hates it is more virtuous.

Two Puritans met on the street. "Isn't this a beautiful day?" said one. "Aye," said the other, "but we'll pay for it."

Puritans will talk about their failures, but hardly ever about their successes and even then, always with a feeling that "God is going to get me, for this." Such "boasting" is too enjoyable!

"FRANKLY, IT'S NOT EASY BEING A PURITAN IN THIS 'HEDONISTIC SOCIETY ! "

Given the Puritan's belief in God, we may speak directly to the Puritan instinct, within that framework of belief. "Look at the birds of the air, and animals at play. You will notice one distinctive fact: **joy follows action.** What you as Puritan fail to recognize is that in human life also, enjoyment isn't a fluke. It's part of God's plan. God wants us to eat; therefore God designs us so that eating is enjoyable. God wants us to sleep; therefore God designs us so that sleeping is enjoyable. God wants us to procreate, love, and make love; therefore God designs us so that sex is enjoyable, and love even more so. And: God gives us unique (or at least unusual) skills and talents; therefore **God designs us so that, when we use the talents He most wants us to use, that is our time of greatest joy.** Joy follows action.

"Furthermore, we gain a sense of achievement from them.

"So, Puritans arise; if you believe in God, believe in One who believes in you. Downgrading yourself is out - - for the duration of your job-hunt."

2. *"I believe in doing this skill identification; but I can't come up with enough good stories about any enjoyable achievements I've ever done in my life."*

If you are trying to think of some enjoyable achievements in your life, but inspiration just isn't coming, try writing a diary of your whole life and your accomplishments, without (at first) stopping to look for "enjoyable" or "remarkable."

This diary method is fully described in a companion book to this one, called *Where Do I Go From Here With My Life?* -- by John C. Crystal and some friend of his.

For now, we will content ourselves here with a mere outline of the method. It has the following directions:

A. Write a diary of your entire life. An informal essay of where you've been, what you've done. Where you were working, what you did there (not in terms of job titles -- forget them -- but in terms of what you feel you achieved).

B. Describe your spare time, in each place where you lived.

What did you do? What did you most enjoy doing? Any hobbies? Avocations? Great. What skills did they use? Were there any activities in your work that paralleled the kinds of things you enjoyed doing in your leisure?

C. Concentrate both on the things you have done, and also on the particular characteristics of your surroundings that were important to you, and that you really enjoyed: green grass, the theater, golfing, warm climate, skiing, or whatever.

D. Keep your eye constantly on that "divine radar": **enjoyable.** It's by no means always a guide to what you should be doing, but it sure is more reliable than any other key that people have come up with. Sift later. For now, put down anything that helped you to enjoy a particular moment or period of your life.

E. Boast a little. Boast a lot. Who's going to see this document, besides you, God, and any twenty people that you choose to show it to? Back up your elation and sense of pride with concrete examples, and figures.

F. Don't try to make this diary very structured. You can bounce back and forth in time, if that's more helpful; go back later, and use the suggestions above to check yourself out.

G. When your diary is all done, you may have a small book -- it can run 30 to 200 pages. (My, you've done a lot of living, haven't you?) Now go back and find just one story in it that you consider to have been an enjoyable achievement for you. Analyze it in the manner explained on page 230. After you are done analyzing it, go back to the autobiography and pick out a second story, in a different time period and a different arena of your life. Do skill identification on that second story. And so on.

This is more work than if you were just trying to write stories cold; but if the story approach isn't working for you, this is your lifeboat. Try it. As the commercials say: "You'll be so glad you did."

3. "I've never had any experience in the world of work. I've been a homemaker all my life. I can think of stories of enjoyable achievements within the home, but I'm not sure I could ever sell an employer on that."

If this is proving to be a hurdle for you, then you will want to write to the Educational Testing Service, Publication Order Services, CN 6736, Princeton, NJ 08541-6736 and ask for their I CAN lists, which are contained in the following inexpensive books, all of which are authored by Ruth B. Ekstrom: *HAVE Skills Women's Workbook -- Finding Jobs Using Your Homemaking and Volunteer Work Experience; How to Get College Credit for What You Have Learned As a Homemaker and Volunteer; HAVE Skills Employer's Guide -- Matching Women and Jobs; HAVE Skills*

Counselor's Guide -- Helping Women Find Jobs Using Their Home-making and Volunteer Work Experience. The I CAN lists classify all the skills of the homemaker under various roles and job titles in business, such as: administrator/manager, financial manager, personnel manager, trainer, advocate/change agent, public relations/communicator, problem surveyor, researcher, fund raiser, counselor, youth group leader, group leader for a serving organization, museum staff assistant, nutritionist, child caretaker, designer, clothing and textile specialist, and so forth. *Very* helpful.

4. *"I have no difficulty finding stories to write up, from my life, that I consider to be enjoyable achievements; but once these are written, I have great difficulty in seeing what the skills are, that I used in doing them -- even with this skills list you have in Appendix A."*

You will want to consider getting two friends or two other members of your family to sit down with you, and do some warm-up on skill identification through the practice of "Trioing." This practice is described at some length in *Where Do I Go From Here With My Life?*

5. *"How do I know if I've done this all correctly? What if I just think I understood what I was supposed to do, but I really didn't? I want to be sure the stuff I've identified is really going to help me in my job-hunt."*

Well, that's a reasonable anxiety, it seems to me. So, here are a few questions, to help you check out how you did:

a. Since all transferable skills are used either with Data, or People, or Things, do you now know which you most prefer working with? Is it some kind of Data, or some kind of People, or some kind of Things? And: which kind?

b. What's your second preference? Your third?

c. Have you described your skills with more than one word? One word is good to start with, but it isn't where you want to end up. In the end, you want to be able to describe what you do in more than just one word. "I'm good at **organizing**" doesn't tell us **anything.** Organizing what? People, as at a party? Nuts and bolts, as on a workbench? Or lots of information, lying in a computer? Those are three entirely different skills. The one word "organizing" doesn't tell us which one, at all. Sooooo, why don't you try going back over the skills you identified as yours, and make sure that each one-word definition gets **fleshed out** with an **object** -- some kind of Data/Information, or some kind of People, or some kind of Thing -- and maybe also an **adverb** or adjective. "I'm good at analyzing people **painstakingly,**" and "I'm good at analyzing people **in a flash, by** intuition," are two entirely different skills. The difference between them is found in the adjectival or adverbial phrase there at the end. So, try expanding each definition of your six favorite skills as much as you can, by an object at least, and maybe an adverb or adjective.

d. Have you got all your skills arranged in order of importance, or priority, for you? **Anytime** you have a bunch of information about yourself, it is relatively useless to you, until you have put it in order of priority. "Here's what I most enjoy doing, this is next, this is next, and so on." This is especially true of your skills. Looking ahead to your next job or career, which skill do you **most** hope you will get to use "on the job," which next, which next? and so on.

e. If you're trying to move into another career, have you avoided stating your skills in the jargon or language of your past career? This is a point on which clergy, in particular, often stumble and fall. "I am good at preaching" is not a very useful skill identification. It is still cloaked in the jargon and language of one career and one career only. What is its larger form? "Teaching?" Perhaps. "Motivating people?" Perhaps. "Inspiring people to the depths of their being?" Perhaps. Only you can say. But get your skills out of any jargon that locks you into your past.

f. Are you hanging loose, willing to look at a number of alternatives, as you move through the homework and research? Or is your desire for finishing this off fast leading you to push prematurely for just one way to go? Stay loose. Preserve **all** your options.

g. Have you thus far steered clear of putting a job title on what you're aiming toward? Skills can point to many different jobs, which have a multitude of titles. Don't lock yourself into a box prematurely. "I'm looking for a job where I can **use** the following skills," is fine. But, "I'm looking for a job where I can **be** a (job title)" is a no-no -- until you've done more homework and more research.

h. As you have been working on the question of your future career or future job, have you begun to get some insights into other aspects of your life and being? Keep yourself open and sensitive to these insights, as they pop up. Properly speaking, what you're engaged in with this systematic approach is not merely career planning, but life planning or life designing, if you prefer. You will become, in all likelihood, increasingly conscious of your values as you go along. As David Maister says, "Play to your evil secrets." They're not really so evil; you just think they are. But, speaking candidly and to yourself alone, what **are** your values? Truth, beauty, color, light, nature, justice, spirituality, righteousness, ambition, compassion, security, service, popularity, status, power, friends, achievement, love, authority, freedom, glamor, giving, integrity, honesty, loyalty, sensitivity, caring - - which holds the most meaning and importance for you? Your values will almost certainly become clearer to you, as you move on through your job-hunting or career-planning homework. Stay alert and sensitive to these. You will get much clearer about who you are willing to work with and for, and who you are not. Those who share your values will be on your hit parade; those who don't, won't.

ARE THERE ANY SHORTCUTS FOR THE LAZY?

You've probably gotten to this point in the chapter, without having yet done the actual identification or inventory of your favorite skills - - not even a peek back at Appendix A - - right? You're doubtless the type who likes to read all the way through and get the overall picture first. But now that you are here, you're debating whether to go do all this work or not. You're maybe in a mood to beg for a shortcut.

Well, what can I tell you? **Anyone** could be forgiven for not wanting to do all this work. And for wanting to know if there are any "Alternatives for the Lazy." Well, sure. I'll tell you at least three ways that some job-hunters have gone about Avoiding All This Job-Hunting Homework:

1. FIRST SHORTCUT: What do you want to be? John Holland first proposed this simple shortcut. In his earliest book, now out of print, he wrote: "Despite several decades of research, the most efficient way to predict vocational choice is simply to ask the person what he wants to be; our best devices do not exceed the predictive value of that method."

So, if you don't want to do a lot of paper and pencil exercises, you might try thinking out the answer to this question: "What do you want to be?" Sit in a quiet place, pen in hand, and write down whatever comes to mind.

2. SECOND SHORTCUT: Whose job do you most admire? One woman I know declined to do any of the skill identification exercises in this book. But she did decide to pose for herself this question: Among all the people that I know or have seen or read about, **whose** job would I most like to have? She decided that the person she most admired, whose job she most coveted, was a woman who appeared as hostess on a television program for children. Accordingly, she went to a local TV station with a carefully written, well-thought-out proposal for a similar children's television program. They not only eventually bought the idea, they asked her to be the hostess of it. Thus did she find her ideal job. "Without," she added triumphantly, "doing a single exercise in your book."

3. THIRD SHORTCUT: Use John Holland's "Self-Directed Search" which is described back on page 276. Instructions on how to order it are there. When you get it, it will take you about an hour to fill it out. Once you have filled it out, and have discovered your "Holland Code" of skills (for example, SIA) buy, borrow or go to your local library for the *Dictionary of Holland Occupational Codes: A Comprehensive Cross-Index of Holland's RIASEC Codes with 12,000 DOT Occupations* and look up all the occupations you could do, with that code (i.e., with those skills). It will not tell you all the things you could do; but it will at least give you a list of **some** places where you could start your Research or Informational Interviewing, as described in the next chapter.

To whet your appetite for John's "Self-Directed Search," you might want to try your hand at the Party Exercise, on the next page. It gives you a "quick fix" on what your "Holland Code" **might** be. You may think of it as a shortcut to a shortcut.

THE PARTY EXERCISE

What Skills You Have and
Most Enjoy Using

Generally speaking, all skills divide into six clusters or families. To see which ones you are *attracted to,* try this exercise:

On the next page is an aerial view of a room in which a two-day (!) party is taking place. At this party, people with the same or similar interests have (for some reason) all gathered in the same corner of the room.

(1) Which corner of the room would you instinctively be drawn to, as the group of people you would most *enjoy* being with for the longest time? (Leave aside any question of shyness, or whether you would have to talk with them.) Write the *letter* for that corner here:

_____

(2) After fifteen minutes, everyone in the corner you have chosen leaves for another party crosstown, except you. Of the groups *that still remain* now, which corner or group would you be drawn to the most, as the people you would most *enjoy* being with for the longest time? Write the letter for that corner here:

_____

(3) After fifteen minutes, this group too leaves for another party, except you. Of the corners, and groups, which remain now, which one would you most enjoy being with for the longest time? Write the letter for that corner here:

_____

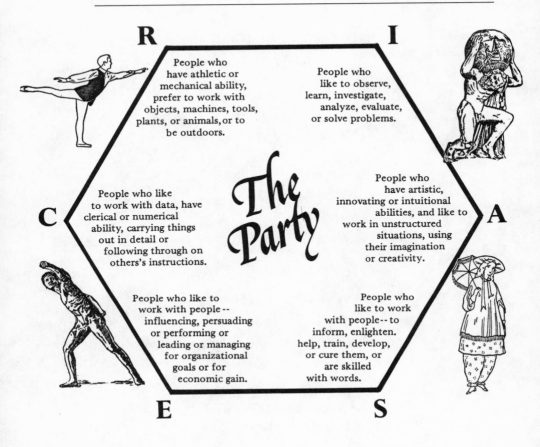

R

People who have athletic or mechanical ability, prefer to work with objects, machines, tools, plants, or animals, or to be outdoors.

I

People who like to observe, learn, investigate, analyze, evaluate, or solve problems.

The Party

C

People who like to work with data, have clerical or numerical ability, carrying things out in detail or following through on others's instructions.

A

People who have artistic, innovating or intuitional abilities, and like to work in unstructured situations, using their imagination or creativity.

People who like to work with people -- influencing, persuading or performing or leading or managing for organizational goals or for economic gain.

People who like to work with people-- to inform, enlighten, help, train, develop, or cure them, or are skilled with words.

E

S

THE PERIL OF SHORTCUTS

Well, there are the shortcuts. Nice, eh? (It's always nice to think that there are shortcuts.) But remember the principle enunciated earlier: the job-hunt in this country is essentially a matter of sheer luck. The more **time** you are willing to spend on some proven job-hunting or career-changing techniques, the more you cut down on how much of your job-hunt depends on luck.

Conversely -- and this is the point you especially want to remember here -- the less time you are willing to spend on your own homework, the more you are willy-nilly returning to a dependence on sheer luck. Shortcuts don't take much time. **Think about it.**

You can try any shortcuts you want to. If you succeed in finding a fabulous job, then luck was obviously on your side.

But, on the other hand if you try these shortcuts and you don't find a job, then **you know what you must do:** go back, and do the skills identification exercises that are back on pages 218ff. in detail.

Practical Exercise
(Cooling Down?)

If two weeks after putting down this chapter, you pick it up again, and realize you still haven't even begun identifying your skills through any of these exercises, then let's face it: you're going to **have to** pay someone to aid you. Too bad, because chances are that if you'd just try this on your own, you could do as well or better by yourself. But better this than nothing: turn to Appendix C, **study** the introductory section there, then in your town choose three possible counselors or places, and go ask them questions. Weigh their answers. Choose one. Pay them for each hour as you go, and **get at this.**

90

Students spend four or more years
learning how to dig data out of the library
and other sources, but it rarely occurs
to them that they should also apply some of
the same new-found research skill to their
own benefit -- to looking up information
on companies, types of professions, sections
of the country that might interest them.

Professor Albert Shapero
The late William H. Davis Professor
of The American Free Enterprise System
at Ohio State University)

CHAPTER FIVE

The Systematic Approach To
The Job-Hunt and Career-Change:

PART II

Where

Do You Want To
Use Your Skills?

Once you've figured out the "WHAT?", you turn to the "WHERE?" Once you've figured out what are your favorite and strongest skills, you turn to the question:

> WHERE do I want to use these skills? What occupation or occupations will use as many of my strongest skills, and on as high a level as possible -- so that I will be doing my most effective work, and also my most enjoyable work?

This "WHERE?" question can be stated in three different forms -- in terms of your **dream job,** or in terms of **the job-market,** or in terms that can guide **your actual job-search.**

"WHERE"
IS THE KEY TO FINDING
YOUR DREAM JOB

Suppose your strongest and most favorite skills involve welding. The "WHERE?" question is: Do you want to weld together a wheel, or do you want to weld the casing of a nuclear bomb? You can see, the "WHERE?" is **terribly** important. Again, suppose your strongest and most favorite skills are secretarial ones. The "WHERE?" question is: Do you want to be working in a legal office, or in an office of a gardening store? Again, the "WHERE?" can make all the difference in the world.

It is not sufficient, therefore, merely to know WHAT are your favorite skills. You must press on, to this next step in your systematic approach to career-change or job-hunting: WHERE do you want to use your favorite skills?

You are starting here at exactly the opposite place from where most job-hunters begin. They begin with Vacancies. They comb the newspapers, professional journals, agencies and other places to try to find out where there are Vacancies. They let the Vacancies call the shots, for their life. You are going about your job-hunt **intelligently** by not beginning there.

You're starting with the issue of where you would **like** to work. Later, you can inquire whether or not there are such jobs, and whether or not the places which have such jobs do in fact have a vacancy. But **you begin with your dreams.** You ask yourself, What would be a dream job for me? So-called Realists scorn this idea of dreaming, of course. At least when it comes to their job. Elsewhere? That's another story.

Elsewhere, almost **everyone** has visions and dreams dreams. We dream of where we'd like to go next summer. We dream of what we're going to do for Christmas next year. We dream of what we'd do if we won the lottery. And so on, and on. It's only when we come to our job that we suddenly think our visions and dreams should be shelved. But the experts have discovered that, quite the contrary, with job-hunting in general and career-change in particular, the more you can tap into your dreams the more you **increase your chances** of being able at last to do what you always wanted to do with your life.

So, dream, dream, dream. Never mind "being realistic." According to the experts, 80% of the workers in this country are "under-employed." That's what comes of "being realistic." You don't want to end up in the same fix. But you will if while you dream you corrupt your dream by keeping one eye fixed on what you **think** you know about the job market. People who fall into this trap, are always saying something like: "I'm dying to be able to do this and that, but I **know** there is no job in the world like that."

You don't know any such thing. So, think out what would truly be your dream job!

Forget the "Yes, buts."

"Yes, but . . . dreams don't always come true in every detail." Well, it's possible that in the end you may not be able to find **all** that you want. But as John Crystal always used to say, why not aim for it, and then settle for less if and when you find out that you simply have to? Just **don't foreclose your future prematurely.** You'd be surprised at what you may be able to turn up.

"Yes, but . . . dreams don't always come true all at once." Well, sometimes they do have to be taken in stages. If you want to be president of a particular enterprise, for example, you may have to work your way toward it through two or three steps. But it is quite likely you will eventually succeed -- if your whole heart is in your dream.

So, take a look at what would be a dream job for you. You may want to do a warm-up exercise to surface some of those forgotten dreams of yours:

ON THE LAST DAY OF MY LIFE

Spend as much time as necessary writing an article entitled "Before I die, I want to . . ." (And then you list things you would like to do, before you die.)

Confess them to a piece of paper now, and maybe you can begin to make them happen in your life.

"Oh, darn, and just as I was beginning
to take charge of my life."

You may prefer to write an article on a similar topic: "On the last day of my life, what must I have done or been so that my life will have been satisfying to me?" Spend an hour or two on this. When finished, go back over it and make three lists: Things Already Accomplished, and: Things Yet To Be Accomplished, and: a third column, beside the second, listing the particular steps that you will have to take, in order to accomplish these things:

1 Things already accomplished.	2 Things yet to be accomplished. *(Then number them in the order in which you would like to accomplish them.)*	3 Steps needed in order to accomplish the things in column 2.

As you get involved with this exercise, you may notice that it is impossible to keep your focus only on your career. You will find some dreams creeping in concerning your leisure or your life-long learning, of places you want to visit, and experiences you want to have that are not on-the-job. **Don't omit these.** Be just as specific as possible.

The above exercise is a general, intuitional way of approaching the matter of your dreams. It's like flying at 30,000 feet. When you want to come in for a landing, however, you need to get a little more specific (maybe a **lot** more specific).

THE ESSENTIAL PARTS OF A DREAM

Dreams, when they concern your future ideal work, should have certain **parts** to them. **You need to be sure you have all those parts,** when you have finished setting your dreams down on paper in detail. Those parts are:

TASKS. What kinds of tasks, using what kinds of skills, do you see yourself doing in your ideal life's work? And with what kind of style? (You defined this in chapter 4, on page 74.)

TOOLS OR MEANS. What do you need in order to be doing your ideal life's work, by way of information, or things, or other people?

OUTCOME. What do you see your work producing, as its result? Immediately? Long-range?

SETTING. In what kind of setting do you see yourself working, in your ideal life's work? Setting means both physical setting and also the invisible stuff: values and the like.

COMPENSATION. What kind of salary or other types of compensation do you want to have, in your ideal life's work? What kinds of rewards do you hope your work will bring you?

These are the "WHERE?" questions, stated in terms of your dream job: WHERE do you want to work, **in terms of tasks, tools, outcomes, setting, and compensation.** (If you don't know the answer to these questions at the moment, don't worry. There are some paper and pen exercises in Appendix A that will enable you to answer these questions easily.)

"WHERE" IS THE KEY TO MASTERING THE JOB MARKET

Now, suppose you were made in such a way that "WHERE" was of no personal importance to you. You feel you could be happy anywhere just as long as you were using your favorite skills. Almost no organization in the country would be ruled out.

So, you're ready to go charging out there **and look at them all.** Lots of luck, my friend. There are 15,000,000 organizations, hence 15,000,000 job markets, out there for you to go look at. We'll see you again in about 43 years.

No, no, no. You have to **cut the territory down.** You have to find some way to narrow down the list of organizations that you will need to weigh, consider, go visit, or research. Otherwise your job-hunting territory will be just too big. If you are to be successful, your job-hunt must look essentially like this:

YOU START WITH
THE WHOLE JOB-MARKET
IN THIS COUNTRY—
15,000,000 JOB MARKETS

1 You narrow this down by deciding just what area, city or county you want to work in. This leaves you with however many thousands of job markets there are in that area or city. **2** You narrow this down by identifying your Strongest Skills, on their highest level that you can legitimately claim, and then thru research deciding what field you *want* to work in, above all. This leaves you with all the hundreds of businesses/community organizations/ agencies/schools/hospitals/projects/associations/ foundations/institutions/firms or government agencies there are in that area and in the field you have chosen. **3** You narrow this down by getting acquainted with the economy in the area thru personal interviews with various contacts; and supplementing this with study of journals in your field, in order that you can pinpoint the places that interest you the most. This leaves a manageable number of markets for you to do some study on. **4** You now narrow this down by asking yourself: *Can I be happy in this place, and do they have the kind of problems which my strongest skills can help solve for them?* **5** This leaves you with the companies or organizations which you will now carefully plan how to approach for a job, in your case, *the* job.

You will see at once the sense of this. The territory **must** be cut down. So, the only question remaining is: **what** questions do you use, to do this?

Experience has revealed that there are **seven basic questions** that are useful for cutting the territory down, (besides your skills, which we saw in the last chapter). These are:

1. WHETHER YOU PREFER TO WORK FOR AN ORGANI-ZATION THAT
   - PRODUCES **INFORMATION**
   - OR INVENTS/PRODUCES/SELLS **A PRODUCT**
   - OR OTHERWISE SERVES **PEOPLE.**

This cuts down the territory for you, because once you've said which you prefer, you only need to look at organizations that "fit your bill."

2. WHAT **KINDS OF INFORMATION** YOU PREFER TO WORK WITH OR HELP OTHERS TO KNOW. By this, we mean two things: FORM AND CONTENT.

   a) By **FORM,** we mean your preferences chosen from the lists which are to be found in Appendix A, e.g., do you prefer to work with books, or computer printouts, or magazines, or articles, or catalogs, etc.?

   b) By **CONTENT,** we mean what is often referred to as SPECIAL KNOWLEDGES -- the subjects you know and enjoy best.

This cuts down the territory for you, because once you've said what these are, you only need to look at organizations that work with such forms and need such special knowledges.

3. WHAT **KINDS OF PEOPLE** YOU PREFER TO SERVE OR WORK WITH. By this, we primarily mean what kinds of people do you want as clients or customers, but we do not want to leave out your co-workers, bosses, etc. -- what kinds of people do you want beside you, above you, below you in the organization?

This cuts down the territory for you, because once you've said what these are, you only need to look at organizations that work with or employ such people.

4. WHAT **KINDS OF THINGS** YOU PREFER TO WORK WITH OR HELP PRODUCE. By this, we mean your preferences chosen from the lists which are to be found in Ap-

pendix A, e.g., do you prefer to work with automobiles, or computers, or adding machines, or telephones, or other tools (which other?), etc.

This cuts down the territory for you, because once you've said what these are, you only need to look at organizations that work with such things.

5. WHAT **PHYSICAL SETTING** YOU WANT FOR YOUR WORK. By this, we mean two things: general and specific.

a) General is the **GEOGRAPHICAL AREA** you would ideally like to have as the setting for your work.

b) Specific is the **WORKING CONDITIONS** you would like to have the organization furnish as the setting for your work.

This cuts down the territory for you, because once you've said what physical setting you want, you only need to look at organizations that exist in or provide such a setting.

6. WHAT **SPIRITUAL OR EMOTIONAL SETTING** YOU WANT FOR YOUR WORK. By this, we mean your:
a) VALUES concerned with TRUTH
b) VALUES concerned with BEAUTY
c) VALUES concerned with MORAL ISSUES
d) VALUES concerned with FAITH, SPIRITUALITY, OR RELIGION

This cuts down the territory for you, because once you've said what spiritual setting you want for your work, you only need to look at organizations that will honor such values.

7. WHAT **SALARY AND LEVEL** YOU WANT AT A MAXIMUM; WHAT SALARY AND LEVEL YOU NEED AT A MINIMUM.

This cuts down the territory for you, because once you've said what salary and level you want for your work, at a maximum and at a minimum, you only need to look at organizations that offer that salary and level.

I know, I know. It makes your head swim the first time you look at this list. But if you are serious about your career-change or job-hunt, you will become **very familiar** with this list, believe me. For now, **many** of you will be helped if you can see these seven questions in a diagram instead of as just a bunch of words. Here 'tis:

The Keys to Cutting Down the Territory

Incidentally, we call this THE FLOWER DIAGRAM for obvious reasons (add a stem at the bottom and some leaves, and it **looks** like a Flower -- if you stand back about 40 feet).

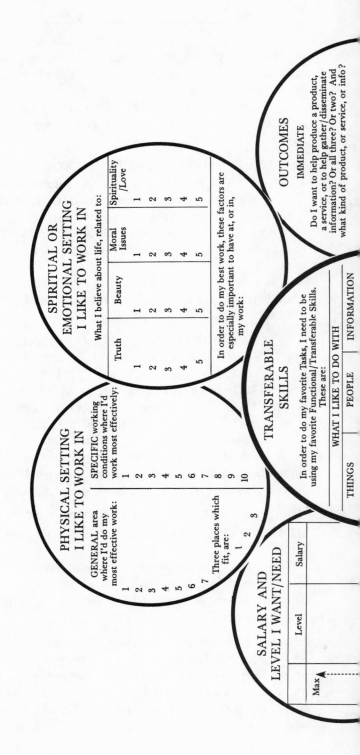

PHYSICAL SETTING I LIKE TO WORK IN

GENERAL area where I'd do my most effective work:

1
2
3
4
5
6
7

SPECIFIC working conditions where I'd work most effectively:

1
2
3
4
5
6
7
8
9
10

Three places which fit, are:
1   2   3

SPIRITUAL OR EMOTIONAL SETTING I LIKE TO WORK IN

What I believe about life, related to:

Truth	Beauty	Moral Issues	Spirituality /Love
1	1	1	1
2	2	2	2
3	3	3	3
4	4	4	4
5	5	5	5

In order to do my best work, these factors are especially important to have at, or in, my work:

OUTCOMES

IMMEDIATE

Do I want to help produce a product, a service, or to help gather/disseminate information? Or all three? Or two? And what kind of product, or service, or info?

TRANSFERABLE SKILLS

In order to do my favorite Tasks, I need to be using my favorite Functional/Transferable Skills. These are:

WHAT I LIKE TO DO WITH

THINGS	PEOPLE	INFORMATION

SALARY AND LEVEL I WANT/NEED

Level	Salary
Max	

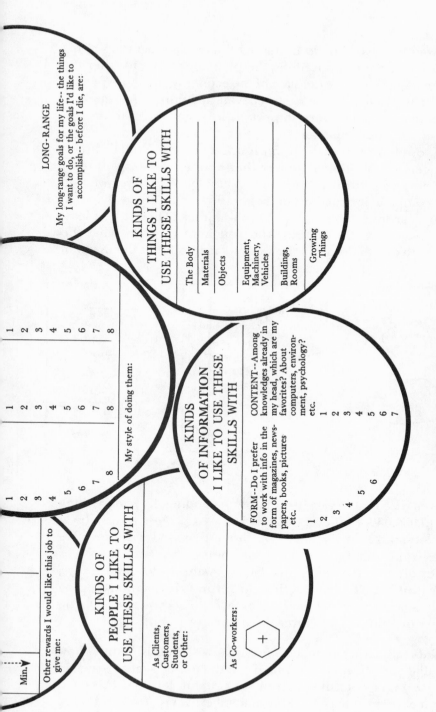

LONG-RANGE

My long-range goals for my life-- the things I want to do, or the goals I'd like to accomplish-- before I die, are:

KINDS OF THINGS I LIKE TO USE THESE SKILLS WITH

The Body

Materials

Objects

Equipment, Machinery, Vehicles

Buildings, Rooms

Growing Things

Other rewards I would like this job to give me:

Min. ▶

1
2
3
4
5
6
7
8

1
2
3
4
5
6
7
8

1
2
3
4
5
6
7
8

My style of doing them:

KINDS OF INFORMATION I LIKE TO USE THESE SKILLS WITH

CONTENT-- Among knowledges already in my head, which are my favorites? About computers, environment, psychology? etc.

1
2
3
4
5
6
7

FORM-- Do I prefer to work with info in the form of magazines, newspapers, books, pictures etc.

1
2
3
4
5
6

KINDS OF PEOPLE I LIKE TO USE THESE SKILLS WITH

As Clients, Customers, Students, or Other:

As Co-workers:

+

FILLING IN THE FLOWER

For a successful career-change, or even a successful job-hunt, you MUST know the answers to the questions above. You must fill out this Flower. You must, you must, you must cut the territory down.

Every hour you spend filling out the above diagram is going to save you **days** of pounding the pavements. The tougher the job-market, the worse the state of the economy, the more people out of work, the bigger a switch you are thinking of making in your career, the **more important** it is that you take time to fill out the above diagram.

If you don't know how to fill it out (and **99.6%** of all career-changers or job-hunters **don't**), then sooner or later you must turn to pages 201ff. in the back of this book, where you will find complete instructions on how to fill out the above diagram.

You may of course be A Lazy Job-Hunter. (There are at least ten of them in the world.) And you want to know what the alternative is, to doing all the work it takes to fill in the diagram

above. Hey, that's easy: just plan on spending 43 years visiting all 15,000,000 employers in the U.S. -- OR: just take stabs at the job-market, hit or miss, and hope that God will prove He loves you by sending a job to your doorstep.

On the other hand, if you DON'T want to do these things, then **you MUST take the time to fill in this diagram** (copied on to a larger piece of paper, **please** -- unless you're practicing for writing the Lord's Prayer on the head of a pin).

Naturally, you will be curious to know -- at this point -- how the diagram above (for cutting down the job-market to manage-ble size) relates to the parts of your dream job that we talked about earlier on page 96. You remember: *Tasks, Tools or Means, Outcome, Setting, Compensation.*

Strangely enough, they are identical, as the following pictorial shows, wherein I have superimposed the "dream" titles on the Flower Diagram above:

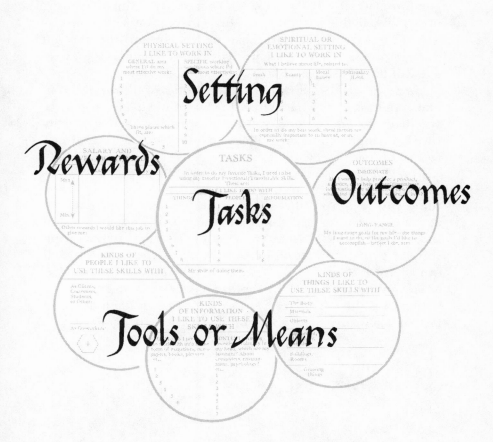

So, you can set about filling out this diagram from either viewpoint. **Think of filling out the Flower as filling out the details of your dream job, and you will automatically cut down the territory of your job-hunt. Or, think of filling out the Flower as trying to cut down the territory, and you will find that in the process of doing that, you are automatically defining your dream job.**

It's always nice when you can do two things at once; and this is one of those times.

ON TO THE RESEARCH
PART OF THIS JOB-HUNT
OR CAREER-CHANGE

Well, we must go on. Of course you probably haven't actually
gone and filled out the Flower Diagram, yet. You're reading
this book all the way through, first, to get the sense of it --
to see the overall plan. To make up your mind whether you
want to do all this work, or just go back to chapter 3 and use
a few of the hints there. I know, ah, how well I know.

However, we have to act as though you **did** fill out the diagram, and ask: now what? What do you do next? The answer is:
you have to go out and gather information -- that activity
which in high school or college we used to call "Research."
Oh no, not that! Yes, that!

Don't let your stomach turn weak, or your knees to jelly. It's
not difficult at all. It never is **when you're researching something you love.** And that was the whole point of the diagram
above, wasn't it: to nail down what it is you **love,** in each of
those eight arenas? When you go out to start your job-hunt,
you are going out first of all to research that diagram: to find
out **what** (out there in the real world) corresponds to the diagram you've drawn (and filled out) on paper.

Courage, then. This research shouldn't be difficult at all, in
fact it usually turns into a lot of fun.

The Process of Career Change

Plan A *The normal process of Career Change in our culture, as practiced by job-hunters left to their own devices, or by some counselors, especially when using the computer.*

Plan B *is the Prescription of the Creative Minority.*

A

1. Start only with the options you are already aware of.

2. Reject any which do not please you.

3. Do interviewing or research in the library and reject any others which do not please you.

4. Settle on one of those which are left; if none of these pleases you very much,

5. Settle on the one that you dislike the least.

B

1. Start with the few options that you are already aware of.

2. Expand your options by taking inventory of your basic building blocks of transferable skills and special knowleges.

3. Use these building blocks to increase your awareness of the many other jobs or careers that you might do and truly enjoy.

4. Then narrow this down to a definite picture of what it is that you would like to do (in your flower), by prioritizing each building block.

5. Now, talk to people and use printed resources to expand your ideas of all the different job-titles and all the different places that would fit your picture above.

6. Then start talking to people and using printed resources in order to eliminate those jobs which do not interest you, or fit in with your skills.

7. Of those which remain, identify the one you love most, the next most, etc. Find the places which have such jobs, and go after them, in that order.

The Prescription of The Creative Minority

DON'T PAY SOMEONE TO DO
THIS RESEARCH FOR YOU,
WHATEVER YOU DO

Now, I know what you're thinking. "Couldn't I pay someone to go do this for me? Aren't there organizations that already know the answers to the questions I need to research?" I would love to be able to tell you, "Yes." Unfortunately, information that organizations have is usually **incredibly** outdated. But even if it were up to date, there are several reasons why *no one else* can do this job-hunting research for you - - not a job-counselor, not your best friend, not your children, not your parents, not your mate, **not anyone.** The reasons are three:

1. Only **you** really know what things you are looking for, and what things you want to avoid if possible, in your next job or career. If anyone else does it for you, they'll cut corners. This is **your** life; no one else has as much interest in making it work, as you do.

2. You need the self-confidence that comes to you as you practice this researching. You need it **before** you go after the organizations that interest you.

3. The skills you use to **find** a job are close to the skills you use **to do** the job, after you get it. Therefore, by doing all this research you are increasing your qualifications for the job itself. Thus, this conclusion: the more research you do, the more qualifications you will have for the job.

It is you yourself who **must** do it. **Can** you do it?

Surrrrrre you can.

SHYNESS VS. LOVE

Of course, just because I say that, doesn't necessarily mean you'll believe it. Many of us, when we go about job-hunting or changing-careers, are sure that we have some handicap no one else in the world has. The favorite is - - you guessed it - - shyness. To be sure, some of us are willing to acknowledge that there are other shy people in the world; but we feel that our case is different. We have Terminal Shyness.

Well me too. Yet our records show that terminally shy people have done **very** effective job-hunts, and very effective research during this "WHERE?" phase. Wanna know why? It's simple. Shyness always yields in the face of Love. If you **love** gardens, you will forget all about your shyness when you're talking to someone else about gardens and flowers. If you **love** movies, you'll forget all about your shyness when you're talking to someone else about movies. If you **love** computers, then you will forget all about your shyness when you're talking to someone else about computers.

So, your shyness will be no obstacle. **If you have taken time to fill in the Flower Diagram on page 100 FIRST, then you are now going out to explore something you just love.** (Don't drop me a line telling me you can't love gardens, movies, computers, etc.; you can only love people. We both know what I mean.) If you're looking for your dream job, you will be **very** motivated. If you **aren't** very motivated, you need to rethink whether this is really your dream job that you've got on that

Flower Diagram. Or did you try to "cut it down" to what you thought was really available out there? Get back to your true dream! Be dying to find it! And then as you go out, your shyness will not bother you.

Do remember this simple truth: your shyness is **your** servant. You are not its servant. Make it serve you. Put on your best clothes, stand tall and straight, shoulders back, and get out there. Conduct yourself as quietly confident that you would be an asset to any organization that you ultimately decide to serve. You will be, indeed. The thoroughness with which you're doing your job-hunting research, shows **that.**

THE PRACTICE JUST FOR PLEASURE

It will help you **a lot** if, before you start your research, you do some Practice first. John Crystal, back in 1972, invented an exercise which he called "The Practice Field Survey." **The purpose of this exercise is simply to get people comfortable about going out and talking to other people, by giving them something that is a pleasure to go out and talk with other people about.**

He suggested that if you are too shy to start doing research on your Flower Diagram (which is your ideal job, and your Principles of Exclusion for cutting down the job-market), **you should practice first on a non-job-related enthusiasm of yours,** that you get great pleasure out of talking about. For example:

- a hobby, *such as skiing, bridge playing, exercise, computers, etc.*
- a curiosity, *such as how do they predict the weather*
- an aspect of the town or city you live in, *such as a new shopping mall that just opened*
- an issue you feel strongly about, *such as the homeless, AIDS sufferers, ecology, peace, health, etc.*
- or any other non-job-related enthusiasm of yours, *such as a movie you just saw that you liked a lot*

You try to find Someone Else who you think might share your enthusiasm -- using your friends or, if you know of no one off the top of your head, turning to the Yellow Pages. When you identify this potential Sharer-of-Your-Enthusiasm, you go then to talk with them. You do this with or without an appointment -- depending on how well you know them, or how accessible they are to the general public.

You ask them whatever questions are on your mind about this hobby, curiosity, aspect, issue, or enthusiasm. Because no job is connected to it **in your present plans,** and because you are talking to someone who (hopefully) shares your enthusiasm, you will normally find that you forget all about your shyness. (And that they forget about **theirs.**)

You may discuss **anything** and ask **any questions** which come to your mind. If nothing occurs to you, these questions have proved to be good conversation starters:

- How did you get involved with/become interested in this? ("This" is the hobby, curiosity, aspect, issue, or enthusiasm you share.)
- What do you like the most about it?
- What do you like the least about it?
- Who else would you suggest I go talk to that shares the same interest?
- Can I use your name?
- May I tell them you recommended that I talk to them?
- Would you be willing to call ahead, so they will know who I am when I go over there?

Then go see whoever they lead you to. If you need some support when you first go out to try this, **it's perfectly okay to take someone with you** -- at this stage of the job-hunt.

Alone or with someone, **keep at this,** until you feel very much at ease in talking with people and asking them questions about things you are curious about. It may take your seeing four people. It may take ten. Or twenty. You'll know.

When you feel comfortable doing this, and it's easy to talk to people about topics in which you take great pleasure, then you are ready for:

THE REAL THING: RESEARCHING OR INFORMATIONAL INTERVIEWING

Here you are into full-blown research or information-gathering on your Flower Diagram. I'll give you an overview, and then we'll tackle the steps one by one (these are the research questions, I mentioned at the beginning of this chapter). So here is the overview: during this phase of your job-hunt or career-change, your research has Four Steps. You are trying to find the answers to four questions:

1 What are the names of jobs that would use my strongest and most enjoyable skills and fields of knowledge?

2 What kinds of organizations have such jobs?

> ## 3
> What are the names of the organizations that I particularly like, among those uncovered in Question #2?

> ## 4
> What needs do they have, or what outcomes are they trying to produce, that my skills could help with?

Now to these Four Questions in detail, one by one. We'll start, of course, with the first.

The First Step in Your Research:
WHAT ARE THE NAMES OF JOBS THAT WOULD USE MY STRONGEST AND MOST ENJOYABLE SKILLS AND FIELDS OF KNOWLEDGE?

Remember what's going on here. **You are genuinely curious to find out what there is out there that matches your Flower/ Ideal Job.** This is **not** just a clever ploy to get in to see employers. In fact, it is not employers you go to see *at all* during this stage of your job-hunt. You go to see **workers who are actually doing the work you think you might like to do.**

In effect, what you are doing here is **trying on jobs to see if they fit you.** It is exactly analogous to your going to a clothing store and trying on different suits (or dresses) that you see in their window. Except instead of suits, it is jobs you are trying on. And why? Well, the suits that look terrific in the window don't always look so terrific when you see them on you. They don't hang quite right, etc., etc. Likewise, the jobs that look so terrific in the books or in your imagination don't always look so terrific when you see them up close, in all their true reality.

To be sure you understand what you are doing here in these **Information or Research Interviews,** let me emphasize how these differ from the **Practice Interview** (which you just did, purely for pleasure) and the **Employment Interview** (which you are not ready for, yet). To explain these differences, study the following diagram which was put together by the job-hunting expert in Europe, Daniel Porot. I use it with his kind permission.

Initial:	Pleasure **P**	Information **I**	Employment **E**
Kind of Interview	Practice Field Survey	Informational Interviewing or Researching	Employment Interview or Hiring Interview
Purpose	To Get Used to Talking with People to Enjoy It; To "Penetrate" Networks	To Find Out If You'd Like a Job, Before You Go Trying to Get It	To Get Hired for the Work You Have Decided You Would Most Like to Do
How You Go to the Interview	You Can Take Somebody with You	By Yourself or You Can Take Somebody with You	By Yourself
Who You Talk To	Anyone Who Shares Your Enthusiasm About a (for You) Non-Job-Related Subject	A Worker Who Is Doing the Actual Work You Are Thinking About Doing	An Employer Who Has the Power to Hire You for the Job You Have Decided You Would Most Like to Do
How Long a Time You Ask For	10 Minutes (and DON'T run over -- asking to see them at 11:50 may help keep you honest, since most employers have lunch appointments at noon)		
What You Ask Them	Any Curiosity You Have About Your Shared Interest or Enthusiasm	Any Questions You Have About This Job or This Kind of Work	You Tell Them What It Is You Like About Their Organization and What Kind of Work You Are Looking For.

Initial:	Pleasure P	Information I	Employment E
What You Ask Them *(continued)*	If Nothing Occurs to You, Ask: 1. How did you start, with this hobby, interest, etc.? 2. What excites or interests you the most about it? 3. What do you find is the thing you like the least about it? 4. Who else do you know of who shares this interest, hobby or enthusiasm, or could tell me more about my curiosity? a. Can I go and see them? b. May I mention that it was you who suggested I see them? c. May I say that you recommended them? ***Get their name and address***	If Nothing Occurs to You, Ask: 1. How did you get interested in this work and how did you get hired? 2. What excites or interests you the most about it? 3. What do you find is the thing you like the least about it? 4. Who else do you know of who does this kind of work, or similar work but with this difference: _____? 5. What kinds of challenges or problems do you have to deal with in this job? 6. What skills do you need in order to meet those challenges or problems? ***Get their name and address***	 You tell them the kinds of challenges you like to deal with. What skills you have to deal with those challenges. What experience you have had in dealing with those challenges in the past.
AFTERWARD: That Same Night	SEND A THANK YOU NOTE	SEND A THANK YOU NOTE	SEND A THANK YOU NOTE

Some of you doubtless like symbols better than words, and for you we have the following diagram. It is like the one above in content, except that it also illustrates how the "P" overlaps with the "I," and how the "I" overlaps with the "E" phase. You will notice that the "P" gives you practice in the "I," and the "I" gives you practice in the "E" phase before you have to go out and do it "for real."

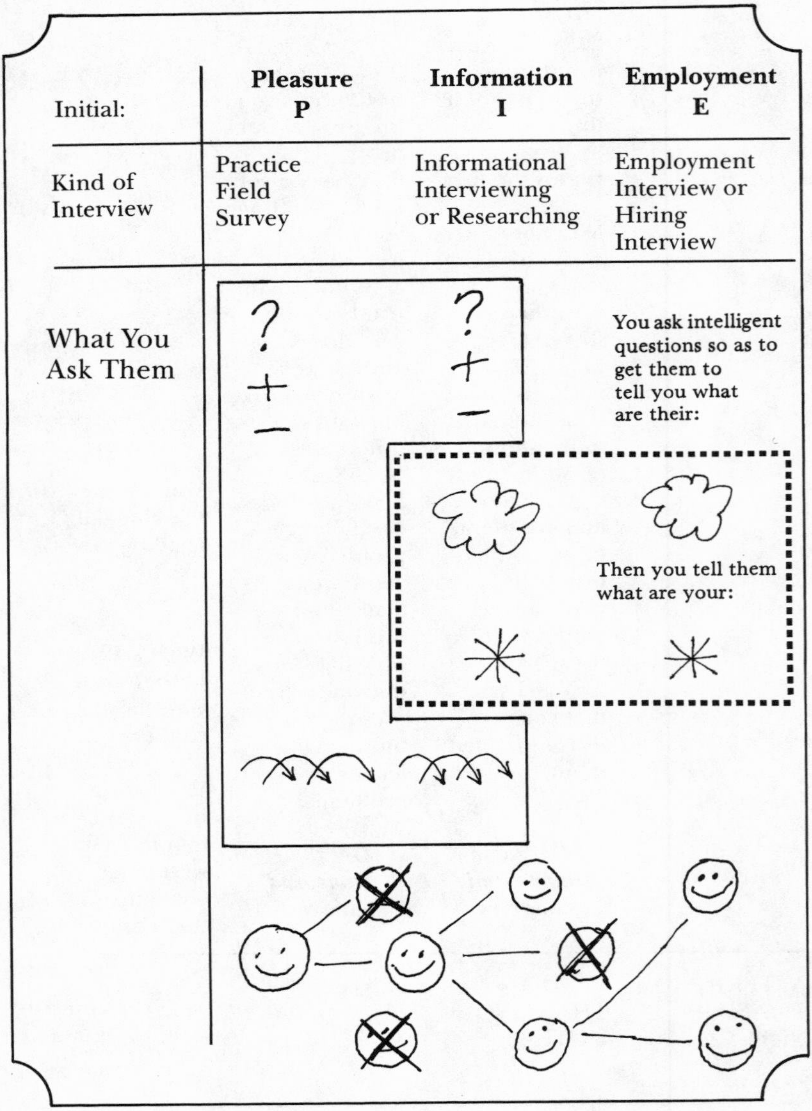
Initial:
Pleasure P
Information I
Employment E
Kind of Interview
Practice Field Survey
Informational Interviewing or Researching
Employment Interview or Hiring Interview
What You Ask Them
?
+
–
You ask intelligent questions so as to get them to tell you what are their:
Then you tell them what are your:

Key
to Porot's
Pie Chart
with symbols

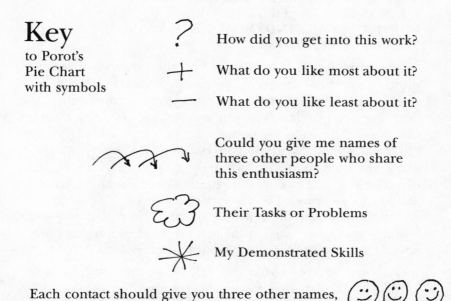

?   How did you get into this work?

+   What do you like most about it?

—   What do you like least about it?

Could you give me names of
three other people who share
this enthusiasm?

Their Tasks or Problems

My Demonstrated Skills

Each contact should give you three other names,

and even though some of them don't pan out,

one or two of the others should, and they will lead you to
still others as the diagram shows.

After studying (and I do mean **studying**) these two diagrams, hopefully you are clear about what you're doing during **this** phase of your job-hunt or career-change.
- You are doing the "I" in the "PIE."
- You are doing Informational Interviewing, or - - if you prefer - - research.
- You are interviewing **workers** doing the work you think you might like to do, or you are interviewing **sources of information,** such as librarians. Or you are poring over **directories** in libraries, such as the *Dictionary of Occupational Titles*.
- You are "trying on" jobs to see if they fit.

**WHY THIS RESEARCH MAKES SENSE
EVEN IF YOU'RE LOOKING
FOR THE SAME KIND OF WORK
YOU'VE ALWAYS DONE**

I am sure you see the sense of all this research **if you are
plotting a career-change.** You are by definition switching from
a job you knew well to some other job or career that you
don't know at all. Naturally, you want to find out all the attractive possibilities that lie before you -- which would fit your
Flower Diagram. Naturally you want to find out what's good
about each possibility, and what's bad about it. So, in the case
of a contemplated career-change, this sort of research obviously
makes a lot of sense. "Look before you leap."

You may not see the sense of all this, however, if all you're
doing is going out looking for just the kind of job you always
have done. *What's the point?* Well, the point is this:

(1) You don't know that you will be able to find the same
kind of work you used to do; those sorts of jobs may all be
taken. Or they may be slowly vanishing off the face of the
earth, replaced by technology or whatever. So, **you've got to
have a plan B.**

(2) You don't know that the same kind of work you used to
do would be the most fulfilling for you. Maybe you can find
something more fulfilling, that even pays better, this time
around. This job-hunt could be your ticket to freedom. It's
worth taking the time and effort to find out if there is something better out there, for you.

"WE'RE OFF TO SEE THE WORKERS . . ."

How do you decide **who** to go see? That's easy. Go back to
the Flower Diagram that you so laboriously filled in (**you did,
didn't you?**) on page 100, following the instructions found on
pages 201ff.

On a separate sheet of paper, now, copy down your favorite
Transferable Skills (the center of the Flower Diagram) and your
favorite Special Knowledges (the bottom petal). Now, show this
list to all your family and friends, and ask them what jobs
come to mind, that they think would use such Skills and such
Knowledges.

You can also ask them where they think you would find the people who do those kinds of jobs (**the workers**).

I repeat, only because countless job-hunters and career-changers have experienced some confusion here no matter how many times one repeats this: **at this stage of your research you are not interested in talking to employers, or people who have the power to hire. Rather, you are only interested in talking to people who are actually doing the work that you think you might enjoy doing.** You are trying to find out if this job fits you; you are trying to find out if this job fits the Ideal Job that you depicted on your Flower Diagram.

Toward this end, the questions you will find most useful to ask of the workers you interview are:

1. **How did you get into this work?**
2. **What do you like the most about it?**
3. **What do you like the least about it?**
4. **And, where else could I find people who do this kind of work?** (OR, if you have discovered from this interview that this kind of job definitely turns you off, then you ask them for ideas as to who you could go talk to about the other kinds of work your friends/family suggested fit your Flower Diagram.) Then you go visit the people they suggest.

You should always ask them for more than one name, so that if you run into a dead end at any point, you can easily go back and visit the other people they suggested.

"SAVING TIME, SAVING MONEY, SCREENING OUT JOBS *BEFORE* WE'RE HIRED"

Please don't think you're doing something screwy, by undertaking this interviewing. **Everybody screens out jobs; it's just that most of them do it after they're hired.** In a survey done in the San Francisco Bay Area it was found that of those people placed in jobs by the U.S. Employment Service, 57% of them were not in that job just thirty days later. Granted that some of them probably only wanted work for a few days, it is still true that many must have tried out the job and found out that they didn't like it -- it just didn't fit them. But, in order to find this out, they had to go through all the hassle of searching for that job, convincing the boss that they were right for that job, taking that job, starting work, telling all their friends that they had found a job, and then finding to their dismay that the job didn't fit them. So they had to quit, or manipulate management into firing them. What a lot of work, for nothing!

How much more intelligent it is to go talk to people about their jobs **before** you get hired in that line of work. How much more intelligent to find out ahead of time that the job doesn't fit you. Or that it does! This is what you are doing with your interviewing of workers, the "I" in the "PIE" process.

"MY RESEARCH KEEPS GETTING BETTER ALL THE TIME"

As you go about this phase of your research, you will discover that the separate and distinct parts of your Flower Diagram/ Ideal Job begin to fit together.

As you go about this phase of your research, you will also discover that you are becoming better and better at figuring out who can give you the information you need.

To illustrate these two points, let us suppose that you have discovered from your Flower Diagram that:
 (a) you are skilled in counseling people, particularly in one-to-one situations;
 (b) you are well-versed in psychiatry; and
 (c) you love carpentry and plants.

How do these three separate ideas start to come together as one unified career?

*"I used to ask myself,
'What can I do to help my fellow man?' but
I couldn't think of anything that wouldn't have put me
to considerable inconvenience."*

Well **that** depends on your becoming better and better at figuring out who can give you the information that you need. To do that you begin by translating each of the skills, knowledges or interests you have, into a corresponding **person.** In this particular case, counseling = a counselor, psychiatry = a psychiatrist, carpentry = a carpenter, plants = a gardener.

Next, ask yourself which of these persons is most likely **to have the largest overview**? This is often, but not always, the same as asking: who took the longest to get their training? The particular answer here: the psychiatrist.

In the place where you presently are, then, plan to go see a psychiatrist (pay them for fifteen minutes of their time, if there is no other way) or go see the head of the psychiatry department at the nearest college or university, and ask them: Do you have any idea how to put all the above together in a job? And if you don't, who might?

In this particular case, you will eventually be told: "Yes, it can all be put together. There is a branch of psychiatry that

uses plants to help heal people. You can use all your skills
and interests. You can even use your carpentry to build planters
for those plants."

You keep at this sort of interviewing until you find some
jobs out there that closely resemble or are identical to the
Dream Job you described on your Flower Diagram. Once you
have begun to get a pretty good idea of what jobs interest you
the most, because they use your favorite Skills and your favorite
Special Knowledges, you are ready for:

The Second Step in Your Research:
WHAT KINDS OF ORGANIZATIONS
HAVE SUCH JOBS?

You will of course have already stumbled upon some of this
information, while you were going about interviewing workers
whose jobs you thought you might like to have. When you
talked with them, usually at their place of business, you got to
know that type of business, **and** they may have told you of
other types of businesses where such jobs exist.

But now it is time to focus your research solely on this issue.
You want to find out all **the different kinds** of organizations
you might consider, in looking for the jobs that most closely
matched your Ideal Job/Flower Diagram, during Step One of
your research here.

To give you an example of what I mean, suppose you found
out during Step One that the job of teacher comes closest to
your Ideal Job. Now, to our question here: what **kinds** of organizations have such jobs? The answer is not what you might first
suppose: *"just schools."* No, no, my friend, not just schools. There
are countless other kinds of organizations and agencies out
there which have a teaching arm, and therefore employ teachers.
For example, corporate training and educational departments,
workshop sponsors, foundations, private research firms, educational consultants, teachers associations, professional and trade
societies, military bases, state and local councils on higher
education, fire and police training academies, and so on, and
so forth. You want to discover **all** such places. Your local town
or city librarian can be a great help.

If during Step One of this research you found there were
four different jobs that seemed close to your Ideal Job/Flower

Diagram, you will now need to discover all the kinds of places that have such jobs, **in each of the four cases.**

"Kinds of places" means many things. It means:

- places that would employ you full-time;
- places that would employ you part-time (maybe you'll end up deciding to hold down two or even three part-time jobs, which altogether would add up to one full-time job, in order to give yourself more variety);
- places which you yourself would start up, **if** you want to be your own boss;
- places that are for profit;
- places that are nonprofit;
- places that take temporary workers, on assignment for one project at a time;
- places that take consultants, one project at a time;
- places that operate with volunteers, etc.

Needless to say, you should plan on devoting a number of days -- **since the average job-hunt lasts three and a half months, you've got the time, believe me** -- to this Step of your research. Stay with it so long as it is fun. Remember, Confucius says: "Never choose a card, except from a full deck."

WRITTEN STUFF AND PEOPLE

If you are a normal job-hunter or career-changer, you will find that during this Step (and the next two Steps, as well) of your research or Informational interviewing, you will be dealing *alternately* with:

written materials -- such as books, journals, magazines, or other materials which librarians can direct you to -- and with

people, who can tell you what you need to know.

In general, the pattern is: you **Read,** until you need some information that no book seems to have. Then you go **Talk** to people until you have found out what you needed to know. Back then to do some more reading.

I caution you to do as much reading as you possibly can before you go and visit people. As a general rule, **people who have jobs are busy people and usually do not appreciate answering questions that you could just as easily have looked up in some directory, book, or annual report.** They are usually glad to answer questions whose answers cannot be found in any printed materials.

HOW TO RECEIVE A CORDIAL WELCOME

You will normally be accorded a cordial welcome by most people you go to see for information. That is obviously true in a small organization with easy public access (like a mom-and-pop grocery store). If you run into a real grumpy person, seek elsewhere for your information. If your information hunt takes you to larger organizations, here are some things to keep in mind. You will be given a **cordial** welcome in most large organizations:

a. **provided** that you know what questions you are trying to find answers to, and the answers can't easily be found in printed materials, microfiche, or on disk.

b. **provided** that you approach no organization until you've first gotten your hands on everything they've got in print, about who they are and what they do -- and provided that you've thoroughly digested this stuff before you go in to see them.

c. **provided** that when it is time for you to approach people, you approach first of all those people whose business it is to give out information to the public, and find out everything they know about the questions or curiosities that are plaguing you. I am thinking of such people as the front desk in personnel offices, receptionists, public relations officers, librarians, and the like.

d. **provided** that when you approach an organization, you talk to those in lesser authority first, to find out everything that they know, before you approach someone higher up in the same organization. The principle here is that you approach people for the information they alone know. Incidentally, visiting a senior person in that organization unannounced ("I just happened to be in the neighborhood") is universally perceived as the conduct of an amateur. If you would like to be seen as a professional, make an appointment; and state at that time that you only need a brief amount of their time (20 minutes, max), plus **what it is that you are trying to find out.** It may be someone else has that information, and they will tell you so over the phone, thus saving you from a fruitless errand.

WHEN IT COMES TO BOOKS, WHAT KINDS OF BOOKS WILL LIKELY PROVE USEFUL?

The kinds of books that you will likely find useful to you at this stage of your research, as well as subsequently, are the following. Most of them are to be found down at your local library.

American Men and Women of Science.
American Society of Training and Development Directory.
Who's Who in Training and Development, Suite 305,
600 Maryland Ave. SW, Washington, DC 20024.
Better Business Bureau report on the organization (call the
BBB in the city where the organization is located).
Business Information Sources, by Lorna M. Daniels.
University of California Press, Berkeley, CA 94720.
Annotated guide to business books and reference sources.
Career Guide to Professional Associations. Garrett Park Press,
Garrett Park, MD 20896.

Chamber of Commerce data on the organization (visit the
    Chamber there).
College library (especially business school library), if there is
    one in your chosen area.
Company/college/association/agency/foundation *Annual
    Reports.* Get these directly from the personnel department
    or publicity person at the company, etc., or from the
    Chamber or your local library.
Consultants and Consulting Organizations Directory, 6th ed.
    Gale Research Co., Book Tower, Detroit, MI 48226.
    Editors: Paul Wasserman and Janice McLean. 1984.
Contacts Influential: Commerce and Industry Directory.
    Business in particular market area listed by name, type
    of business, key personnel, etc. Contacts Influential,
    Market Research and Development Services, 321 Bush St.,
    Suite 203, San Francisco, CA 94104, if your library doesn't
    have it.
Dictionary of Holland Occupational Codes.
Dictionary of Occupational Titles.
Directory of Corporate Affiliations. National Register
    Publishing Co., Inc.

Directory of Information Resources in the United States.
(Physical Sciences, Engineering, Biological Sciences)
Washington, DC. Library of Congress.
Dun & Bradstreet's Million Dollar Directory. Very helpful.
Dun & Bradstreet's Middle Market Directory. Very helpful.
Dun & Bradstreet's Reference Book of Corporate Managements.
Encyclopedia of Associations, Vol. I, National Organizations.
Gale Research Co. Lists organizations that are in the
business of giving out information.
Encyclopedia of Business Information Sources, 4th ed.
(2 volumes). Gale Research Co.
Fitch Corporation Manuals.
F & S Indexes (recent articles on firms).
F & S Index of Corporations and Industries.
Lists "published articles" by industry and by company
name. Updated weekly.
Fortune Magazine's 500.
Fortune's Plant and Product Directory.
The Foundation Directory.
How to Reach Anyone Who's Anyone, by Michael Levine.
Price/Stern/Sloan Publishers, Inc. 410 N. La Cienega Blvd.,
Los Angeles, CA 90048.
Industrial Research Laboratories of the United States.
R.R. Bowker Co., 205 E. 42nd St., New York, NY 10017.
Investor, Banker, Broker Almanac.

MacRae's Blue Book.
Moody's Industrial Manual (and other Moody manuals).
National Directory of Addresses and Telephone Numbers.
    Concord Reference Books, 240 Fenel Lane, Hillside, IL
    60162.
*National Recreational Sporting and Hobby Organizations of
    the U.S.* Columbia Books, Inc., 777 14th St. NW, Washington,
    DC 20005.
*National Trade and Professional Associations of the United States
    and Canada and Labor Unions.* Garrett Park Press, Garrett
    Park, MD 20766.
Occupational Outlook Handbook.
Occupational Outlook Handbook for College Graduates.
Plan Purchasing Directory.
Register of manufacturers for your state or area
    (e.g., *California Manufacturers Register*).
Research Centers Directory, 6th ed. Gale Research Co.
    Also: *New Research Centers,* updating the original 1979
    volume.
Standard and Poor's Corporation Records.
Standard and Poor's Industrial Index.
Standard and Poor's Listed Stock Reports (at some brokers'
    offices).
*Standard and Poor's Register of Corporations, Directors and
    Executives.* Key executives in 32,000 leading companies,
    plus 75,000 directors.
Telephone Contacts for Data Users. Customer Services Branch,
    Bureau of the Census, 301-449-1600 for statistical
    information on any subject.
Thomas' Register of American Manufacturers.
    Thomas Publishing Co.
Trade association periodicals.
Trade journals.

Training and Development Organizations Directory, 3rd ed.
    Gale Research Co., Book Tower, Detroit, MI 48226.
    Editor: Paul Wasserman. 1983.
United States Government Manual. Or call the Federal
    Information Center of the General Services Administration
    at 202-755-8660 to find the names of experts in any field.
    For help on a question no one seems to know the answer
    to, try the National Referral Center at the Library of
    Congress, 202-287-5670.
Value Line Investment Survey, from Arnold Bernhard and Co.,
    5 E. 44th St., New York, NY 10017. (Most libraries have a set.)
Walker's Manual of Far Western Corporations and Securities.
*Ward's Business Directory, 3 vols. (Vol. 1, Largest U.S.
    Companies; Vol. 2, Major U.S. Private Companies; Vol. 3,
    Major International Companies).* Information Access Com-
    pany, 1201 Davis Dr., Belmont, CA 94002. Updated yearly.
Who's Who in Finance and Industry, and all the other Who's
    Who books. Useful once you have the name of someone-
    who-has-the-power-to-hire, and you want to know more
    about them.

Some of you will look at the above list, and faint. *Too much!*
Well, you don't need to use all of the above. Just keep clearly
in mind what you're trying to find out. If you're trying to find
out, for example, what are all the kinds of organizations that
use teachers, then you go to your helpful local librarian and
tell him or her so. See what they suggest. If there's no librarian,
or no helpful librarian, then look over the above list and take
a stab at what directories you think might have the information
you're looking for. If you don't know which directory to consult,
see:

• Klein's *Guide to American Directories*
    or
• Gale Research Company's *Directory of Directories*

Besides these directories, some periodicals are worth perusing: *Business Week, Dun's Review, Forbes, Fortune,* and the *Wall Street Journal.*

Some of you will find this research tedious but necessary. Others of you will find it great fun. You will enjoy discovering how much you can find out in this "Information Society" of ours, if you just set your mind to it. If you really get into this and want to find out more about how one finds **any** information about **anything,** here are some books for you to browse at your leisure:

Todd, Alden, *Finding Facts Fast: How to Find Out What You Want and Need to Know.* Ten Speed Press, Box 7123, Berkeley CA 94707. 1979.

Ferraro, Eugene, *You Can Find Anyone!* Marathon Press, 407 W. Santa Clara Ave., Santa Ana, CA 92706. 1988.

Mann, Thomas, *A Guide To Library Research Methods.* Oxford University Press, Inc., 200 Madison Ave., New York, NY 10016. 1987.

Pryor, Bill, *Secret Agent, Vol. 1.* Eden Press, Inc., P.O. Box 8410, Fountain Valley, CA 92728. 1986.

Harry, M., *The Muckraker's Manual: How to Do Your Own Investigative Reporting.* Revised and expanded. Loompanics Unlimited, Box 1197, Port Townsend, WA 98368. 1984.

Ullmann, John, with Honeyman, Steve, Ed., *The Reporter's Handbook.* St. Martin's Press, Inc., 175 Fifth Ave., New York, NY 10010. 1983.

I have gone into all of this at some length in order to show you that finding out what **kinds** of organizations have the jobs you are interested in is not a very difficult job. It just takes determination and persistence. Anyhow, one way or another, through people or books, once you have identified the kinds of organizations that have the kinds of jobs you are interested in, you are ready for:

The Third Step in Your Research:
WHAT ARE THE NAMES OF SUCH ORGANIZATIONS THAT I PARTICULARLY LIKE?

CUTTING DOWN THE NUMBER OF ORGANIZATIONS

Your problem here is that you must first of all cut down the territory. The kinds of organizations may total some twenty-five or thirty, and the list of the names of organizations which are of those thirty kinds may total 2,000. You can't go visit 2,000 organizations. So your task will be much more manageable if before you start collecting names, you first look over your list of organizations that have your Ideal Dream Job, and cross out **the kinds of organizations you don't like.** Here are some questions that may help you do this:

• 1. "Do I want to do the same kind of work I've always done, or do I want to start a new career now?"

• 2. "Do I want to work for somebody else, or would I rather start my own business at this time of my life?"

• 3. "If I want to start my own business, who among the people I visited would be the best models, as to how my own business should be set up?" You will need to go back and talk to them, to pick their brains for everything they're worth.

• 4. "Do I want to hold down just one job, or have several part-time jobs?" If you are interested in several part-time jobs, you might want to look at temporary agencies; they exist for many different fields now, not just for secretaries (as in days of old).

• 5. "If I choose to work for somebody else, do I want to work for a large organization or a small one?"

• 6. "Do I want to work for an older and larger organization, or get in on the ground floor of a new and smaller one, with growth possibilities?" If you're in an area where hiring is "tight," look long and hard at the new and smaller organizations. It's true that their failure rate is high; but it's also true that that's where two-thirds of all new jobs get created -- in businesses with twenty or less employees.

• 7. "Do I want to work for a profit-making company, a nonprofit firm, agency, college, association, foundation, small business, the government, or what?"

• 8. "Do I want to work for a 'going concern' or for 'a problem child' type of operation?" *As the experts say, a company in trouble is a company in search of leadership. The same goes for foundations, agencies, etc. If that is your cup of tea (well, is it?), you can probably find such places without too much investigation. Some experts say if you go for such a challenge, give yourself a time limit, say three to five years, and then if you can't solve it, get out. The average job in this country only lasts 3.6 years, anyway. If your goal is to advance rapidly, you'll probably need to look at an organization with solid plans for expansion - - overseas or at home.*

• 9. *Other questions:* "What do I want to accomplish with my skills? what working circumstances do I want? what opportunities? what responsibilities? what kinds of job pressures am I willing to exist under, and do I feel capable of handling? what kinds of people do I want to work with? starting salary? salary five years from now? promotion opportunities?"

DON'T TRY TO STAY VAGUE AND 'WIDE-OPEN' TO 'ANYTHING THAT COMES ALONG'

As you undoubtedly realize by now, **the more you can cut the territory down, the easier it will be to conduct your job-hunt. And the more detailed you are, the easier it will be for you to cut the territory down, and find the names of organizations that truly interest you.** Conversely, the less specific you are willing to be, the harder it will be for you to find the names of specific organizations which might hire you for the job you most want.

For example, let us see how two of the exercises you did earlier for your Flower Diagram/Ideal Job can be of particular relevance and helpfulness, at this point: General Physical Setting (i.e., Geography), and Specific Physical Setting (i.e., Working Conditions).

Geography, for one, can save you from saying, "I'm looking for the names of organizations which hire welders," which is much too broad. Suppose the San Jose area of California is your preferred physical setting for your future Ideal job. You will be helped by your Geography statements then to a statement which cuts your job-hunting area down to a more manageable size, such as: "I'm looking for the names of organizations in the San Jose area which hire welders."

Your preferred **Working Conditions** will further aid you in cutting down the territory. If you stated that you preferred to work for an organization with fifty or less employees, then you add this to your statement, so that it now reads: "I'm looking for the names of organizations having fifty or less employees which hire welders, in the San Jose area."

If, on top of this, you can throw in any other statements from your Flower Diagram or your earlier research, your task will get easier still. Suppose you decided you want to work for an organization which produces wheels. Then your statement gets further modified, to: "I'm looking for the names of organizations in the San Jose area, which produce wheels, hire welders, and have fifty or less employees." Now, you're talking! That's a manageable area in which to do your job-search!

CONTACTS, CONTACTS, CONTACTS
USE THOSE CONTACTS!

Once you're able to say just exactly and most specifically what **kinds** of organizations you want to find, how do you go about discovering their **names**?

Well, you know: the same kind of research that you've been doing. You use books, and people, people and books.

In this quest for names, you use every **contact** that you have. That means members of your family. Every friend. Your relatives. Your doctor, dentist, gas station attendant (a vanishing race), and the check-out clerk at your supermarket. **Everyone** you meet, anywhere, during the week.

They can not only tell you names of organizations, they often know what's going on at those places.

You see, to do your job-hunt well, you need to be in twenty places at once, with your eyes and ears wide open. And you just can't be. But your contacts can -- **if** they know what you are looking for, and **if** you have enlisted them to keep their eyes and ears open on your behalf.

Whenever a job-hunter writes me and tells me they've run into a brick wall, as far as finding out the names of organizations is concerned, I know what the problem will usually turn out to be. They aren't making sufficient use of their contacts. **The more people you know, the more people you meet, the more people you talk to, the more people you enlist as part of your own personal job-hunting network, the better your job-finding success is likely to be.**

Now, to be sure, your memory is going to be overloaded during your job-hunt or career-change, so do think about keeping the names of your contacts on 3 x 5 file cards with addresses, phone numbers, and anything about where they work or who they know that may be of use at a later date. Go back over those cards **frequently.**

Some job-hunters have written to tell me they cultivate new contacts wherever they go. For example, if they go to hear a speaker on some subject that interests them, they make it a point to join the crowd that gathers 'round the speaker at the end of the talk, and -- with notepad poised -- ask such questions as: "Is there anything special that people with my technical expertise can do?" And here they mention their specialty: computer scientist, health professional, chemist, writer, or whatever. Very useful information has thus been turned up. You can also ask if you can contact the speaker for further information -- "and at what address?" Conventions, likewise, afford rich opportunities to make contacts. Says one college graduate: "I snuck into the Cable Advertisers Convention at the Waldorf in N.Y.C. That's how I got my job."

Another way people have gathered contacts, is -- if they have a phone answering machine -- to leave a message on that machine which tells everyone who calls that they are looking for work. One job-hunter used the following message: "This is the recently laid off John Smith. I'm not home right now because I'm out looking for a good job in the telecommunications field; if you have any leads or just want to leave a message, please leave it after the tone."

If you decide that your target is in some entirely different geographical area from where you presently reside, you can still find out the names of organizations **there.** Detailed instructions on how to do this will be found in Appendix E.

A CAUTIONARY WORD:
CHECK AND CROSS-CHECK

In gathering information from people, one person's word should rarely be taken as gospel. There are people who will tell you something that absolutely isn't so, but they will tell it to you with every conviction in their being because **they think** it's true. Sincerity they have, one hundred percent. Accuracy is something else again. You will need to check and cross-check any information that people tell you or that you read in books (even this one).

For example, if someone tells you that the only way you can get into a certain kind of job is to have had fourteen years of post-high school education, make a quiet mental note to check it out. *"It ain't necessarily so. . . ."* Your response, while you're still talking to that person, should be, "Yes, but do you know of **anyone** who got into this kind of job **without** having had all that education?"

Anyway, be careful. Be thorough. Be persistent. This is your life you're working on, and your future. Make it glorious. Whatever it takes, find out the names of those organizations. That will bring you, then, to:

The Fourth and Last Step in Your Research:
WHAT NEEDS DO THEY HAVE OR WHAT OUTCOMES ARE THEY TRYING TO PRODUCE THAT MY SKILLS COULD HELP WITH?

"**Needs**" is a polite word. So is "**challenges.**" You know what we're **really** talking about here. We're talking about:

AN ORGANIZATION'S PROBLEMS

All organizations have some success. What you want to do is increase their success. What you are looking for are their problems -- specifically, problems that your skills can help solve. What problems are bugging this organization? Ask; look. But you should probably avoid direct use of the word "problems" since few organizations like to admit to outsiders that they have any problems. So, if you know some people within a company or organization that looks interesting to you, ask them ever so gently: What is the biggest **challenge** you are facing there?

The problem, or challenge, does not have to be one that is bothering only **that** organization. You want to ask if there is a problem common to the whole industry or field -- low profit, obsolescence, inadequate planning, or what? Or it may be there is a problem that is common to the geographic region: labor problems, minority employment, etc. All you really need is to put your finger on one major problem that you would truly delight to help solve.

If you feel you have no skills at analyzing an organization's problems or needs, think again. Visualize five stores you have been in, where you debated whether you would ever go back. Why was that? Well, of course, because of some problem they had. And don't tell me you didn't know what the problem was. You know very well that you did, and do. You weren't waited on, when it was your proper turn. You weren't told all the information you needed to know, in order to make an intelligent purchase. The person with whom you were dealing insisted on going by the rule book, no matter what common sense and compassion would otherwise dictate. The person with whom you were dealing had some small amount of power but was misusing that power for all it was worth. The organization had installed a computer where a person used to be, and the person between you and the computer seemed to be taking orders from it, rather than vice versa. The organization had, in a word, lost the human touch. You could tick off every one of those problems. It doesn't take a genius. You saw it all. You're not blind.

All you're doing at this stage of your job-hunt is putting this old skill to a new use. You will quickly realize that you are more skilled at analyzing an organization's problems than you thought you were. All you have to do now is polish this awareness of yours. (A detailed set of instructions on how to do this will be found in Appendix E: it's called, "Rules for Finding Out in Detail the Needs or Problems of an Organization.")

Anyway, assuming you did the work outlined on the previous pages, you have a manageable list of specific places now that interest you, and their names. What you want to do before you go there (or back there) is to identify -- within the area, department or tasks that interest you -- what kinds of problems you could help solve, if they hired you.

Some of this you can figure out, just by thinking, and using logical analysis. You may, for example, want to think how an unsatisfactory employee would behave in the job you are going to go after, and what problems such behavior would create.

YOU'LL LIKE THIS JOB, EXCEPT EVERY NOW AND THEN, WHEN THEY DUMP A LOT OF PAPER WORK ON YOU.

ANALYZING AN ORGANIZATION'S PROBLEMS

☐ If it's a decent-sized company, send for (or go pick up) their annual report to stockholders; granted it's a public relations piece, it still may help quite a bit. If the organization is too small to have an annual report, get whatever pamphlets they have, describing their work. Also, use your contacts to try to find people who know a lot about them. Then, after studying what you find out, you will want to weigh the following questions:

IF IT IS A LARGE COMPANY:

☐ How does this organization rank within its field, or industry? Is this organization family owned? If so, what effect has that on promotions? Where are its plants, offices or branches? What are all its projects or services? In what ways have they grown in recent years? New lines, new products, new processes, new facilities, etc.? Existing political situations: imminent proxy fights, upcoming mergers, etc.? What is the general image of the organization in people's minds? If the organization sells stock, what has been happening to it (see an investment broker and ask).

**QUESTIONS TO BE ASKING YOURSELF
REGARDLESS OF THE COMPANY'S SIZE:**

☐ What kind of *turnover of staff* have they had? What is the attitude of employees toward the organization? If you've been there, are their faces happy, strained, or what? Is promotion generally from within, or from outside? How long has the chief executive been with the organization?

☐ Do they encourage their employees to further their educational training? Do they help them pay for it?

☐ How do *communications* work within the organization? How is information collected, and by what paths does it flow? What methods are used to see that information gets results — to what authority do people respond there? Who reports to whom?

☐ Is there a "time-bomb" — a problem that will kill the organization, or drastically reduce its effectiveness and efficiency if they don't solve it real fast?

You of course intend to be just the opposite: a very competent, and enthusiastic employee, if you get that job. Therefore, you will automatically eliminate the problems that an unsatisfactory employee would cause. Just know what they are, before you ever go for an employment interview.

Beyond 'just thinking about it,' there is research. You want to go talk to every contact you have to learn as much as you can about the workings of the companies or organizations that interest you: what they are trying to accomplish, how they go about it, and - - like that.

As you go through all this intensive research concerning the places where you might like to work, two things will happen:

1. **Your list will get smaller,** as you discover some of the places that at first interested you **did not upon inspection turn out to have the kind of problems or difficulties that your strongest skills would enjoy solving.** Eliminate these places from your list. You would be unhappy there, even if they hired you. Know that now, and cross them off.

2. You will get to know **a great deal** about the remaining organizations which still interest you, including - - most specifically - - their problems, and what you could do to help solve them.

SELF-EMPLOYMENT, TEMPORARY WORK, VOLUNTEER WORK, INTERNSHIPS

I have, throughout this chapter, assumed that you are looking to be employed by someone else in a permanent, full-time job. That is what the vast majority of job-hunters and career-changers in this country are looking for. But you may be an exception. And you will then want to know how all of this chapter applies to you.

It's not hard to make the translation. For example, if you are thinking of starting your own business, you need to go out and interview everyone you can who is running that kind of business in your broad geographical area. I say 'broad' geographical area, because it is best not to go see someone in your same town; they will only see you as potential competition, and may be very reluctant to tell you what you want to know. (There are exceptions: generous souls who cheerfully tell you all they know, because they believe that that is the only way to live.

May their tribe increase!) But if you are thinking of starting your own business in, say, Passaic, New Jersey, you would do well to conduct your informational interviewing in New York City. What you of course want to find out is: what skills and knowledges does it take to run such a business successfully? (We will call this **List A.**). Then, when you have checked and cross-checked this information, you take from the Flower Diagram the inventory of the skills and knowledges *you* already have. (We will call this **List B.**) You subtract B from A, which

results in a list we shall call **List C.** List C is a list of the skills and knowledges you **don't** have; that is therefore a list of the skills and knowledges you will **have** to go out and hire, if your business is to be a success.

When you find people running the same kind of business or organization or service that you would like to start up, you ask them (of course) the four questions that are on page 117. Later, when it comes time to think about problems, you try to think of what problems your potential clients or customers have, and then how your product/service/information would help them. Or sometimes it is a matter of researching to see **who** has the kinds of problems you are trying to solve with your product/service/information. This helps to target your marketing.

Applying the steps in this chapter to any other path that you want to follow will likewise help you immensely. That includes volunteer work, internships, temporary work (which agency should you sign up with), etc. It's just a detailed common-sense application of the old refrain, "Look before you leap."

Many job-hunters **and career-changers** have found that a useful way to explore organizations is to sign up with some temporary agency. Temporary agencies, in the old days, were solely for clerical workers and secretarial help. But the field has seen an explosion of services in recent years -- according to the Bureau of Labor Statistics, temporary or part-time workers now number over 35 million in number, and represent 29% of the total civilian labor force -- and now there are temporary agencies (at least in the larger cities) for many different occupations. See your local phone book, under "Temporary Agencies." The advantage to you of temporary work is that if there is an agency which loans out people with your particular skills and expertise, you get a chance to visit a number of different

organizations over a period of several weeks, and see each one **from the inside.** Not so coincidentally, a number of employers now use temporary agencies as a way for **them** to shop for permanent employees. Both of you get a chance to look at each other, without any long-range commitment.

Another useful way to explore a field, particularly if you're new to the job-market, or contemplating a career-change to a new field, is volunteer work. Again, because you're a volunteer, it's relatively easy to get them to let you work there for a while at the target of your choice; and thus you get a chance to know them from the inside. Not so coincidentally, if you decide you would really like to work there permanently, they've had a chance to see you in action, and when you are about to end your volunteer time there, may want to hire you permanently. It has happened, very often; though you cannot absolutely count on this.

THE END OF THE 'I' IN THE 'PIE'

Well, that's it. Once you've found the answers to these four questions,

1. WHAT ARE THE NAMES OF JOBS THAT WOULD USE MY STRONGEST AND MOST ENJOYABLE SKILLS AND FIELDS OF KNOWLEDGE?

2. WHAT KINDS OF ORGANIZATIONS HAVE SUCH JOBS?

3. WHAT ARE THE NAMES OF THE ORGANIZATIONS THAT I PARTICULARLY LIKE, AMONG THOSE UNCOVERED IN QUESTION 2?

4. WHAT NEEDS DO THEY HAVE OR WHAT OUTCOMES ARE THEY TRYING TO PRODUCE THAT MY SKILLS COULD HELP WITH?

you're done with this phase of your job-hunt or career-change. You're done with the "WHERE?" You've defined your Ideal Job, you've found what out there most closely corresponds to that Ideal Job. Now you're ready for the "HOW." "How do I get that job?" But before we turn to that, in our next chapter, we have one final problem to consider here.

WHAT IF I GET OFFERED A JOB
ALONG THE WAY, WHILE I'M
STILL GATHERING INFORMATION?

You probably won't. During this information gathering, you're not talking primarily to employers. You're talking to workers. Do remember this, please. Of course, an occasional employer **may** stray across your path during all this research. And that employer **may** be so impressed with the carefulness you're showing, in going about your career-change or your job-hunt, that they want to get their hands on you **immediately.** So, it's possible that you might get offered a job while you're still doing your information gathering. Not "likely" but "possible." And if that happens, what should you say?

Why, of course, you simply tell them what you're doing. You tell them that the average job-hunter tries to screen a job **after** they take it. But you are doing what you are sure this employer would do if they were in your situation: you are examining careers, fields, industries, jobs, organizations **before** you decide where you can do your best and most effective work.

You tell them that during this part of your job-hunt, it is premature for you to be thinking about accepting a job offer; you don't know where you can be most effective, until you've concluded this part of your research.

And then you add something along these lines: "Of course, I'm tickled pink that you would want me to be working here. I'm sure you understand, however, that until I've finished my survey and am clearer about where my skills could best be used, I just can't say Yes or No to your kind invitation. But, when I've finished my personal survey, I'd sure be glad to get back to you about this, as this seems to me to be the **kind** of place I'd like to work in, and the kind of people I'd like to work with."

You don't walk through any opened doors yet; but neither do you slam them shut.

HUNGRY EMPLOYERS

Except in the most difficult of job-hunting times, there are more places out there which would like to hire you, than you will ever imagine. The problem is, they don't know how to find you, any more than you know how to find them.

The great thing about your taking such care about your job-hunt as we have discussed in this chapter, is that by doing this research thoroughly, you will make it possible for **both of you** to find each other. You are doing the employer a service, as well as yourself. That's why this is **the most effective** method of job-hunting in the world.

It has worked successfully for hundreds of thousands of job-hunters before you, many of them with unimaginable handicaps. There is **no** reason why it cannot also work for you.

A SUMMARY FOR THOSE WHO LIKE SUMMARIES

This has been a chapter filled with many ideas. Your head is swimming. You want a simple digest of the whole chapter, so you can remember it. Voila!

Job-hunting is a two-way street. For the time being, whether the places you visit during your research happen to have a vacancy, or happen to want you, is premature and irrelevant. In this dance of life, you get first choice: you get to decide first of all whether or not **you** want **them.** Only after you have decided that you **do** want them, is it appropriate to ask if they also want you.

You're a bunch of jackasses. You work your rear ends off in a trivial course that no one will ever care about again. You're not willing to spend time researching a company that you're interested in working for. Why don't you decide who you do want to work for and go after them?

Professor Albert Shapero
(again) to his students

CHAPTER SIX

The Systematic Approach To
The Job-Hunt and Career-Change:

PART III

How

Do You Find The
Person Who Has The Power
To Hire You For
The Job That You Want?

The answer, in a nutshell, is: through your research and then through your contacts.

But let's back up for a moment. As we saw earlier, in chapter 3, the three parts of a systematic job-hunt, and career-change are WHAT, WHERE, and HOW. Having traversed the WHAT and the WHERE, we come now to the HOW.

Assuming you didn't just open this book to this chapter, and assuming you read chapters 4 and 5, and assuming you actually did the exercises those two chapters told you to do, by this point you will have:

- found the career field you like best,
- found what kind of organization within that field appeals to you the most,
- found the names of specific organizations of that kind, that truly interest you,
- found what kinds of needs these organizations have and what sorts of problems or challenges they are facing,
- narrowed down the possible organizational targets to four or five places that stand out above all the rest.

And now what do you do? You go talk to **the person in each such organization who has the power to hire you.** And as Daniel Porot, the job-hunting expert in Europe puts it, you go not as a **"job beggar"** but as a **"resource person."** That is to say, you are not going there because there is something you want to beg from them; you are going there because there is something you have to offer them, in return for a salary: your brains, your hands, your skills.

We call this the HOW phase of the job-hunt, because the questions facing you here are three HOW questions:

1. HOW do I find out who has the power to hire me, there?
2. HOW do I get in for a job interview with that person?
3. HOW do I **convince** them that they should hire me?

The answer to the first question, as I said above, is: "Through the research you already did, and through your contacts." Contacts, you recall, means every single person that you meet, talk to, blunder into, stumble across, can write letters to, phone up, or whatever. It does **not** mean "just business people." It means **everyone you know.**

Let us say it is a mythical Capachin Corporation that interests you, but you can't find out who has the power to hire you there. What do you do? Well, you use your library, and search the directories there that we saw listed in the previous chapter. Hopefully that will yield the information you want. If it doesn't, which will particularly be the case with smaller organizations, **then you use your contacts.** You approach as many people as necessary among all those you know, and the question you ask them all is, "Do you know anyone who works at Capachin Corporation?" Once you find someone who does, you then ask them:

- What is the name of the person at Capachin?
- May I tell them it was you who recommended that I talk with them?
- Would you be willing to call ahead, to set up an appointment for me, and tell them who I am?

Then you keep that appointment (**always** arriving promptly or slightly ahead of time) and talk to that person. Because they are inside the organization that interests you, they are usually able to give you the exact answer to your HOW Question #1: "Who would have the power to hire me here, for this kind of position (which you then describe)?"

Discovering this information is not as difficult as job-hunters and career-changers presume. It simply takes time and persistence to uncover it. Either the library or your contacts should yield up the answer. People assume this is difficult information to discover, because when they think of going out looking for a job they are always picturing themselves approaching some large organization, where they can't figure out whether it's somebody on the twenty-first floor or the fourteenth that they should be approaching. However, since as we have said **two-thirds of all new jobs are in fact to be found in organizations of twenty employees or less,** in most cases this is not a difficult information search at all. If the place that interests you is basically a "mom-and-pop" operation, then the issue of identifying "who has the power to hire" is pretty simple: it's either mom or pop.

THE DREADED 'PERSONNEL DEPARTMENT'

In all cases, you will likely discover that the individual (or committee) who has the power to hire you is **not** within the Personnel Department. There are two reasons why this is so.

First, as we saw in chapter 3, **only 15% of all organizations even have personnel departments.** Ergo, 85% of the organizations you may approach are too small or too understaffed or whatever, to have such departments.

Secondly, even in those organizations which do, it is not *normally* the function of the personnel department to do the hiring (except for entry-level or lower-level positions). The function of the personnel department is to *screen out* applicants and then send the ones who survive that screening on 'upstairs' to be interviewed by the person who actually has the power to hire. You will see immediately that **from the point of view of the organization,** the personnel department is a great idea. It saves busy executives from being bothered by too many applicants, when the time for hiring has come. But, from the point of view of the job-hunter or career-changer (namely, you or me) this passage through the hands of the personnel department is not necessarily something to look forward to.

There are actually two kinds of personnel departments in those organizations which have them. **Some** personnel departments harbor the kindest and warmest souls in the entire building, who will move heaven and earth to help you find a job there. But other personnel departments harbor souls who either a) get some perverse delight out of screening people out, or b) are overzealous about protecting the people "upstairs," or c) are frightened about losing their own job. If you fall into **their** hands, you can get screened out -- and thus never get to see the person who actually has the power to hire -- even though in fact you might be exactly the person he or she is looking for. So, going through the personnel department when you don't have to, is a big fat gamble: The Lady or the Tiger?

THE MOST LIKELY SCENARIO

Of these two scenarios, **the more likely one** is that by going to personnel you will get screened out. Because no personnel executive wants to hear some "upstairs" executive who is hiring say, "You're sending me too many people to see," personnel tends to **overscreen** -- i.e., *"when in doubt, screen them out"* -- which means that **you can get screened out by the personnel department even if you were absolutely right for the job.** This is to **your** disadvantage, obviously; but do not forget it is also to the disadvantage of the person "upstairs" who would like to have seen you and would have hired you -- but now will never know. And because personnel may not be clear about exactly what is wanted "upstairs," they may in fact be sending up people who are not exactly what the job demands. Hence, the hiring executive **may** end up having to hire someone with less qualifications than yours.

To repeat the point of earlier chapters, the whole job-hunting process in this country is Neanderthal. And, this "Neanderthalness" **hurts the employer** as much as it does the job-hunter.

In any event, all this that I have said concerning the personnel department dictates that the intelligent job-hunter (generally speaking) **avoid that department.** It is better to identify the person who has the power to hire you, through research and use of your contacts as described previously, and then to get in to see him or her directly, without first going through this unnecessary extra step, where you risk getting screened out.

This leads us, then, directly into our second HOW question: how do I get in for a job interview with that person? The traditional answer, as you know, is "By sending a resume." Unfortunately, this isn't the best or most effective way, by a long shot. So let's see why.

A CRASH COURSE IN RÉSUMÉS

My conversations with job-hunters, over the years, have convinced me that there is a passionate belief in resumes that is out of all proportion to how often they in fact ever get anyone an interview for a job. I think the faith placed in resumes is a very misplaced faith. For every person *you* know who did get a job-interview by sending out resumes, I know ninety-nine who didn't.

I said this once to a group of college placement people, many of whom were devoting large blocks of time to teaching students how to write a resume. When I sat down afterward, I found myself next to the personnel director for a huge public utility company, which employed thousands of people. He leaned across to me. "I listened to what you said about resumes," he began. I waited for the axe to fall. However, he went on: "I've been trying to tell these counselors for years to get off this obsession they have with resumes. I'll interview anyone. But I don't read resumes. Haven't read one in five years. I can't tell a thing about a candidate from a resume. I was so glad you said what you did. Maybe they'll listen if they hear it from you."

Okay, so much by way of introduction to this crash course. Perhaps now I ought to briefly summarize what we know about resumes.

RÉ-SU-MÉ **rez-e-mā** n [F. *resume* fr. pp. of *resumer*
to resume, summarize] SUMMARY *specif:* a short
account of one's career and qualifications prepared
typically by an applicant for a position.   —Webster's

FRANK AND ERNEST *by Bob Thaves*

Resumes serve four different functions:

(1) they can serve as a **self-inventory,** preparing you before
the job-hunt to recall all that you've accomplished thus far in
your life;

(2) they can be an **extended calling card,** whose purpose is
to get you invited in for an interview, by the employer(s) to
whom you send that "calling card";

(3) they can be an **agenda for an interview,** affording the
interviewer a springboard from which to launch his or her
inquiry about you, after you have been invited in;

(4) and, finally, resumes can be a **memory jogger** for the
employer after the interview, or for a whole committee -- if a
group is involved in the hiring decision.

SENDING A RESUME
TO GET AN INTERVIEW

It is as **extended calling card** that the resume is most often
used. Indeed, as calling card it may be sent out to hundreds
of prospective employers. Its lack of effectiveness in this role
I cited in chapter 2. But let me remind you here: only one
job-offer is tendered for every 1,470 resumes that the average
company receives.

Well, okay, so maybe they don't always work. But what's the
harm in trying out a resume, just in case? Well, if you've got

the money and the time, fine. But do keep in mind what we have discovered in the past: that **job-hunters who invest a lot of time on sending out their resume, often suffer tremendous damage to their self-esteem by having depended exclusively upon resumes.** This damage is created by the following facts:

a) The odds being what they are, with some 6 million job-hunters out there hunting for a job at any given moment, it is predictable that **some** job-hunters do actually get an interview, and subsequently a job, because they sent out resumes.

b) But **many, many more** job-hunters do **not** get a job by means of a resume. In fact, an incredible number do not even get **one** invitation to an interview, in spite of sending out 800 or 900 resumes.

c) The ones who do get a job thereby, talk a lot about it; the ones who find their resumes don't work for them, rarely say much. Consequently, there is a widespread **mythology** in our culture that 'this is a method which works for almost everyone.'

d) When resumes don't work at all for a particular job-hunter, he or she is usually devastated, and assumes something is drastically **wrong with them.**

The result: plummeting self-esteem. It is not that a method has been tried, and failed. It is that a method **which you think works for almost everyone else has failed for you.** Hence, depression, emotional paralysis, and even worse symptoms often come in the wake of this rejection shock. It has happened to tens of thousands of job-hunters. It has even happened to me. Don't let it happen to you.

Well, so much for resumes as **extended calling cards.** If they have such a lousy track record in this capacity, how then **do** you get in to see the person who has the power to hire? The method that we know is effective most of the time has three parts to it:

a) **Commitment.** Devoting eight hours a day, five days a week, to the job-hunt.

b) **Going Face-to-Face.** Knocking on the door, personally, at every organization that looks the least bit interesting to you, whether you think they have a vacancy or not.

c) **Using Contacts.** When you find a place you like, or are curious about, but you can't get an interview there, asking every person you know if they know someone who works there. And when someone says they do, asking them to set up an appointment for you to see them. Then go ask the person on the inside for the name of the person who has the power to hire there, for the kind of job you want to do.

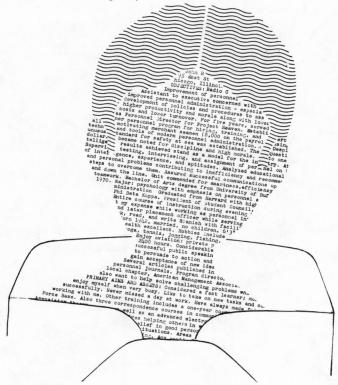

An engineer friend of mine used to sum up this whole matter thusly: Paper is an insulating material. Never insert it between you and another person.

THE OTHER THREE USES OF RESUMES

Given the fact that the resume as **extended calling card** is tremendously ineffective, what can we say about its other three roles? Well, generally speaking the exercises in both our previous two chapters really supplant any need for the resume as **self-inventory.** So the only time you might need a resume for that purpose would be if you're too lazy to do the exercises. And your own research about organizations that interest you, as described in the previous chapter, really supplants any need for the resume as **agenda for an interview.** But, after talking with countless numbers of successful job-hunters, I am bound to say that there is one place where a resume may be **very useful,** and that is if you send it to the employer **after** the interview. The resume as **memory-jogger for the employer** has

a very high effectiveness rate.

This explains the ancient saying in career-counseling: "A resume is something you should never send ahead of you, but always leave behind you." Based on the experience of successful job-hunters, I think there is great wisdom in that saying.

Further, I believe it is often -- if not always -- wise **not** to carry a resume on your person when you go into an interview, so that if you are asked for your resume you can say absolutely truthfully, "I don't have one with me, but I can mail it to you tonight." This saves you from having to hand the employer your "general-purpose one-size-fits-all" resume which mentions all your possible skills and every sterling attribute you possess;

and you have time to go home, edit your resume so that it mentions only the skills and experience needed in the job you both just discussed, **while leaving out all information that is not relevant to that job,** type it neatly (or have it typed up at a professional place if you wish), and then mail it that same night, along with a thank-you note as your cover letter.

In today's job-market, I think there is a genuine need for this use of the resume **as memory jogger.** Many hiring decisions these days, even in small organizations, are made by a committee; and you do not always have a chance to meet them all, at least in the first round or two. Furthermore, even where it is an individual who is making the hiring decision, you will oftentimes be called back for one or more additional interviews, before they decide who they want. Your resume, mailed to them after the first interview, will remind them of who you are, and keep them from confusing you with one or more among the nineteen other candidates they are looking at.

FOR THAT FARAWAY CITY,
YOU MAY NEED TO SEND A RESUME

If you're interested in leaping across the country (or even part of the country) for your next job, it may be impractical for you to go there, at least in the beginning. You may want to research it first. I have therefore given detailed suggestions on page 374 as to how you do this. But suppose **that** research is completed. You have discovered some organizations that, at this distance, look like "possibles." But you still aren't ready to invest the time or money to go there, just yet. So, what should you do?

Well of course you will begin by using every contact that you have developed **there.** (Again, see page 374.) If they know any of the organizations that interest you, and -- better yet, the name of the person who has the power to hire you -- a letter which mentions the name of a mutual friend in that faraway city, will always receive more favorable attention than would be the case if you were a total stranger. (Unless -- the job-hunter's nightmare -- your mutual friend/contact has **misrepresented** how close he or she is to your target employer, and as a matter of fact said employer can't stand the sight of your "mutual friend." **It has happened.** It is to die.)

In any event, **generally speaking** your letter to employers in that faraway city will be **much** stronger if you mention some mutual friend. Now, should you also enclose a resume? Opinions vary widely. **Everything** depends on the nature of the resume, and the nature of the person you are sending it to.

RESUMES AND DATING

Resumes, after all, are a lot like dating. There is virtually no man who is liked by all the women he dates. There is virtually no woman who is liked by all the men she dates. And so with resumes: some employers like resumes, others hate them. Some will like your resume; others won't.

The only question that should concern you is: never mind if not all employers would like my resume -- will the employers **I care about** like it? And that is the $64,000 question.

I used to have a hobby of collecting resumes that had actually gotten someone an interview and, ultimately, a job. I delighted in showing them to employers whom I knew. Many of them didn't like the winning resume at all. "That resume will never get anyone a job," they would say. Then, being basically a mischievous man, I would tell them, "Sorry, you're wrong. It already has. What you are saying is that it wouldn't get them a job **with you.**"

The resume reproduced on the next page is an example of what I mean. *(You did want an example of a good resume, didn't you?)* Jim Dyer, who had been in the Marines for twenty years, wanted a job as a salesman for heavy construction and mining equipment thousands of miles from where he was then living. He devised the resume you see, and had fifteen copies made. "I used," he said, "a grand total of seven before I got the job in the place I wanted!"

Like the employer who hired him, I loved this resume. Yet, when I've shown it to other employers, they criticized it for using a picture, for being too long (or too short), etc., etc. In other words, had Jim sent his resume to **them,** they wouldn't have been impressed enough to invite him in for an interview.

So, don't believe anyone who tells you there's one right format for a resume, or one style that's guaranteed to win. It's still a gamble, where you're hoping that the employer(s) you like will also like your resume. Generally speaking, the most endearing quality needed in it, besides neatness and clarity, is that **you**

E.J. DYER   Street, City, Zip   Telephone No.

I SPEAK
THE LANGUAGE
OF
MEN
MACHINERY
AND
MANAGEMENT
...

OBJECTIVE: Sales of Heavy Equipment

QUALIFICATIONS * Knowledge of heavy equipment, its use and maintenance.

                * Ability to communicate with management and with men in the field.

                * Ability to favorably introduce change in the form of new
                  equipment or new ideas... the ability to sell.

EXPERIENCE   * Maintained, shipped, budgeted and set allocation priorities for
                  85 pieces of heavy equipment as head of a 500-man organization
Men and   (1975-1977).
Machinery
                * Constructed twelve field operation support complexes, employing
                  a 100-man crew and 19 pieces of heavy equipment (1965-1967).

                * Jack-hammer operator, heavy construction (summers 1956-1957-1958).

Management   * Planned, negotiated and executed large scale equipment purchases
                  on a nation to nation level (1972-1974).

Sales   * Achieved field customer acceptance of two major new computer-
                  based systems:
                  - Equipment inventory control and repair parts expedite system
                    (1968-1971)
                  - Decision makers' training system (1977-1979).
                * Proven leader ... repeatedly elected or appointed to senior posts.

EDUCATION   * B.A. Benedictine College, 1959. (Class President; Editor
                  Yearbook; "Who's Who in American Colleges").

                * Naval War College, 1975. (Class President; Graduated "With
                  Highest Distinction").

                * University of Maryland, 1973-1974. (Chinese Language).

                * Middle Level Management Training Course, 1967-1968
                  (Class Standing: 1 of 97).

PERSONAL   * Family: Sharon and our sons Jim (11), Andy (8) and Matt (5)
                  desire to locate in a Mountain State by 1982, however, in
                  the interim will consider a position elsewhere in or outside
                  the United States ... Health: Excellent ... Birthdate: December
                  9, 1937 ... Completing Military Service with the rank of
                  Lieutenant Colonel, U.S. Marine Corps.

SUMMARY   A seeker of challenge ... experienced, proven and confident of
                closing the sales for profit.

shine through it all. One job-hunter, for example, found this unique truthful way of describing her period of job-hunting: "Job-Hunter (Self-Employed) January 1988 — January 1989:
- Developed and executed all phases of marketing and advertising for product
- Targeted markets and identified the needs of diverse consumers
- Developed sales brochure
- Designed packaging, and upgraded visual appeal of product
- Scheduled and conducted oral presentations"

So, **she** shone through it all.

Here endeth our crash course on resumes. If you decide you do want a resume, preferably to leave behind you **after** the interview, and the guidance I have given you here is not enough, I refer you to the books listed on page 284. The best of these, by a long shot, is Richard Lathrop's *Who's Hiring Who (newly revised),* wherein he describes and recommends "a qualifications brief" -- an idea akin to one which John Crystal used to propose: that in approaching an employer you should think of offering him or her **a written proposal** -- rather than "a resume." Of course there are those who say, "No matter what you try to call it, it's still a resume in the end." The second most helpful resume book (in my opinion) calls the thing plainly: *The Damn Good Resume Guide,* by Yana Parker.

THE ALTERNATIVE TO RESUMES

Now, back to our second HOW question. If resumes are not the preferred route to a job-interview, then how *do* you get in to see the person who has the power to hire?

The answer is: Through your contacts.

If you have found out that X is the name of the person who has the power to hire you for the kind of position you are interested in, then you ask *everyone* you meet and everyone you know, "Do you personally know X, over at Capachin Corporation, or do you know someone who does?"

If you persist with **every** person you know, in the family, among your friends, in your former places of employment, in the congregation of your church/synagogue/mosque the odds are 20 to 1:

a) that you are going to come across someone who knows X, and therefore

b) that you are going to get in to see him or her.

To the first person who says, "Yes, I know X," you of course are going to respond with the familiar litany:

• May I use your name?

• May I say you recommended that I talk with them?

• Would you be willing to call ahead, to set up an appointment for me, and tell them who I am?

And if you do this part successfully, you will then (and only then) need the answer to the third HOW question, namely, How do I convince them that they should hire me?

INFORMATION IS THE KEY TO A SUCCESSFUL INTERVIEW

Briefly stated, the answer is that you sell yourself by finding out as much about that organization as you possibly can **before you ever go in there for an interview.** You lay your hands on **everything** you can that is in print about them. If this is a large organization, you read all their brochures, annual reports, addresses of the chairman or boss -- whatever. If they have a personnel department or a public relations department, that's where you'll find the stuff. Also, you go to the library and ask the librarian or reference librarian (if they have one) to see every clipping they have about that organization.

If it is a small organization, you still find out if there is anything in print about their work or what they do. (Even places that only have two employees often have **something** in print about what the organization is trying to achieve. The small local paper may have run an article about them.) Also, you talk to **everybody** you know, to find out everything you can about the organization in question: their work, their history, who used to work there, etc.

If this strikes you as sort of prying into their private life, then recall to your mind the purpose of all this research. There are actually two honorable purposes:

1. As we saw in the last chapter, the tradition in our country is to find a job, take it, and then try to find out after you're in it whether it was a good job or not. You're trying to go against that tradition, as any sensible job-hunter or career-changer should, by finding out whether or not you'd like to work there **before** you ever accept a job there. You're saving **them** grief as well as saving yourself grief.

2. Organizations, be they large or small, profit or nonprofit, love to be loved. If you have gone to the trouble to learn a great deal about them before you ever walk in their doors, **you make that organization feel important.** Most job-hunters don't ever go to this trouble. They walk in knowing little or nothing about the organization. According to the chairman of the National Association of Corporate and Professional Recruiters, a survey of theirs revealed "Candidates too often are so unknowledgeable about the company, industry, the situation of the culture that they cannot ask the right questions." Taking the trouble to learn something about the place before you have a job-interview there, makes you stand out from the other job-hunters, and greatly increases your chances of getting a job there. How much information should you gather? If possible, **more than you are ever going to have to use,** at least during the hiring interview. But the depth of your research will pay off in the quiet sense of confidence you exude.

WELL, YOU WANT TO SEE THEM, BUT DO THEY WANT TO SEE YOU?

This is the question which bothers almost everyone new to the job-hunt or new to career-change. We sort of just assume the answer is "No." This mental attitude is what Daniel Porot calls "our job beggar mentality." We feel the employer would be doing us a tremendous favor by offering us a job; and particularly so, if we have some real or imagined handicap or some bad history working against us, such as age, or a psychiatric history, or a prison record, or whatever.

You need to remember, no matter what your real or imagined handicap may be, this simple but profound truth (post it on your bathroom mirror):

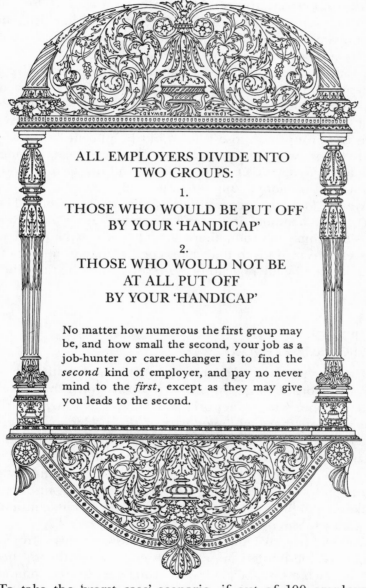

ALL EMPLOYERS DIVIDE INTO
TWO GROUPS:

1.
THOSE WHO WOULD BE PUT OFF
BY YOUR 'HANDICAP'

2.
THOSE WHO WOULD NOT BE
AT ALL PUT OFF
BY YOUR 'HANDICAP'

No matter how numerous the first group may be, and how small the second, your job as a job-hunter or career-changer is to find the *second* kind of employer, and pay no never mind to the *first*, except as they may give you leads to the second.

To take the 'worst case' scenario, if out of 100 employers, 90 would be bothered by your handicap or your history, but 10 wouldn't care about it in the slightest so long as you can do the work well that needs to get done, **your job is to make your way as quickly as you can through the 90, and find those other 10. They are the only ones you really want to work for, anyway.** You wouldn't **really** want to work for those who are prejudiced against your history or your handicap, now would you? We all want to work for an employer who's rootin' for us, not one who's waiting for us to fall on our face.

I can hear your objections, right now. You think **you've** got a handicap that's the exception to this rule. For example, that you're over 60 years old, and employers wouldn't want someone that old. Okay, let's repeat it together: "All employers divide into two groups: 1) those who would be put off by your age, and 2) those who would not be put off by your age, so long as you are a good worker. Your job is to find the second kind of employer, and not pay any attention to the first."

Please! Make no generalizations about "employers." There isn't any such animal. In any and all circumstances that you can possibly come up with, **there are always two kinds of employers.** Your job is to find the second kind, and to try not to be bothered by the rejections you receive from the first kind.

'JOB BEGGAR' VS. 'RESOURCE PERSON'

Having said that, remember this. You're not visiting an employer in order to get him or her to do **you** a big favor. If you've done your homework, you know you can be part of the solution there, and not part of the problem. Therefore you're going in to see this employer in order that you may do a favor **for each other.** That's not an arrogant posture for you to take. It **is** the truth, and it can be stated very quietly but confidently. You are coming to see this employer, in order to make an oral proposal, followed hopefully by a written proposal, of what **you** can do for **them.**

You will perceive immediately what a switch this is from the way **most** job-hunters approach an employer! And will he or she, in such a case, be glad to see you, when you're coming in to offer them skills and knowledges which will help them, with what they're trying to accomplish there? **In most cases,** you bet they will.

WHAT DO YOU SAY, ONCE YOU 'GET IN'?

Once you get in to see her or him, the interview has begun. The term "interview" shouldn't frighten you by this time. You will have had rich experience in interviewing people for information all along the way, up 'til now. From an objective standpoint, this is just another such interview. *So much for what your mind tells you!*

We all know in our gut that the Employment Interview **does** feel different from all previous interviews -- so let's see what its special characteristics are. For, if you understand what an employment interview is, you will be ahead of 98% of all other job-hunters who go into the Interview as a lamb goes to the slaughter. Moreover, you will then automatically know the kinds of things you ought to talk about.

So, what's to understand about the Employment Interview? There are two fundamental truths about it:

THE FIRST FUNDAMENTAL TRUTH
ABOUT THE INTERVIEW:

Each of you has questions in the interview -- both you **and** the employer. The essence of the interview is that each of you is trying to find out the answers to those questions.

YOUR QUESTIONS ARE:

First you report to them just exactly how you've been conducting your job-hunt, and what impressed you so much about their organization during your research, that you decided you wanted to come in and talk to them about a job. Then you get to your questions (or bow to theirs first, if the employer is anxious to talk).

If this is an interview for a job that already exists,
your questions are:
1. What does this job involve?
2. Do my skills truly match this job?
3. Are you the kind of people I would like to work with?
4. If we do match, can I persuade you to hire me?

"I'll tell you why I want this job. I thrive on challenges. I like being stretched to my full capacity. I like solving problems. Also, my car is about to be repossessed."

You will rarely, if ever, say these questions out loud during the interview; but you will keep them in the front of your mind (or written on a pad) because these are the questions you came there to find the answers to, one way or another.

If the job in question is a job that you want them to create for you, then your four questions get changed into four statements:
1. What you like about this organization.
2. What sorts of **needs** you find intriguing in this field and in this organization (don't **ever** use the word "problems," as

most employers resent it - - unless you hear the word coming out of their mouth, first).

3. What skills seem to you to be needed in order to meet such needs.
4. Your presentation of your claim, backed by evidence, that you have the very skills in question.

THEIR QUESTIONS ARE:

Well, **many.** In fact, some books publish a list of eighty-nine questions (or so) that an employer may ask you. They list things like:
- Tell me about yourself.
- Why are you applying for this job?
- What do you know about this job or company?
- How would you describe yourself?
- What are your major strengths?
- What is your greatest weakness?
- What type of work do you like to do best?
- What are your interests outside of work?
- What accomplishment gave you the greatest satisfaction?
- What was your worst mistake?
- Why did you leave your last job?
- Why were you fired (if you were)?
- How does your education or experience relate to this job?
- Where do you see yourself five years from now?
- What are your goals in life?
- How much did you make at your last job?

And so on. Fortunately, however, as John Crystal once taught us all, beneath the dozens of Possible Questions, there are really only four. These four are:

1. **Why are you here?** They mean by that, why did you pick out our organization?
2. **What can you do for me?** They mean by that, what are your skills and your special knowledges?
3. **What kind of person are you?** They mean by that, do you have a personality that they will enjoy working with, or not? What are your values and how do you get along with people?
4. **Can they afford you?** They want to know what your minimum salary needs are, and what your maximum salary hopes are.

Now that you see the kinds of questions you each are bound to have, remember the object of the interview is:

1) to find out the information that **you** need to know, in order to decide whether **you** want to work there or not; and

2) to help the employer find out the information that **he or she** needs to know, in order to decide whether **they** want to hire you or not.

And this is the case, even if the interview begins and ends without either of you ever putting these questions precisely into words, during the entire time.

HOW DO YOU ANSWER THEIR QUESTIONS?

1. **"Why are you here?"** If you did all your research, as described in the previous chapter, you'll know the answer. If you didn't, you won't. End of story. There's no reward for laziness in the job-hunt. There is a reward for hard work, and this is where it pays off.

Incidentally, the essence of a good answer to this question is some variation on: "I have become interested in organizations which are _____, and yours particularly attracted me because _____."

2. **"What can you do for me?"** What the employer is essentially wanting to know here, is: "Will you help this organization to do its work better, and achieve its goals more completely -- and if so, in what way?" Again, **if** you did your research, you will know what that company's work and goals are, what their problems and challenges are, **and** in what ways you would be an asset toward the accomplishing of that work, the achieving of those goals, and the overcoming of those problems and challenges. If you didn't do your research, you won't know the answer. Even bluffing usually won't save you here.

3. **"What kind of person are you?"** This is a crucial question, but unhappily there's no right answer for you to memorize. You will answer this question by **everything** you say during the interview, and everything you do during the interview. It is likely that **nothing** will escape the scrutiny of the person across the desk from you. And I mean: your haircut or hairdo; your manner of dress; your posture; your use of your hands; your body odor or perfume; your breath (good or bad); your finger-nails (dirty or clean, clipped or not); the sound of your voice;

the way in which you do or don't interrupt; the hesitant or assured manner in which you ask your questions or give your answers; your values as evidenced by the things which impress you or don't impress you in the office, in your history, and so on; the carefulness with which you did or didn't research this company before you came in; the thoroughness with which you know your skills and strengths; your awareness of what you are willing to sell in order to get this job **and** what you aren't willing to sell in order to get this job; your enthusiasm for your work; and that's just for openers. We can also throw in whether or not you smoke (in a race between two equally qualified people, the nonsmoker will win out over the smoker 94% of the time, according to a study done by a professor of business at Seattle University); whether, if at lunch, you order a drink or not; whether you show courtesy to the receptionist, secretary, waiter or waitress, or not; and -- like that. Everything is grist for the mill, as the employer tries to divine "what kind of person is this?" What the employer is typically looking for, so as to screen you out, are:

- any sign of dishonesty or lying;
- any sign of irresponsibility or tendency to goof off;
- any sign of arrogance or excessive aggressiveness;
- any sign of tardiness or failure to keep appointments and commitments on time;
- any sign of not following instructions or obeying rules;
- any sign of complaining or blaming things on others;
- any sign of laziness or lack of motivation;
- any sign of a lack of enthusiasm for this organization and what it is trying to do;
- any sign of instability, inappropriate response, and the like.

Since the employer will probably end up having to fire anyone with these signs, the employer would like to find these things out **now** rather than later.

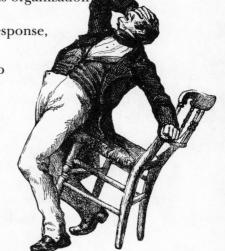

Beyond these tangibles, there are the intangibles of **making a good impression.** Study after study has confirmed that if you are a male, you will make a better impression if:
- your hair and beard are neatly trimmed;
- you have obviously freshly bathed, used a deodorant and mouthwash, and have clean fingernails;
- you have freshly laundered clothes on, and a suit rather than a sports outfit, and sit without slouching;
- your breath does not dispense gallons of garlic, onion, stale tobacco, or strong drink, into the enclosed office air;
- your shoes are neatly polished, and your pants have a sharp crease;
- you are not wafting tons of after-shave cologne fifteen feet ahead of you.

And, if you are a female, you will make a better impression if:
- your hair is newly 'permed' or 'coiffed';
- you have obviously freshly bathed, used a deodorant and mouthwash, and have clean or nicely manicured fingernails;
- you wear a bra, freshly cleaned clothes, a suit or sophisticated-looking dress, and sit without slouching;
- your breath does not dispense gallons of garlic, onion, stale tobacco, or strong drink, into the enclosed office air;
- you wear shoes rather than sandals;
- you are not wafting tons of perfume fifteen feet ahead of you.

Now please, dear reader, do not send me mail telling me how asinine you think some of these 'rules' are. I **know** that. I'm only reporting that study after study reveals these things **do** affect whether or not you get hired. There are of course employers who care about none of these things, and will hire you if you can do the job. Period. Do remember, however, that where you have to work with other people, these things are given a lot of weight. This employer already has other employees; he or she wants to know that you will not alienate them, or cause friction. You must somehow 'fit in.'

If you don't want to 'fit in,' then you might want to consider forming your own (one-person) business, and -- particularly if it is a mail-order business -- you can dress or conduct yourself any way you like, and no one will be the wiser.

If, however, you want to work for someone else, you are in a sense on trial during this interview. All of the above factors are a part of that trial.

Of course, what makes the job interview tolerable or sometimes even **fun,** is that **you** are studying **everything** about this employer, at the same time that they are studying everything about you. You are just as much in need of making up your mind about what kind of person **they** are, and whether or not you would like to work with them, as they are doing with you.

Two people, both sizing each other up. Well, that's what the

employment interview is; and you know what it reminds you of. Dating. The job interview is indeed every bit like 'the dating game.' **Both** of you have to like the other, before you can get on to the question of 'going steady.' Thus the employer is just as much 'on trial' during the job interview as you are. Realizing **that,** can take some of the stress away.

4. **"How much are you going to cost me?"** Until they have said "We **want** you," **and** you have decided, "I want them," all discussion of salary is highly inappropriate. And that's true, even if it is the employer who brings up the subject early on, in the interview.

IN SALARY NEGOTIATION,
TIMING IS EVERYTHING

You may of course think to yourself, "Yes, but what if they have a fixed salary figure in mind, and it is way below what I could accept -- shouldn't I find that out as early as possible, so that I can graciously excuse myself, and go elsewhere?" That's logical, except for one minor little point: if you're the first person they've interviewed, and they haven't yet had a chance to get to know you very well, they may assume you are 'average material' and so mention merely an average kind of salary. But if they have seen a lot of people, **and** have had a chance to get to know you over two or three interviews, say. And **if** they are very impressed with you by this time, **obviously** they are going to be willing to do whatever they can to get a hold of you. And **if** that takes more money than they were originally prepared to offer, they may push themselves to find it. **This happens very often.**

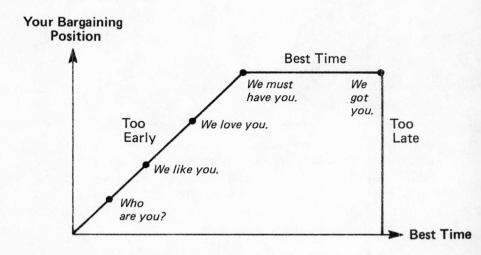

If you allow discussion of salary to take place prematurely, you will be told **the lowest** figure they had in mind, but it will be presented as though it were **the highest.** They haven't yet seen you in all your splendor. They don't know what they would be getting if they got you. Or, what they would be losing, if they let you go. Therefore, generally speaking until a firm offer has been made, **postpone** all discussion of salary.

There is more to be said about salary negotiation, but since such negotiation should **always** take place at the end of the interview, this discussion is at the end of this chapter.

TWENTY SECONDS TO TWO MINUTES

Well, we have now seen the first fundamental truth about the employment interview: it's two people trying to get answers to natural questions. If you understand that, then you're ahead of most other job-hunters.

Beyond the issue of **what** to say, is the issue of **how** to say it. Studies have revealed that generally speaking the people who get hired are those who mix speaking and listening fifty-fifty in the interview. That is, half the time in the interview the job-hunter **listens** and lets the employer do the talking, half the time in the interview the job-hunter does the **talking.**

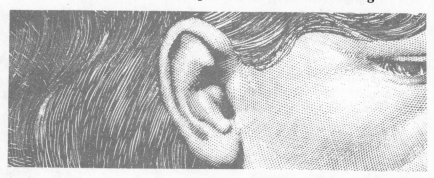

When it is your turn to speak, studies conducted by Daniel Porot have revealed that to make the most favorable impression **you should not speak any longer than two minutes at a time.** In fact, a good answer to an employer's question sometimes only takes twenty seconds to give. This is useful information for you to know, in conducting a successful interview -- as you certainly want to do.

Okay, now let's turn to:

THE SECOND FUNDAMENTAL TRUTH
ABOUT THE EMPLOYMENT INTERVIEW:

If the employment interview were simply two people, job-hunter and employer, trying to get answers to natural questions, the interview would be a snap. Unfortunately, this simple exchange is corrupted by the fact that **both** individuals sitting there are filled with a number of fears and anxieties, **which they don't feel free to discuss openly.** So they try to allay their fears by asking clever questions.

Hence, you must examine **every** question the employer asks, to see what fear lies beneath it, **so that you can answer the fear, and not just the surface question.** Because, in the employment interview questions don't always mean what they seem to mean at first sight.

Now, I emphasize this fundamental truth about the employment interview, because it is hardly ever mentioned in any discussion of job interviews that I have seen. Everyone assumes that **the job-hunter** is filled with fears in the interview, but that the employer is sitting there like some cool cat, wonderfully at ease. Not true. That employer, sitting across the desk from you, in the employment interview, usually has as many fears as you do. Maybe more.

For openers, the employer has the following ten major fears when you, the job-hunter or career-changer, are face-to-face with him or her:

1. That You Won't Be Able to Do the Job; That You Lack the Necessary Skills or Experience

2. That If Hired, You Won't Put In a Full Working Day

3. That If Hired, You'll Be Frequently "Out Sick," or Otherwise Absent Whole Days

4. That If Hired, You'll Only Stay Around for a Few Weeks or At Most a Few Months

5. That It Will Take You Too Long to Master the Job, and Thus Too Long Before You're Profitable to That Organization

6. That You Won't Get Along with the Other Workers There, or That You Will Develop a Personality Conflict with the Boss Himself (or Herself)

7. That You Will Do Only the Minimum That You Can Get Away With, Rather Than the Maximum That You Are Capable Of

8. That You Will Always Have to Be Told What to Do Next, Rather Than Displaying Initiative; That You Will Always Be in a Responding Rather Than an Initiating Mode (and Mood)

9. That You Will Have a Work-Disrupting Character Flaw, and Turn Out to Be: Dishonest, a Spreader of Dissention at Work, Lazy, an Embezzler, a Gossip, Totally Irresponsible, a Liar, Incompetent - - in a Word: No Fun to Have Around

10. (If This Is a Large Organization, and Your Would-Be Boss Is Not the Top Person): That You Will Bring Discredit upon Them, and Upon His or Her Department/Section/Division, etc., for Ever Hiring You in the First Place - - Possibly Costing Your Would-Be Boss a Raise or Promotion

Moreover, employers don't usually talk with each other about this sort of thing. So, oftentimes an employer is facing the job-interview thinking that he or she is the only employer in the world going into job-interviews with so many fears. They've never had a chance to check it out, and discover that other employers feel exactly the same way.

This makes the employer feel extremely isolated and alone. That's why, in larger organizations, the person who has the power to hire often begs to share the hiring decision with a committee or a veritable army of his or her peers in that organization. The rationale for this popular style of hiring might well be stated as: "Deliver me from my fears."

THE FEAR BENEATH THE QUESTIONS

The most important thing to keep in mind during the interview is that no employer cares about your past. The only thing any employer can possibly care about is your future. Therefore, the more a question **appears** to be about your past, the more certain you may be that some Fear is behind it. And that Fear is about your future - - i.e., what will you be like, **after** the employer decides to hire you, **if** they decide to hire you.

So, let's run down nine typical employer questions to see
a) what they are, and
b) what fear typically lies behind those questions, and
c) some key phrases that you can use to answer the questions, so as to allay the employer's Fear.

THE EMPLOYER'S QUESTION:
"Tell me about yourself."

The Fear Behind the Question: The employer is afraid they won't ask the right questions during the interview. **or:** The employer is afraid there's something in your background or in your attitude toward your work that will make you a Bad Employee.

The Point You Try to Get Across to Answer Their Fear: You would make a good employee, and you have proved that by your past.

Ideas or Phrases You Might Use: The briefest history in the world, of where you were born and raised, hobbies, interests, etc. The briefest description of where you have worked or the kind of work you have done.

Any sentence or phrase which describes your past attitude toward your work in a positive way:

"Hard worker"

"Came in early, left late"

"Always did more than was expected of me," etc.

THE EMPLOYER'S QUESTION:
"What kind of work are you looking for?"

The Fear Behind the Question: That it isn't the same kind of job the employer needs to fill -- e.g., they are looking for a secretary, you are looking to be office manager; they are looking for somebody who can work alone, you are looking for a job where you would be rubbing shoulders with other people.

The Point You Try to Get Across to Answer Their Fear: You have picked up many skills, which are transferable from one field to another.

Ideas or Phrases You Might Use: You are looking for work where you can use your skills with People (specify what those skills are -- that you most enjoy).

and/or

You are looking for work where you can use your skills with Data or Information (specify what those skills are, that you most enjoy).

and/or

You are looking for work where you can use your skills with

Things/Machines/Tools/Plants, etc. (specify what those skills are, that you most enjoy).

If you are applying for a known vacancy, you can **first** respond to this question by saying, "I'd be happy to answer that, but first it seems to me it's more important for you to tell me what kind of work this job involves."

Once the employer has told you, **don't forget** to then answer their question. But now you can couch your answer in terms of the skills you have, which are **relevant** to the work the employer has described.

THE EMPLOYER'S QUESTION:
"Have you ever done this kind of work before?"

The Fear Behind the Question: The employer is afraid you can't do the work, that you don't possess the necessary experience or skills.

The Point You Try to Get Across, to Answer This Fear: You have transferable skills.

Ideas or Phrases You Might Use: The same ones as in the last question, plus:

"I pick up stuff very quickly."

"I have quickly mastered any job I have ever done."

"Every job is a whole new universe, but I make myself at home very quickly."

THE EMPLOYER'S QUESTION:
"Why did you leave your last job?"
OR
"Why did your last job end?"
OR
"How did you get along with your former boss and co-workers?"

The Fear Behind the Question: The employer is afraid that you don't get along with people, especially bosses.

The Point You Try to Get Across, to Answer This Fear: That you do get along well with people, and your attitude toward your former boss(es) and co-workers proves it.

Ideas or Phrases You Might Use:

"My **job** was terminated." (if you were fired)

"My boss **and I** both felt I would be **happier** and **more effective** in a job where (here describe your strong points: e.g., I would be under less supervision and have more room to use my initiative and creativity)."

Say as many positive things as you can about your boss and co-workers (without telling lies).

THE EMPLOYER'S QUESTION:
"How is your health?"

The Fear Behind the Question: The employer is afraid that you will miss work because of sickness.

The Point You Try to Get Across, to Answer This Fear: You are a hard worker, and you have no health problem **that keeps you from being at work daily.**

If you do have a health problem: You stress your attendance average in terms of how many days per month you have been absent at previous jobs, and you stress how hard you work on the days that you are there.

Ideas or Phrases You Might Use: Your productivity, compared to other workers, at your previous jobs.

Your determination to produce more than other workers, if you get this job (or more than your predecessor did).

THE EMPLOYER'S QUESTION:
"How much were you absent from work during your last job?"

The Fear Behind the Question: The employer is afraid that you will be absent from work a lot, if they hire you.

The Point You Try to Get Across, to Answer This Fear: You Will Not Be Absent from Work.

Ideas or Phrases You Might Use: If you **were** absent quite a bit on a previous job, say why, and stress that it is a **past** difficulty (if it is).

If you were not absent on your previous job, stress your good attendance record, and **the attitude** you have toward the importance of always being at work.

THE EMPLOYER'S QUESTION:
"Can you explain why you've been out of work so long?"

OR

"Can you tell me why there are these gaps in your work record or work history?" (Usually asked, after studying your resume)

OR

"How long have you been out of work?"

The Fear Behind the Question: The employer is afraid that you don't really like to work, and will quit the minute things aren't going "your way."

The Point You Try to Get Across, to Answer This Fear: You like to work, and you regard times when things aren't going well as Challenges.

Ideas or Phrases You Might Use: You were working hard during the times when you weren't employed. Either: studying, doing volunteer work, sitting down to do lots of hard thinking about how you could most effectively use the talents you have been given, trying to get beyond merely "keeping busy" to finding some sense of mission for your life.

THE EMPLOYER'S QUESTION:
"Doesn't this work (or this job) represent a step down for you?"   OR
"Don't you think you would be underemployed if you took this job?"

OR

"I think this job is way beneath your talents and experience."

The Fear Behind the Question: The employer is afraid that you could command more salary and more responsibility, that you are only taking this job as a stopgap measure, and that you will leave him (or her) as soon as something better turns up.

The Point You Try to Get Across, to Answer This Fear: You will stick with this job just as long as you possibly can, so long as you **and the employer** agree this is where you should be.

Ideas or Phrases You Might Use: "This job isn't a step down for me. It's a step up - - from being on welfare, or unemployment."

"I like to work, and I give my best to every job I've ever done."

"Every employer is afraid the employee will leave too soon, and every employee is afraid the employer might fire him (or her). We have mutual fears. I'll do the finest job I know how, and I'll stay as long as we both agree this is where I should be."

THE EMPLOYER'S QUESTION:
"Tell me, what is your greatest weakness?"

The Fear Behind the Question: The employer is afraid you have some work-flaw or character-flaw, and is hopeful you will confess to it, **now.**

The Point You Try to Get Across, to Answer This Fear: You have limitations just like any other person but you work constantly to improve them and make yourself into a more effective worker.

Ideas or Phrases You Might Use: Mention some weakness of yours that has a positive aspect to it. Stress that positive aspect, e.g., "I don't respond well to being over-supervised, because I have a great deal of initiative, and I like to use it, anticipating problems before they even arise."

There are many other interview questions we could look at; but the above nine should give you the principles which you can now apply to all.

From the foregoing you will see: if it turns out to be a successful interview, the fears of each of you will get allayed, and you will both feel pretty good about each other. If that is the case, further interviews may be in store for you there, either with the same person, or with a committee. But for now, the first interview is over, and you are free to go home.

THE ABSOLUTELY CRUCIAL
THANK-YOU NOTE

That evening, you put your feet up, turn on the TV, and have a pleasant evening to yourself or with your loved one, right? Wrong. That evening **you work.**

Each evening, you **MUST** take time to sit down and write (pen or typewriter) a brief thank-you note to **each person that you saw that day.** That includes employers, **secretaries, receptionists,** or anyone else who gave you a helping hand that day. It should be regarded as basic to the simplest rules of common

courtesy and kindness, that you write such notes. After all, you are presenting yourself as one who has skills at treating people as people. Prove it. Your actions must be consistent with your words. This thank-you note serves several purposes, in addition to common courtesy:

First of all, it helps them to remember you. Even if the interview did not go well, and you lost all interest in working **there,** they may still hear of **other** openings, elsewhere, that might be of interest to you. In the thank-you note, you can mention this, and ask them to keep you in mind. Thus the thank-you note may gain you additional leads.

Secondly, if the interview went rather well, and you are hopeful of being invited back, then the thank-you letter can reiterate your interest in further talks.

Thirdly, the thank-you note gives you an opportunity to **correct** any wrong impression you left behind you. You can **add** anything you forgot to tell them. You can **underline** anything that you want to stand out in their minds, from among all those things you two discussed.

The importance of sending a thank-you letter to everyone is one of the most essential steps in the entire job-hunt. It is talked about *endlessly* **in job-hunting books and job-hunting seminars. Yet it is the most overlooked step in the entire job-hunting process.** We know of one woman who was told she was hired because she was **the only** interviewee, out of thirty-nine, who sent a thank-you letter after the interview.

That's right, the thank-you letter may actually get you the job. **You cannot afford to think of this as simply an optional exercise. It is critical to your getting hired.**

You may want to include with the thank-you note two other documents. The first, and preferred piece of paper, would be a written **proposal** from you as to what it is you would like to be able to do for that organization, what it is you hope you could accomplish for them. As evidence, you will want to cite **relevant** past accomplishments of yours, taking care **in each case** to cite:

a) what the problem was

b) what you did to solve it

c) what means you used

d) what the results were, of your actions, stated as concretely as possible in terms of things accomplished, money saved, money earned, etc.

The virtue of such a written proposal is that it looks forward rather than (as the resume does) backward. And it puts into writing the essence of the hiring interview: you are not asking them merely to do something for you. More importantly, you are offering to do something for them.

The second piece of paper you may wonder if you should include with your thank-you letter is a resume as **memory jogger.**

If you have included a proposal, this is really unnecessary. If you haven't included a written proposal, then your resume or some kind of summary of your background and history should be included, to remind them of who you were in that parade of people that they interviewed.

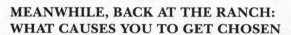

MEANWHILE, BACK AT THE RANCH: WHAT CAUSES YOU TO GET CHOSEN

While **you** are sitting there, writing out your thank-you letter, the employer you saw that day is also sitting at home, very likely reflecting on the day's interview. What's going on in his or her head, do you suppose? Well, you know. They are mentally sifting through all the candidates they saw, trying to decide **who stands out,** so far.

Usually, they've seen a number of candidates who - - in terms of skills and experience - - are basically equal. We will assume you are among those. Sooooooo, the problem the employer faces is trying to decide who stands out, **on other grounds.** And just how do you think they are going to decide that? On what grounds will they give the nod to one person over the other seventeen who are equally qualified? The answer will vary from employer to employer, but according to a survey we did, this is how the employer **typically** chooses one candidate over all the others. **They ask themselves:**

1) "Does this prospective employee **fit in** with the people who are already here? Does this person share compatible perspectives, exhibit integrity, manifest a desire to work as part of a team, and have similar values and sense of humor?"

2) "Does this prospective employee give the feeling of great **enthusiasm for this particular job?** How much does he or she seem to **want** it?"

3) "Does this prospective employee have an **appearance** that I like?" This is an intangible thing, and one can't define it, but

it has to do with the employer's intuition about the person, their face, the way they dress, and how reliable or stable the employer feels them to be, beneath all the externals. One looks for a quiet self-confidence.

4) "Does this prospective employee give me the feeling that he or she would give that **extra boost of energy** to their work that I like to see, rather than just trying 'to get by'?" This seems to be dependent on how much the prospective employee truly has their own individual goals, toward which they are striving.

5) "Finally, does this prospective employee seem to have a genuine **enthusiasm for this organization** and what it is trying to do? Does he or she seem to like its goals, appreciate its style, and want to work for its success?"

If you get chosen, it will probably be because you **stood out** from the other applicants, in these five areas. Therefore, in your thank-you note, and in your written proposal, **anything** you can point to that demonstrates you stand out in these areas, will be very much in your favor: particularly, your enthusiasm for that place and for that job.

WHEN YOU GET INVITED BACK

Assuming things are going favorably, you will be invited back for another interview, or interviews. If you still like them, and they increasingly like you, a job offer will eventually be made. **That's** the time to deal with the fourth question that we saw earlier has got to be on the employer's mind:

"How much are you going to cost me?" As I said earlier, **if** this matter gets raised before you have each decided you want to work together, **turn the question gently aside.** If early on in the game the employer says, "How much salary are you looking for?", you can respond with gentleness and grace: "I think that's a fair question once we have **both** decided that this is where I should be working. First, however, there are other areas we need to explore."

But if you have explored those areas, and are agreeing 'to go steady,' **then** the subject of "how much are you going to cost me?" is not only legitimately raised, it is crucial that it be raised. "The laborer is worthy of his (or her) hire," says the Scriptures. Which, roughly translated, means: "You are entitled to get what

you are worth, and not a penny less." So, **you** are interested
in getting as much as possible.

There are times when the employer is in total sync with you,
and offers you exactly what you were hoping for, or more, so
that your jaw drops open in amazement. This does happen,

"Let's talk salary. How does 'astronomical' sound to you?"

but my advice would be not to count on it. Halley's comet
happens too, but only once in every 86 years. Usually, your
would-be **employer** is interested in saving as much money as
possible -- therefore, in **getting you for as little as possible.**
So, you two are (for the moment) at odds. Hence you need to
negotiate. That's why this part of the job-interview is called
"salary negotiation." And few of us are born knowing how to go
about this. We need some instruction. So, here we go:

SALARY NEGOTIATION

A woman was once describing her very first job to me. It was
at a soda fountain. I asked her what her biggest surprise at
that job was. "My first paycheck," she said. "I know it sounds
incredible, but I was so green at all this, that during the whole
interview for the job it never occurred to me to ask what my
salary would be. I just took it for granted that it would be a
fair and just salary, for the work that I would be doing. Did I
ever get a shock, when my first paycheck came! It was so small,
I could hardly believe it. Did I ever learn a lesson from that!"
Yes, and so may we all.

AT ITS SIMPLEST LEVEL

To speak of salary negotiation is to speak of a matter which can be conducted on several levels. The simplest kind - - as the above story reminds us - - involves remembering to ask during the job-hiring interview what the salary will be. And then stating whether, for you, that amount is satisfactory or not. **That** much negotiation, everyone who is hunting for a job must be prepared to do.

It is well to recognize that you are at a disadvantage if salary negotiation is approached on this simplest level, however. A figure may be named, and if you have not done any research, you may be totally unprepared to say whether or not this is a fair salary for that particular job. You just don't know.

AT ITS NEXT HIGHEST LEVEL

If you're really serious about finding out ahead of time what the job should pay, you will have to do a little research.

• If it's a non-supervisory job you are interested in, you can find out a "ballpark figure" for that industry, by having your library unearth for you the latest monthly issue of the U.S. Department of Labor's *Employment and Earnings.*

• If it's a manager's or supervisory job you are interested in, you will find many of the directories listed in our previous chapter will unearth the information you want. For those graduating from college, some of this information is to be found in the "Salary Surveys" put out by the College Placement Council, from Bethlehem, Pennsylvania. See your library, or the career counseling/placement office of a nearby college.

• *The Occupational Outlook Handbook* will also give you ballpark figures for a selected list of jobs. The job you are interested in **may** be included.

• The other books that you will find most helpful are listed on pages 123ff. See if your local library has them.

If your librarian simply cannot find or help you find the salary information that you want, do remember that almost every occupation has its own association or professional group, whose business it is to keep tabs on what is happening salarywise within that occupation or field. To learn the association or professional group for the field or occupation you are interested in, consult the *Encyclopedia of Associations, Vol. 1,* at your library.

In all dealings with this kind of information, you must keep in mind that there are often **serious** variations in salary from region to region. Such regional differences in salary reflect, of course, a variety of factors, such as differences in cost of living, differences in supply and demand, etc.

MORE SOPHISTICATED YET

Some job-hunters want to get beyond these "ballpark figures" into more detailed salary negotiation. You may want to walk into an interview knowing **exactly** what That Place pays for a job. Why? Well, for one thing, the pay may be too low for you -- and thus you are saved the necessity of wasting your precious time on that particular place. Secondly, and more importantly, many places have -- as John Crystal used to so insistently point out -- a **range** in mind. And if you know what that range is, you can negotiate for a salary that is nearer the **top** of the range, than the **bottom.**

By way of example, let's assume you have done all the home-work outlined in the previous two chapters. You have done your research, gone out and knocked on doors, as well as visited libraries. And you have gotten your search down to three or five places that really interest you. You know in general what

sort of position you are aiming at, in those particular places --
and you are ready to go for a job interview **as soon as you
know what the salary range is for the position that interests
you** (it matters not whether that position already exists, or is
one you are going to ask them to create). How do you find
out what the salary is, or should be, by way of range?

It's relatively easy to define. The rule of thumb is that you
will, generally speaking, be paid **more** than the person who is
below you on the organizational chart, and **less** than the person
who is **above** you. There are, needless to say, exceptions to
this rule: people who don't quite fit in the organizational chart,
such as consultants or researchers who are financed by a grant.
But in general, the rule of thumb holds true.

This makes the matter of salary research which precedes
salary negotiation relatively (I said "relatively") simple. If through
your own information search you can discover who is or would
be **above** you on the organizational chart, and who is or would
be **below** you, and what they are paid, you would then automatically know what your salary range is, or would be.

a) If the person who would be below you makes $22,000,
and the person who would be above you makes $27,000, your
range will be something like $23,000 to $26,000.

b) If the person below you makes $10,000, and the person
who would be above you makes $13,500, then your range will
be something like $10,500 to $12,500.

c) If the person below you makes $6,240, and the person
who would be above you makes $7,800, your range would be
$6,400 to $7,600.

That's not so hard to figure out, is it? *Not as hard as you
thought it was going to be, at any rate!*

Only one minor problem in the above equation: how do you
find out what those who would be above and below you, make?
Well, first -- to emphasize the obvious -- you have to find out
the **names** of those who would be above or below you, or at
least the names of their **positions.** If it is a small organization
you are going after -- one with twenty or less employees --
finding this information out should be duck soup. Any employee will likely know the answer. And, since two-thirds of all
new jobs are created by companies of that size, you would be
wise beyond your years to be looking at such sized organizations, **anyway.**

But if you still like "the Big Guys," the large corporations with row upon row of cubicles, and floor after floor of offices, laboratories, or classrooms, then you need to fall back with mercy and pleading on our two familiar life preservers:

your local reference **librarian** (at the library, you will be surprised at how much of this information is in the organization's annual report, or in other books available there)

every **contact** you have (family, friend, relative, business or church acquaintance) who might know the company, and therefore, the information you seek.

Try the library first, but when it has produced all it can for you, and you are still short of what you want to know, go to your contacts. You are looking for Someone Who Knows Someone who either is working, or has worked, at that particular place or organization that interests you, and therefore has or can get this information for you.

If you absolutely run into a blank wall on a particular organization (everyone who works there is pledged to secrecy, and they have shipped all their ex-employees off to Siberia), then seek out information on their nearest **competitor** in the same geographic area (e.g., if Citicorp were inscrutable, you would then try Chase Manhattan as your research base; or vice versa).

Perseverance and legwork pay off, in this. And if your enthusiasm flags along the way, just picture yourself sitting in the interview for hiring, and now you're at the end of the interview. The prospective employer likes you, you like them, and they say: "How much salary were you expecting?" And because you have done your homework, you know the range, and you name a figure near or at the **top** of their range -- justified, you hasten to add, by what you anticpate will be your superior performance in that job.

But suppose you **didn't** do your research. Then you're Shadow-Boxing in the Dark -- as they say. If you just take a stab at it and end up naming a figure way too high, you're out of the running -- and you can't back-track. *("Sorry, we'd like to hire you, but we just can't afford you.")* If you take a stab at it and end up naming a figure way too low, you're also out of the running. *("Sorry, but we were hoping for someone a little, ah, more professional.")* And if you're in the right range, but at the bottom of it, you've just gotten the job -- **but you have needlessly lost as much as $2,000 a year or more that could have been yours.**

So, salary research/salary negotiation, no matter how much time it takes, pays off handsomely. Let's say it takes you a week to ten days to run down this sort of information on the three or four organizations that interest you. And let us say that because you've done this research, when you finally go in for the hiring interview you are able to ask for and obtain a salary that is $2,000 higher in range, than you would otherwise have known enough to ask for. In just three years, you'll have earned $6,000 extra, because of that research. Not bad pay, for ten days' work! And it could be much more. As we have said earlier, **information is the key to a successful job-hunt.** And there is no reward for those too lazy to go gather that information.

AT ITS MOST SOPHISTICATED LEVEL

Job-hunters with incredibly developed bargaining needs, always ask how salary negotiation is conducted at its most sophisticated level. By way of answering, let me say first of all that it is my personal conviction most job-hunters will **never** operate at this level, and therefore do **not** need this sort of information.

But in case you do, or in case you are simply dying of curiosity to know how it's done, it is completely described in

Where Do I Go From Here With My Life? pages 140-42, as honed to a fine point by John Crystal. Briefly summarized, it goes like this:

You do all the steps described previously, so that you discover what the employer's range would likely be. Let us say it turns out that the range is one that varies two thousand dollars. You then "invent" in your mind a new range, for yourself, that "hooks" on the old one, in the following fashion:

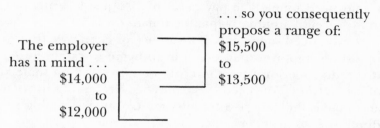

The employer
has in mind . . .
$14,000
to
$12,000

. . . so you consequently
propose a range of:
$15,500
to
$13,500

During the job-interview, then, when the employer says, "What kind of a salary did you have in mind?" you can respond, "I believe my productivity is such that it would **justify** a salary in the range of $13,500 to $15,500." This keeps you, at a minimum, near *the top* of their range; and, at a maximum, challenges them to go **beyond the top** that they had in mind, either immediately, or in the future, by means of promised raises. (Don't be afraid to ask "When?")

FRINGES

During your salary negotiation, do not forget to pay attention to so-called fringe benefits. 'Fringes' such as life insurance, health benefits or health plans, vacation or holiday plans, and retirement programs add another 25% to many workers' salaries, such as manufacturing workers. That is to say, if an employee receives $800 salary per month, the fringe benefits are worth another $200 per month. So, if the employee who is beneath you on the organizational chart gets $700 plus benefits, and the employee who is above you gets $1,100 plus benefits, while you are offered this new job at $800 and no benefits, you are being acquired rather cheaply. You should therefore remember to ask for similar benefits to those above and below you. If no benefits are possible, then you are justified in asking for a higher salary, which in this case ought to be $1,000.

FINALLY, THE MATTER OF A
RAISE AND/OR PROMOTION

In 75 out of the last 100 years, the cost of living increased. That means that your initial salary will annually **decline** in value, as inflation takes its toll. You will need a regular series of raises, just to protect your starting salary against erosion.

Furthermore, many people -- particularly women and minorities -- start out at too low a salary. The average woman would need immediate pay raises of 70% just to bring her up to the level of a similarly qualified man.

So, you need some kind of assurance or guarantee from your would-be employer **before you even begin working there** that **if** you do superior work, there will be raises and on some kind of a timetable. You need this assurance **preferably in writing,** and **now** is the very best time to get it. Your bargaining power diminishes to near zero once they've 'got you.'

Therefore, this question should be a part of your salary negotiation, without fail: *"If I accomplish this job to your satisfaction, as I fully expect to -- and more -- when could I expect to have my salary raised, and by how much? Would there be promotions in this job, and if so, on what kind of timetable?"* If you have certain needs or wishes in this area, you may wish to state what they are.

Once this part of the salary negotiation is concluded to your satisfaction, do ask to have it included in any letter of agreement or employment contract that they may be sending you. It may be you cannot get it in writing, but **do try!** The Road to Hell is paved with oral promises that went unwritten, and - - later - - unfulfilled. Many executives conveniently "forget" what they told you, or later deny they ever said it. Many executives leave the company for another position and place, and their successor or the one over you all may disown any **unwritten** promises: *"I don't know what caused them to say that to you, but they clearly exceeded their authority, and of course we can't be held to that."*

But even if you do get the promise in writing, raises and promotions are still something **you** have to justify, and on an annual basis. You will be amazed at how little attention your superiors will probably pay to your noteworthy accomplishments, and how little they are aware at the end of the year that you really are **entitled** to a raise. Noteworthy your accomplishments may be, but usually no one is taking notes . . . unless **you** do. Accordingly, career experts such as Bernard Haldane have suggested that you keep a weekly diary of your accomplishments, once you are on the job. I know employees who do just that. They take time each Friday afternoon or early evening to jot down reminders to themselves of just what it is that they accomplished that past week (or helped others to accomplish, if they were part of a team effort). **Do take this seriously.** Then, when the yearly anniversary of your hiring comes around, you can read through the diary, make up **a one-page summary** of its contents for that past year, and take that summary in with you to support your request for a raise and/or promotion.

CONCLUSION

We have covered now the techniques of successful job-hunters. We discussed in chapter 3 some brief hints that should help you in your job-hunt, if all you are looking for is hints. We discussed in chapters 4 and 5 as well as in this chapter, the three secrets of **successful career-change** or truly **systematic** job-hunting: WHAT, WHERE and HOW.

If you have not merely read (never mind, just skimmed) those chapters, but you have actually done the exercises in those chapters **and in Appendix A,** you will have mastered the systematic techniques that successful job-hunters and career-changers use. With a little bit of luck, these techniques should work for you as they have worked for them.

Assuming they do, when you are in that next job (hopefully that Dream Job), you will know the truth of something Dick Lathrop first said many many years ago, in his book *Who's Hiring Who:*

There may be others out there who could do this job better than you. But it is true today, and it will ever be true: the person who gets hired is not necessarily the one who can do that job best; but, the one **who knows the most about how to get hired.**

POSTSCRIPT

Twenty years ago, during one of the times that I was myself job-hunting, I devoured everything in print about job-hunting, hoping someone had the magic key. I noticed one thing that all these books and articles had in common. They described what you should do, and then the very next line said, "Now, that you've gotten a job." And I thought to myself, "Oops. But what if you do everything they tell you to do, and it **doesn't** lead to a job? What then?"

I have a built-in suspicion of anyone who claims they have discovered some magic job-hunting formula that never fails. I hope you do, too. Certainly I want to make no such claim in these pages. We have tried to **improve your chances -- I would even say greatly improve your chances --** at conducting an effective and successful job-hunt or career-change. And we have tried to do this by describing what we have learned from talking to thousands of successful job-hunters. This is akin to what you would instinctively do if you wanted to learn how to run well, or how to play tennis, or master a craft. You would talk to successful runners, tennis players, or craftspeople, and pick their brains for everything they were worth.

In these pages I've carefully described all the techniques which successrul job-hunters use. But I know the next question out of your mouth will be:

DOES THIS CREATIVE METHOD OF THE JOB-HUNT ALWAYS WORK?

Ah, dear reader, how I wish I could assure you that it does. There are two things that *are* absolutely true:

(1) It works **most of the time for most people** who diligently and persistently give the time and effort to their job-hunt that is required. And:

(2) **It works better than any other job-hunting technique in the world.**

But does it **always** work, and for everyone? Ah, now we're talking about a perfect world and perfect techniques. There is no such animal, at least not on this earth.

Follow every instruction in this book *precisely,* do every exercise **slavishly,** follow every prescription **religiously,** you still are not absolutely 100% guaranteed that you will find the job you are looking for. Or at least not right away.

There are two reasons why this is so: people don't follow the techniques in this book as thoroughly as they think they do; and, some part of job-hunting still depends on **luck,** no matter what you do to try to change that.

NOT BEING THOROUGH
WHEN YOU THINK
YOU ARE BEING THOROUGH

Each year, about 300,000 people purchase, read, and use this book. Each year, as many as 10,000 of them write to us. Most people write to tell the story of how the book helped them, or to make helpful suggestions for next year's update. But each year, about two of those letter-writers write to say that they tried all the ideas in this book, and they just didn't work **for them.**

I am prepared even before I read such a letter, to believe them. I can always picture exceptions to anything. It does not matter if these techniques work for **most** people; I can still picture someone in a small village where every job is not only taken, but numbered. I can picture someone with a handicap so formidable that no one is sympathetic enough to hire them. So, I have been ever ready with a sympathetic ear and heart. We have followed up these letters very carefully.

But over the years of such follow-up I have learned something I had not anticipated. Namely, it has been astounding to me how often people claimed they had followed every prescription in this book, but under questioning revealed they had skipped over some step that I had said was crucial. Like what? Well, like sending thank-you notes.

Just to be sure we were talking on the same wavelength, I would go down a little check-list with the person who said they'd tried everything I'd suggested, and it just hadn't worked. In due time I'd come to "Send thank-you notes." "How many thank-you notes did you send out during your job-hunt?" I'd ask. "Thank-you notes? Was I supposed to send thank-you notes?" would come the reply. It is to tear out your hair. "My dear fellow, it says thank-you notes have actually gotten people the job." "Oh. I don't recall reading that."

So, in due time, we prepared a little checklist, which I am reproducing here. Some of you may find it helpful.

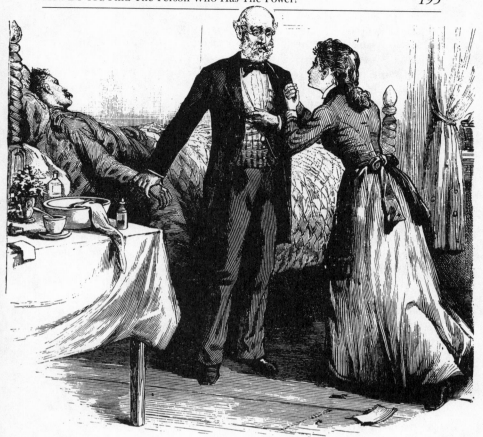

CHECKLIST FOR THOSE TIMES
WHEN YOUR JOB-HUNT
ISN'T GOING WELL

1. Are you devoting at leat six hours a day, five days a week to your job-hunt?

    IF NOT, **THAT** IS YOUR DIFFICULTY. GO DO IT.

2. If you're having trouble in getting going, are you recruiting some other job-hunters to meet with you regularly, in a group?

    IF NOT, **THAT** IS YOUR DIFFICULTY. GO DO IT.

3. Are you clear exactly what your skills are?

    IF NOT, **THAT** IS YOUR DIFFICULTY. GO DO IT.

4. Have you put your skills in their order of priority for you?

    IF NOT, **THAT** IS YOUR DIFFICULTY. GO DO IT.

5. Have you got your skills described with more than one word -- e.g., not just "organizing" but, say, "organizing data into meaningful groups" or "organizing people into motivated small groups"?
   IF NOT, **THAT** IS YOUR DIFFICULTY. GO DO IT.

6. Have you decided just exactly where it is you want to use your skills, in terms of factors?
   IF NOT, **THAT** IS YOUR DIFFICULTY. GO DO IT.

7. Have you gone out and done intensive research, devoting at least two or three hours a day to it, for twenty days?
   IF NOT, **THAT** IS YOUR DIFFICULTY. GO DO IT.

8. Are you looking for exceptions, rather than the rule -- e.g., most employers may be prejudiced against someone over forty, but are you looking for those who aren't?
   IF NOT, **THAT** IS YOUR DIFFICULTY. GO DO IT.

9. If after finishing your research you are getting in to be interviewed for hire, but you are getting turned down, are you going back to ask them for helpful feedback as to how you could improve the way in which you are presenting yourself?
   IF NOT, **THAT** IS YOUR DIFFICULTY. GO DO IT.

10. After seeing someone, either for information or for hire, do you always remember to send a thank-you note that night?
    IF NOT, **THAT** IS YOUR DIFFICULTY. GO DO IT.

11. Are you really *determined* to find that job that fits you, no matter what, rather than just giving it a twirl of the wheel, so you can say, Well, I knew it wouldn't work?
    IF NOT, **THAT** IS YOUR DIFFICULTY. GO DO IT.

THE OTHER PROBLEM:
THE NEED FOR JUST
A LITTLE BIT OF LUCK

Even if you **have** done everything right, and left no stone unturned, there is still always the chance that the job-hunt won't go well. That's because, over and above everything else, over and above all the hard work and thinking that you expend on your job-hunt, you must have on your side at least a little bit of **luck.** By luck, I mean that accidental meeting with **just** the right person, or being in **just** the right place at **just** the right time, so that a door opens for you that leads to that job.

That seems to leave a lot to chance. So why not just start with chance, and chuck all the homework and other stuff we've talked about on these pages? Well wait just a minute.

HOW TO GET LUCKY

Based on interviews with countless numbers of successful job-hunters, we now know that "getting lucky" is not the random chance that it would seem to be. Articles and books have been written about who "gets lucky" and who does not. If you would "get lucky," there are things you can do. Here's what we now know:

(1) **Luck favors the prepared mind.** The reason for this is not difficult to understand. If you've done all the homework on yourself, diligently identified your favorite skills, *put them in order,* and if you've gotten a pretty complete picture of the kind of job you are looking for, **you will be more sensitive and alert to luck, when it crosses your path.**

(2) **Luck favors the person who is working the hardest at the job-hunt.** In a word, the person who is devoting the most hours to getting out there and pounding the pavement, doing their research, making contacts. Luck favors the person who is putting in thirty-four hours a week on their job-hunt much more than it favors the person who is putting in five hours a week. The more you are 'out there' the more you're going to run across that fortunate coincidence that others call 'luck.'

(3) **Luck favors the person who has told the most people clearly and precisely what he or she is looking for.** The more ears and eyes you have out there, looking on your behalf for the kind of job you want, the more likely that you will 'get

lucky.' Forty eyes and ears are 'luckier' than two. Eighty, a hundred and twenty, are 'luckier' still. But before you get 'this lucky,' you must have done your homework so carefully that you can tell those other eyes and ears just exactly what it is you want. Luck does not favor the vague.

(4) **Luck favors the person who has alternatives up his or her sleeve,** and doesn't just **bull-headedly** persist in following just one method, or going after just one place, or one kind of job.

(5) **Luck favors the person who WANTS WITH ALL THEIR HEART to find that job.** The ambivalent job-hunter, who is looking half-heartedly, for a job that inspires no enthusiasm in them, is rarely so 'lucky.'

(6) **Luck favors the person who is going after their dream -- the thing they really want to do the most in this world.** When you want something so much that it brings tears to your eyes at the thought of getting it, you will always be 'luckier' than the person who is settling for 'what's realistic.'

(7) **Luck favors the person who is trying hard to be 'a special kind of person' in this world, treating others with grace and dignity and courtesy and kindness.** The person who runs roughshod over others in their race to 'get ahead,' usually is not so 'lucky.' During the job-hunt you need 'favors' from others. If you treated them cavalierly in another day and age, now is their time to say, "Sure, I'll help you out," and then do nothing. **Getting even** is more popular than being helpful, if there is a score to be settled.

So, if you would have 'luck' on your side during this phase of the job-hunt, **do** take seriously the above **ways of improving your luck.**

My friend, I wish you **good luck.** I wish you **persistence.** I wish you **success,** not only with your job-hunt or career-change, but -- even more -- with your life.

WHAT IS SUCCESS?

To laugh often and much;

To win the respect of intelligent people
and the affection of children;

To earn the appreciation of honest critics
and endure the betrayal of false friends;

To appreciate beauty;

To find the best in others;

To leave the world a bit better, whether by
a healthy child, a garden
patch or a redeemed social condition;

To know even one life has breathed
easier because you have lived;

This is to have succeeded.

—*Ralph Waldo Emerson*

Appendix A

How To Create
A Picture
of
Your Ideal Job
or
Next Career

The 1989 Quick Job-Hunting
(And Career-Changing)
Map

(Portions of the Map are in Chapters 4 and 5)

by
Richard N. Bolles

*W*e make a living by what we get,
but we make a life
by what we give.

—*Winston Churchill*

Introduction

In order to hunt for your ideal job, or even something close to your ideal job, you must have a picture of it, in your head. The clearer the picture, the easier it will be to hunt for it. The purpose of this Appendix is to guide you as you draw that picture.

We have chosen a "Flower" as the model for that picture. While such phrases as "plugging in," "turning on," and other common phrases portray you as a machine, you are actually much more like a Flower than a machine. That is to say, you flourish in some climates, wither in others. In choosing your next job or career you need to remind yourself that you flourish in some job-environments, but wither in others. Therefore, the purpose of putting together this Flower Picture of yourself is to help you identify what kind of a work climate you will flourish in, and thus do your very best work. Your twin goals here should be to be as happy as you can be at work, while at the same time you do your most effective work.

The Flower model is depicted on the next page, but it is only there to give you a feeling for a sort of overview. That picture of the Flower isn't large enough, nor does each petal have enough detail, to be really useful as a worksheet.

The actual worksheets, dealing with one petal at a time, are scattered throughout the remainder of this Appendix. You will deal with the petals in a logical order, beginning with the ones that are easiest to fill out, and working on through to the harder ones.

A Picture of My Ideal Job

Setting

PHYSICAL SETTING I LIKE TO WORK IN

GENERAL area where I'd do my most effective work:
1
2
3
4
5
6
7

Three places which fit, are:
1
2 3

SPECIFIC working conditions where I'd work most effectively:
1
2
3
4
5
6
7
8
9
10

SPIRITUAL OR EMOTIONAL SETTING I LIKE TO WORK IN

What I believe about life, related to:

Truth	Beauty	Moral Issues	Spirituality /Love
1	1	1	1
2	2	2	2
3	3	3	3
4	4	4	4
5	5	5	5

In order to do my best work, these factors are especially important – to have at, or in, my work:

Rewards

SALARY AND LEVEL I WANT/NEED

	Level	Salary
Max.		
Min.		

Other rewards I would like this job to give me:

KINDS OF PEOPLE I LIKE TO USE THESE SKILLS WITH

As Clients, Customers, Students, or Other:

As Co-workers:

Tasks

In order to do my favorite Tasks, I need to be using my favorite Functional/Transferable Skills. These are:

WHAT I LIKE TO DO WITH

THINGS	PEOPLE	INFORMATION
1	1	1
2	2	2
3	3	3
4	4	4
5	5	5
6	6	6
7	7	7
8	8	8

My style of doing them:

Outcomes

IMMEDIATE

Do I want to help produce a product, a service, or to help gather/disseminate information? Or all three? Or two? And what kind of product, or service, or info?

LONG-RANGE

My long-range goals for my life-- the things I want to do, or the goals I'd like to accomplish-- before I die, are:

KINDS OF THINGS I LIKE TO USE THESE SKILLS WITH

The Body
Materials
Objects
Equipment, Machinery, Vehicles
Buildings, Rooms
Growing Things

KINDS OF INFORMATION I LIKE TO USE THESE SKILLS WITH

FORM--Do I prefer to work with info in the form of magazines, newspapers, books, pictures etc.
1
2
3
4
5
6

CONTENT--Among knowledges already in my head, which are my favorites? About computers, environment, psychology? etc.
1
2
3
4
5
6
7

Tools or Means

The order in which you will work on the eight petals is:

1. Physical Setting
2. Spiritual or Emotional Setting
3. My Favorite Skills -- what I like to do with <u>Things</u>, <u>People</u> and/or <u>Information</u>
4. My Favorite Kinds of People I Like to Use These Skills with
5. My Favorite Kinds of Information I Like to Use These Skills with
6. My Favorite Kinds of Things I like to Use These Skills with
7. Outcomes: Immediate and Long-range
8. Rewards: Salary, Level & Other

And when you are done, you will put all the petals together, so that they form one complete Flower picture of your Ideal Job.

Okay? Then, get out your pen or pencil and let's get started.

Step One. Physical Setting

1

In order to fill out the petal dealing with The Physical Setting I like to Work In (pages 210-211), you will need to think about two questions: your ideal Geography, and your ideal Working Conditions. Both of these are essentially memory exercises. That is to say, if you can remember all the places you have lived -- and what you liked or didn't like about them -- you will have answered the Ideal Geography question. And if you can remember all the places you have worked -- and what you liked or didn't like about them -- you will have answered the Ideal Working Conditions question. It's as easy as that.

First, to the Geography. Where are the places you have lived, and what did you like or dislike about them? On

(continued on page 208)

Geography

Decision Making for One

Names of Places I Have Lived	From the Past: Negatives	Transferring the Negatives into Positives	Ranking of My Positives
I/We	Factors I Disliked and Still Dislike About That Place		1.
			2.
			3.
			4.
			5.
			6.
			7.
			8.
			9.
			10.
		Factors I liked and Still Like About That Place	11.
			12.
			13.
			14.
			15.

Preferences

	Decision Making for Two		
Places Which Fit These Criteria	Ranking of My Partner's List	Ranking of Our Combined List	Places Which Fit These Criteria
	a.	a.	
		1.	
	b.	b.	
		2.	
	c.	c.	
		3.	
	d.	d.	
		4.	
	e.	e.	
		5.	
	f.	f.	
		6.	
	g.	g.	
		7.	
	h.	h.	
		8.	
	i.	i.	
		9.	
	j.	j.	
		10.	
	k.	k.	
		11.	
	l.	l.	
		12.	
	m.	m.	
	n.	14.	
		n.	
	o.	15.	

pages 206-207 you will find a chart to help you answer this question. The first column is (obviously) for the names of the towns or cities.

The second column is for you to list all the things you disliked and still dislike about that city or town (e.g., "cloudy or foggy too much of the year," "terrible newspaper," etc.). You do not need to put these things directly opposite the name of the city or town you are thinking of. Put them anywhere in the second column. But do write small!

The third column serves two purposes. The top part is for you to list the **opposite** for each of your negative factors (e.g., "sunny most of the year," "good newspaper," etc.) The bottom part of that same column is for you to list any positive factors that you liked about the places you have lived (e.g., "we had a big yard," etc.). Again, these factors do not have to be listed directly opposite the name of the city you are thinking of.

In the fourth column, you are asked to put all the positive factors you listed in the third column (top or bottom) in their order of importance for you. For example, if "sunny most of the year" is the most important factor for you, that becomes #1. If "has a good newspaper" is the next most important for you, that becomes #2, etc. You will note in that column that #13 is missing, for the sake of the superstitious. If you are not superstitious, a space has been left for you to put it back in. Of course, you may find some difficulty in deciding which Positive factor is most important to you, which is second, and so on; if that is the case, we urge you to use the Prioritizing Grid which you will find on page 213, complete with instructions.

The fifth column requires your friends to help you. You read to them the list of Positive factors that you have arranged, in order, in the fourth column, and see what cities or towns they can think of, that have these characteristics. Don't stumble over two factors that seem to be contradictory, like "sunny all year round" and "skiing nearby." There's usually an answer (like, "Palm Springs with the tram up Mt. San Jacinto to the snow"). When your friends are through suggesting places, pick the one you like best, next best, and third best, and put them on the bottom left-side of the petal on pages 210-211. If you don't know enough about them, put your three favorites in any order, and write away to their chambers of commerce, to find out more about them. The library also can help!

The last three columns are only to be used if you have a wife, husband, or partner, and you are doing joint decision-making about where you eventually want to move to. In that case, your partner will need to photocopy the Geography chart (before you fill it out, obviously) and do their own first five columns. If your preferred geographical areas turn out to be identical, then you are done with the chart. But if they don't, then go on to column #6 ("Ranking of my partner's list") and put down your partner's positive factors from their column #4.

Now, on to column #7. Merge together, there, your "Ranking of My Positives" and your partner's ranking. Your factors, obviously, are numbered 1,2,3,4,5, etc. while your partner's are numbered a,b,c,d,e, etc. You will notice that column #7 asks you first to list your partner's top priority, then your top one, then your partner's second priority, then your second one, etc.

When done, move on to column #8. It involves exactly the same procedure as column #5. Show column #7 to all your friends and ask them what cities or towns they think of, when they read this (combined) list of factors. Again, don't be put off by apparently contradictory factors. There's usually some place, somewhere, that can give you both factors.

Incidentally, you may have looked at this chart and sort of shrugged your shoulders, because you already know your geographical destination, and by name. It's either where you already are, or some place you both have to move to, or some place you both would love to move to. Nonetheless, try filling out columns #1 through #4, anyway. It helps a lot if you know, in that city or town, which characteristics you like best (or you each like best) -- and in what order.

Working Conditions

Now, to the other half of the Physical Settings petal: Working Conditions. You use the same method as you did for Geography. In fact you can make up a chart where you copy the first four columns (only) of the Geography Chart.

(continued on page 212)

The Physical Setting I Like to Work In

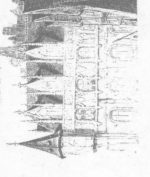

GENERAL

The geographical area which would please me most, and therefore help me to do my most effective work, would have the following characteristics (e.g., warm dry summers, skiing in the winter, a good newspaper, etc.):

1.

2.

3.

SPECIFIC

At my place of work I could be happiest and do my most effective work, if I had the following working conditions (e.g., working indoors or out, not punching a timeclock, a boss who gave me free rein to do my work, having my own office, etc.):

1.

2.

3.

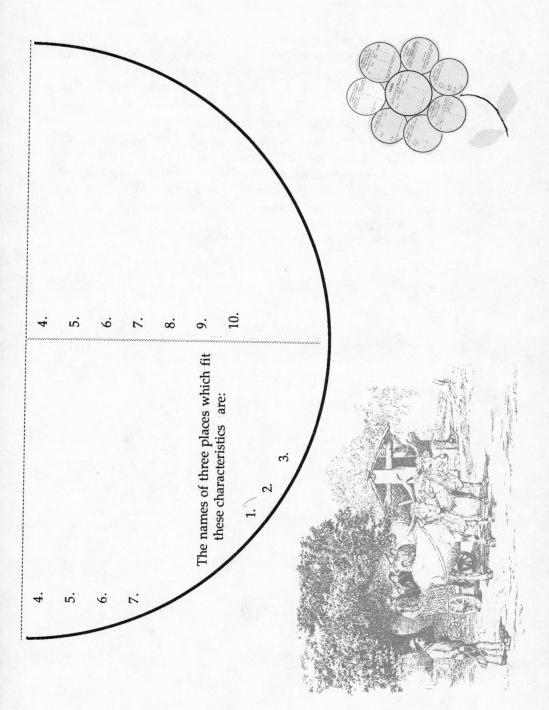

The names of three places which fit these characteristics are:

1.
2.
3.

4.
5.
6.
7.
8.
9.
10.

4.
5.
6.
7.

The only change you will need to make is to re-label column #1 as "Names of Places I Have Worked." Here name all the companies, or all the jobs you have ever held.

Column #2, now, is "Factors I Disliked and Still Dislike About That Job." Examples would be "no windows," "a boss that oversupervised me," "had to come in too early," etc.

Columns #3 and #4 remain the same. List, and then prioritize, the positive factors about the working conditions you like best. Remember, these are also the working conditions under which you can do your best and most effective work. When you're done, list them on the right hand side of the petal, page 211.

And voila! The first petal is all finished.

```
1    1    1    1    1    1    1    1    1
  2    3    4    5    6    7    8    9    10

2    2    2    2    2    2    2    2
  3    4    5    6    7    8    9    10

3    3    3    3    3    3    3
  4    5    6    7    8    9    10

4    4    4    4    4    4
  5    6    7    8    9    10

5    5    5    5    5
  6    7    8    9    10

6    6    6    6    6
  7    8    9    10

7    7    7
  8    9    10

8    8
  9    10

9
  10
```

PRIORITIZING GRID

Here is a method for taking (say) ten items, and figuring out which one is most important to you, which is next most important, etc.

• <u>LIST</u>, <u>COMPARE</u>. First make a list of the items and number them. In the case of geographical factors, list the ten factors you care most about, then number them 1 thru 10. Now, look at the top line of this grid. You see a 1 and a 2 there. So, compare items one and two on your list. Which one is more important to you? State the question any way you want to: In the case of geographical factors you might ask If I were being offered two jobs, one in an area that had factor #1, but not factor #2; the other in an area that had factor #2, but not factor #1, all other things being equal, which job would I take? <u>Circle it</u>. Then go on to the next pair, etc.

When you are all done, count up the number of times each number got circled, all told. Enter these totals here:

1____ 2____ 3____ 4____ 5____ 6____ 7____ 8____ 9____ 10____

• <u>RECOPY</u>. Finally, recopy your list, beginning with the item that got the most circles. This is your *new* #1. Then the item that got the next most circles. This is your *new* #2.

In case of a tie (two numbers got the same number of circles), look back on the grid to see when you were comparing those two numbers there, which one got circled. That means you prefer That One over the other; thus you break the tie.

(See next page for a larger grid which enables you to compare up to 24 items.)

1 1 1 1 1 1 1 1 1 1 1 1 1 1 1 1 1 1 1 1 1 1 1
2 3 4 5 6 7 8 9 10 11 12 13 14 15 16 17 18 19 20 21 22 23 24

2 2 2 2 2 2 2 2 2 2 2 2 2 2 2 2 2 2 2 2 2 2
3 4 5 6 7 8 9 10 11 12 13 14 15 16 17 18 19 20 21 22 23 24

3 3 3 3 3 3 3 3 3 3 3 3 3 3 3 3 3 3 3 3 3
4 5 6 7 8 9 10 11 12 13 14 15 16 17 18 19 20 21 22 23 24

4 4 4 4 4 4 4 4 4 4 4 4 4 4 4 4 4 4 4 4
5 6 7 8 9 10 11 12 13 14 15 16 17 18 19 20 21 22 23 24

5 5 5 5 5 5 5 5 5 5 5 5 5 5 5 5 5 5 5
6 7 8 9 10 11 12 13 14 15 16 17 18 19 20 21 22 23 24

6 6 6 6 6 6 6 6 6 6 6 6 6 6 6 6 6 6
7 8 9 10 11 12 13 14 15 16 17 18 19 20 21 22 23 24

7 7 7 7 7 7 7 7 7 7 7 7 7 7 7 7 7
8 9 10 11 12 13 14 15 16 17 18 19 20 21 22 23 24

8 8 8 8 8 8 8 8 8 8 8 8 8 8 8 8
9 10 11 12 13 14 15 16 17 18 19 20 21 22 23 24

9 9 9 9 9 9 9 9 9 9 9 9 9 9 9
10 11 12 13 14 15 16 17 18 19 20 21 22 23 24

10 10 10 10 10 10 10 10 10 10 10 10 10 10
11 12 13 14 15 16 17 18 19 20 21 22 23 24

11 11 11 11 11 11 11 11 11 11 11 11 11
12 13 14 15 16 17 18 19 20 21 22 23 24

12 12 12 12 12 12 12 12 12 12 12 12
13 14 15 16 17 18 19 20 21 22 23 24

13 13 13 13 13 13 13 13 13 13 13
14 15 16 17 18 19 20 21 22 23 24

14 14 14 14 14 14 14 14 14 14
15 16 17 18 19 20 21 22 23 24

15 15 15 15 15 15 15 15 15
16 17 18 19 20 21 22 23 24

16 16 16 16 16 16 16 16
17 18 19 20 21 22 23 24

17 17 17 17 17 17 17
18 19 20 21 22 23 24

18 18 18 18 18 18
19 20 21 22 23 24

19 19 19 19 19
20 21 22 23 24

20 20 20 20
21 22 23 24

21 21 21
22 23 24

22 22
23 24

23
24

PRIORITIZING GRID
FOR UP TO 24 ITEMS

Total times each number got circled

1	2	3	4	5	6
7	8	9	10	11	12
13	14	15	16	17	18
19	20	21	22	23	24

Step Two: Spiritual or Emotional Setting

2

Every job or career has not merely a physical setting, but a spiritual or emotional one also: the realm of things we cannot see. For example, a man once phoned me to ask what he should do about a crooked contract his firm had just executed. I asked him who drew it up. He said, "I did." I asked him why. He said, "My boss told me it was that, or I'd lose my job."

You need to think out, as part of your picture of your Ideal Job, what is important to you in life -- in the area of things we cannot see: values, principles, what you are willing to stand up for, and what you are not willing to stand up for, what you care about.

The most useful way to do this is to take a piece of blank paper (or two) and write out on it your *philosophy about life:* which typically might include some statement of why you think we are here on earth, what it is that you believe we are supposed to do while we are here, what you think is important in life and what is not important, and which values of our society you agree with, and which ones you disagree with. As a suggested framework only, the upper part of the Spiritual/Emotional petal on pages 216-217 suggests you might include your thoughts about the importance of *truth* (in what areas, particularly, does truth most matter to you?), the importance of *beauty* (what kinds of beauty do you like best?), *moral issues* (which ones are you most concerned about -- justice, feeding the hungry, helping the homeless, comforting AIDS sufferers, or what?), and the importance of *spirituality* and/or *love* (if you believe in a Higher Power, or Being, or God, include that, and how it affects your philosophy about life). Don't just write; take time also to think!

When you are done writing your philosophy of life, the bottom part of the petal on pages 216-217 asks you to lift out of that philosophy any factors which are especially important to you at your future place of work, or in your future work. For example, your philosophy of life might have reminded you: "I have to work in a place where I am never asked to do anything dishonest." Or: "I want to be among

(continued on page 218)

Spiritual or Emotional Setting I Like to Work In

MY PHILOSOPHY OF LIFE.
What I believe about life in general,
and my life in particular,
as it relates to:

Matters of the mind	Matters of the heart	Matters of the will	Matters of the whole self and the universe
TRUTH	BEAUTY	MORAL ISSUES	SPIRITUALITY OR LOVE
1.	1.	1.	1.
2.	2.	2.	2.
3.	3.	3.	3.

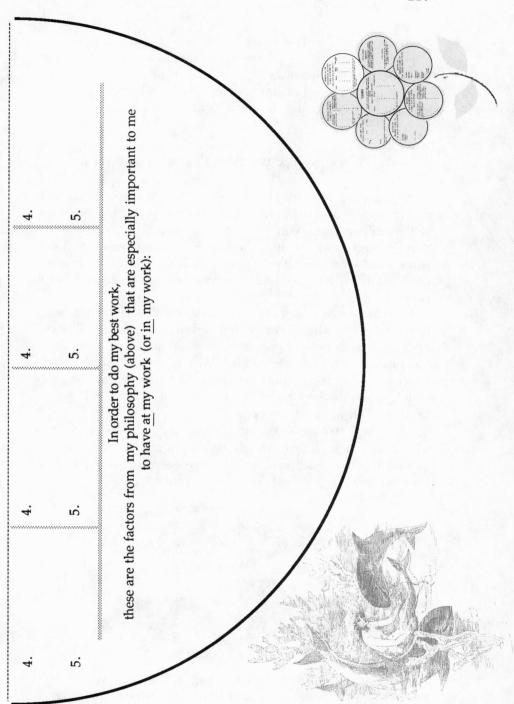

In order to do my best work,
these are the factors from my philosophy (above) that are especially important to me
to have at my work (or in my work):

4.

5.

4.

5.

4.

5.

4.

5.

loving, supportive co-workers, and not among people who are always backbiting or gossiping about everyone." Whatever occurs to you, after studying your philosophy, put this stuff down, in the bottom part of that petal.

And, voila! The second petal is all finished.

Step Three: My Favorite Transferable Skills

If you have already read chapter 4, you know what it is you're going to do here. You are going to figure out what skills you use when you are enjoying yourself the most -- either in your work, or in your home, or when you are doing some hobby or recreation. These skills, no matter where you used them in the past, are transferable now to other jobs or careers.

In order to find out this information, it will be necessary for you eventually to write out seven (7) stories of some enjoyable and satisfying experiences or achievements which you have done in your life. Which stories should you choose? Ah, that's a good question. Not necessarily the ones which occur to you right off the top of your head. Sometimes you have to dig deeper.

To guard yourself against impulsively choosing stories which may not tell you much about your skills, it is helpful to construct a basic outline of your life, for yourself, first. One way to do this is through a Memory Net.

That Net may be found on pages 220-221. You should take at least a couple of hours (with some hard thinking, as well as writing) to fill it in.

In the first column of the Memory Net are the years of your life, divided into five-year periods (cross out the years before your birth, of course). Some of you will be able to remember what activities you were doing during each of these five-year periods, just from seeing the dates. Use this column, then, to jog your memory, and fill in the rest of the Net.

The second column is for those of you who don't remember things by Dates, but by what job you were holding down (or what school you were attending). Use this column, then, to jog your memory -- fill it in, and then fill in the rest of the Net.

The third column is for those of you who don't remember things by either Years or Jobs, but by where you were living at the time. Use this column, then, to jog your memory -- fill it in, and then fill in the rest of the Net.

Once you've tackled the first three columns, as you go across the rest of the Memory Net you will generally find it pays to fill in the three Activities columns first, and then go back to the Achievements columns. That is to say, once you remember what you were doing (activities) in the way of Leisure, Learning, or Labor (Work), you will then find it easier to think of specific achievements in your Leisure or your Learning or your Labor. Put down titles only, or a few words to jog your memory, rather than attempting any more detailed description of your achievements, at this time.

Once you have the Net all filled in, you will need to take seven blank sheets of notebook paper.

On each of these sheets you are going to write one of your stories, picked from the Memory Net -- which you will then analyze as we shall show you, to see what skills you were using.

Memory

In Terms of Five-Year Periods	In Terms of Jobs You Have Held	In Terms of Places You Have Lived	Leisure	
			Activities	Accomplishments
1985-1989				
1980-1984				
1975-1979				
1970-1974				
1965-1969				
1960-1964				
1955-1959				
1950-1954				
1945-1949				
1940-1944				
1935-1939				
1930-1934				
1925-1929				
1920-1924				
1915-1919				

Learning		Labor	
Activities	Accomplishments	Activities	Accomplishments

For the time being, you start by writing just one of those stories.

Look over your Memory Net, and most particularly at the three columns devoted to achievements or accomplishments -- whether they were early in your life, or more recently, whether they were in your leisure life, or your learning life, or your labor/work life. It does not matter.

What does matter is that this first story you choose to tell in greater detail, should have the following characteristics. There was:

> 1. A TASK. Something you wanted to do, just be-cause it was fun or would give you a sense of adven-ture or a sense of accomplishment Normally there was a problem that you were trying to solve, or a challenge you were trying to overcome, or something you were trying to master or produce or create.
>
> 2. TOOLS OR MEANS. You used something to help you do the task, solve the problem, overcome the challenge. Either you had certain Things to help you -- objects, materials, tools or equipment, or you had other People to help you, or you got a hold of some vital Information. Tell us what tools or means you used, and how you used them.
>
> 3. AN OUTCOME OR RESULT. You were able to finish the task or solve the problem, overcome the challenge, master a process or produce or create something. You had a sense of pride, even if no one else knew what it was you had accomplished. [1]

1 © *Copyright 1988 by D. Porot. Adapted and used by his permission.*

Once you have selected your first story, write it out in detail -- but keep it comparatively brief -- two or three paragraphs at most. Be sure that it is *a story* you tell -- that is, that it moves step by step. It may help if you pretend that you are telling it to a small whining child who keeps saying, "An' then whadja do?" "An' then whadja do?"

Be sure also that it deals in turn with TASK, TOOLS, AND MEANS, and OUTCOME or RESULT. See the example that follows here:

THIS WON'T DO

THIS WILL DO

SAMPLE

"The Halloween Experience.
I won a prize on Halloween
for dressing up as a
horse."

SAMPLE

"My Halloween Experience When
I Was Seven Years Old. Details:

When I was seven, I decided I wanted
to go out on Halloween dressed as a
horse. I wanted to be the front end of
the horse, and I talked a friend of mine
into being the back end of the horse.
But, at the last moment he backed out,
and I was faced with the prospect of
not being able to go out on Halloween.
At this point, I decided to figure out
some way of getting dressed up as the
whole horse, myself. I took a fruit
basket, and tied some string to both
sides of the basket's rim, so that I could
tie the basket around my rear end. This
filled me out enough so that the
costume fit me, by myself. I then fixed
some strong thread to the tail so that
I could make it wag by moving my
hands. When Halloween came I not
only went out and had a ball,
but I won a prize as well."

When you are done, label that sheet "#1".

(continued on page 230)

My transferable skills dealing with

THINGS

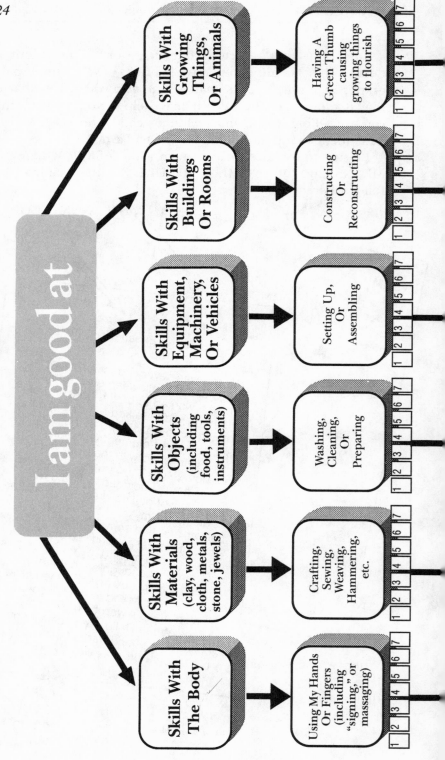

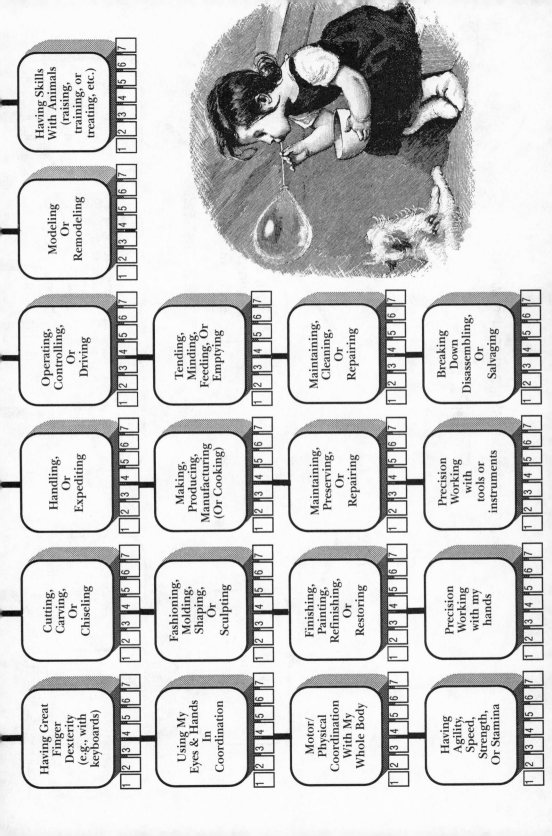

| Having Skills With Animals (raising, training, or treating, etc.) | 1 2 3 4 5 6 7 |

| Modeling Or Remodeling | 1 2 3 4 5 6 7 |

| Operating, Controlling, Or Driving | 1 2 3 4 5 6 7 |

| Tending, Minding, Feeding, Or Emptying | 1 2 3 4 5 6 7 |

| Maintaining, Cleaning, Or Repairing | 1 2 3 4 5 6 7 |

| Breaking Down Disassembling, Or Salvaging | 1 2 3 4 5 6 7 |

| Handling, Or Expediting | 1 2 3 4 5 6 7 |

| Making, Producing, Manufacturing (Or Cooking) | 1 2 3 4 5 6 7 |

| Maintaining, Preserving, Or Repairing | 1 2 3 4 5 6 7 |

| Precision Working with tools or instruments | 1 2 3 4 5 6 7 |

| Cutting, Carving, Or Chiseling | 1 2 3 4 5 6 7 |

| Fashioning, Molding, Shaping, Or Sculpting | 1 2 3 4 5 6 7 |

| Finishing, Painting, Refinishing, Or Restoring | 1 2 3 4 5 6 7 |

| Precision Working with my hands | 1 2 3 4 5 6 7 |

| Having Great Finger Dexterity (e.g., with keyboards) | 1 2 3 4 5 6 7 |

| Using My Eyes & Hands In Coordination | 1 2 3 4 5 6 7 |

| Motor/ Physical Coordination With My Whole Body | 1 2 3 4 5 6 7 |

| Having Agility, Speed, Strength, Or Stamina | 1 2 3 4 5 6 7 |

My transferable skills dealing with

PEOPLE

I am good at

With Groups, Organizations, or the masses

Managing, Supervising, Or Running (a business, fund drive, etc.)

1 2 3 4 5 6 7

Playing Games, or a particular game, Leading Others in recreation or exercise

1 2 3 4 5 6 7

Communicating Effectively to a group or a multitude

1 2 3 4 5 6 7

With Individuals one at a time

Diagnosing, Treating, Or Healing

1 2 3 4 5 6 7

Taking Instructions, Serving, Or Helping

1 2 3 4 5 6 7

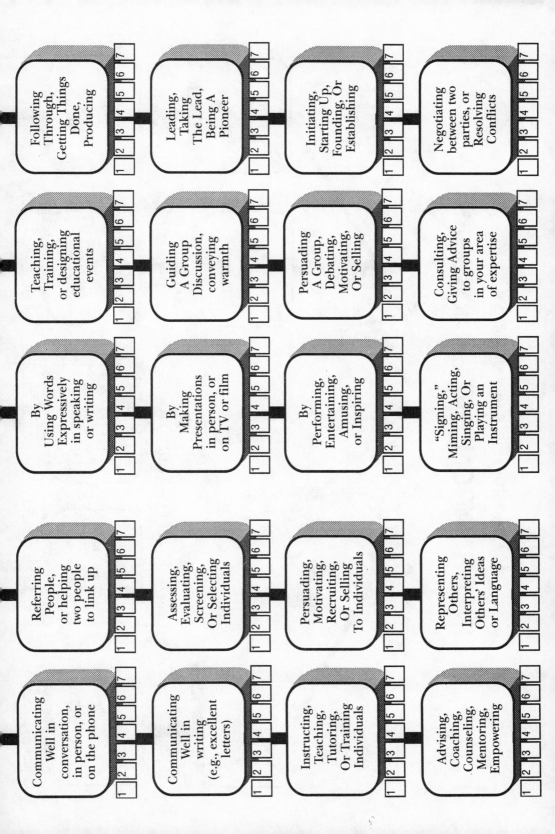

Communicating Well in conversation, in person, or on the phone
1 2 3 4 5 6 7

Communicating Well in writing (e.g., excellent letters)
1 2 3 4 5 6 7

Instructing, Teaching, Tutoring, Or Training Individuals
1 2 3 4 5 6 7

Advising, Coaching, Counseling, Mentoring, Empowering
1 2 3 4 5 6 7

Referring People, or helping two people to link up
1 2 3 4 5 6 7

Assessing, Evaluating, Screening, Or Selecting Individuals
1 2 3 4 5 6 7

Persuading, Motivating, Recruiting, Or Selling To Individuals
1 2 3 4 5 6 7

Representing Others, Interpreting Others' Ideas or Language
1 2 3 4 5 6 7

By Using Words Expressively in speaking or writing
1 2 3 4 5 6 7

By Making Presentations in person, or on TV or film
1 2 3 4 5 6 7

By Performing, Entertaining, Amusing, or Inspiring
1 2 3 4 5 6 7

"Signing," Miming, Acting, Singing, Or Playing an Instrument
1 2 3 4 5 6 7

Teaching, Training, or designing educational events
1 2 3 4 5 6 7

Guiding A Group Discussion, conveying warmth
1 2 3 4 5 6 7

Persuading A Group, Debating, Motivating, Or Selling
1 2 3 4 5 6 7

Consulting, Giving Advice to groups in your area of expertise
1 2 3 4 5 6 7

Following Through, Getting Things Done, Producing
1 2 3 4 5 6 7

Leading, Taking The Lead, Being A Pioneer
1 2 3 4 5 6 7

Initiating, Starting Up, Founding, Or Establishing
1 2 3 4 5 6 7

Negotiating between two parties, or Resolving Conflicts
1 2 3 4 5 6 7

My transferable skills dealing with

INFORMATION, DATA, AND IDEAS

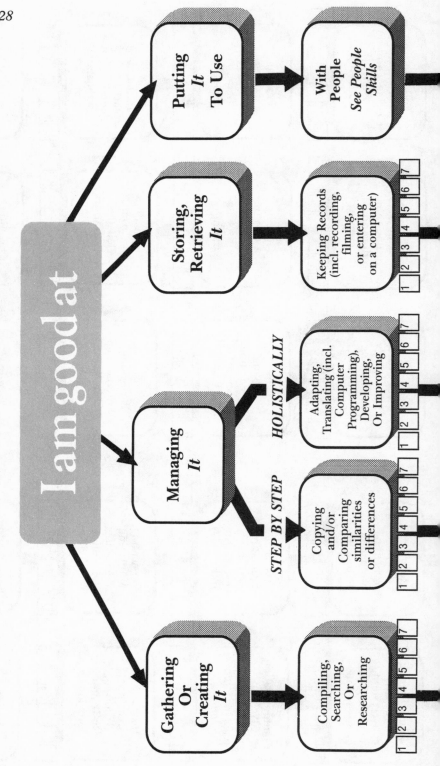

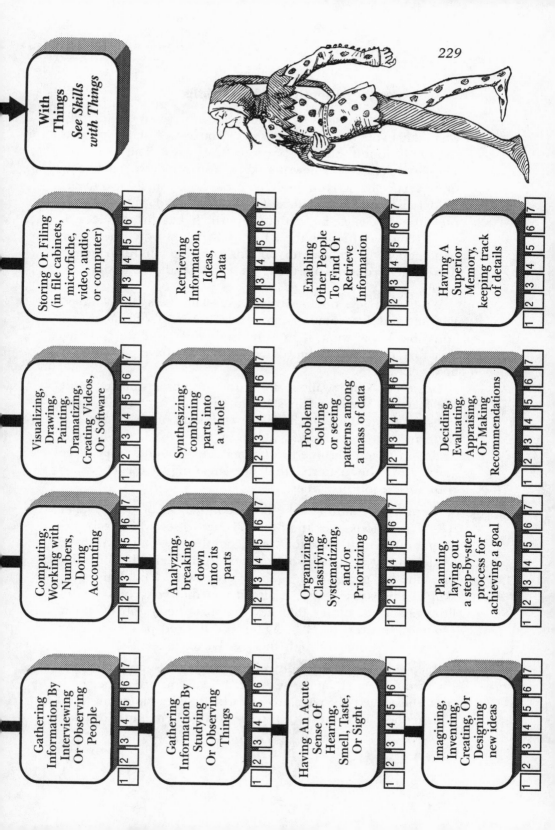

229

With
Things
*See Skills
with Things*

Storing Or Filing
(in file cabinets,
microfiche,
video, audio,
or computer)
1 2 3 4 5 6 7

Retrieving
Information,
Ideas,
Data
1 2 3 4 5 6 7

Enabling
Other People
To Find Or
Retrieve
Information
1 2 3 4 5 6 7

Having A
Superior
Memory,
keeping track
of details
1 2 3 4 5 6 7

Visualizing,
Drawing,
Painting,
Dramatizing,
Creating Videos,
Or Software
1 2 3 4 5 6 7

Synthesizing,
combining
parts into
a whole
1 2 3 4 5 6 7

Problem
Solving
or seeing
patterns among
a mass of data
1 2 3 4 5 6 7

Deciding,
Evaluating,
Appraising,
Or Making
Recommendations
1 2 3 4 5 6 7

Computing,
Working with
Numbers,
Doing
Accounting
1 2 3 4 5 6 7

Analyzing,
breaking
down
into its
parts
1 2 3 4 5 6 7

Organizing,
Classifying,
Systematizing,
and/or
Prioritizing
1 2 3 4 5 6 7

Planning,
laying out
a step-by-step
process for
achieving a goal
1 2 3 4 5 6 7

Gathering
Information By
Interviewing
Or Observing
People
1 2 3 4 5 6 7

Gathering
Information By
Studying
Or Observing
Things
1 2 3 4 5 6 7

Having An Acute
Sense Of
Hearing,
Smell, Taste,
Or Sight
1 2 3 4 5 6 7

Imagining,
Inventing,
Creating, Or
Designing
new ideas
1 2 3 4 5 6 7

Identifying Your Skills

Once this first story is written, you are ready to identify what skills you used, in that story. The list of skills you are to use is found on the previous six pages. The skills resemble a series of typewriter keys. You go down each column vertically. As you look at each key, you ask yourself, "Did I use this skill **in this story?**" If you did, you color in the little box *right under* that key which has the number 1 in it (color right *over* the "1"). We suggest you use a red pen, pencil, or crayon, to do this coloring in. Keep going down each column, in turn, on each of the following six pages.

When you are done with all the skills keys, for Things, People, and Information, you have finished with story #1. You now know what skills you used while you were doing this first enjoyable achievement, that you have selected to analyze.

However, "one swallow doth not a summer make," and the fact you used certain skills in this one accomplishment doesn't yet tell us much. What you want to look for are patterns: i.e., which skills keep getting used, again and again, in accomplishment after accomplishment, story after story. It is the patterns that are meaningful for choosing your future job or career.

So now it is time to take the second sheet of paper, label it "#2", and look over the Memory Net to see which achievement you want to pick for your second story. Once you have written it out in detail, you go back to the Skills Keys on the previous six pages, and again ask yourself, "Did I use this skill **in this story?**" And, again, if you did, you color in the little box right under that key that has the number 2 in it (color right over the "2"). Again, use the red pen, pencil, or crayon. Continue through the six skill pages.

Take the third sheet and repeat the process, and continue on through sheet (and story) #7. When you are done, look over these next six pages to see which skills stand out (i.e., which ones have the little boxes under them most colored in).

Choosing Your Favorite Transferable Skills

You must now choose your favorites, from the Skills pages you just filled out. How you make that choice is entirely up to you. Here are two different methods for doing this:

a) **The Top Ten**. Look at all the Skills pages you just filled out, and put a big check mark by your ten favorite skills -- never mind whether they are with Things, People, or Information. It could turn out, for example, that eight of your favorite skills are with Things, and one with People and one with Information. On a sheet of scratch paper, list all ten and then rearrange them so that they end up being listed *in their order of importance for you.* You can do this prioritizing either by guess and by gosh, *or* by using the Prioritizing Grid on page 213. What you want to end up with is a *prioritized list* -- on which the skill that is most important to you is listed first, the skill that is next most important to you is listed second, next most important is third, next most important is fourth, and so on.

b) Alternative Method: **Eight, Eight and Eight**. Look at the Skills pages (pages 224-229) and pick your eight favorites off *each diagram*: your eight favorite Skills with Things, your eight favorite Skills with People, and your eight favorite skills with Information. Put each eight in order, again either by guessing, or by using the Prioritizing Grid three times. You will end up with three lists: your eight favorite Skills with Things, *in order of priority for you;* and your eight favorite Skills with People, *in order of priority for you;* and your eight favorite Skills with Information, *in order of priority for you.*

Optional:
Restating Your Favorite Skills in Your Own Language

Now (and only now) that you have a list of your favorite skills -- either The Top Ten or the Eight, Eight and Eight -- you *may* want to restate them in other language than was on the Skills diagrams, language that is more uniquely and personally yours. *If so,* turn to the vocabulary section called "Uniquely You," beginning on page 265. Look up the skills which you picked as your favorites, and see if you prefer any of the words that are offered as alternatives there. You can,

of course, rephrase even *these* words so that your list, in the
end, is completely in your own language.

'Fleshing Them Out'

As explained on page 83, a *complete* identification of a
transferable skill of yours *should* have three parts to it: verb,
object, and modifier (adjective or adverb). Now that you
have *the verb* in your own language you *may* want to flesh
out each of your favorite skills so that each one also has
some general *object* and *modifier.* Again, consult page 83 for
guidance.

Copying Them Onto the Skills Diagram

When you have your list of your favorite skills in a final
form that is satisfying to you, copy the list on to either (or
both) of two pages:

The Block diagram on page 233, which allows you to put
Your Top Ten favorite skills, in order of priority.

The Tasks Petal on page 234, which allows you to list
your *Eight, Eight and Eight.* (If you *only* worked with the
Eight, Eight and Eight, and now want to also hammer out a
top ten list, you can do that very easily by taking these
twenty-four and prioritizing them together - - listing the re-
sulting top ten of the twenty four, *in order of priority,* on the
Block diagram on page 233.) Use the Prioritizing Grid if
you need to, on page 214.

Your *Style* of Working

At the bottom of *The Tasks Petal* on page 235, space is
provided for you to list **the style** with which you do the skills
that you do. Often it is this style which sets you apart from
nineteen other people who can do the same tasks as you
can. Therefore, *this part of the exercise should not be skipped
over.* Following is a list of styles (they are often called **personal traits** or **self-management skills**; you will further note
that many of them can serve as the **modifier** when you are
fleshing out your skill verbs, above). Put a checkmark in

(continued on page 236)

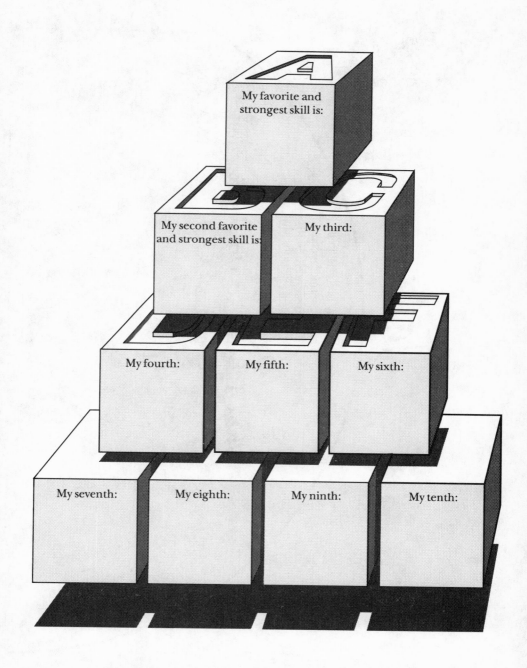

234

Tasks

In order to do my favorite Tasks,
I need to be using my favorite
Functional / Transferable Skills.
These are:

What I Like to Do With

THINGS	PEOPLE	INFORMATION
1.	1.	1.
2.	2.	2.
3.	3.	3.
4.	4.	4.

5.	5.	5.
6.	6.	6.
7.	7.	7.
8.	8.	8.

My Style
of Doing Them: (so-called "traits" or "self-management skills")
e.g., "quickly," "thoroughly," "painstakingly," etc.

front of any word (or phrase) below that you think applies to you in your work. Add any others that occur to you, which are not on this list. Then when you are done checking, pick the ten that you think are **most** important, and copy them on to the bottom part of *The Tasks Petal -- in their order of importance to you, if you can.* This matter of *importance* will most often come down to a question of which style you are proudest of, next proudest of, and so forth. Use the Prioritizing Grid if you need to (on page 213).

STYLE WITH WHICH I DO THESE SKILLS

I am VERY:

- ☐ Accurate
- ☐ Achievement-oriented
- ☐ Adaptable
- ☐ Adept
- ☐ Adept at having fun
- ☐ Adventuresome
- ☐ Alert
- ☐ Appreciative
- ☐ Assertive
- ☐ Astute
- ☐ Authoritative
- ☐ Calm
- ☐ Cautious
- ☐ Charismatic
- ☐ Competent
- ☐ Consistent
- ☐ Contagious in my enthusiasm
- ☐ Cooperative
- ☐ Courageous
- ☐ Creative
- ☐ Decisive
- ☐ Deliberate
- ☐ Dependable/ have dependability
- ☐ Diligent
- ☐ Diplomatic
- ☐ Discreet

- ☐ Driving
- ☐ Dynamic
- ☐ Extremely economical
- ☐ Effective
- ☐ Energetic
- ☐ Enthusiastic
- ☐ Exceptional
- ☐ Exhaustive
- ☐ Experienced
- ☐ Expert
- ☐ Firm
- ☐ Flexible
- ☐ Humanly oriented
- ☐ Impulsive
- ☐ Independent
- ☐ Innovative
- ☐ Knowledgeable
- ☐ Loyal
- ☐ Methodical
- ☐ Objective
- ☐ Openminded
- ☐ Outgoing
- ☐ Outstanding
- ☐ Patient
- ☐ Penetrating
- ☐ Perceptive
- ☐ Persevering

- ☐ Persistent
- ☐ Pioneering
- ☐ Practical
- ☐ Professional
- ☐ Protective
- ☐ Punctual
- ☐ Quick/ work quickly
- ☐ Rational
- ☐ Realistic
- ☐ Reliable
- ☐ Repeatedly
- ☐ Resourceful
- ☐ Responsible
- ☐ Responsive
- ☐ Safeguarding
- ☐ Self-motivated
- ☐ Self-reliant
- ☐ Sensitive
- ☐ Sophisticated, very sophisticated
- ☐ Strong
- ☐ Supportive
- ☐ Tactful
- ☐ Thorough
- ☐ Unique
- ☐ Unusual
- ☐ Versatile
- ☐ Vigorous

I am a person who:

With respect to execution of a task, and achievement
- [ ] Takes initiative
- [ ] Is able to handle a great variety of tasks and responsibilities simultaneously and efficiently
- [ ] Takes risks
- [ ]   Takes calculated risks
- [ ] Is expert at getting things done

With respect to time, and achievement
- [ ] Consistently tackles tasks ahead of time
- [ ] Is adept at finding ways to speed up a task
- [ ] Gets the most done in the shortest time
- [ ] Expedites the task at hand
- [ ] Meets deadlines
- [ ]   Delivers on promises on time
- [ ]   Brings projects in on time and within budget

With respect to working conditions
- [ ] Maintains order and neatness in my workspace
- [ ] Is attendant to details
- [ ] Has a high tolerance of repetition and/or monotonous routines
- [ ] Likes planning and directing an entire activity
- [ ] Demonstrates mastery
- [ ] Promotes change
- [ ] Works well under pressure and still improvises
- [ ] Enjoys a challenge
- [ ] Loves working outdoors
- [ ] Loves to travel
- [ ] Has an unusually good grasp of.......
- [ ] Is good at responding to emergencies
- [ ] Has the courage of his or her convictions

When you are done with this exercise, you are ready to move on.

The Things You Like to Act Upon

These next three steps, and the next three petals as a matter of fact, are called "**Tools or Means.**" Skills *always* require some tool or means. A tool or means is something you love **to handle**, or something you like **to use**, or something you like **to work on**, or **act upon**. It may be *people*, or *information*, or a *thing*.

For example, if you love to hammer things, you need both a hammer and a thing to hammer -- let us say a nail. The hammer and the nail are the tools or means that enable you to use your skill -- of hammering. And, in this case, they are *things*. Of course, you also need some knowledge of *how to hammer*, and that means that some *information* is also used here, as a tool or means.

On the succeeding three petals, and in the succeeding three steps, we will look first at People, and then at Information, and then at Things, to see which of these are your favorites.

Step Four: My Favorite People to Work With

If you checked any skills with People, as your favorites, in Step Three, it is important that you now specify *what kind* of People you prefer to work with. Let us say, for example, that you checked "teaching" as one of your favorite skills. The question now is: *What* people do you most enjoy teaching? All people? Particular age groups? If so, which ones? People with particular problems? If so, which ones? People who are working on particular issues in their life? If so, which ones?

Following is a list of people. Put a checkmark in front of any description that describes people you particularly like (or think you would particularly like) to work with -- as clients, customers, students or whatever, in your work. Add any others that may occur to you, which are not on the list. Then when you are done checking, pick the ten that you think are m**ost** important, and copy them on to the Petal called *Tools or Means: I* (found on page 240) -- *in your order of preference. "I would most enjoy working with these people, next with these people, next with these people,"* etc. Use the *Prioritizing Grid if you need to (on page 213).*

KINDS OF PEOPLE YOU PREFER TO SERVE, OR TRY TO HELP:

☐ Men
☐ Women
☐ Individuals
☐ Groups of eight or less
☐ Groups larger than eight
☐ Babies
☐ School-age children
☐ Adolescents or young people
☐ College students

☐ Young adults
☐ People in their thirties
☐ The middle-aged
☐ The elderly
☐ The retired
☐ All people regardless of age
☐ Heterosexuals
☐ Homosexuals
☐ All people regardless of sex

☐ People of a particular cultural
    background:

☐ People of a particular economic
    background:

☐ People of a particular social
    background:

☐ People of a particular educational
    background:

☐ People of a particular philosophy
    or religious belief:

☐ Certain kinds of workers (blue-
    collar, white-collar, executives,
    or whatever):

☐ People who are poor:

☐ People who are powerless:

☐ People who wield power:

☐ People who are rich:

☐ People who are easy to work with:

☐ People who are difficult to work with:

☐ People in a particular place (the
    Armed Forces, prison, etc.)

KINDS OF PROBLEMS YOU LIKE TO TRY TO HELP PEOPLE WITH:

☐ Physical handicaps
☐ Overweight
☐ Mental retardation
☐ Pain
☐ Disease in general
☐   Hypertension
☐   Allergies
☐   Self-healing, psychic healing
☐   Terminal illness
☐   Holistic health
☐ Life/work planning or life
    adjustment
☐ Identifying and finding meaning-
    ful work
☐ Job-hunting, career change, unem-
    ployment, being fired or laid off
☐ lliteracy, educational needs
☐ Industry in-house training
    Performance problems, appraisal
☐   Low energy
☐   Nutritional problems
☐   Physical fitness
☐   Work satisfaction
☐   Discipline problems, self-discipline
☐   Stress
☐   Sleep disorders
    Relationships
☐   Personal insight, therapy
☐   Loneliness
☐   Boredom
☐   Complaints, grievances
☐   Anger
☐   Anxiety
☐   Fear
☐   Shyness
☐   Meeting people, starting
      friendships

☐   Communications, thoughts,
    feelings
    Love
☐   Self-acceptance and acceptance
    of others
☐   Learning how to love
☐   Marriage
☐   Competing needs
☐   Sexual education, sexual
    problems
☐   Sexual dysfunction
☐   Pregnancy and childbirth
☐   Parenting
☐   Physical abuse
☐   Rape
☐   Divorce
☐   Death and grief
☐ Addictions
☐   Drug problems
☐   Alcoholism
☐   Smoking
☐ Mental illness
☐   Depression
☐   Psychiatric hospitalization
☐ Personal economics
☐   Financial planning
☐   Possessions
☐   Budgeting
☐   Debt bankruptcy
☐ Values
☐ Ethics
☐ Philosophy or religion
☐   Worship
☐   Stewardship
☐   Life after death
☐   Psychic phenomena

(continued on page 242)

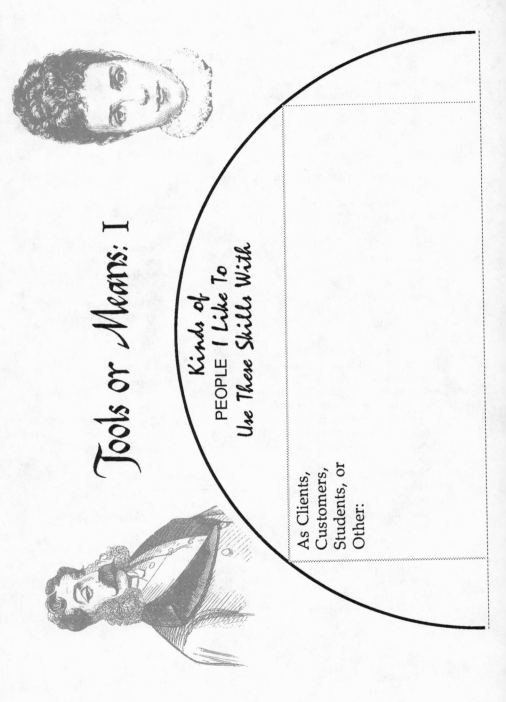

Tools or Means: I

Kinds of
PEOPLE I Like To
Use These Skills With

As Clients,
Customers,
Students, or
Other:

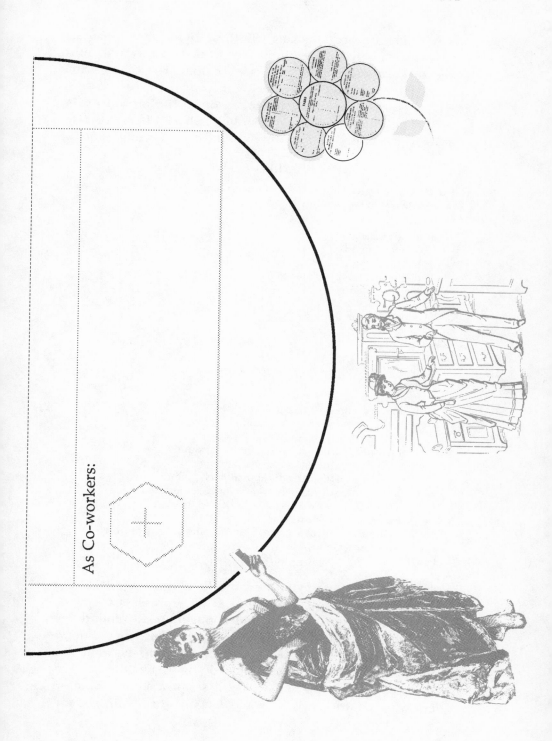

As Co-workers:

If while you are checking off these descriptions, you see any which apply to the kind of **co-workers** you would most like to have, copy them onto the bottom part of the same petal. (You may also find clues about your preferred co-workers, in *the Styles list* that you worked on in the previous exercise.) The following list may also help. Check off the descriptions which apply, or add any others which occur to you:

MY PREFERRED CO-WORKERS:

I prefer to work with what kinds of co-workers
or colleagues, bosses, or subordinates?

☐ Both sexes
☐   Men primarily
☐   Women primarily
☐ People of all ages
☐   Adolescents or young people
☐   College students
☐   Young adults
☐   People in their thirties
☐   The middle-aged
☐   The elderly
☐   The retired
☐ All people regardless of sexual orientation
☐   Heterosexuals
☐   Homosexuals
☐ All people regardless of background
☐   People of a particular background:
☐   People of a particular cultural background:
☐   People of a particular economic background:
☐   People of a particular social background:
☐   People of a particular educational background:
☐   People of a particular philosophy or religious belief:
☐   Certain kinds of workers (blue-collar, white-collar,
        executives, or whatever):
☐   People in a particular place (the Armed Forces, prison, etc.):
☐ People who are easy to work with:
☐ People who are difficult to work with

In the bottom part of this same Petal, on page 241, you will see an outline of a hexagon. This represents the Party Exercise, found on page 87, and is put there to remind you that you *may* want to put down *the descriptions* from your *favorite* corners of the hexagons, as descriptions of what you would like your co-workers to be doing (true, the corners you chose were supposed to be descriptive of *you*, but in identifying co-workers you would like to work with, the ancient truth is that birds of a feather tend to like to flock together -- e.g., artistic types tend to like to work and communicate with other artistic types, not accountants in three-piece suits -- and vice versa). Within the hexagon on that petal, you will see a figure resembling a cross -- to remind you (you are at the center of the figure) to think out what kind of person you want *over* you as boss (top of the figure), *beside* you as co-workers (middle of the figure) and *below* you, as subordinates (bottom of the figure).

When you are all done with this exercises, you will have now finished the fourth petal out of eight; the picture of your ideal job should be starting to get clearer. Also you can begin to see how you are cutting down the size of the job-market that you will need to explore, to a much more manageable territory. On to the next step.

Step Five: My Favorite Kinds of Information That I Like to Work With   5

If you checked any skills with Information, as your favorites, in Step Three, it is important that you now specify *what kind* of Information you prefer to work with. This will break down, as you can see from the next petal, on page 246, into **Form** and **Content**.

Form is a matter of: Do you prefer to work with information in the form of newspapers, magazines, books, computer output, reports, pictures, or what?

Following is a more complete list of such forms. Put a checkmark in front of any word (or phrase) below that describes forms of information you enjoy (or think you would enjoy) working with at your place of work. Add any others that occur to you, which are not on this list. Then when you are done checking, pick the ten that you think are **most** important to you, and copy them on to the lefthand side of the petal called *Tools or Means: II* (page 246) -- *in their order of importance to you, if you can. Use the Prioritizing Grid if you need to (on page 213).*

FORMS OF INFORMATION I PREFER TO WORK WITH, OR HELP PRODUCE:

☐ Books
☐ Magazines
☐ Newspapers
☐ Catalogs
☐ Handbooks
☐ Records, files
☐ Trade or professional literature
☐ Videotapes
☐ Audiotapes
☐ Computer printouts
☐ Seminars, learning from trainers
☐ Courses, learning from teachers
☐ Words
☐ Numbers or statistics
☐   Specifications
☐   Precision requirements
☐   Statistical analyses
☐   Data analysis studies
☐   Statistical analyses
☐   Financial needs
☐   Costs
☐   Accountings

☐ Symbols
☐ Designs
☐   Blueprints
☐   Wall-charts
☐   Time-charts
☐   Schema
☐ Facts
☐   History
☐ Ideas
☐   Conceptions
☐ Investigations
☐ Opinion-collection
☐   Points of view
☐   Surveys
☐ Research projects, research and
☐   development
     projects, project reports
☐ Procedures
☐ Guidebooks
☐ Manuals

DO I LIKE TO COLLECT OR DEAL WITH INFORMATION ABOUT ANY OF THE FOLLOWING:

☐ Principles
☐   Physical principles
☐   Spiritual principles
☐ Values
☐ Standards
☐   Repeating requirements
☐   Variables
☐ Frameworks
☐   Organizational contexts
☐   Boundary conditions
☐   Parameters

☐ Systems
☐ Programs
☐ Operations
☐ Sequences
☐ Methods
☐   Techniques
☐   Procedures
☐   Specialized procedures
☐ Analyses
☐   Data analysis studies
☐   Schematic analyses
☐   Intuitions

DO I LIKE TO HELP PUT INFORMATION TO USE IN ANY OF THE FOLLOWING PRACTICAL WAYS:

☐ Principles' applications
☐ Recommendations
☐   Policy recommendations
☐ Goals
☐   Project goals
☐ Objectives
☐ Solutions
☐   New approaches

☐ Plans
☐   Tactical needs
☐ Performance characteristics
☐   Proficiencies
☐   Deficiencies
☐   Reporting systems
☐   Controls systems

When you are done with this checklist, and have listed your top seven on the left hand side of the petal on page 246, then it is time to turn from **Form** to **Content**. Content is on the right hand side of that same petal.

Content is a matter of: Among the knowledges *you already have in your head*, which knowledges are your favorites? Do you love the knowledge you have about computers, or the knowledge you have about cars, or the knowledge you have about the Environment, or your knowledge of antiques, or gardening, or skiing, or painting, or psychology, or the Bible -- or what?

Knowledges are always *a subject*, or a *major* (as in college), or "*Principles of...*," or "*How to...*," or "*Rules for...*," or "*The Secrets of...*," etc. (These are also known as **specific knowledges**, or **specific content skills**, or **special knowledge skills**.)

Generally speaking, you picked up such knowledges in four different ways (at least), and these four ways form a handy chart for recalling to yourself what are your knowledges. Copy this chart on a larger piece of scratch paper, if you wish.

Special Knowledges I Picked Up

In School or College (At Home or Work)	On The Job, Or Just By Doing	From Seminars or Workshops	By Personal Instruction from People Avidly

You want to list *all* knowledges you possess, this first time 'round, whether you like them a lot or not. You can go back later and check off your favorites, as well as cross out the ones you just hate.

Here are some *examples* to guide you in filling in the chart:

(continued on page 248)

Tools or Means: II

Kinds of
INFORMATION I Like To
Use These Skills With

FORM	CONTENT
e.g., "Do you prefer to work with information in the form of newspapers, magazines, books, computer output, reports, or pictures?" etc.	Among the knowledges you already have in your head, which knowledges are your favorites? Do you love your knowledge about computers, or the environment, or antiques, or gardening, or psychology, or what?
1.	1.
2.	2.

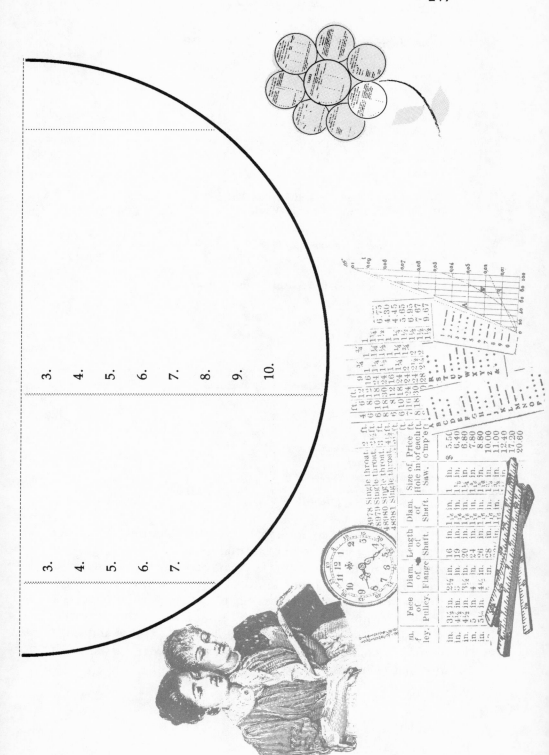

**Special Knowledges I Picked
Up in School or College**

*e.g., Spanish
Psychology
Biology
Geometry
Accounting
Music appreciation
Typing
Sociology*

**Special Knowledges I Picked Up On The Job,
Or Just By Doing(At Home or Work)**

*e.g., How to operate a computer
How a volunteer organization works
Principles of planning and management*

**Special Knowledges I Picked Up From Seminars
or Workshops**

*e.g., The way the brain works
Principles of art
Speed reading
Drawing*

**Special Knowledges I Picked Up By Personal
Instruction from
People or by Reading Avidly**

*e.g., How to sew
How to drive an automobile
How computers work
Principles of comparison shopping
Knowledge of antiques
Principles of outdoor survival*

You may want to look back at your Memory Net, page
220, at this point, for help in filling in the preceding chart.
And, to further aid you, you may want to see a list, or at
least a sampler, of other kinds of specific knowledges -- just
to jog your memory. Following is such a list. Put a checkmark in front of any word (or phrase) below that describes
special knowledges that you already possess and would enjoy
getting a chance to use in your ideal job. Write in any others that occur to you, as you go down this list.

A SAMPLER OF SPECIFIC KNOWLEDGES

Primarily about People

☐ Sociology
☐ The *how to* of customer relations and service
☐ Principles of group dynamics
☐ Principles of behavioral modification
☐ Instructional principles and techniques
☐ Organization planning
☐ Manpower requirements analysis and planning
☐ Personnel administration
☐ Recruiting
☐ Performance specifications

Primarily about Things

☐ Physics
☐ Chemistry
☐ Astronomy
☐ Computer programming
☐ Knowledge of a particular computer and its applications
☐ Design engineering
☐ Interior decorating
☐ How to run a particular machine
☐ Horticulture
☐ Car repairs
☐ Industrial applications
☐ Government contracts
☐ Maintenance

☐ Financial planning and management
☐ Bookkeeping
☐ Fiscal analysis, controls, reductions and Programming
☐ Accounting
☐ Taxes
☐ R & D Program and Project Management
☐ Merchandising
☐ Systems analysis
☐ Packaging
☐ Distribution
☐ Marketing/sales

Other specific knowledges (not easily categorized)

☐ Principles of art
☐ Cinema
☐ Principles of recording
☐ Knowledge of foreign countries (which ones?)
☐ Musical knowledge and taste
☐ Graphic arts
☐ Photography
☐ Broadcasting
☐ How to make videos
☐ Linguistics or languages
☐ Spanish
☐ Music
☐ Policy development
☐ Religion

You will of course want to know if you can put down some knowledge that you have **not** yet picked up, but think you would just love to have and to use in your future ideal job. Well, sure, if you are absolutely, one hundred per cent, planning on picking up that knowledge in the near future. Or if you want to find a volunteer job or an apprenticeship where you could pick up that knowledge *on the job*. But let's not just talk about what you do not yet have; in addition to these, **do** list knowledges *you already possess*, as well. (In other words, don't duck the exercise above.)

When you are all done listing or checking off all the special knowledges you have, **then** go back over the list and check your favorites, as well as cross out the ones you just hate. And, from among your favorites, pick the ten that you feel are **most** important to you to be able to use in your future ideal job, (from both the chart *and* this list), and copy these ten onto the right hand side of the petal called *Tools or Means: II* (page 246) -- *in their order of importance to you, if you can. Use the Prioritizing Grid if you need to (on page 213).*

When you are done, you are now ready to move on to:

6 Step Six: My Favorite Kinds of Things That I Like to Work With

If you checked any skills with Things, as your favorites, in Step Three, it is important that you now specify *what kind* of Things you prefer to work with.

You may do this either of two ways. The first way is to turn to the Petal called *Tools or Means: III,* on page 254, and jot down any of your favorite things that occur to you, under the various headings there: The Body, Materials, Objects, etc. You will note that these headings correspond to the headings under "Skills with Things," on pages 224-225. If you will look back at those pages, and see what skills you checked there, that may bring to your remembrance what particular kinds of things you most like to use those skills with. When you are done with filling in the petal, number the top ten, in your order of preference. *Use the Prioritizing Grid if you need to (on page 213).*

If you do not like the way described in the previous paragraph, there is an alternative. It involves, as the two previous petals did, a list -- a sampler. Following is such a list of Things. Put a checkmark in front of any word that describes *things* you particularly like (or think you would particularly like) to use, or act upon, or help produce in your work. Add any others that may occur to you, which are not on the list. Then when you are done checking, pick the ten that you think are **most** important, and copy them onto the Petal on page 254, ignoring the titles that are there. Just copy your top ten favorite *things*, in your order of preference. *"I would most enjoy **using** this thing in my work, next this thing, next this thing,"* etc. Use the Prioritizing Grid if you need to (on page 213).

THINGS I ENJOY WORKING WITH

Types of Material

- ☐ Paper
- ☐ Pottery
- ☐ Pewter
- ☐ Paraffin
- ☐ Papier-mâché
- ☐ Wood
- ☐ Other crafts materials
- ☐ Bronze
- ☐ Brass
- ☐ Cast iron, ironworks
- ☐ Steel
- ☐ Aluminum
- ☐ Rubber
- ☐ Plywood
- ☐ Bricks
- ☐ Cement
- ☐ Concrete, cinder-blocks
- ☐ Plastics
- ☐ Textiles
- ☐ Cloth
- ☐ Felt
- ☐ Hides
- ☐ Synthetics
- ☐ Elastic
- ☐ Crops
- ☐ Plants
- ☐ Trees

Types of Manufactured Stuff

- ☐ Machines
- ☐ Tools
- ☐ Toys
- ☐ Equipment
- ☐ Controls, gauges
- ☐ Products

☐ Housing Items

- ☐ Tents
- ☐ Trailers
- ☐ Apartments
- ☐ Houses
- ☐ Chimneys
- ☐ Columns
- ☐ Domes
- ☐ Carpenter's tools
- ☐ Paint
- ☐ Wallpaper
- ☐ Heating elements, furnaces
- ☐ Carpeting
- ☐ Fire extinguishers, fire alarms, burglar alarms
- ☐ Household items
- ☐ Furniture
- ☐ Beds
- ☐ Sheets, blankets, electric blankets
- ☐ Laundry
- ☐ Washing machines, dryers
- ☐ Washday products, bleach
- ☐ Kitchen appliances, refrigerators, microwaves, ovens, dishwashers, compactors
- ☐ Kitchen tools
- ☐ Dishes
- ☐ Pots and pans
- ☐ Can openers
- ☐ Bathtubs
- ☐ Soaps
- ☐ Cosmetics
- ☐ Toiletries
- ☐ Drugs
- ☐ Towels
- ☐ Tools, power tools

☐ **Foods or Food Manufacturing Equipment**
  ☐ Wells, cisterns
  ☐ Meats
  ☐ Breads and other baked goods
  ☐ Health foods
  ☐ Vitamins
  ☐ Dairy equipment
  ☐ Winemaking equipment

☐ **Clothing items**
  ☐ Clothing
  ☐ Raingear, umbrellas
  ☐ Spinning wheels, looms
  ☐ Sewing machines
  ☐ Patterns, safety pins, buttons, zippers
  ☐ Dyes
  ☐ Shoes

☐ **Old equipment**
  ☐ Clocks
  ☐ Telescopes
  ☐ Microscopes

☐ **Electrical and electronics**
  ☐ Radios
  ☐ Records
  ☐ Phonographs
  ☐ Stereos
  ☐ Tape recorders
  ☐ Cameras
  ☐ Television cameras
  ☐ Television sets
  ☐ Videotape recorders
  ☐ Movie cameras, film
  ☐ Electronic devices
  ☐ Electronic games
  ☐ Lie detectors
  ☐ Radar equipment

☐ **Amusement, recreation**
  ☐ Games
  ☐ Cards
  ☐ Board games, checkers, chess, Monopoly, etc.
  ☐ Kites
  ☐ Gambling devices or machines

☐ **Musical instruments**

☐ **Financial Things**
  ☐ Calculators
  ☐ Adding machines
  ☐ Cash registers
  ☐ Financial records
  ☐ Money

☐ **Office Related Things**
  ☐ PBX switchboards
  ☐ Desks, tables
  ☐ Desktop supplies
  ☐ Pens, ink, felt-tip, ballpoint
  ☐ Pencils, black, red or other
  ☐ Typewriter
  ☐ Computers
  ☐ Copying machines, mimeograph machines, printers

☐ **Communication things**
  ☐ Telephones, answering machines
  ☐ Cellular phones
  ☐ Telegraph
  ☐ Fax machines, teleprinters
  ☐ Voice mail machines
  ☐ Ship to shore radio, shortwave, walkie-talkies

☐ **Printing materials**
  ☐ Printing presses, type, ink

☐ **Art materials**
  ☐ Woodcuts, engravings, lithographs
  ☐ Paintings, drawings, silk-screens

☐ **Reading materials**
  ☐ Books, braille books
  ☐ Newspapers
  ☐ Magazines

☐ **Educational materials**
  ☐ Transparencies

☐ **Manufacturing or Warehouse Supplies**
  ☐ Dollies, handtrucks
  ☐ Containers
    ☐ Bottles
    ☐ Cans
    ☐ Boxes
  ☐ Automatic machines
  ☐ Valves, switches, buttons
  ☐ Cranks, wheels, gears, levers
  ☐ Hoists, cranes

☐ **Things that produce Light**
☐ Matches
☐ Candles
☐ Lanterns, oil lamps
☐ Light bulbs, fluorescent lights
☐ Laser beams

☐ **Energy Things**
☐ Fuel cells
☐ Batteries
☐ Transformers, electric motors,
    dynamos
☐ Engines, gas, diesel
☐ . Windmills
☐ Waterwheels
☐ Water turbines
☐ Gas turbines
☐ Steam turbines
☐ Steam engines
☐ Dynamite
☐ Nuclear reactors

☐ **Transportation Things**
☐ Land
☐   Roads
☐   Bicycles
☐   Motorcycles
☐   Mopeds
☐   Automobiles
☐   Parking meters
☐   Traffic lights
☐   Trains
☐   Subways
☐ Air
☐   Gliders
☐   Balloons
☐   Airplanes
☐   Parachutes

☐   Sea
☐   Rivers
☐   Lakes
☐   Streams
☐   Canals
☐   Ocean
☐   Boats
☐   Steamships
☐ Other vehicles

☐ **Medical Materials or Equipment**
☐ Medicines
☐ Vaccines
☐ Anesthetics
☐ Thermometers
☐ Hearing Aids
☐ Dental equipment
☐ X-ray machines
☐ False parts of the human body
☐ Spectacles, glasses, contact lenses

☐ **Gym equipment**

☐ **Sports equipment**
☐ Fishing rods, fishhooks, bait
☐ Traps, guns

☐ **Gardening or Farm Equipment**
☐ Garden tools
☐ Shovels
☐ Picks
☐ Rakes
☐ Lawnmowers
☐ Ploughs
☐ Threshing machines, reapers,
    harvesters
☐ Fertilizers
☐ Pesticides
☐ Weed killers

(continued on page 256)

254

Tools or Means: III

Kinds of
THINGS I Like To
Use These Skills With

The Body
Materials

Objects

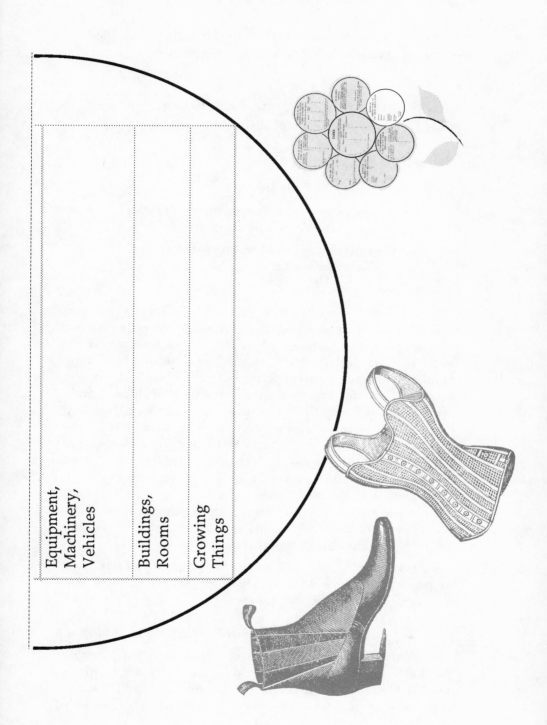

Equipment,
Machinery,
Vehicles

Buildings,
Rooms

Growing
Things

When you are done with this checklist, and have filled
out the petal on page 254, you are ready for:

Step Seven: My Favorite Outcomes, Immediate and Long Range

Now that you know:

- what your favorite skills are, and

- what **things**, **people**, and **information** you most
  like to use these skills on, as well as

- what physical and spiritual **setting** you do your
  most effective work in,

we turn to the question of outcomes.

In the world of work, it is not enough merely to keep
busy. One must be keeping busy for some purpose. We are
talking about o**utcomes**, or **where does it all lead to?** In the
world of work, this is often called "the bottom line." I remember some years ago sending out two of my staff to find
some materials for me, and after four hours' fruitless search,
one turned to the other and said, "Well let's go back. At
least we tried." And the other replied, "Unfortunately, in the
world of work you're not usually rewarded for *trying*; you're
only rewarded for *succeeding*." So they kept on, until they
found what they were looking for. This underlines the point
here: generally speaking, when you set about to use your
skills in the world of work, you must be aiming at some result - - in accordance with some **purpose** or **goal**, that either
you or the organization has (preferably *both*).

So, turn now, if you will, to the petal entitled **Outcomes**,
on page 258. There you will see that *Outcomes* divides into
two parts: **Immediate** and **Long-range**.

Immediate Results of Your Work

Immediate results, at your place of work, is a matter of:
"At the work I'd most love to do, what result am I aiming
at? Do I want to help produce a **product**, or do I want to
help offer some **service** to people, or do I want to help

gather, manage, or disseminate **information** to people? Or all three? Or two? And in what order of priority? Do I think the world basically needs me to help it have: more information, or more service, or more of some product -- such as food, clothing, or shelter?

Once you've answered that, the next question *of course* is: **what** product, or service, or information?

Well, the *what* is relatively easy to answer (I said *relatively*). If your preferred outcome is some **product** that you'd like to help produce or market, you'll probably find it identified on your *Favorite Things* petal, in the previous Step (Six). If your preferred outcome is some **service** to people, you'll probably find it identified on your *Favorite People* petal, in Step Four. And if your preferred outcome is some kind of **information** that you'd like to help gather, manage, or disseminate, you'll probably find it identified on your *Favorite Information* petal, in Step Five.

Fill in the top part of the *Outcomes* petal, on page 258, accordingly. But do take some time to think (hard) about all of this, rather than just hurriedly copying something down. Then, on to:

The Long-range Results of Your Work

As a result of **all** the work you do here on earth, what results or outcome do you want to achieve by the time that you die? What goals do you want to accomplish, what things do you want to do? Your answer to this should be written out, thoughtfully, on a one page piece of scratch paper -- and then the most important points in your statement should be copied onto the bottom part of the petal on page 259.

You may want to refer back to the exercise on page 94 in chapter 5, if you filled it out. It was called "Before I die..." and deals with parallel issues to the ones you are writing about, here.

Incidentally, if while you are writing this statement, you find yourself setting down some long-range goals that really have nothing to do with *your work* as such, but have to do

(continued on page 260)

258

Outcomes

Immediate

At the work I'd most love to do,
do I want to help produce a product
or do I want to help offer some service to people,
or do I want to help gather, manage or disseminate
information to people? Or all three? Or two?
And what kind of product, service, or info?

Long-range

My long-range goals for my life - - the things I want to do, or the goals
I'd like to accomplish - - before I die, are:

more with your overall *life* - - such as, "Before I die, I want to travel all over the world" - - write them down *anyway*. You just never know when a job might be offered to you some- where down the road that would make it possible for you to achieve some of your life-goals, and not just your work or achievement-goals.

And now on to the last step in your putting together a picture of your ideal job:

8 Step Eight: My Favorite Rewards at Work

If you turn to page 262, you will see the final petal of your *flower* picture of the ideal job for you. It is entitled "Re- wards." Virtually all of us hope for some reward from our job that is different than, and distinguishable from, *the out- comes* which we saw in the previous Step. That is to say, in addition to producing a product, service, or information, we (usually) want our work to put bread on our table, clothes on our back, and a roof over our head - - at a minimum.

The petal, on page 262, speaks of **Level** and **Salary**. It asks you to think out what is the *minimum* salary you would need from your next job or career, and what is the *maximum* salary you would like to have if things were ideal.

Hand in hand with *salary* goes the question of *level*. If you aspire, in matters of salary, to $70,000 a year, but you aspire, in the matter of level, to being an office boy, there is some- thing flawed about your dream. Level and salary usually go hand in hand. Office boys don't make $70,000 a year.

On this petal, salary is relatively easy to figure out. Mini- mum is what you simply *must* make, or you will starve. It requires a little budget figuring, and that's all. Maximum is what you would *like* to make. It requires a little searching of your daydreams, and that's all.

Level is harder to figure out. To some degree, it's what you find out as you conduct your informational interviewing. For example, let us say that you discover from your flower picture, that your ideal job would involve doing research into how one prolongs human life. As you visit the various places that are involved in such research, you discover that an apprentice researcher makes barely your minimum desired salary. A team member with ten years experience makes $10,000 more than your minimum salary, while only a senior researcher who is head of a research team makes the maximum salary that you have put on your petal here. It is at this point (and this point only) that you can really fill out the level part of this petal.

But, there are some questions about *level* -- let's call them "some preliminary hunches" that you *can* put down, even now. For example, in your ideal job do you want to work:

☐ by yourself and for yourself;

☐ by yourself but for another person or organization;

☐ in *tandem* with one other person;

☐ as a member of a team of equals;

☐ as a member of a hierarchy where you have no
       major responsibilities;

☐ as a member of a hierarchy where you are the boss or
       supervisor or owner;

☐ or what?

Jot down, on the petal, as many ideas or hunches as occur to you at the moment. You can always change them later (as, indeed, you can change *any* petal) after you have conducted your own research or informational interviewing about your *flower* picture, as described in chapter 5.

(continued on page 263)

Rewards

Salary and Level I Want/Need

	LEVEL	SALARY
MAX ↑		
↓ MIN		

Other rewards I would like this job to give me:

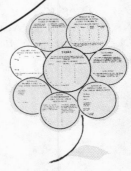

At the bottom of this petal, page 262, you will see that space has been provided for you to add any other rewards that you would like your ideal job to give you. What do we mean by this? Well, many people hope their job will give them more by way of reward, than just money. *For example* (put a checkmark in front of any that apply to you):

☐ Social contact
☐ A chance to help others
☐ A chance to bring others closer to God
☐ Intellectual stimulation
☐ A chance to use my expertise
☐ A chance to make decisions
☐ A chance to be creative
☐ A chance to exercise leadership
☐ A chance to be popular

☐ Respect
☐ Adventure
☐ Challenge
☐ Influence
☐ Security
☐ Independence
☐ Wealth
☐ Power
☐ Fame

Jot down any others that may occur to you, which are not on this list. When you are done, rank them in their order of importance to you (you may use the Prioritizing Grid, on page 213, if you wish), and then copy them in order, on the bottom part of the petal, page 262.

Conclusion

Now that you have completed all of the petals, it is time to put them all together on one piece of paper. Why do you need to put all the petals together? Because, your ideal job is not going to be found lying about the countryside in eight separate pieces; it will be a unity, and so must your picture of it be, that you carry in your mind (or in your notebook) as you go job-hunting.

So, don't leave the filled-out picture of the petals as they presently are -- all separated from each other, lying on separate sheets in this Appendix. Please cut them out and paste them, or copy them -- all of them -- on to one piece of paper.

Obviously, you will need a large sheet of blank paper on which to do this. You may make this sheet most easily by simply taping together nine sheets of plain 8 1/2 x 11" paper as shown here:

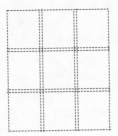

Or, if you want to avoid all this taping, you may go to any art supply or large stationery store, and buy a sheet of paper or cardboard there that is about 24 x 36" in size. When you have this larger paper, **please** paste (or copy) all your filled-out petals onto it, so that the overall picture resembles the Flower Picture on page 204 (or 100).

When you are done, you will be staring at the completed picture of your Ideal Job. Study it for a while. See if anything new strikes you about it. Anything you want to change? Do it! It's your picture. It's your Ideal Job.

When you are satisfied with it, please turn back to page 104 in chapter Five, and follow the instructions there for the next stage in your job-hunt or career-change.

Uniquely You:
A Dictionary of Skill Synonyms
or Related Words

This is a supplemental section to *The 1989 Quick Job-Hunting (and Career-Changing) Map*.

It is only designed to be used **after** you have identified your skills **and** chosen your favorites -- either your Top Ten or your Eight, Eight and Eight.

You don't need to use this section at all, if you are basically satisfied with the way your skills were described on the Transferable Skills charts (pages 224-229). But most job-hunters, and career-changers in particular, **will** want to get their skills out of the standard language and into language they feel more comfortable with, because it describes their uniqueness. If you are one of those, this section is for you. You need only look up those skills which you checked off as your favorites.

See if anything in this section describes the skill you actually have, in a better way. You do not need to slavishly copy any phrases here. If you can think of any way to adapt them, and make them even more uniquely your own, by all means do so.

 **Skills with Things**

If some of your favorite skills were with **Things,** those skills are listed below (in **bold** type), with the synonyms or related skills (if any) in regular type, immediately after each. Circle any that you think more accurately describe what it is you do.

I AM GOOD AT

Using my hands or fingers: good with my hands, feeling, fingering, having manual dexterity, gathering, receiving, separating, sorting, applying, pressing

Having great finger dexterity: having keen sense of touch, keyboarding, typing, playing (a musical instrument)

Using my eyes and hands in coordination: balancing, juggling, drawing, painting

Motor/physical coordination with my whole body: possessing fine motor coordination, raising, lifting, carrying, pushing, pulling, moving, unloading, walking, running, backpacking, swimming, hiking, mountaineering, skiing

Having agility, speed, strength or stamina: displaying great physical agility, possessing great strength, demonstrating outstanding endurance, maintaining uncommon physical fitness, acting as bodyguard

Crafting, sewing, weaving, hammering, etc: knitting, collecting

Cutting, carving or chiseling: logging, mining, drawing samples from the earth

Fashioning, molding, shaping or scuplting: working (materials)

Finishing, painting, refinishing, or restoring: binding, sandblasting, grinding,

Precision working with my hands: making miniatures, skilled at working in the micro-universe

Washing, cleaning or preparing:

Handling, or expediting: using particular tools (say which), placing, guiding, receiving, shipping, distributing, delivering

Making, producing, manufacturing (cooking): having great culinary skills

Maintaining, preserving, or repairing objects, tools, instruments:

Precision working with tools or instruments: precise attainment of set limits, tolerances, or standards, having great dexterity with small instruments (e.g., tweezers), keypunching, drilling, enjoy working within precise limits or standards of accuracy

Setting up or assembling: clearing, laying, installing, displaying

Operating, controlling, or driving: piloting, navigating, guiding, steering, mastering machinery against its will

Tending, minding, feeding, or emptying: monitoring machines or valves, giving continuous attention to, regulating controls of, watching to make sure nothing goes wrong, making a ready response in any emergency, checking, pushing buttons, starting, flipping switches, switching, adjusting controls, turning knobs, making adjustments when machine threatens to malfunction, placing, inserting, stacking, loading, dumping, removing, disposing of

Maintaining, cleaning or repairing equipment, machinery, or vehicles: changing, refilling, tuning, adjusting, fitting, doing preventative maintenance, trouble-shooting, restoring, fixing

Breaking down, disassembling, or salvaging: mopping up, cleaning up, knocking down

Constructing or reconstructing: erecting, putting together

Modeling or remodeling: able to perform magic on a room

Having a green thumb, causing growing things to flourish: helping to grow, farming, digging, plowing, tilling, seeding, planting, nurturing, groundskeeping, landscaping, weeding, harvesting

Having skills with animals, raising, training, or treating, etc.: animal training, ranching, sensing, persuading, etc. *With higher animals, the skills used are very similar to people skills (which see, below)*

  ## Skills with People

If some of your favorite skills were with **People**, those skills are listed below (in **bold** type), with the synonyms or related skills (if any) in regular type, immediately after each. Circle any that you think more accurately describe what it is you do.

I AM GOOD AT
• WITH INDIVIDUALS •

Taking instructions, serving, or helping: following detailed instructions, rendering support services, preparing (something for someone), hostessing, waiting on tables, protecting, rendering services to, dealing patiently with difficult people

Communicating well in conversation, in person or on the phone: hearing and answering questions perceptively, adept at two-way dialogue, being sensitive and responsive to the feelings of others, empathizing, showing warmth, good telephoning skills, developing warmth over the telephone, creating an atmosphere of acceptance, keen ability to put self in someone else's shoes, signaling, talking, telling, informing, giving instructions, exchanging information

Communicating well in writing: (see above), also: expressing with clarity, verbalizing cogently, uncommonly warm letter composition

Instructing, teaching, tutoring, or training individuals: guiding, interpreting and expressing facts and ideas

Advising, coaching, counseling, mentoring, empowering: facilitating personal growth and development, helping people identify their problems, needs, and solutions, interpreting others' dreams, raising people's self-esteem

Diagnosing, treating, or healing: prescribing, attending, caring for, nursing, ministering to, caring for the handicapped, having true therapeutic abilities, having healing abilities, powerful in prayer, rehabilitating, curing, raising people's self-esteem

Referring people, or helping two people to link up: recommending, making and using contacts effectively, acting as a resource broker, finding people or other resources, adept at calling in other experts or helpers as needed

Assessing, evaluating, screening, or selecting individuals: having accurate gut reactions, sizing up other people perceptively, quickly assessing what's going on, realistically assessing people's needs, perceptive in identifying and assessing the potential of others, monitoring behavior through watching, critical evaluation, and feedback

Persuading, motivating, recruiting, or selling individuals: influencing, moving, inspiring, displaying charisma, inspiring trust, evoking loyalty, convincing, motivating, developing rapport or trust, recruiting talent or leadership, attracting skilled, competent and creative people, enlisting, demonstrating (a product), selling tangibles or intangibles

Representing others, interpreting others' ideas or language: translating jargon into relevant and meaningful terms, helping others to express their views, speaking a foreign language fluently, serving as an inter-

preter, clarifying values and goals of others, expert at liaison roles, representing a majority or minority group in a larger meeting or assembly

• WITH GROUPS •
Communicating effectively to a group or a multitude, by...

using words expressively in speaking or writing: outstanding writing skills, making oral presentations, exceptional speaking ability, addressing large or small groups confidently, very responsive to audiences moods or ideas, thinking quickly on my feet, speechwriting, playwriting, writing with humor, fun and flair, employing humor in describing my experiences, ability to vividly describe people or scenes so that others can visualize them, very explicit and concise writing, making people think, doing excellent promotional writing, creating imaginative advertising and publicity programs, keeping superior minutes of meetings

making presentations in person, or on TV or film: using voice tone and rhythm as unusually effective tool of communication, giving radio or TV presentations, giving briefings, making reports

performing, entertaining, amusing, or inspiring: exhibiting showmanship, having strong theatrical sense, understudying, provoking laughter, making people laugh, distracting, diverting,

signing, miming, acting, singing, or playing an instrument: dramatizing, modeling, dancing, playing music, giving poetry readings, relating seemingly disparate ideas by means of words or actions, exceptionally good at facial expressions or body language to express thoughts or feelings eloquently

Playing games, or a particular game, leading others in recreation or exercise: excellent at sports, excellent at a particular sport (tennis, gymnastics, running, swimming, golf, baseball, football), helping others to get fit, creating, planning and organizing outdoor activities, leading backpacking, hiking, camping, mountain climbing expeditions, outdoor survival skills, excellent at traveling

Teaching, training, or designing educational events: lecturing, explaining, instructing, enlightening, demonstrating, showing, detailing, modeling (desired behavior), patient teaching, organizing and administering in-house training events, planning and carrying out well-run seminars, workshops or meetings, fostering a stimulating learning environment, ability to shape the atmosphere of a place so that it is warm, pleasant and comfortable, instilling in people a love of the subject being taught, explaining difficult or complex concepts or ideas, putting things in perspective, showing others how to take advantage of a resource, helping others to experience something, making distinctive visual presentations

Guiding a group discussion, conveying warmth: skilled at chairing meetings, group-facilitating, refusing to put people into slots or categories, treating others as equals, without regard to education, authority or position, discussing, conferring, exchanging information, drawing out people, encouraging people, helping people make their own discoveries, helping people identify their own intelligent self-interest, adept at two-way dialogue, ability to hear and answer questions perceptively

Persuading a group, debating, motivating, or selling: publicizing, promoting, reasoning persuasively, influencing the ideas and attitudes of others, selling a program or course of action to decison-makers, obtaining agreement after the fact, fundraising, arranging financing, writing a proposal, promoting or bringing about major policy changes, devising a systematic approach to goal setting

Consulting, giving advice to groups in my area of expertise: advising, giving expert advice or recommendations, trouble-shooting, giving professional advice, giving insight concerning

Managing, supervising, or running a business, fund drive, etc.: coordinating, overseeing, heading up, administering, directing, controlling (a project), conducting (an orchestra), directing (a production, or play), planning, organizing and staging of theatrical productions, adept at planning and staging ceremonies, deft at directing creative talent, interpreting goals, promoting harmonious relations and efficiency, encouraging people, organizing my time expertly, setting up and maintaining on-time work schedules, establishing effective priorities among competing requirements, coordinating operations and details, sizing up situations, anticipating people's needs, deals well with the unexpected or critical event, skilled at allocating scarce financial resources, bringing projects in on time and within budget, able to make hard decisions

Following through, getting things done, producing: executing, carrying out decisions reached, implementing decisions, expediting, building customer loyalty, unusual ability to work self-directedly without supervision, able to handle a variety of tasks and responsibilities simultaneously and efficiently, instinctively gathering resources even before the need for them becomes clear, recognizing obsolescence of ideas or procedures before compelling evidence is yet at hand, anticipating problems or needs before they become problems, decisive in emergencies, continually searching for more responsibility, developing or building markets for ideas or products, completing, attaining objectives, meeting goals, producing results, delivering as promised, increasing productivity, making good use of feedback

Leading, taking the lead, being a pioneer: determining goals, objectives, and procedures, making policy, willing to experiment with new approaches, recognizing and utilizing the skills of others, organizing diverse people into a functioning group, unifying, energizing, team-building, delegating authority, sharing responsibility, taking manageable risks, instinctively understand political realities, acting on new information immediately, seek and seize opportunities

Initiating, starting up, founding, or establishing: originating, instituting, establishing, charting, financing startups

Negotiating between two parties, or resolving conflicts: mediating, arbitrating, bargaining, umpiring, adjudicating, renegotiating, reconciling, resolving, achieving compromise, charting mergers, getting diverse groups to work together, adept at conflict management, accepting of differing opinions, handling prima donnas tactfully and well, collaborating with colleagues skillfully, handling super-difficult individuals in situations, without stress, skilled at arriving at jointly agreed-upon decisions or policy or program or solutions, working well in a hostile environment, confronting others with touchy or difficult personal matters, treating people fairly

 ## Skills with Information

If some of your favorite skills were with **Information**, those skills are listed below (in **bold** type), with the synonyms or related skills (if any) in regular type, immediately after each. Circle any that you think more accurately describe what it is you do.

I AM GOOD AT

Compiling, searching, or researching: have exceptional intelligence tempered by common sense, like dealing with ideas, information and concepts, exhibit a perpetual curiosity and delight in new knowledge, relentlessly curious, have a love of printed things, reading avidly, reading ceaselessly, committed to continual personal growth and learning, continually seeking to expose self to new experiences, love to stay current, particularly on the subjects of..., continually gathering information with respect to a particular problem or area of expertise (say w*hat*), finding and getting things not easy to find, searching databases, discovering, discovering resources, ways and means, investigating, detecting, surveying, identifying, ascertaining, determining, finding, assembling, compiling, gathering, collecting, surveying organizational needs, doing economic research

Gathering information by interviewing, or observing people: skilled at striking up conversations with strangers, talking easily with all kinds of people, adept at gathering information from people by talking to them, listening intently and accurately, intuiting, inquiring, questioning people gently, highly observant of people, learns from the example of others, studies other people's behavior perceptively, accurately assessing public moods

Gathering information by studying, or observing things: paying careful attention to, being very observant, keenly aware of surroundings, examining, concentrating, focussing on minutiae

Having an acute sense of hearing, smell, taste, or sight: ability to distinguish different musical notes, perfect pitch, having uncommonly fine sense of rhythm, possessing color discrimination of a very high order, possessing instinctively excellent taste in design, arrangement and color

Imagining, inventing, creating, or designing new ideas: devising, generating, innovating, formulating, conceptualizing, having conceptual ability of a high order, hypothesizing, discovering, conceiving new concepts, approaches, interpretations, being an idea man or woman, having "ideaphoria," demonstrating originality, continually conceiving, generating and developing innovative and creative ideas, creative imagining, possessed of great imagination, having imagination and the courage to use it, improvising on the spur of the moment, composing (music), continually conceiving, generating and developing music, continually creating new ideas for systems, methods and procedures

Copying, and/or comparing similarities or differences: addressing, posting, making comparisons, checking, proofreading, perceiving identities or divergences, developing a standard or model, estimating (e.g., the speed of a moving object), comparing with previous data

Computing, working with numbers, doing accounting: counting, taking inventory, counting with high accuracy, having arithmetical skills, calculating, performing rapid and accurate manipulation of numbers, in my head or on paper, having very sophisticated mathematical abilities, solving statistical problems, using numbers as a reasoning tool, preparing financial reports, estimating, budgeting, projecting, ordering, purchasing, acquiring, auditing, maintaining fiscal controls

Analyzing, breaking down into its parts: reasoning, dissecting, atomizing, figuring out, finding the basic units, breaking into its basic elements, defining cause and effect relationships, doing financial or fiscal analysis, doing effective cost analysis

Organizing, classifying, systematizing, and/or prioritizing: putting things in order, bringing order out of chaos (with ideas, data or things), putting into working order, perceiving common denominators, giving a definite structure and working order to things, forming into a whole with connected and interdependent parts, formulating, defining, clustering, collating, tabulating, protecting, keeping confidential

Planning, laying out a step-by-step process for achieving a goal: determining the sequence of tasks after reviewing pertinent data or requirements, planning on the basis of learnings from the past, determining the sequence of operations, establishing logical, sequential methods to accomplish stated goals, making arrangements for the functioning of a system, planning for change

Adapting, translating, computer programming, developing, or improving: updating, expanding, improving, upgrading, applying, arranging (e.g., music), redesigning, improvising, adjusting, interpreting, extrapolating, projecting, forecasting, creating a new form of something, taking what others have developed and applying it to new situations, making practical applications of theoretical ideas, deriving applications from other people's ideas, able to see the commercial possibilities in a concept, idea or product, revising goals, policies and procedures, translating numbers and words into computer electronically coded data

Visualizing, drawing, painting, dramatizing, creating videos, or software: continually conceiving, generating and developing pictures, able to visualize shapes, able to visualize in three dimensions, conceiving shapes, colors, or sounds, having form perception, skilled at symbol formation, creating symbols, conceiving symbolic or metaphoric pictures of Reality, designing, designing in wood or other media, fashioning, shaping, making models, designing handicrafts, creating poetic images, thinking in pictures, visualizing concepts, illustrating, sketching, coloring, drafting, graphing, mapping, photographing, doing computer graphics, doing mechanical drawing, able to read blueprints, able to read graphs quickly, using video or other recording equipment to produce imaginative audio/visual presentations, good at set designing

Synthesizing, combining parts into a whole: transforming apparently unrelated things or ideas, by forming them into a new whole, relating, combining, integrating, unifying, producing a clear, coherent unity, seeing 'the big picture', always seeing things in a larger context

Problem solving, or seeing patterns among a mass of data: diagnosing, intuiting, figuring out, perceiving patterns or structures, recognizing when more information is needed before a decision can be reached, proving, disproving, validating

Deciding, evaluating, appraising, or making recommendations: love making decisions that require personal judgment, making judgments about people or data or things, keeping confidences, keeping secrets, encrypting, inspecting, studying data to determine compliance with an established norm, checking, testing, weighing, appraising, assessing, determining the fair market value of an object, reviewing, critiquing, discriminating between what is important and what is unimportant, separating the wheat from the chaff, summarizing, editing, reducing the size of a database, judging, selecting, screening, screening out, extracting, reviewing large amounts of material and extracting its essence, writing a precis, conserving, making fiscal reductions, eliminating, simplifying, consolidating

Keeping records, including recording, filming, or entering on a computer: transcribing, reproducing, imitating, keeping accurate financial records, operating a computer competently, word processing, maintaining databases

Storing, or filing, in file cabinets, microfiche, video, audio, or computer: good clerical ability

Retrieving information, ideas, data: extracting, reviewing, restoring, reporting, giving out information patiently and accurately, good at getting materials that are needed

Enabling other people to find or retrieve information: filing in a way to facilitate retrieval, classifying expertly, organizing information according to a prescribed plan, am an excellent 'resource broker'

Having a superior memory, keeping track of details: easily remembers facts and figures, having a keen and accurate memory for detail, recalling people and their preferences accurately, retentive memory for rules and procedures, expert at remembering numbers and statistics accurately and for a long period, having exceedingly accurate melody recognition, exhibiting keen tonal memory, accurately reproducing sounds or tones (e.g., a foreign language, spoken without accent), easily remembering faces, accurate spatial memory, having a memory for design, having a photographic memory.

Now, you will want to finish the statement of skills in your own language, by describing **degree.** Here are some possible modifiers you may want to put in front of **the skills you are best at** (*one usually omits the words "I..." or "I have..." or "I am...", which are understood*):

> Good at...,
> Exceptionally good at...,
> Adept at...,
> Expert at...,
> Deft at...,

> Excel at...,
> Unusually skillful at...,
> Unusual ability to...,
> Skilled at ...,
> Demonstrated exceptional ability to...

When you are done with this section, before you copy them on to the *Tasks/Transferable Skills* petal, on page 234, go back to page 83 and 84 and jot down on scratch paper any *expansions* you care to make, in describing your favorite skills, viz., adding to the verb an object and a modifier. The phrases above can be used as modifiers of particular skills, if they are used in their adjective or adverb form, e.g., *"Exceptional," "uncommon," "adeptly," "expertly," "skillfully," "unusually,"* and so forth.

My son, be admonished:
of making many books there is no end;
and much study is a weariness of the flesh.

Ecclesiastes

Appendix B

Special Problems in the Job-Hunt

additional readings and comments

BOOKS

Every book has a different voice. That's fortunate. No one book (least of all this one) can reach every reader. If you find *Parachute* didn't give you what you needed or wanted, here are some other books that may succeed for you. Different voices.

It may also be that while *Parachute* helped you, there are still some areas where you need or want more light shed. These books should help. Different lights.

IN GENERAL: HIGHLY RECOMMENDED

Lathrop, Richard, *Who's Hiring Who?* Ten Speed Press, Box 7123, Berkeley, CA 94707. 1977. Simply excellent resource. Used more often by our readers than any other book (besides *Parachute*).

Holland, John L., *Making Vocational Choices*. A Theory of Vocational Personalities and Work Environments, 2nd ed., Prentice-Hall, Inc., Sylvan Avenue, Englewood Cliffs, NY 07632. 1985. John Holland is one of my favorite people, and this is one of my favorite books. I think it is a **must** for counselors, and very **helpful** to any job-hunter who is looking for a system by which to understand all jobs. Unfortunately, Prentice-Hall has raised its price until it is now $19.93 -- for a 150-page **paperback**. (I have a policy of not mentioning prices in this book -- because they change so constantly -- but this one is **worth** mentioning.) Also since I have never seen this book in a bookstore, except a college bookstore where it was one of the required texts for some course, if you cannot find it in your local library or you want a permanent copy for your very own, you will **have** to order it directly from the publisher, address above. Phone: 800-223-1360, or 201-767-5937. In so doing you **have** to mention the title code number 547596, or else the chances are ten to one that Prentice-Hall's computer will **claim** it is out of print. (The **hardback** copy is, and apparently that's all their computer was ever introduced to.) Once you have found your "Holland code" from the SDS (Self-Directed Search) instrument, I would recommend you use the *Dictionary of Holland Occupational Codes* (below), instead of the more limited *Occupations Finder*.

Holland, John L., "Self-Directed Search, 1985 Revision." As I mentioned in chapter 4, this is a self-marking test which you can use to discover your "Holland code" and what occupations you might **start** your research with. You can order an SDS Specimen Set for less than $5, which includes the SDS, a brief *Occupations Finder* and a booklet "You and Your Career," from the publisher, Psychological Assessment Resources, Inc., Box 998, Odessa, FL 33556.

Holland, John L., Ph.D., *The Alphabetized Occupations Finder*. This puts the little *Occupations Finder*, mentioned above, into alphabetical order. For use with the Self-Directed Search. Psychological Assessment Resources, Inc., Box 998, Odessa, FL 33556. 1-800-331-TEST. In Florida 1-813-968-3003. 1986.

Holland, John L., and Gottfredson, Gary D., and Ogawa, Deborah Kimiki, *Dictionary of Holland Occupational Codes: A Comprehensive Cross-Index of Holland's RIASEC Codes with 12,000 DOT Occupations*. Consulting Psychologists Press, Inc., 577 College Ave., Palo Alto, CA 94306. 1982. 520 pp. This immensely helpful book, if you are working with Holland's system, gives a comprehensive list of occupations which your "code" suggests, plus the DOT number for each of 12,000 occupations, thus enabling you to go to the *Dictionary of Occupational Titles* and look up more detailed information on each occupation that looks of interest -- before you go out to do your informational interviewing or research. It does, however, have some 'glitches' in it, where occupations you would expect to find in it are nowhere to be seen. So, don't take it as 'gospel.'

Wegmann, Robert, and Chapman, Robert, and Johnson, Miriam, *Work in the New Economy: Careers and Job Seeking into the 21st Century.* JIST Works, 720 North Park Ave., Indianapolis, Indiana 46202. 1989. Updated, great. Highly highly recommended.

Wallach, Ellen J., and Arnold, Peter, *The Job Search Companion: The Organizer for Job Seekers.* The Harvard Common Press, 535 Albany St., Boston, MA 02118. 1984. Primarily a book of very useful "forms" for keeping track of your job search. Intended as a supplement to other job-hunting books. If I myself were going job hunting tomorrow, I would definitely use the forms in this book to help organize my job hunt.

Sher, Barbara, *Wishcraft - How to Get What You Really Want.* Ballantine Books, 201 E. 50th St., New York, NY 10022. 1983. A very helpful book.

Jackson, Tom, *Guerrilla Tactics in the Job Market* (revised). Bantam Books, 666 Fifth Ave., New York, NY 10103. 1980. A very popular and useful book.

Jackson, Tom, and Mayleas, Davidyne, *The Hidden Job Market for the Eighties.* Quadrangle/The New York Times Book Co., 3 Park Ave., New York, NY 10016. 1981.

Figler, Howard E., *The Complete Job Search Handbook: Presenting the Skills You Need to Get Any Job, And Have A Good Time Doing It.* Holt, Rinehart and Winston, 383 Madison Ave., New York, NY 10017. 1979. Tries to identify twenty skills the job-hunter needs in order to pull off a job hunt **successfully**.

Germann, Richard, and Arnold, Peter, *Bernard Haldane Associates' Job and Career Building.* Ten Speed Press, Box 7123, Berkeley, CA 94707. 1981, 1980. A detailed description of how to find a job, once you know what it is you want to do.

Miller, Arthur F., and Mattson, Ralph T., *The Truth About You: Discover What You Should Be Doing with Your Life.* People Management Incorporated, 10 Station St., Simsbury, CT 06070. 1977. A greatly revised edition of this book is scheduled to be published this year or next by Ten Speed Press, Box 7123, Berkeley CA 94707. Until that comes out, you can get the old edition from the address in Simsbury. A first class book, very helpful. I like it a lot.

Haldane, Bernard, *How to Make a Habit of Success.* Acropolis Books, Ltd., 2400 17th St. NW, Washington, DC 20009. One of the pioneer books in this field, first published in 1960.

Haldane, Bernard, and Jean, and Martin, Lowell, *Job Power: The Young People's Job Finding Guide.* Acropolis Books Ltd., 2400 17th St. NW, Washington, DC 20009. 1980. Undoubtedly the best book available for high school students.

Irish, Richard K., *Go Hire Yourself An Employer*. Anchor Press, Doubleday, New York, NY. 1987. An old classic, now reissued (in its third edition).

Campbell, David P., *If You Don't Know Where You're Going, You'll Probably End Up Somewhere Else*. Argus Communications, Niles, IL. 1974. Useful for those who need to be convinced of the need for career planning.

OTHER RESOURCES FOR THE JOB-HUNTER OR CAREER-CHANGER BY RICHARD BOLLES

Crystal, John C., and Bolles, Richard N., *Where Do I Go From Here With My Life?* 272 pages. Ten Speed Press, Box 7123, Berkeley, CA 94707. 1974.

Bolles, Richard N., *The Three Boxes of Life, and How To Get Out of Them*. 480 pages. Ten Speed Press, Box 7123, Berkeley, CA 94707. 1978.

Bolles, Richard N., *The New Quick Job-Hunting Map, Advanced Version*. 48 pages. Ten Speed Press, Box 7123, Berkeley, CA 94707. 1985. An 8-1/2 x 11-inch workbook version of most of the exercises found in *Parachute*.

Bolles, Richard N., *The Quick Job-Hunting Map for Beginners*. 32 pages. Ten Speed Press, Box 7123, Berkeley, CA 94707. 1977. A workbook version of the Map for high school students just entering the labor force, and those other job-hunters who may prefer a simpler alternative to the Map above.

Bolles, Richard N., "How to Choose and Change Careers." A 57-minute *Psychology Today* audio cassette. Available from Education Services Corporation, 1725 K St. NW, #408, Washington, DC 20006. 202-298-8424.

OTHER VERSIONS OF PARACHUTE

Bolles, Richard N., *Job-Hunting, Ein Handbuch für Einsteiger und Aufsteiger*. Goldmann Rageber, München. 1987.

Bolles, Richard, N., *¿De Qué Color Es Su Paracaidas?* Editorial Diana, S.A., Roberto Gayol 1219, Mexico, D.F. 1983.

Bolles, Richard N., *Chercheurs d'emploi, n'oubliez pas votre parachute*. Translated by Daniel Porot. Sylvie Messinger, éditrice, 31 rue de l'Abbé-Grégoire, Paris 6e, France. 1983.

Bolles, Richard N., *Chercheurs d'emploi, n'oubliez pas votre parachute*. Translated by Daniel Porot. Guy Saint-Jean Editeur Inc. 674 Place Publique, Laval, Quebec H7X 1G1, Canada. 1983.

Bolles, Richard N., *Werk zoeken-een vak apart, Een professionele aanpak voor het vinden van een (nieuwe) baan*. Translated by F.J.M. Claessens. Uitgeverij

Intermediair, Amsterdam/Brussels. 1983.

   Bolles, Richard N., *'87 What Color Is Your Parachute?* (In Japanese) Japan UNI Agency, Inc., Ten Speed Press and Writers House, Inc., N.Y. 1986.

SPECIAL PROBLEMS IN THE JOB-HUNT

   Most of you will find that *Parachute* gives you everything you need to successfully conduct your job-hunt. Others of you, however, may feel the need for some additional guidance or information in particular areas. The areas covered in the following bibliography are:

1. **Skills** Identification
2. Physical Setting: **Geography** including Overseas
3. Physical Setting: **Working Conditions**
4. Spiritual or Emotional Setting: **Values**
5. **Goals and Outcomes**
6. **Resumes**
7. **Interviewing**
8. **Salary** Negotiation
9. After You Get Hired: **Promotions, Raises**, Hanging On To Your Present Job
10. After You Get Hired: **Quitting, Getting Fired**, Getting Laid Off
11. **Second Careers**, Career Change, **Mid-Life** through Retirement
12. Going Back to **School** or Getting an External Degree
13. Alternative Forms of Jobs: **Volunteering**
14. Alternative Forms of Jobs: **Internships**
15. Alternative Forms of Jobs: **Temporary Work**, Temporary Rest
16. Alternative Forms of Jobs: **Part-time Work** or Holding Several Small Jobs

If you have a particular interest, and you don't find here any book that helps, there are two alternative routes still open to you: one is your local bookstores -- go there, browse, and see what they have that is even newer than those listed in this bibliography. The other is your friendly local reference librarian. If your library has such a person, he or she can often be worth their weight in gold to you. Tell them your problem or interest, and see what they can dig up. They often know of hidden treasures, buried in books, articles and clippings, which will be an answer to your prayers.

1. SKILLS IDENTIFICATION

Pearson, Henry G., *Your Hidden Skills: Clues to Careers and Future Pursuits.* Mowry Press, Box 405, Wayland, MA 01778. 1981.

Myers, Isabel Briggs and Peter, *Gifts Differing.* Consulting Psychologists Press, Inc., 577 College Ave., Palo Alto, CA 94306. 1980. Related to the increasingly popular Myers-Briggs Test.

Scheele, Adele, *Skills for Success: A Guide to the Top for Men and Women.* Ballantine Books, 201 E. 50th St., New York, NY 10022. 1979.

Fine, Sidney A., *Functional Job Analysis Scales: A Desk Aid.* Methods for Manpower Analysis, No. 5. April 1973. Available from The W.E. Upjohn Institute for Employment Research, 300 S. Westnedge Ave., Kalamazoo, MI 49007.

2. PHYSICAL SETTING: GEOGRAPHY
INCLUDING OVERSEAS

Friedenberg, John E., Ph.D. and Bradley, Curtis H., Ph.D., *Finding a Job in the United States.* VGM Career Books, 4255 W. Touhy Ave., Lincolnwood, IL 60646-1975. 1986. A guide for immigrants, refugees, limited-English-proficient job-seekers, foreign-born professionals - - anyone who is baffled by the process of finding, and keeping, a job in the U.S. It contains job information based on the successful experience of job-seekers, plus advice from the U.S. Department of Labor. Includes information about American job customs and laws related to immigration, as well as a systematic plan for job-hunting.

Boyer, Richard, and Savageau, David, *Places Rated Almanac: Your Guide to Finding the Best Places to Live in America.* Rand McNally & Co., Box 7600, Chicago IL 60680.

Fraser, Jill Andresky, *The Best U.S. Cities for Working Women.* Plume Books, New American Library, 1633 Broadway, New York, NY 10019. 1986.

Now to overseas work: many people assume you find an overseas job by packing a bag, buying a ticket and passing out resumes at your foreign destination. But work permit requirements and high unemployment make finding jobs at foreign destinations difficult or impossible. The wiser approach is to conduct your overseas job search in the U.S. If you're hired in the U.S. by a company who'll send you overseas, they'll take care of the visa and work permit red tape, pick up your travel bill, and provide other lucrative benefits.

Every successful search for an overseas job starts with (unfortunately) a resume and a source of information on "who's hiring now." Major metropolitan newspapers, professional association magazines, and "networking" will provide leads on current employers. Beware of directories listing overseas employers. Many are out of date and tend to report on "who **was** hiring" versus "who is hiring *now.*"

If you choose to do your own research about overseas work, how do you go about it? Well, first of all, talk to everyone you possibly can who has in fact been overseas, most especially to the country or countries that interest you. A nearby large university will probably have such faculty or students (ask). Companies in your city which have overseas branches (your library should be able to tell you which they are) should be able to lead you to people also -- possibly to the names and addresses of personnel who are still "over there" to whom you can write for the information you are seeking. Alternatively, try asking every single person you meet for the next week (at the supermarket checkout, at your work, at home, at church or synagogue, etc.) if they know someone who used to live overseas and now is in your city or town. By doing research with such people, you will learn a great deal.

Talking to the consulate of the country in question (should you live in or near a major city) may also be very enlightening. Books from your local library or local bookstore in the travel section, if they are recent, may also tell you much.

As for the general facts about living overseas, books on this subject keep getting regularly published, regularly flourish for a season, and then regularly die. But currently these are:

International Employment Hotline, Box 6170, McLean, VA 22106. Provides job search advice and names and addresses of employers hiring for international work in government, nonprofit organizations, and private companies.

For teachers wishing to work overseas, the Department of Defense publishes a pamphlet with application entitled *Overseas Employment Opportunities for Educators.* Write to U.S. Department of Defense Dependent Schools, Recruitment and Assignments Section, Hoffman Bldg. I, 2461 Eisenhower Ave., Alexandria, VA 22331-1100, 703-325-0885, for the pamphlet/application.

Schuman, Howard, *Making It Abroad -- The International Job Hunting Guide.* John Wiley & Sons, 605 Third Ave., New York, NY 10158-0012. 1988.

Cantrell, Will and Marshall, Terry, *101 Ways to Find an Overseas Job.* Cantrell Corp., Box 2018, Merrifield, VA 22116. 1987.

Mullett, Joy and Darley, Lois, *Careers for People Who Love to Travel.* Arco Books, One Gulf + Western Plaza, New York, N.Y. 10023. 1986.

Casewit, Curtis W., *How to Get a Job Overseas.* Arco Publishing, Inc., One Gulf + Western Plaza, New York, N.Y. 10023. 1984.

Your library should also have books such as Angel, Juvenal, *Dictionary of American Firms Operating in Foreign Countries* (World Trade Academy Press).

And to research overseas public companies which sell stock in this country, the Securities Exchange Commission will have their Form 6-K, which they filed in order to be able to sell that stock.

In general, the principles found on page 374 will apply here with equal or greater force.

3. PHYSICAL SETTING: WORKING CONDITIONS

Levering, Robert, *A Great Place to Work.* Random House, Inc., 201 E. 50th St., New York, NY 10022. 1988. A study of what makes some employers so good and most so bad.

Krantz, Les, *The Jobs Rated Almanac.* Pharos Books, 200 Park Ave., New York, NY 10166. 1988.

Naisbitt, John, and Aburdene, Patricia, *Re-inventing the Corporation: Transforming Your Job and Your Company for the New Information Society.* Warner Books, Inc., 75 Rockefeller Plaza, New York, NY 10019. 1985.

Levering, Robert; Moskowitz, Milton; and Katz, Michael, *The 100 Best Companies to Work for in America.* Addison-Wesley Publishing Co., Route 128, Reading, MA 01876. 1984. The problem is: is there any such animal as "the 100 best companies to work for," or are some companies excellent on the fifth floor, but poor down on the second floor? Nonetheless, this is a fascinating book, as is everything these authors have written.

Peters, Thomas J., and Waterman, Jr., Robert H., *In Search of Excellence: Lessons from America's Best Run Companies.* Harper & Row, 10 E. 53rd St., New York, NY 10022. 1982. An instant classic. The title says it all.

4. SPIRITUAL OR EMOTIONAL SETTING: VALUES

Lydenberg, Steven D., with Marlin, Alice Tepper, and Strub, Sean O'Brien, and the Council on Economic Priorities, *Rating America's Corporate Conscience: A Provocative Guide to the Companies Behind the Products You Buy Every Day.* Addison-Wesley, Route 128, Reading, MA 01876. Has rated major companies on corporate social responsibility, as to which companies are "best" in the moral sense.

Hagberg, Janet, and Leider, Richard, *The Inventurers: Excursions in Life and Career Renewal.* Addison-Wesley Publishing Co., Route 128, Reading, MA 01867. 1988.

Anderson, Nancy, *Work With Passion: How to Do What You Love for a Living.* A co-publication of Carroll & Graf Publishers, Inc., 260 Fifth Ave., New York, NY 10001, and Whatever Publishing, Inc., Box 137, Mill Valley, CA 94942. 1984. Good on how to establish contact with people.

Long, Charles, *How to Survive Without a Salary.* Summerhill Press, Ltd., Toronto, Ontario Canada. Distributed by Collier Macmillan Canada, 50 Gervais Dr., Don Mills, Ontario M3C 3K4, Canada. Coping in today's inflationary times by learning how to live the Conserver Life-style.

Edwards, John F., *Starting Fresh.* Prima Publishing & Communications, P.O. Box 1260SF, Rocklin, CA 95677. 1988. How to plan for a simpler, happier, and more fulfilling new life in the country.

Kirkpatrick, Frank, *How to Find and Buy Your Business in the Country.* Storey Communications, Inc., Pownal, VT 05261. 1985. While this would appear to belong to the geography section, what it is talking about is a simpler life-style, away from the hustle and bustle of the city. Therefore it is talking primarily about the emotional setting, not the physical.

5. GOALS AND OUTCOMES FOR YOUR WORK

Straat, Kent L. with Sabin, Nellie, *What Your Boss Can't Tell You: How to Evaluate Your Company, Your Job, Your Goals and Your Performance.* AMACOM, 135 West 50th St., New York, NY 10020. 1988.

Caple, John, *The Right Work: Finding It and Making It Right.* Dodd, Mead & Company, Inc., 71 Fifth Ave., New York, NY 10003. 1987.

Cohen, Steve and de Oliveira, Paulo, *Getting to the Right Job.* Workman Publishing Company, Inc., 1 W. 39th St., New York, NY 10018. 1987.

Snelling, Robert O., Sr., *The Right Job.* Viking Penguin Inc., 40 W. 23rd St., New York, NY 10010. 1987.

Wegmann, Robert and Chapman, Robert, *The Right Place at the Right Time.* Ten Speed Press, Box 7123, Berkeley, CA 94707. 1987.

6. RESUMES

Lathrop, Richard, *Who's Hiring Who?* Ten Speed Press, Box 7123, Berkeley, CA 94707. 1977, updated 1980. The very best book on how to write a resume, or "qualifications brief," as the author prefers it be called.

Parker, Yana, *The Resume Catalog: 200 Damn Good Examples.* Ten Speed Press, Box 7123, Berkeley, CA 94707. 1988.

Parker, Yana, *The Damn Good Resume Guide.* Ten Speed Press, Box 7123, Berkeley, CA 94707. 1986. Describes how to write a **functional** resume.

Washington, Tom, *Resume Power: Selling Yourself on Paper.* Mt. Vernon Press, 1750 112th Northeast C-247, Bellevue, WA 98004. 1988.

Miller Kaplan, Robbie, *Resumes: The Write Stuff.* Garrett Park Press, Box 190, Garrett Park, MD 20896. 1987.

Feld, Warren S., *How High Can You Fly: The Ultimate Career and Resume Guide For the Upwardly Mobile Professional.* Prentice Hall Press, Sylvan Ave., Englewood Cliffs, N.J. 07632. 1986.

Jackson, Tom, *The Perfect Resume.* Anchor Press/Doubleday. Garden City, NY 11530. 1981.

Teeple, Barbara, *Barbara Teeple's Guide through the Resume Workbook.* Rainbow Word Pros Ltd., 1002 Knottwood Rd. E., Edmonton, Alberta T6K 3R5, Canada. 1982.

Williams, Eugene, *Getting the Job You Want with the Audiovisual Portfolio.* Comptex Associates, Inc., Box 6745, Washington, DC 20020. 1982. Manual for job-seekers and career changers in professions other than teaching, who want to present something audiovisual rather than a written resume.

7. INTERVIEWING

Biegeleisen, J.I., *Make Your Job Interview A Success.* Arco Books, One Gulf + Western Plaza, New York, N.Y. 10023. 1987.

Yate, Martin John, *Knock 'Em Dead with Great Answers to Tough Interview Questions.* Bob Adams, Inc., 840 Summer St., Boston, MA 02127. 1987.

Hellman, Paul, *Ready, Aim, You're Hired!: How to Job-Interview Successfully Anytime, Anywhere with Anyone,* AMACOM, 135 W. 50th St., New York, NY 10020. 1986.

Robert Half on Hiring. Crown Publishers, Inc., One Park Ave., New York, NY 10016. 1985.

Merman, Stephen K. and McLaughlin, John F., *Out-Interviewing The Interviewer. A Job Winner's Script for Success.* Prentice-Hall Press, Sylvan Ave., Englewood Cliffs, N.J. 07632. 1983.

Allen, Jeffrey G., J.D., C.P.C., *How to Turn an Interview Into a Job.* Fireside Edition, Simon & Schuster, Inc., Rockefeller Center, 1230 Avenue of the Americas, New York, NY 10020. 1983.

Medley, H. Anthony, *Sweaty Palms: The Neglected Art of Being Interviewed.* Ten Speed Press, Box 7123, Berkeley, CA 94707. 1978. *The* classic on interviewing.

Zimbardo, Phillip G., *Shyness, What It Is, What to Do About It.* Jove Publications, 757 Third Ave., New York, NY 10017. 1977.

8. SALARY NEGOTIATION

Wright, John W., *The American Almanac of Jobs and Salaries, 1987-1988.* Avon Books, Dept. FP, 1790 Broadway, New York, NY 10019. 1987.

Snelling, Robert O., *Jobs! What They Are...Where They Are...What They Pay!* Fireside Edition, Simon & Schuster, Inc., Rockefeller Center, 1230 Avenue of the Americas, New York, NY 10020. 1986.

9. AFTER YOU GET HIRED: PROMOTIONS, RAISES, HANGING ON TO YOUR PRESENT JOB

There is not enough said, generally, in job-hunting books about surviving after you get the job. The enemy is both within, and without. From within, the now-familiar problem of burnout. From without, various adversaries - - both animate and inanimate.

Mackay, Harvey B., *Swim with the Sharks without Being Eaten Alive.* William Morrow & Co., 105 Madison Ave., New York, NY 10016. 1988. A best-seller already and probably destined to be a classic.

Hochheiser, Robert M., *How to Work for a Jerk.* Vintage Books, a division of Random House, New York, NY. 1987.

Schwimmer, Larry, *Winning Your Next Promotion In One Year (Or Less!).* Harper & Row, 10 E. 53rd St., New York, NY 10022. 1986.

Layard, Richard, *How To Beat Unemployment.* Oxford University Press, Walton St., Oxford, OX2 6DP, U.K. 1986.

Nakell, Mark, *Job Sight: A New Way to Look at Your Job.* The Kit Group, 418 Fore St., Portland, ME 04101. 1986.

Kennedy, Marilyn Moats, *Office Politics: Seizing Power, Wielding Clout.* Warner Books, 666 Fifth Ave., New York, NY 10103. 1981.

———, *Career Knockouts: How to Battle Back.* New Century Publishers, Inc., 275 Old New Brunswick Rd., Piscataway, NJ 08854. 1980.

You will also find some helpful words on this subject in John Crystal's book, *Where Do I Go From Here With My Life?* (Ten Speed Press, Box 7123, Berkeley, CA 94707, 1974), pages 241-245 ("Understanding the Nature of the World of Work"), and 150-160 ("How to Survive After You Get the Job").

10. AFTER YOU GET HIRED: **QUITTING, GETTING FIRED, GETTING LAID OFF**

Pines, Ayala and Aronson, Elliot, *Career Burnout: Causes and Cures.* The Free Press, 866 Third Ave., New York, NY 10022. 1987.

Levinson, Jay Conrad, *Quit Your Job! Making The Decision, Making The Break, Making It Work.* Dodd, Mead & Co., 71 Fifth Ave., New York, NY 10003. 1987.

Employment Law in the 50 States: A Reference for Employers. CUE/NAM, 1331 Pennsylvania Ave. NW, Suite 1500 - North Lobby, Washington, DC 20004-1703. 1987.

Avrutis, Raymond, *How to Collect Unemployment Benefits: Complete Information for All 50 States.* Prentice-Hall, Sylvan Ave., Englewood Cliffs, N.J. 07632. 1983. There is much mythology about unemployment -- for example, that you cannot collect if you were fired. That's only true if you were fired for misconduct.

May, John, *The RIF Survival Handbook: How to Manage Your Money if You're Unemployed.* Tilden Press, 1737 DeSales St. NW, Suite 300, Washington, DC 20036.

11. SECOND CAREERS, CAREER-CHANGE, MID-LIFE THROUGH RETIREMENT

Robbins, Paula I., *Successful Midlife Career Change: Self-Understanding and Strategies for Action.* Amacom, 135 W. 50th St., New York, NY 10020. Very thorough, very helpful. Probably the best book dealing with this problem.

Golzen, Godfrey and Plumbley, Philip, *Changing Your Job After 35.* Kogan Page Ltd., 120 Pentonville Rd., London N1 9JN. 1988.

Kanchier, Carole, *Questers: Dare to Change Your Job and Your Life.* R&E Publishers, P.O. Box 2008, Saratoga, CA 95070. 1987.

Falvey, Jack, *What's Next? Career Strategies After 35.* Williamson Publishing, Charlotte, VT 05445. 1987.

Durkin, Jon, "Mid-Life Career Changes." Johnson O'Connor Research Foundation, Human Engineering Laboratory, 701 Sutter St., San Francisco, CA 94109.

Allen, Jeffrey G. and Gorkin, Jess, *Finding the Right Job at Midlife.* Fireside Edition, Simon & Schuster, Inc., Rockefeller Center, 1230 Avenue of the Americas, New York, N.Y. 10020. 1985.

Kouri, Mary K., Ph.D., *Elderlife: A Time to Give -- A Time to Receive.* A workbook for the elder adult who wants to put meaning and satisfaction into life after 55. Human Growth and Development Associates, 1675 Fillmore St., Denver, CO 80206. 303-320-0991. 1985.

Best-Rated Retirement Cities & Towns, Consumer Guide. Publications International, Ltd., 7373 N. Cicero Ave., Lincolnwood, IL 60646. 1988. A review of 100 of the most attractive retirement locations across America.

Boyer, Richard, and Savageau, David, *Places Rated Retirement Guide: Finding the Best Places in America for Retirement Living.* Rand McNally and Co., Box 7600, Chicago, IL 60680. 1983.

12. GOING BACK TO SCHOOL OR GETTING AN EXTERNAL DEGREE

Mendelsohn, Pam, *Happier By Degrees: A College Reentry Guide for Women.* Ten Speed Press, Box 7123, Berkeley, CA 94707. 1986.

Bear, John, *How to Get the Degree You Want: Bear's Guide to Non-Traditional College Degrees.* Ten Speed Press, Box 7123, Berkeley, CA 94707. 280 pages.

To get equivalency examinations for the knowledge or experience you've already acquired out of life, write to CLEP (College-Level Examination Program), College Entrance Examination Board, Box 1822, Princeton, NJ 08541, or Box 1025, Berkeley, CA 94701. It is a national standardized examination program for college credit.

Gross, Ronald, *The Independent Scholar's Handbook: How to Turn Your Interest in Any Subject into Expertise.* Addison-Wesley, General Books Division, Route 128, Reading, MA 01867. 1982.

13. ALTERNATIVE FORMS OF JOBS: **VOLUNTEERING**

If you are interested in volunteering full-time to work for social justice, primarily with the poor. the elderly, and the handicapped, working either in the U.S. or in the developing countries, you should contact The St. Vincent Pallotti Center for Apostolic Development, Inc., 34 Mt. Auburn St., Cambridge, MA 02138. They act as a resource center for anyone interested in such work. Most programs are for a summer or for one to two years. However, **some** are as short as a long weekend, and some for as long as five years. A directory, called CONNECTIONS, is free to anyone who requests it. The East Coast office's phone is 617-876-1717; the West Coast office's phone is 415-989-0508. Incidentally, when volunteers complete their term of service, the Center assists them in finding relevant work that pays a living wage, using *Parachute.*

Shenk, Ellen J., ed., *Directory of Volunteer Opportunities.* Career Information Centre, University of Waterloo, Waterloo, Ontario, N2L 3G1 Canada. 1986.

See also the next section and the section on "Jobs Dealing with Social Change"

14. ALTERNATIVE FORMS OF JOBS: **INTERNSHIPS**

Jobst, Katherine, *1988 Internships: 38,000 On-the-Job Training Opportunities for All Types of Careers.* Writer's Digest Books, 1507 Dana Ave., Cincinnati, OH 45207. 1987.

Community Jobs, 1516 P St. NW, Washington, DC 20005, 202-667-0661. Published monthly by Community Careers Resource Center. Will list jobs and internships in nonprofit, community organizations. Write directly to them for subscription information.

National Directory of Internships, published by the National Society for Internships and Experiential Education (NSIEE), 122 St. Mary's St., Raleigh, NC 27605, 919-834-7536.

Directory of Internships, Work Experience`Programs, and On-the-Job Training Opportunities. Ready Reference Press, Box 5169, Santa Monica, CA 90405. Also available -- *The First Supplement to the Directory.*

15. ALTERNATIVE FORMS OF JOBS: **TEMPORARY WORK, TEMPORARY REST**

Mayall, Donald, and Nelson, Kristin, *The Temporary Help Supply Service and the Temporary Labor Market.* Olympus Research Corp., 1670 E. 13th South, Salt Lake City, UT 84105. 1982.

Rubin, Bonnie Miller, *Time Out.* W.W. Norton & Company, 500 Fifth Ave., New York, NY 10110. 1987. How to take a year (or more or less) off without jeopardizing your job, your family, or your bank account.

16. ALTERNATIVE FORMS OF JOBS: **PART-TIME WORK, OR HOLDING SEVERAL SMALL JOBS**

One in every 20 workers, currently, holds two or more jobs.

Levinson, Jay Conrad, *Earning Money Without a Job: The Economics of Freedom.* Holt, Rinehart, and Winston, 521 Fifth Ave., New York, NY 10175. 1979. The first part of this book is the best, as Jay sets forth his idea of "modular economics" -- putting together several small jobs, rather than one big one -- and having plenty of time left over for leisure.

Employee Benefits for Part-Timers. Association of Part-Time Professionals, P.O. Box 3419, Alexandria, VA 22302. Primarily directed at employers of part-time workers. Describes benefit packages put together by various private firms for their part-time employees; intended to serve as models for others.

If you are thinking of part-time work, please see also the agencies listed in the next section.

17. ALTERNATIVE FORMS OF JOBS: **JOB-SHARING**

People are discovering there are all kinds of alternatives to the traditional nine-to-five, Monday-through-Friday job. Job-sharing with another worker, flex-time, where you decide which hours of the day you want to work, the four-day work week, holding down three to five small jobs rather than one full-time job, working long and hard two or three days a week, then having the other days to yourself, etc. If such alternatives appeal to you, do your informational interviewing with people who have already gone that route, first; and then with smaller employers, who are often more open than are larger employers, to new patterns of work.

Olmstead, Barney, and Smith, Suzanne, *The Job Sharing Handbook.* Ten Speed Press, Box 7123, Berkeley, CA 94707. 1983. How to share a full-time job with another person, if you don't want to work full-time.

Work Times Newsletter, published by New Ways to Work, 149 Ninth St., San Francisco, CA 94103. An international information exchange on alternative work time.

There are centers dedicated to helping people who want to find flexible work-time options, such as job-sharing. They often have helpful pamphlets and other publications. Among them are:

Work/Life Options
6101 S. Rural Rd., #128
Tempe, AZ 85283
602-839-8284

New Ways to Work
149 Ninth St.
San Francisco, CA 94103
415-552-1000

Flexible Career Associates
Box 6701
Santa Barbara, CA 93111
805-687-2575

Innovative Career Options
School of Business - Box 13
Metropolitan State College
1006 Eleventh St.
Denver, CO 80204
303-629-3245

Family and Career Together
(FACT)
Eight N. Main St., Ste. 143
W. Hartford, CT 06107
203-521-1603

Association of Part-Time
Professionals
Atlanta Chapter
c/o Debbie Weil
77 28th St. NW
Atlanta, GA 30309
404-351-6637

Division of Women's Programs Alternative Working Arrangements Project
27000 University Ave.
Drake University
Des Moines, IA 50311
515-271-2181

Work Options for Women
1358 N. Waco
Wichita, KS 67203
316-264-6604

Work Options Limited
645 Boylston St.
Boston, MA 02116
617-247-3600

Nancy Viehmann
Pier Rd., Box 78
Cape Porpoise, ME 04014
207-967-3462

Lansing Women's Bureau
Human Resources Dept.
City of Lansing
119 N. Washington Sq.
Lansing, MI 48933
517-483-4479

Workshare
311 E. 50th St.
New York, NY 10022
212-832-7061

Work Time Options, Inc.
966 Summer Pl.
Pittsburgh, PA 15243
412-261-0846

Austin Women's Center
1700 S. Lamar, #203
Austin, TX 78704
512-447-9666

Phoenix Institute
383 S. 600 E.
Salt Lake City, UT 84102
801-532-5080

Association of Part-Time
Professionals
Box 3419
Alexandria, VA 22302
202-734-7975

Focus
509 Tenth Ave. E.
Seattle, WA 98102
206-329-7918

18. ALTERNATIVE FORMS OF JOBS: **WORKING AT HOME**

An estimated 16 million people work out of their homes, 4.7 million full-time and 11.3 million part-time -- many of them women. Computers, modems, fax machines, cellular telephones, voice/electronic mail all help make this possible even for those who, technically, have offices elsewhere. Thus people can work out of their preferred environment, even including a skiing chalet. Two problems: according to one expert, home-based workers earn only 70% of what their full-time office-based equals do. Also, it's often difficult to separate business and family time, so sometimes the family time gets short-changed, while in other cases the demands of

family (particularly with small children) may become so interruptive, that the business time gets short-changed.

Behr, Marion, and Lazar, Wendy, *Women Working Home: The Homebased Business Guide and Directory*. Women Working Home, Inc., 24 Fishel Rd., Edison, NJ 08820. 1983. The authors were co-founders of the National Alliance of Homebased Businesswomen, a New Jersey based group, with 1500 members currently.

Arden, Lynie, *The Work-at-Home Sourcebook*. Live Oak Publications, 6003 N. 51st St., #105, Boulder, CO 80306. 1987.

Edwards, Paul and Sarah, *Working from Home: Everything You Need to Know about Living and Working under the Same Roof*. J.P. Tarcher, Inc., 9110 Sunset Blvd., Los Angeles, CA 90069. 1985. 420 pages. Has a long section on computerizing your home business, and on telecommunicating.

Brabec, Barbara, *Homemade Money: The Definitive Guide to Success in a Home Business*. Betterway Publications, Inc., White Hall, VA 22987. 1984. 272 pages. A very fine book, with an A to Z business section, and a most helpful summary of which states have laws regulating (or prohibiting) certain home-based businesses.

The Home Office Newsletter. A monthly publication for individuals who run businesses from their homes. Newsletter is also available in electronic database form through Genie and Delphi information services. Subscribe to Compusystems Management, 4734 E. 26th St., Tucson, AZ 85711. 602-790-6333.

Homeworking Mothers, a quarterly newsletter for women who want to start their own businesses and work from their homes. Mother's Home Business Network, Box 423, East Meadow, NY 11554.

Hoge, Cecil C., Sr., *Mail Order Know-How*. Ten Speed Press, Box 7123, Berkeley, CA 94707. 1982.

Hoge, Cecil C., Sr., *Mail Order Moonlighting*. Ten Speed Press, Box 7123, Berkeley, CA 94707. 1976.

19. ALTERNATIVE FORMS OF JOBS: **SELF-EMPLOYMENT**

The self-employment route is exceedingly attractive to the unemployed, because it is a beautiful way to avoid the job-hunt. Unable to find work, we figure we have nothing to lose.

But of course you do. Your shirt. Or your blouse. The statistics on new businesses are depressing. You've probably heard them already, but in case you haven't: 65% of all new businesses fail within five years. That means, for example, that of the approximately 250,000 new businesses started in 1986, 162,500 will fail. That's the bad news.

The good news, if you're the type who likes to look on the bright side of things, is that -- as David Birch points out in his great book (below) -- only about 25% of new businesses fail **in any given year**; so, year by year, you have a 75% chance of succeeding. Furthermore, there are about 28 old businesses in this country, for every new business that starts up. This keeps the national bankruptcy/failure rate much lower than most people think. In 1986, for example, out of every 10,000 businesses in this country 120 failed. That means that 9880 out of every 10,000 businesses survived - right? So, **if** you can make it through the first few **very** difficult years in a new business, you'll probably survive.

Everything therefore depends on how you start up. That's why you must not even for a moment think that the self-employment route is a good way to avoid the job-hunt. On the contrary, you'll have to work harder at your research, harder at setting up your business, harder at finding customers (should you be offering a service or product) than you ever would in a normal job-hunt if your experience is at all like the self-employed from whom I regularly hear. You will look back at the job-hunt as an elementary school exercise by comparison.

Many people try to cut the risk down by going after a franchise. There are more than 600,000 franchised businesses operating in this country, employing more than 5 million people. If the idea of becoming involved in an already established business interests you, do your research **very** thoroughly. Books on franchising are listed below. Also, go talk to everyone you can who is doing the type of franchised work that you are thinking of doing.

The ten riskiest small businesses, according to experts, are local laundries and dry cleaners, used car dealerships, gas stations, local trucking firms, restaurants, infant clothing stores, bakeries, machine shops, grocery or meat stores, and car washes.

If I could move **gradually** into self-employment, doing it as a moonlighting activity first of all, I certainly would. Test out your enterprise, as you would a floorboard in a very old run-down house, stepping on it cautiously without putting your full weight on it, at first, to see whether or not it will hold you. If you're not presently employed, and you're determined to go the self-employment or franchise route, for heaven sakes have a plan B. "I'm going to try out this self-employment, and my plan B is that if after a certain number of months it doesn't look like it's going to make it, then I'm going to ... (fill in the blank)." And give some time to the exploration of that alternative before you start your self-employment thing, so that plan B is "all in place," as they say.

No matter how inventive you are about self-employment, you're probably *not* going to create a job no one has ever heard of; in all likelihood you're only going to create a job that *most* people have never heard of. But someone, somewhere, in this world of endless creativity, has probably already put together the kind of job you're dreaming about. Your task: to go find her, or him, and interview them to death. Why should you have to invent the wheel all over again? They've already stepped on all the landmines for you. They know where all the pitfalls are in this business you're dreaming of starting.

But suppose you can't find such a person? Well, then, figure out who is doing something that is **close** to what you're dreaming of doing, and go interview *that* person. For example, let's suppose your dream is to use computers to monitor the growth of plants at the Arctic. And you can't find anybody who's ever done such a thing. Well, then, break it down into its parts: computers, plants, and Arctic. Try combining **two** parts with each other, and you'll see what your research task is: to find someone who's used computers with plants, or computers at the Arctic, or someone who's worked with plants at the Arctic (yes, I know this is a moderately ridiculous example, but I want to stretch your imagination). My point is a simple one: you can **always** find someone who has done something that approximates what it is you want to do, and from her or him you can learn a great deal. Better yet, they may lead you to others who have done something even closer to what it is you want to do.

How do you get funded for a new job no one has ever heard of? Well, if it's a product or service you are offering, you get funded by convincing people to buy it. (And you ask people already offering a similar product or service how they got people to buy theirs, so you'll know what the general principles are, regarding what works and what doesn't work.)

But admittedly, this **can** be "the pits" if you have to go out and convince people, one by one, to buy your product, services, or whatever. No wonder, then, that a number of (hopefully) soon-to-be self-employed persons find the idea of a foundation grant or government grant tremendously attractive and winsome. How, they ask, can I find such a grant? Well, basically the same way you find a job. Thorough-going research. To get you started, consult your library (or else your banker) for one of the directories of grants (already) given. Such directories as:

Annual Register of Grant Support, published by Marquis Academic Media, 200 E. Ohio St., Rm. 5608, Chicago, IL 60611. The directory or register covers 2300 current grant programs, and has four helpful indexes.

The Foundation Center, 79 Fifth Ave., New York, NY 10003, is an independent, nonprofit organization offering assistance in locating grants. It publishes *The Foundation Directory,* which lists over 4,400 U.S. foundations, whose grants accounted en toto for 92% of all U.S. dollars awarded in three typical years. There are four reference collections operated by the Center, in New York, Washington, DC, Cleveland, and San Francisco. There are also dozens of cooperating collections nationwide. For information on locations nearest you, call 800-424-9836.

If you decide that applying for a grant is the way in which you would like to try to get funded, there are some rules. As Matthew Lesko (author of *Getting Yours*) points out:

1. If it is a government grant you seek, look at state and local governments as well as the Federal.
2. The money may not be where logic would suggest it should be. For example, the Department of Labor funds doctoral dissertations, the Department of Agriculture funds teenage entrepreneurs, and the like.
3. Talk to the people at the agency who are in charge of dispersing the grant funds.

4. When you have located an appropriate agency for what you want to do, ask to see a copy of a successful application (under the Freedom of Information Act).

5. If they make clear that they will not give you a large amount, ask for a small amount for a year; and let them get to know you.

And now to the books:

Birch, David, *Job Creation In America.* The Free Press, 866 Third Ave., New York, NY 10022. 1987. Where the new jobs are coming from and how our smallest companies put the most people to work. David is an excellent researcher, and knows more about small businesses than anyone else in the country.

Davidson, Jeffrey P., *Avoiding the Pitfalls of Starting Your Own Business.* Walker & Company, 720 Fifth Ave., New York, NY 10019. 1988.

Starting a Small Business in Ontario. Ministry of Industry, Trade, and Technology, Small Business Branch, 7th Floor, Hearst Block, 900 Bay Street, Toronto, Ontario M7A 9Z9, Canada.

Golzen, Godfrey, *Working for Yourself.* Kogan Page Ltd., 120 Pentonville Rd., London N1 9JN. 1987. How to start a business, raise capital, etc.

Hawken, Paul, *Growing A Business.* Simon & Schuster, Inc., Rockefeller Center, 1230 Avenue of the Americas, New York, NY 10020. 1987. This is the companion volume to the public television series by the same name.

Jones, Constance, *The 220 Best Franchises to Buy.* Philip Lief Group, 319 E. 52nd St., New York, NY 10022. 1987. A sourcebook for evaluating the best franchise opportunities.

Kamoroff, Bernard, *Small-Time Operator.* Bell Springs Publishing, P.O. Box 640, Laytonville, CA 95454. 1987. How to start your own small business, keep your books, pay your taxes and stay out of trouble.

Lesko, Matthew, *Getting Yours: The Complete Guide to Government Money.* Viking Penguin Inc., 40 W. 23rd St., New York, NY 10010. 1987.

Lant, Dr. Jeffrey L., *The Consultant's Kit.* JLA Publications, a division of Jeffrey Lant Associates, Inc., 50 Follen St. Suite 507, Cambridge, MA 02138. 1986.

Levinson, Jay Conrad, *Guerrilla Marketing: Secrets for Making Big Profits from Your Small Business,* Waldentapes, Box 1084, Stamford, CT 06904. 1985. Listen & Learn Cassettes, ISBN 0-681-30739-0.

Revel, Chase, *168 More Businesses Anyone Can Start and Make a Lot of Money.* Bantam Books, Inc., 666 Fifth Ave., New York, NY 10103. 1984.

Nicholas, Ted, *How to Form Your Own Corporation Without a Lawyer for Under $50.00. Complete with Tear-Out Forms, Certificate of Incorporation, Minutes, By-Laws.* Enterprise Publishing Co., Inc., 1000 Oakfield Lane, Wilmington, DE 19810. 1973.

And now, a special word about women and self-employment. There are over 15 million small business enterprises in the U.S. Women own 25% of them but only take in 9% of all small business income. According to experts, that's mostly because they price goods and services too low, are not able to take risks to the same degree as men are, and often get turned down for financing because of their sex. Of course, this is slowly changing.

Women who are thinking of starting their own business can get counseling over the phone, from the American Women's Economic Development Corporation (AWED), Monday through Friday, between 9 a.m. and 6 p.m. eastern time, at a cost of $10 for up to ten minutes. The hotline offers an expert in the area in which the caller needs help. Longer counseling, up to one and a half hours, is also offered, at a cost of $35. If calling from New York City, Alaska or Hawaii, call 212-692-9100. If calling from New York State, call 1-800-442-AWED. If calling from any other area, call 1-800-222-AWED. Both services may be charged to major credit cards.

20. GENERAL DIRECTORIES OF JOBS

Guide for Occupational Exploration. Supt. of Documents, U.S. Govt. Printing Off., Washington, DC 20402. Occupations organized by interest and job title.

U.S. Dept. of Labor, Employment and Training Admin., *Selected Characteristics of Occupations Defined in the Dictionary of Occupational Titles.* Supt. of Documents, U.S. Govt. Printing Off., Washington, DC 20402. 1981.

Bureau of Labor Statistics, *Occupational Outlook Handbook,* Supt. of Documents, U.S. Govt. Printing Off., Washington, DC 20402. 670-page encyclopedia of careers, covering hundreds of occupations and 35 major industries.

Feldman, Beverly Neuer, *Jobs/Careers Serving Children and Youth* (including Supplement: Appendix C and Index - - inserted into the book, but separate). Till Press, Box 27816, Los Angeles, CA 90027. 1978. Groups the jobs and careers according to how much education the job-hunter has had. For all those who want to work with youth or children

Rucker, T. Donald and Keller, Martin D., *Planning Your Medical Career: Traditional and Alternative Opportunities.* This manual describes the many options open to doctors today, listing the numerous new specialties now available. Garrett Park Press, Box 190, Garrett Park, MD 20896, 301-946-2553.

Collard, Betsy A., *The High-Tech Career Book: Finding Your Place in Today's Job Market.* William Kaufmann, Inc., 95 1st St., Los Altos, CA 94022. 1986.

21. PARTICULAR KINDS OF JOBS: JOBS DEALING WITH SOCIAL CHANGE

Careers in this arena are often called "public service careers."

Public service careers may be with **government** (federal, state, or local), with **nonprofit organizations**, with **agencies** (independent of state or local government, but often cooperating with them) or with **colleges** (particularly community colleges), etc.

Public service careers include such varied occupations as *Community Services Officer* at a community college, *recreation educator, city planner, social service technician* (working with any or all agencies that deliver social services), *welfare administration, gerontology specialist* (for further information, contact - - among others - - your State Commission on Aging), etc.

Other public service careers: *Workers with the handicapped, public health officials* (see your State Department of Public Health, or the Chief Medical Doctor at the county Public Health Agency - - the Doctor often being the best informed person about *opportunities*), *officials dealing with the foster parent program for mentally retarded persons, workers in the child welfare program,* and so forth.

If you are interested in this general field of social service, you ought to do extensive research, including talking with national associations in the fields that interest you, state departments, county, city.

"I'm hoping to find something in a meaningful, humanist, outreach kind of bag, with flexible hours, non-sexist bosses, and fabulous fringes."

Drawing by Donald Reilly; © 1981 The New Yorker Magazine, Inc. Used by permission.

Potential employers for social or public service occupations include social welfare agencies, public health departments, correctional institutions, government offices, colleges, economic opportunity offices, hospitals, rest homes, schools, parks and recreation agencies, etc.

Thorough research on your part will often reveal other ways in which **funding can be found for positions not yet created if you know exactly what it is you want to do**, and find a person who knows something about **that**.

And now to the books:

Smith, Devon, ed., *The Fourth of July Resource Guide for the Promotion of Careers in Public, Community, and International Service.* The Middle Atlantic

Placement Association, Special Project for Public & Community Service, 3041 Elm Drive, Allentown, PA 18103. 1987. Very useful list of directories, places, and other helpful information.

Powell, Thomas J., *Self-Help Organizations and Professional Practice.* National Association of Social Workers, Inc., Silver Springs, MD. 1987.

Schmolling, Paul, Jr., with Burger, William R. and Youkeles, Merrill, *Careers in Mental Health: A Guide to Helping Occupations.* Garrett Park Press, Box 190, Garrett Park, MD 20896.

Hughes, Kathleen, ed., *Good Works: A Guide to Social Change Careers.* Center for Study of Responsive Law, Box 19367, Washington, DC 20036. 1982.

Reynolds, Akie N., *Planning Your Career in Peacemaking.* From: Career Services Center, University of California, Santa Cruz CA 95064.

Human Service Organizations: A Book of Readings, University of Michigan Press, 615 E. University, Ann Arbor, MI 48106. Deals with an analysis of the structure of schools, employment agencies, mental health clinics, correctional institutions, welfare agencies and hospitals. If you're thinking about going to work in one of these human service organizations, this could help your research.

Brand, Stewart, editor emeritus. *The Essential Whole Earth Catalog.* Doubleday & Co., Inc., Garden City, NY.

22. PARTICULAR KINDS OF JOBS: **ARTS AND CRAFTS**

If your creativity is not out of the left-hemisphere of your brain (words, words, words), but out of the right-hemisphere (pictures, art, crafts, and so forth), there are books for you too; issued annually:

Gibson, James, *Getting Noticed: A Musician's Guide to Publicity & Self-Promotion.* Writer's Digest Books, 1507 Dana Ave., Cincinnati, OH 45207. 1987.

Whaley, Julie, *1989 Songwriter's Market.* Writer's Digest Books, 1507 Dana Ave., Cincinnati, OH 45207. 1988.

Eidenier, Connie, *1989 Photographer's Market.* Writer's Digest Books, 1507 Dana Ave., Cincinnati, OH 45207. 1988.

Conner, Susan, *1989 Artist's Market.* Writer's Digest Books, 1507 Dana Ave., Cincinnati, OH 45207. 1988.

Lapin, Lynne, ed., *1989 Craftworker's Market.* Writer's Digest Books, 1507 Dana Ave., Cincinnati, OH 45207.

If it is the visual arts that interest you, you may contact the Alliance of Independent Colleges of Art, 633 E St. NW, Washington, DC 20004. They have a quarterly magazine.

23. PARTICULAR KINDS OF JOBS: **WRITING, OR PUBLISHING**

I used to live in an apartment-complex, and as I walked through the courtyard each day, I could hear typewriters going incessantly, out of every open window. They couldn't **all** be part-time secretaries, working at home. Obviously, there are a lot of budding authors and authoresses in the land. For them, some helps:

Appelbaum, Judith, *How to Get Happily Published (Third Edition)*. Harper & Row, Inc., 10 E. 53rd St., New York, N.Y. 10022. 1988. A good and helpful book, by an expert.

Miller, Casey and Swift, Kate, *The Handbook of Nonsexist Writing, 2nd Ed.* Harper & Row, Inc., 10 E. 53rd St., New York, NY 10022. 1988. Newly revised, and a classic in its field.

Neff, Glenda Tennant, *1989 Writer's Market.* Writer's Digest Books, 1507 Dana Ave., Cincinnati, OH 45207. 1988.

Jerome, Judson, *1989 Poet's Market.* Writer's Digest Books, 1507 Dana Ave., Cincinnati, OH 45207. 1988.

Boswell, John, *The Awful Truth about Publishing: Why They Always Reject Your Manuscript - and What You Can Do about It.* Warner Books, 666 5th Ave., New York, NY 10103.

24. PARTICULAR KINDS OF JOBS: **TEACHING**

Teachers teach in schools. That has been the assumption that has dominated teacher-training for ages, as I mentioned in chapter 5.

You would do well not to make this error. The range of places that use people with teaching skills is mind-boggling: but as just a sampling, there are all the places we cited in chapter 5. An indication of some of the further possibilities you may want to research, can be found in *Education Directory: Education Associations*. It's available in your local library, or from the Supt. of Documents, U.S. Govt. Printing Off., Washington, DC 20402.

Moreover, the range of jobs that are done under the broad umbrella of Education is multitudinous and varied; just for openers, there is: *teaching* (of course), *counseling* (an honorable teaching profession, where it isn't just used by a school system as the repository for teachers who couldn't 'cut it'), *general administration, adult education programs, public relations, ombudsman, training, human resource development,* and the like. If the latter - - i.e., training and development - - is of particular interest to you, you will find there is a very useful description of the particular competencies, skills, and knowledges needed in the training and development fields. You'll find it in *Training and Development Competencies,* Patricia A. McLagan, Volunteer Study Director. Published in 1983, it is available from the American Society for Training and Development. Also see: Stump, Robert W., *Your Career in Human Resource Development: A Guide to Information and Decision Making.* American Society for Training and Development, 1630 Duke St., Box 1443, Alexandria, VA 22313. 31 pages. 1985. Our Canadian friends, namely the Ontario Society for Training and Development, have put out also a helpful guide, entitled *Competency Analysis for Trainers: A Personal Planning Guide.* It is available from O.S.T.D., Box 537, Postal Station K, Toronto, Ontario, M4P 2G9, Canada. It outlines the kinds of skills which people who are entering this field ought to possess, and provides a checklist against which one can compare one's own skills.

All of which is to say, just because you have defined your dream of life for yourself as "teacher" doesn't mean you have even begun to narrow the territory down sufficiently for you to start looking for a job. You still have more research, and information gathering to do, before you have defined exactly *what kind* of teaching, *with what* kind of *groups, in what* kind of *place.* In other words, chapters 4 through 6 in this book apply to you as much as, or even more than, anyone else.

If you decide to look elsewhere than teaching, there are aids produced for various teaching specialties, that you may want to seek out, e.g., for history majors there is: *Careers for Students of History,* from the American Historical Association, 400 A St. SE, Washington, DC 20003. 1977. While, for English majors, there is: *Aside from Teaching English, What in the World Can You Do?* by Dorothy K. Bestor, available from: University of Washington Press, Seattle, WA 98105. 1982, revised.

A more general guide for you, regardless of major, is:

Kimeldorf, Martin, *Educator's Job Search, A Guide To Finding Positions In Education.* Ednick Communications, Inc., PO Box 3612, Portland, OR 97208. 1988. Also:

Bastress, Frances, *Teachers in New Careers: Stories of Successful Transitions.* The Carroll Press. 1984. From: Career Development Services, Box 30301, Bethesda, MD 28104. See also:

Beard, Marna L. and McGahey, Michael J., *Alternative Careers for Teachers.* The complete job-changing handbook for educators. Arco Publishing, Inc., One Gulf + Western Plaza, New York, N.Y. 10023. 1985.

25. PARTICULAR KINDS OF JOBS: **WORKING FOR THE GOVERNMENT**

As with any other kind of job, you've got to decide **where** it is you want to work, what skills you want to be able to use, and what it is you want to do (in other words, chapters 4 and 5 in this book apply to you as much as to non-governmental workers).

If you are new to the idea of the government as your employer, you will of course suppose that researching them won't do you any good, because you are going to have to take a Civil Service examination of one kind or another. Well, eventually you probably **are** going to have to take that exam. But all the principles in chapter 6 apply just as much to government managers as they do to other employers. Government managers, too, are tired of hiring people ill-suited for the job. Civil service exams don't give these managers any better clues than resumes do for non-governmental employers. So if, in the course of your research, you happen to visit the government person who has the power to hire you, and if he or she takes a real liking to you, you can bet your bottom dollar they will do everything *they can* to guide you through the examination maze, so that you can end up in their office. Any government manager worth her or his salt knows how to manipulate -- ah, excuse me, creatively use -- standard operating procedures, so that it all works out to their best advantage.

Federal Jobs Digest, Billing Dept., P.O. Box 594, Millwood, N.Y. 10546-9989. 800-824-5000. They have a special edition called "Introduction to the Federal Employment Process," which some of our readers have found **very** helpful. The *Digest* is published bi-monthly. Can often be found at your local public library, as can the following:

Federal Research Service, Inc., *Federal Career Opportunities.* Federal Research Service, Inc., 370 Maple Ave. W., Box 1059, Vienna, VA 22180, 703-281-0200. Bi-weekly 64-page magazine. Six issues. Up-to-date listing of available federal jobs plus application instructions.

Federal Yellow Book. An organizational directory of the top-level employees of the Federal departments and agencies. See your library. The publisher (Washington Monitor, Inc., 1301 Pennsylvania Ave., NW, Washington, DC 20004) also publishes *Congressional Yellow Book,* an up-to-date loose-leaf directory of members of Congress, their committees and their key aides.

Phillips, David Atlee, *Careers In Secret Operations - How to Be a Federal Intelligence Officer.* Stone Trail Press, P.O. Box 17320, Bethesda, MD 20817. 1984.

Lesko, Matthew, *Information U.S.A.,* rev. ed. Viking Penguin Inc., 40 W. 23rd St., New York, NY 10010. 1986.

Guide to Careers in World Affairs, published by the Foreign Policy Association, 205 Lexington Ave., New York, NY 10016, 212-481-8450. Lists more than 250 sources of employment in the world affairs field.

26. SPECIAL PROBLEMS: **ELEMENTARY SCHOOL STUDENTS, HIGH SCHOOL STUDENTS, AND SUMMER JOBS**

Griffith, Susan, *1988 Summer Jobs in Britain.* Writer's Digest Books, 1507 Dana Ave., Cincinnati, OH 45207. 1988.

Woodworth, David, *1988 Directory of Overseas Summer Jobs.* Writer's Digest Books, 1507 Dana Ave., Cincinnati, OH 45207. 1987.

Beusterien, Pat, *1988 Summer Employment Directory of the United States.* Writer's Digest Books, 1507 Dana Ave., Cincinnati, OH 45207. 1987.

Groves, Josh, *The Student's Guide to the Best Summer Jobs in Alaska.* Mustang Publishing, Box 9327, New Haven, CT 06533. 1986.

Schocket, Sandra, *Summer Jobs, Finding Them, Getting Them, Enjoying Them.* Peterson's Guides, Dept. 5602, Princeton, NJ 08540, 800-225-0261. 1985.

Kennedy, Joyce Lain, and Laramore, Dr. Darryl, *Joyce Lain Kennedy's Career Book.* VGM Career Books, 4255 West Touhy Ave., Lincolnwood, IL 60646-1975. 1988. Joyce is a very popular and knowledgeable syndicated writer on the subject of careers, while Darryl has written other books on youth and jobs. See below.

The Guide to Basic Skills Jobs, Vol. 1. RPM Press, Inc., Verndale, Minnesota. 1986. A catalog of viable jobs for individuals with only basic work skills. This volume identifies 5,000 major occupations within the U.S. economy which require no more than an eighth grade level of education, and no more than one year of specific vocational preparation.

Mosenfelder, Donn, *Vocabulary for the World of Work.* Educational Design, Inc., 47 W. 13th St., New York, NY 10014. 1985. The 300 words that people entering the work force most need to know.

Feldman, Beverly Neuer, *Kids Who Succeed.* Rawson Associates, Macmillan Publishing, 866 Third Ave., New York, NY 10022. 1987.

Reprinted with permission from *Trever's First Strike*, Brick House Publishing, 1983

Kimeldorf, Martin, *Pathways to Work: A Workbook for Finding Job Opportunities*. Meridian Education Corporation, 236 E. Front St., Bloomington, IL 61701. 1989.

Kimeldorf, Martin, *Pathways to Leisure*. Meridian Education Corporation, 236 E. Front St., Bloomington, IL 61701. 1989.

Kimeldorf, Martin, *Job Search Education*. Educational Design, Inc., 47 W. 13th St., New York, NY 10014. 1985. Worksheets for the young job-hunter.

Otto, Luther B., *How to Help Your Child Choose a Career*. M. Evans & Co., 216 E. 49th St., New York, NY 10017. 1984.

Jones, Ilene, *Jobs for Teenagers*. Ballantine Books, 201 E. 50th St., New York, NY 10022. 1983.

Henderson, Douglass, *Get Ready: Job-Hunters Kit* (for high school students). This package includes: *Get Ready, Teachers Manual; Get Ready, Students Manual;* and cassette. Get Ready, Inc., a subsidiary of Educational Motivation, Inc., Box 18865, Phildelphia, PA 19119. 1980.

Laramore, Darryl, *Careers - A Guide For Parents And Counselors*. Brigham Young University Press, Provo, UT 84602. 1979.

Hummel, Dean L. and McDaniels, Carl, *How To Help Your Child Plan A Career*. Acropolis Books, Ltd., Colortone Bldg., 2400 17th St., NW, Washington, DC 20009. 1979.

27. SPECIAL PROBLEMS: **COLLEGE STUDENTS**

Phifer, Paul, *College Majors and Careers: A Resource Guide for Effective Life Planning*. Garrett Park Press, Box 190, Garrett Park, MD 20896, 301-946-2553. 1987.

Cohen, Steve and de Oliveira, Paulo, *Getting to the Right Job, A Guide for College Graduates*. Workman Publishing Co., 1 W. 39th St., New York, NY 10018. 1987.

Falvey, Jack, *After College: The Business of Getting Jobs*. Williamson Publishing, Charlotte, VT. 05445. 1986.

Elsman, Max, *How to Get Your First Job.* Crown Publishers, Inc., One Park Ave., New York, NY 10016. 1985.

Moore, Ph.D., Richard W., *Winning the Ph.D. Game: How to Get Into and Out of Graduate School with a Ph.D. and a Job.* Dodd, Mead & Co., 79 Madison Ave., New York, NY 10016. 1985. This seems to me to be an unusually helpful and well-researched book for Ph.D. graduates.

Kingstone, Brett, *The Student Entrepreneur's Guide.* Ten Speed Press, Box 7123, Berkeley, CA 94707. 1981. What college students are able to do as entrepreneurs, while still in college, has always staggered my imagination. One of them tells how it's done.

Figler, Howard E., *Path: A Career Workbook for Liberal Arts Students.* The Carroll Press Publishers, Box 8113, Cranston, RI 02920. 1979, 1975. Second edition, completely revised. Good stuff.

Books on summer jobs are listed in
the previous section.

28. SPECIAL PROBLEMS: **WOMEN**

> Books aimed at women in the world of work appear faster than one can possibly record them. I tried, for years, but finally gave up. They come into print and then go out of print, faster than a speeding bullet. This listing was always hopelessly out of date. So now I leave it to you to browse your local bookstore to see the full range of what's currently available. Books you may not find in your bookstore are listed below.

Ekstrom, Ruth B., Harris, Abigail M., and Lockheed, Marlaine E., *How to Get College Credit for What You Have Learned as a Homemaker and Volunteer.* 1977. Project HAVE SKILLS, Education Testing Service, Princeton, NJ 08541. They also publish the: *Have Skills Women's Workbook, Have Skills Counselor's Guide,* and *Have Skills Employer's Guide.* All of these include the famous "I CAN" lists, based upon the pioneering work, in the assessment of volunteer skills and knowledge, of the Council of National Organizations for Adult Education. Even for those not interested in college credit, but only in assessing the skills they picked up or sharpened as a volunteer or homemaker, this is an excellent resource. Classifies the skills under the various roles: administrator/manager, financial manager, personnel manager, trainer, advocate/change agent, public relations/communicator, problem surveyor, researcher, fund raiser, counselor, youth group leader, group leader for a serving organization, museum staff assistant (docent), tutor/teacher's aide, manager of home finances, home nutritionist, home child caretaker, home designer and maintainer, home clothing and textile specialist, and home horticulturist. *Very* helpful book, with accompanying aids.

Alston, Anna with Miller, Ruth, *Equal Opportunities: A Careers Guide.* Viking Penguin Inc., 40 W. 23rd St., New York, NY 10010. 1987.

Doss, Martha Merrill, *Women's Organizations: A National Directory.* Lists over 2,000 women's organizations nationwide as well as locally, plus much more. Garrett Park Press, Box 190, Garrett Park, MD 20896. 1986.

If you are interested in sales positions, you will want to know about the National Association for Professional Saleswomen, Box 255708, Sacramento, CA 95865. They have chapters across the country, and they publish a newsletter, called *Successful Saleswoman.*

29. SPECIAL PROBLEMS: MINORITIES

Minority Student Enrollments in Higher Education: A Guide to Institutions with Highest Percent of Asian, Black, Hispanic, and Native American Students. Garrett Park Press, Box 190, Garrett Park, MD 20896. 1987.

There is a *Financial Aid for Minority Students Series,* for which there is a booklet on each of the following subjects: *Financial Aid for Minorities: Awards Open to Students with any Major; in Business and Law; in Education; in Engineering and Science; in Health Fields, and in Journalism/Mass Communications.* Garrett Park Press, Box 190, Garrett Park, MD 20896. 1987.

The Black Resource Guide. Black Resource Guide, Inc., 501 Oneida Pl., NW, Washington, DC 20111. 1987. A comprehensive list of over 3,000 black resources or organizations in the U.S.

Johnson, Willis L., Ed., *Directory of Special Programs for Minority Group Members: Career Information Services, Employment Skills Banks, Financial Aid Sources, 4th ed.* Garrett Park Press, P.O. Box 190, Garrett Park, MD 20896. 1986.

Cole, Katherine W., ed., *Minority Organizations: A National Directory.* Garrett Park Press, Box 190, Garrett Park, MD 20896. 1987. An annotated directory of 7,000 Black, Hispanic, Native, and Asian American organizations.

Financial Aid for Minority Students in: Allied Health, Business, Education, Engineering, Law, Mass Communications, Medicine, or Science. Available from Garrett Park Press, Box 190, Garrett Park, MD 20896.

The national periodical for black college students is called *The Black Collegian.* Kuumba Kazi-Ferrouillet is the Managing Editor. It is published four times yearly. If you are interested in it, their address is: The Black Collegian, 1240 South Broad Street, New Orleans, LA 70125.

30. SPECIAL PROBLEMS: CLERGY

The first five resources are not restricted to clergy alone, but are written for people of faith whether ordained or not (they are written primarily, however, from a Christian orientation):

Rinker, Richard N. and Eisentrout, Virginia, *Called to Be Gifted and Giving: An Adult Resource for Vocation and Calling.* United Church Press, 132 W. 31st St., New York, NY 10001. 1985.

Staub, Dick; Trautman, Jeff; and Cutshall, Mark, eds., *Intercristo's CAREER KIT: A Christian's Guide to Career Building.* Intercristo, Seattle 98133. 1985. Booklets (6) and cassette tapes (3) enclosed in binder.

Wehrheim, Carol and Cole-Turner, Ronald S., *Vocation and Calling. Introduction/Hearing God's Call/Sharing Gifts: An Intergenerational Study Guide.* United Church Press, 132 W. 31 St., New York, NY 10001. 1985.

Moran, Pamela J., *The Christian Job Hunter.* Servant Publications, 840 Airport Blvd., Box 8617, Ann Arbor, MI 48107. 1984.

Mattson, Ralph, and Miller, Arthur, *Finding a Job You Can Love.* Thomas Nelson Publishers, Nelson Place at Elm Hill Pike, Nashville, TN 37214. 1982. Very helpful and useful book, written from the Christian perspective.

If a book doesn't give you everything you need, there are some religious centers you can turn to. Probably no profession has developed, or had developed for it, so many resources to aid in career assessment as has the clerical profession. Many of them have broadened their services to include helping Church members, and not just clergy. All counselors in these centers are sincere; many are also very skilled. When you run into a clerical counselor who is sincere but inept, you will probably discover that the ineptness consists in an inadequate understanding of the distinction between career **assessment** -- roughly comparable to taking a snapshot of people as they are in one frozen moment of time -- vs. career **development** -- which is roughly comparable to teaching people how to take their own motion pictures of themselves, from here on out.

Having issued this caution, however, we must go on to add that at some of these centers, listed below, are some simply excellent counselors who fully understand this distinction, and are well trained in that empowering of the client which is what career *development* is all about.

THE OFFICIAL INTERDENOMINATIONAL CAREER DEVELOPMENT CENTERS

The Career and Personal Counseling Service
St. Andrews Presbyterian College, Laurinburg, NC 28352
919-276-3162
Also at: 4108 Park Rd., Suite 200,
Charlotte, NC 28209
704-523-7751
Elbert R. Patton, Director

The Career and Personal Counseling Center
Eckerd College
St. Petersburg, FL 33733
813-864-8356, Ext. 356
John R. Sims, Director

The Center for Ministry
7804 Capwell Dr.
Oakland, CA 94621
415-635-4246
Robert Charpentier, Director

Lancaster Career Development Center
561 College Ave.
Lancaster, PA 17603
717-397-7451
L. Guy Mehl, Director

North Central Career Development Center
3000 Fifth St. NW
New Brighton, MN 55112
612-636-5120
John Davis, Director

Northeast Career Center
83 Princeton Ave.
Suite 2D
Hopewell, NJ 08525
609-466-0774
Roy Lewis, Director

Career Development Center of the Southeast
531 Kirk Rd.
Decatur, GA 30030
404-371-0336
Robert M. Urie, Director

Midwest Career Development Service
Box 7249
Westchester, IL 60153
312-343-6268
Ronald Brushwyler, Director

Southwest Career Development Center
Box 5923
Arlington, TX 76011
817-265-5541
William M. Gould, Jr., Director-Counselor

Center for Career Development and Ministry
70 Chase St.
Newton Centre, MA 02159
617-969-7750
Harold D. Moore, Director

The centers listed above are all accredited and coordinated by the Career Development Council, Room 774, 475 Riverside Dr., New York, NY 10115. Some of them are accepting directors of Christian Education, ministers of music, and others in addition to clergy; some centers are open to all and not merely to church-related clients; some are open to high school students, as well as to adults.

ALSO DOING WORK IN THIS FIELD:

CareerWorks -- a division of Intercristo. 19303 Fremont Ave. N., Seattle, WA 98133, 206-546-7395. Jeff Trautman, Director.

Enablement Information Service, Inc., 14 Beacon St., Rm. 707, Boston, MA 02108, 617-742-1460. James L. Lowery, Jr., Executive Director.

Mid-South Career Development Center, Box 120815, Acklen Station, Nashville, TN 37121, 615-327-9572. W. Scott Root, Director.

Career and Personal Counseling Center, 1904 Mt. Vernon St., Waynesboro, VA 22980, 703-943-9997. Lillian Pennell, Director.

Bernard Haldane, Wellness Education Council, 4502 54th NW, Seattle, WA 98105. 206-525-2205. A pioneer in the clergy career management and assessment field, Bernard teaches (totally independently of the agency which bears his name) seminars and training of volunteers (particularly in churches) to do job-finding counseling.

Life/Career Planning Center for Religious, 10526 W. Cermak Rd., Suite 111, Westchester, IL 60153. 312-531-9228. Dolores Linhart, Director. Doing work with Roman Catholics.

31. SPECIAL PROBLEMS: **EX-OFFENDERS**

Federal/State Employment Offices often can be of particular assistance to ex-offenders. All offices can provide for bonding of ex-offenders, if needed to obtain employment. They also have information on tax-breaks for employers who hire ex-offenders. The larger offices even have Ex-Offender Specialists.

You can obtain a "Pre-Employment Curriculum" from the American Correctional Association, 4321 Hartwick Rd., College Park, MD 20740. There is also: *A Survival Source Book for Offenders,* from Contacts, Inc., Box 81826, Lincoln, NB 68501.

32. SPECIAL PROBLEMS: **EXECUTIVES AND THE BUSINESS WORLD**

Lucht, John, *Rites of Passage at $100,000+: The Insider's Guide to Absolutely Everything About Executive Job-Changing.* The Viceroy Press, New York, NY. 1988.

Kidron, Michael and Segal, Ronald, *Business Money and Power, What You Need to Know.* Simon & Schuster/Touchstone Books, Rockefeller Building, Rockefeller Center, 1230 Avenue of the Americas, New York, NY 10020. 1987.

Figueroa, Oscar, and Winkler, Charles, *A Business Information Guidebook,* Amacom, 135 W. 50th St., New York, NY 10020. 1980.

Jablonski, Donna M., ed., *How to Find Information about Companies,* Washington Researchers, 918 16th St. NW, Washington, DC 20006.

Boll, Carl R., *Executive Jobs Unlimited.* Updated edition. Macmillan Publishing Co., Inc., 866 Third Ave., New York, NY 10022. 1979, 1965. **The** classic in the executive job-hunting field.

Drucker, Peter, *Management: Tasks, Responsibilities, Practices.* Harper & Row, Publishers, 10 E. 53rd St., New York, NY 10022. 1973. Should be absolutely required reading for anyone contemplating entering, changing to, or becoming a professional within the business world, or any organization.

33. SPECIAL PROBLEMS: **TWO-WORKER FAMILIES**

With more and more married women in the work-force, a body of literature has appeared concerning the problem of Both Partners Working:

Bastress, Frances, *The Relocating Spouse's Guide to Employment: Options and Strategies in the U.S. and Abroad.* Woodley Publications, 4620 Derussey Parkway, Chevy Chase, MD 20815.

Bird, Caroline, *The Two-Paycheck Marriage.* Pocket Books, 1230 Avenue of the Americas, New York, NY 10020. 1979.

Hall, Francine S., and Hall, Douglas T., *The Two-Career Couple.* Addison-Wesley, Route 128, Reading, MA 01867. 1979.

34. SPECIAL PROBLEMS: **THE HANDICAPPED**

The National Library Service for the Blind and Physically Handicapped, Library of Congress, 1291 Taylor St. NW, Washington, DC 20542 has many books on career planning and job-hunting (such as *Parachute*) on tape, which they will send, with special playback equipment, to your home and back, free, if you are able to prove a "print-handicap."

Recording for the Blind, Inc., 20 Roszel Rd., Princeton, NJ 08540 likewise has translated job-hunting books for the print-handicapped and visually-impaired.

Resource on Disabilities: McBurney Resource Center, 905 University Ave., Madison, WI 53706. Access to Independence, Inc., 1954 E. Washington Ave., Madison, WI 53704. These resources help with psychological aspects of job-hunting.

Kimeldorf, Martin and Edwards, Jean, *Numbers That Spell Success, Transitions to Work and Leisure Roles for Mildly Handicapped Youth.* Ednick Communications, Box 3612, Portland, OR 97208. 1988.

Klein, Karen with Hope, Carla Derrick, *Bouncing Back From Injury: How to Take Charge of Your Recuperation.* Prima Publishing & Communications, P.O. Box 1260BB, Rocklin, CA 95677. 1988.

Ryan, Colleen, *Job Search Workshop for Disabled, Dislocated and Discouraged Workers.* Adult Life Resource Center, Division of Continuing Education, The University of Kansas. 1985.

Bruck, Dr. Lilly, Producer, *The Assertive Jobseeker: A Telecommunications Conference of Nationally Prominent Experts.* In Touch Networks, 322 W. 48th

St., New York, NY 10036. A three-cassette series, with speakers on such subjects as job-hunting and assertiveness, including *Parachute*'s author.

Addendum:

IF YOU ARE A CAREER COUNSELOR,
OR WANT TO BE

Those just getting started in the field of career counseling (inside or outside academia) will, of course, want to read this current edition of *Parachute* from cover to cover, and then **do** all the exercises within it, before they inflict them on their helpless students or clients. *Teaching is Sharing, and Sharing should only follow Experiencing.*

Among the following listings, you will find a number of aids designed to help you with that Sharing.

Periodicals:

Career Planning & Adult Development Newsletter, published monthly by the Career Planning and Adult Development Network, 1190 S. Bascom Ave., Suite 211, San Jose, CA 95128.

CNews: Career Opportunities News, Garrett Park Press, Box 190, Garrett Park, MD 20896. Useful news for counselors (and job-hunters) about employment fields, fellowships, new books, etc.

The Vocational Guidance Quarterly, a professional journal concerned with research, theory, and practice in career development, career guidance, career resources, and career education. The official publication of the National Vocational Guidance Association, a division of the American Association for Counseling and Development, 5999 Stevenson Ave., Alexandria, VA 22304.

Books:

The Guide to Basic Skills Jobs, Vol. 1. RPM Press, Inc., Verndale, MN 56481. 1986. A catalog of viable jobs for individuals with only basic work skills. This volume identifies 5,000 major occupations within the U.S. economy which require no more than an eighth grade level of education, and no more than one year of specific vocational preparation. Immensely useful book if you counsel that kind of job-hunter.

Career & Job Search Instruction Made Easy, JIST Works, Inc., The Job Search People, 720 North Park Ave., Indianapolis, IN 46202. 1-800-648-JIST.

Job Information and Seeking Training Program Instructor's Guide and Job Seekers Workbook. JIST, 1001 W. 10th St., Indianapolis, IN 46202. 1980.

Kimeldorf, Martin, *Job Search Education.* Educational Design, Inc., 47 W. 13 St., New York, NY 10011. 1985.

Johnson, Miriam, *The State of the Art in Job Search Training,* Olympus Publishing Co., Box 9362, Salt Lake City, UT 84109. 1982. "The state of the art" at least as it was back in '82.

Baxter, Neale, *Opportunities in Counseling and Development.* VGM Career Horizons, 4255 W. Touhy Ave., Lincolnwood, IL 60646-1975. 1986.

Edwards, Patsy B., *Leisure Counseling Techniques.* Constructive Leisure, 511 N. La Cienega Blvd., Los Angeles, CA 90048.

Porot, Daniel, *Comment Trouver Une Situation.* Les Editions d'Organisations, 5, rue Rousselet, F-75007 Paris. 1985. If you read French, this is Daniel's approach to the job-hunt. Since he is the expert in Europe, this is well worth reading.

Raelin, Joseph A., *Building a Career: The Effect of Initial Job Experiences and Related Work Attitudes on Later Employment.* W.E. Upjohn Institute for Employment Research, 300 S. Westnedge Ave., Kalamazoo, MI 49007. 1980.

Lathrop, Richard, *The Job Market.* The National Center for Job-Market Studies, Box 3651, Washington, DC 20007. What would happen if we decreased the length of the job-hunt in America, and other iconoclastic ideas which are also eminently sensible.

U.S. Dept. of Labor, Bureau of Labor Statistics, *Handbook of Labor Statistics.* Supt. of Documents, U.S. Govt. Printing Off., Washington, DC 20402.

Feingold, S. Norman and Hansard-Winkler, Glenda Ann, *900,000 Plus Jobs Annually: Published Sources of Employment Listings.* Garrett Park Press, Box 190, Garrett Park, MD 20896

"Computers in Career Planning," Summer 1987 issue of *Career Planning: An Adult Development Journal.* To order call (408) 559-4946.

See also the entries in sections dealing with the specific kind of client you desire to counsel. For example, if you wish to counsel people with limited education, see section 26; if you wish to counsel college students, see section 27.

Audio-Visuals:

Wallach, Ellen J., with Fulford, Nancy, *Career Management: When Preparation Meets Opportunity. Leader's Guide.* AMA Film/Video, 85 Main St., Watertown, MA 02172. An excellent manual, designed to go with the film of the same title, in order to help you to use the film to serve a number of purposes: if you (as counselor) are trying to sell decision makers on the benefits of career management to their organization; or if you want to inform managers about the benefits of career management as part of an overall human resource system; or if you are working with HR professionals to assess organizational career management needs and/or to design a systems approach to career management; or if you want to give individual employees, their managers, or HR professionals an overview of career management; or if you are training personnel who are charged with career guidance responsibilities; or if you want to conduct a career management workshop; or if you are approached by an employee or manager seeking individual career counseling.

Sladey, Pat, *Find the job you want...and get it!* A four audio cassette program, on the subjects: Find the Hidden Job Market; Sell Yourself in the Interview; Prepare Winning Resumes & Letters; and Stay Motivated During the Search. Available from: Pat Sladey & Associates, P.O. Box 440352, Aurora, CO 80044.

Training:

There are countless training opportunities for career counselors in the U.S. and abroad. *Career Planning & Adult Development Newsletter,* mentioned earlier (published monthly by the Career Planning and Adult Development Network, 1190 S. Bascom Ave., Suite 211, San Jose, CA 95128) maintains a very good calendar of these events, and anyone interested in further training would be well advised to be receiving this *Newsletter.*

I do training for career counselors myself, but only once a year. We call it:

Life/Work Planning
at the Inn of the Seventh Mountain

No, this is not held in the Orient. The Inn of the Seventh Mountain is a lovely resort on the outskirts of Bend, Oregon, which -- as everyone knows -- is in the center of the United States (Honolulu is 3,000 miles to the West, New York City is 3,000 miles to the East).

The workshop is two weeks in length. It is always in August, always the first Friday through the third Friday. It is led, in its entirety, by Daniel Porot and myself; we teach as a team. Daniel, as you know if you have worked your way through this book already, is the job-hunting expert in Europe. His expertise is really quite dazzling. And since we wish this to be the very finest training that career counselors can find anywhere, we often have other distinguished leaders in the career development field, who lecture in the evening. In the past these have included the late John Crystal, Sidney Fine, Arthur Miller, and Bob Wegmann. The total number of hours of training exceeds 100. Normally between 40 to 70 people are enrolled, each year. In the past they have come from the U.S., Canada, England, France, Holland, Switzerland, New Zealand, Australia, and Indonesia. They have included all ages, and all ethnic groups.

Tuition for the two weeks is $1,000. Room and board are additional.

If you wish additional information, you should write to:

> Erica Chambré, Registrar
> Two-Week Workshop
> What Color Is Your Parachute?
> P.O. Box 379
> Walnut Creek, CA 94597

The workshop is designed primarily as training for counselors in the art of life/work planning and career-changing; **it is, however, open to anyone who wishes two weeks of study with Dick Bolles and Daniel Porot, whether you are a counselor, job-hunter or career-changer.**

Two are better than one;
   for if they fall,
the one will lift up his fellow;

but woe to him that is alone when he falleth,
and hath not another to lift him up.

Ecclesiastes

Appendix C

*when books are not enough
and
you want a live person
to help you:*

Career Counselors
and
Other Resources

REQUIRED READING:

If You're Thinking of Hiring a Career Counselor to Help You

Okay, you're back here in this section either because you're just curious to know what it says, or because you're ready to admit you've just got to hire *somebody* to help you, with all this.

And you've decided you've got to find somebody to help you because either:

a)   you *tried* doing the exercises in the book, and you just aren't getting anywhere; or

b)   you've read the book -- sections of it anyway -- and without even trying the exercises, you know yourself well enough to know you need someone who will explain it all to you, step by step. You're an "ear" person, more than an "eye" person, and you do better when a human being is explaining something to you, than when you're trying to read it for yourself; OR

c)   you've not read the book, nor tried any of the exercises, but you **have** counted the number of pages in the book, and the very thickness of it all was so intimidating, that you've decided to toss in the towel before you even begin. (*"Help!"*)

You've turned to this section because you figure that back here must be some sort of "authorized list" of names: people who understand this whole job-hunting process thoroughly, know how to do all the exercises in this book, have been through some kind of careful credentialing process, and received the Parachute Seal of Approval.

Ah, dear reader, how I wish it were so. But, unhappily, there is no such list. First of all, while I do train people once a year, I haven't trained all that many, over the years. Moreover, I can't **guarantee** that simply because they've been through my hands, they truly understand. So, publishing a list of their names wouldn't necessarily give you the information you want.

Secondly, there are lots of people "out there" who understand the whole job-hunting process thoroughly and well, even though they've never been trained by me and may not even (necessarily) have read this book. In most cases, of course, I've never met them, and consequently I don't know who they are or where they are. I simply know **that** they are.

What this all adds up to, you've already guessed. Hunting for a decent person or place to help you is just like hunting for a job. You've got to do your own research, and your own interviewing, in your own area. Getting somebody else's opinion, in effect letting them do your research for you, isn't very effective. First of all, their information is often somewhat outdated, and therefore questionable. Maybe the counselor or place they're telling you about is one they ran into a year ago. The counselor was excellent, at that time. But since then (unbeknownst to your friend) that counselor has been through a really rough time, personally: divorce, burnout, overwhelming fatigue -- the works. It's affected their counseling, to say the least; they're no longer functioning at the top level they were a year ago. Your friend's recommendation is outdated -- at least for the present. And, of course, it can be just the other way around. Your friend tells you someone is terrible, as a counselor, because when your friend ran into them, two or three years ago, it was true. But, that counselor has had dozens and dozens of clients since then, and learned a lot (most career counselors are trained by their clients, you know). That counselor is now very good. Your friend's "dis-recommendation" is now outdated.

Secondly, the three things you absolutely want from anyone you're paying good money to, are:

a) a firm grasp of the whole job-hunting process, at its most creative and effective level;

b) the ability to communicate that information lucidly and clearly to others;

c) rapport with you.

This last is a very difficult thing to pin down. Maybe this counselor is simply wonderful on the first two counts, but he reminds you of your Uncle Harry. You've always **hated** your Uncle Harry. No go. But how could anyone have known that, except you?

I repeat: no one can do this research about which job counselor is best, except you. Because the real question is not "Who is best?" but "Who is best **for you**?" Those last two words change everything.

What I want to do for you is:

1. Give you a brief crash course about this whole field of career counseling.
2. Tell you where to find some names with which **to start** your search for "who is best for you."
3. Give you some questions, that will help you separate the sheep from the goats, and make an intelligent decision.

Okay, here we go:

1. A CRASH COURSE ABOUT THIS WHOLE FIELD OF CAREER COUNSELING

In the whole big field of The Job Hunt, all professional help divides (one regrets to say) into the following three categories, so far as the job-hunter is concerned:

> 1. Professionals who are sincere and skilled.
> 2. Professionals who are sincere but inept.
> 3. Professionals who are insincere and inept.

The problem we all face when we decide to seek help with our job-hunt, is: which is which. Or, who is who. We want a career counselor who falls into category No. 1; if he or she falls into the other categories, which of the other two they fall into is really irrelevant: ineptness is ineptness, whether it is sincere or not.

The various clues which may at first occur to us, for identifying good career counselors, are upon more serious examination not terribly fruitful. Let us tick off some of them, and see why:

★ **Clue No. 1**: Perhaps we can tell who is sincere and skilled, by the name of the specialist or their agency. Difficulty: names vary greatly from one operation to another, even when the operations are similar. Among the names which some counselors or agencies bear, you will find: executive career counselors, executive career consultants, career management teams, vocational psychologists, executive consulting counselors, career guidance counselors, executive advisors, executive development specialists, executive job counselors, manpower experts, career advisors, employment specialists, executive recruitment consultants, professional career counselors, management consultants, placement specialists, executive search specialists, vocational counselors, life/work planners, etc. If, tomorrow, some legitimate counselor who is sincere and skilled takes on a new name, the day after that some counselor who is insincere and inept will copy the name directly. What it all comes down to, is this: Wolves need sheep's clothing. Names are sheep's clothing. Trouble is, hidden in there are some genuinely helpful people. We need another clue.

★ **Clue No. 2**: Perhaps we can tell who is sincere and skilled by reading everything that the agency or counselor has written. Difficulty: both good and bad counselors know the areas where the job-hunter feels exceedingly vulnerable. Consequently, there are "turn on" words which occur in almost everybody's advertisements, brochures, and books: we will give you help, say they, with evaluating your career history, in-depth analysis of your background, establishment of your job objective, in-depth analysis of your capabilities, writing an effective resume, names of companies, preparing the covering letter, background materials on companies, interviewing techniques, salary negotiations, filling out forms, answering ads, aptitude tests, special problems -- unemployment, age, too broad a background, too narrow a background, too many job changes, too few job

changes, poor references, etc. We will, they say, open doors for you, tell you which companies are hiring, and so forth. Both the counselors who are skilled and those who are inept will never get anyone in their doors if they don't mention the areas that have put the job-hunter in Desperation City. So how they describe their services (real or alleged) doesn't separate the sheep from the goats, unfortunately. Next clue?

★ **Clue No. 3**: Perhaps we can tell who is sincere and skilled by the fee they charge? I mean, they wouldn't charge a high fee, would they, if they weren't skilled? Difficulty: as insiders say, low fees may mean well-intentioned but amateurish help. However, the reverse of this is **not** true. As we have already mentioned, the vacuum created by the chaotic condition of our job-hunting process has attracted both competent people **and** people who are determined to prey upon the acute state of anxiety that job-hunters are often in. And when the latter say "Let us prey" they **really** prey. And they **thrive**. They can charge anywhere between $2,000 and $10,000 (it's solely dependent on your previous salary) **up front**, before they've given you **any** services or help at all. And if you are later dissatisfied, your chances of getting your money back are remote, indeed - - no matter what the contract said. (They've fashioned every legal loophole in the book, into that contract, so that they can keep your money, no matter what.) P. T. Barnum knew what he was talking about. [1] Next.

★ **Clue No. 4**: Perhaps we can tell which professionals are both sincere and skilled, by talking to satisfied clients -- or asking our friends to tell us who was helpful to them. If you stop to think about it, you will realize this most crucial truth: **all your friends can possibly speak to you about is the particular counselor or counselors that they worked with, at that agency, in that particular city**. Should you go to the same place, and get a different counselor, you might have a very different experience. One bad counselor in an agency that has say, six good ones, can cost you much money, time, and self-esteem, if **you** get that bad one as **your** counselor. The six good ones might as well be in Timbuktu, for all the good they'll do you. So should any of your friends recommend a place they went to, be sure to find out the counselor (or counselors) they worked with, there, **by name**, so you will know who to ask for, if you decide to investigate or follow their lead.

Before we leave this clue, let us also observe that while most professional career counselors will show you letters from satisfied customers, or even give you (in some cases) their names to check out, it is impossible to find out what percentage of their total clientele these satisfied persons represent: 100%? 10? 1? .1? a fluke? If you want a clue, you may make what you will out of the fact that the top officers of the largest executive counseling firm, which allegedly did over 50% of the business in the industry before it declared bankruptcy in the U.S. in the fall of 1974 (*namely*, Frederick Chusid & Co.) gave testimony during a civil suit in a New York Federal district court which indicated that only three or four out of every ten clients had been successful in getting a new job,

---

1. "A sucker is born every minute." Or as the post office has updated it: "A sucker is shorn every minute."

during a previous six-month period (a 60-70% failure rate). More recently, another prominent executive counseling firm was reported by the Attorney General's Office of New York State to have placed only 38 out of 550 clients (a 93% failure rate, right?).[1] Are these figures average for the industry? Better than average? Worse? Nobody knows. But they should certainly be enough to make you wary. Do you want to bet $600 to $8,000 (or whatever their fee is), where there is a 60 to 93% chance that you **won't** find a job?

In any event, virtually no career counselor or career counseling firm will **ever** show you letters from **dis**satisfied clients. Were you to be given access to such letters (the files of the Better Business Bureaus, the Consumer Fraud division of your state or city Attorney General's office, not to mention the Federal Trade Commission, are loaded with such letters) you would find the complaints have certain recurrent themes: the career counseling firm being complained about, they say, did not do what they **verbally** promised to do, have exclusive lists of job openings they claimed to have, nor the success rate they claimed, nor did they give the amount of time to the client they **verbally** promised in advance (sometimes it turned out to be as few as six hours). 'Job campaigns' for the clients were slow to start, usually not until the full advance fee was paid, promised lists were slow in being provided and often were outdated and full of errors, the friendly 'intake counselor' was actually a salesperson, and is never seen again once the contract is signed, the actual counselor was often difficult (or impossible) to get ahold of after a certain period of time (sometimes coinciding with the final payment by the client of the advance fee), the 'plan' was often no news at all to the client, the promised contact with employers on the client's behalf was not forthcoming, phone calls or letters of complaint were ignored, and the fee was not refunded in whole or in part, when the client was dissatisfied, despite implicit (or explicit) promises to the contrary. Whew!

Well, that's enough of a crash course on career counseling, and the pitfalls that await the unwary or the innocent. If you are **dying** to know more, and your local library has back files of magazines and newspapers (on microfiche, or otherwise) you can look up:

"Career-Counseling Industry Accused of Misrepresentation," *New York Times*, Sept. 30, 1982, p.C1.

"Consumer Law: Career Counselors and Employment Agencies" by Reed Brody, *New York Law Journal*, Feb. 26, 1982, p. 1. Reed was Assistant Attorney General of the State of New York, and more recently Deputy Chief of the Labor Bureau within that State's Department of Law; in this capacity he became the leading legal expert in the country, on career counseling malpractices.

"Career Counselors: Will They Lead You Down the Primrose Path?" by Lee Guthrie, *Savvy Magazine*, Dec., 1981, p. 60ff.

"Franklin Career Search Is Accused of Fraud In New York State Suit," *Wall Street Journal*, Jan. 29, 1981, p. 50.

---

1. "Career Counselors: Will They Lead You Down The Primrose Path?" by Lee Guthrie, in the December 1981 issue of *Savvy Magazine*, p. 60 ff.

"Job Counseling Firms Under Fire For Promising Much, Giving Little," *Wall Street Journal*, Jan. 27, 1981, p. 33

Stuart Alan Rado has been raging a sort of "one man crusade" against career counseling firms which take advantage of the job-hunter. **His** advice, as the result of counseling many victims, is: don't go to **any** firm which requires the fee all in advance. If you are reading this too late, did pay some firm's fee all in advance, and feel you were ripped off, if you will send Mr. Rado a self-addressed stamped envelope, he will send you a one-page sheet of some actions you can take. His address is: 1500 23rd St., Sunset Island #3, Miami Beach, FL 33140. 305-532-2607. He is working to help bring about new state laws, which will make it at least a little more difficult for unconscionable career counseling firms to take advantage of the hapless job-hunter or career-changer. Some states, such as California, have already adopted such laws.

2. WHERE TO FIND SOME NAMES TO START YOUR SEARCH FOR WHO IS BEST FOR YOU

You start, of course, by asking everyone you know -- family, friends, and people you've just met -- if they know any really helpful career counselors.

You supplement this by looking in the Yellow Pages of your local telephone book. Possible headings to check out (they vary from phone book to phone book) are: vocational counselors, executive career counselors, career counselors, job counseling, guidance counselors, career consultant, employment counselors. Also any cross-references that these lead you to.

I am printing in this Appendix a Sampler (only) of some of the kinds of places to be found around the country, including a number of private counselors who aren't very easy to stumble across. The sampler starts on page 322. This is not a complete directory of anything. Countless good people, agencies, and places exist, which will not be found in this Sampler. Also, countless bad people, places, and agencies. To list all such, would require an encyclopedia.

The listing of an organization, agency or person in this Sampler is NOT a recommendation or endorsement of that organization, agency or person: Likewise, the failure to list a particular organization, agency or person in this Sampler is NOT a condemnation of that organization, agency or person. It is what its name implies: a sample only. In any event, you **must** do your own comparison shopping, and ask some sharp questions. If you don't comparison shop, you will deserve whatever you get (or don't get).

There is **no way** this Sampler can stay up-to-date and accurate, for more than about two days. Places fold, almost weekly in this field. Places move. The staff changes. Their phone numbers and hours change. I apologize for any information or listing that proves to be inaccurate. You could be of great service by dropping us a line, if you find a place that is no longer in existence, or impossible to get a hold of, or is -- in your opinion -- totally unhelpful (Box 379, Walnut Creek, CA 94597).

3.   SOME QUESTIONS, BY MEANS OF
WHICH YOU MAY BE ABLE TO SEPARATE
THE SHEEP FROM THE GOATS

Choose, from your friends' recommendations, from the phone book, from the Sampler attached hereto, **at least three places or counselors**. **VISIT IN PERSON EACH OF THE THREE PLACES YOU HAVE CHOSEN.** These are exploratory visits only. Leave your wallet and your checkbook home, please! You are only comparison shopping at this point, not decision reaching!!

Make this unmistakably clear, when you are setting up the appointment for the interview.

You will need a notebook. In this notebook, **before** you go to see each career counselor (or firm), you will need to write out the following questions.   And, as you ask the questions at each place, take time to write down some notes, (or direct quotes) of their answers. **Don't** trust your memory.

You may prefer to make four columns across your notebook, so that it will be easier to compare the places, after you have visited all three:

At each place, with each counselor, ask every one of these questions — omitting none.

• *What is their program?* When all gimmicks are set aside (and some have great ones, like rehearsing for interviews on closed circuit TV, or using video-tape or cassettes to record your skills or your resume, etc.) what are they offering: is it basically "the numbers game" **or** is it basically some variation of the creative minority's prescription?

• *Who will be doing it?* Do you get the feeling that you must do most of it, with their basically assuming the role of coach?   (if so, three cheers); or do you get the feeling that everything (including decision making about what you do, where you do it, etc.) will be done for you (if so, three warning bells should go off in your head)?

• *What guarantee is there that it will work?* If they make it clear that they have had a good success rate, but if you fail to work hard at the whole process, then there is no guarantee you are going to find a job, give them three stars.   On the other hand, if they practically guarantee you a job, and say they have never had a client that failed to find a job, no matter what, **watch out.**   Pulmotor job-counseling is very suspect; lifeless bodies make poor employees.

• *Are you face-to-face, and talking, with the actual persons who will be working with you, should you decide to become a client?* It might help you to be aware that some job-hunting or career counseling firms have professional salespeople who introduce you to the company, convince you of their 100% integrity and charm, secure your decision, get you to sign the contract, and then you never see them again. You work with someone entirely different (or a whole team). *Ask the person you are talking to, if they are the one*

MY SEARCH FOR A GOOD CAREER COUNSELOR

Questions	Answer from Counselor #1	Answer from Counselor #2	Answer from Counselor #3
1. What is their program?			
2. Who will be doing it?			
3. Guarantee?			
4. Who is the actual counselor?			

(and the only one) you will be working with, should you eventually decide to become a client. If they say No, ask to meet those who would actually be working with you -- even if it's a whole battery of people. When you actually meet them, there are three considerations you should weigh:

(1) *Do you like the counselor?* Bad vibes can cause great difficulties, even if this person is extremely competent. Don't dismiss this factor!

(2) *How long has the counselor been doing this?* Ask them! And what training did they have for it? (Legitimate questions; if they get huffy, politely thank them for their time, and take your leave gently **but firmly.**) Some agencies hire former clients as new staff. Such new staff are sometimes given only "on the job training." Since you're paying for Expertise already acquired, you have a **right** to ask about this before making up your mind. Incidentally, beware of such phrases as "I've had eighteen years' experience in the business and career counseling world." What that may mean is: seventeen and a half years as a fertilizer salesman, and one half year doing career counseling. Persist. "How long have you been doing **formal career counseling**, as you are now?"

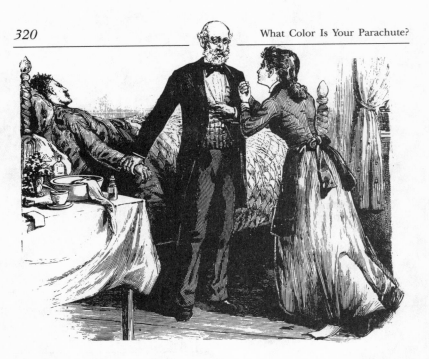

(3) *How much time will they give you?* As a minimum? As a maximum? (There's got to be a maximum, no matter what they may at first claim. Every career counselor runs into extremely dependent types as clients, who would be there all day every day if the counselor or the firm didn't have some policy about time limits. **Press** to find out what it is, just so you'll know.) Over how long a period can you use their services? And, **will they put this in writing?** That's the question that separates the men from the boys, and the women from the girls.

• *What is the cost of their services? Is it paid hourly, as you go along, or must it all be paid "up front" before you even start?* You will discover that there are some career counselors that charge you an hourly rate, just as a therapist might. The fee normally ranges between $50 and $85 an hour. Each time you keep an appointment, you pay them at the end of that hour (or hours) for their help. There is no written contract. You signed nothing. You can stop seeing them at any time, if you feel you are not getting the help you wish. Obviously, this sort of arrangement is very much **to the advantage of the job-hunter**. However, you will also discover that there are some career counselors or agencies that, by contrast, have a policy of requiring you to pay for the entire "program" before you start -- or shortly after you start. There is **always** a written contract. You **must** sign it. (If you are married, your spouse will usually be invited to come in, before the contract is signed; you may suspect this is to help "sell" them on the idea of the contract, so they then can sell you. You may be right.) The fee normally ranges between $600 and $8,000.

The contract sometimes allows it to be paid in installments, but you **are** obligated to pay it, one way or the other. You are sometimes **verbally** told that you can get your money back, or a portion of it, at any time, should you be dissatisfied with the career counselor's services. This is often **not** in the written contract. Verbal promises, without witnesses, are difficult if not impossible to enforce. The written contract takes precedence. Sometimes the written contract will provide for a partial refund, up to a certain cut-off point in the program. There is **always** a cut-off point; and many times it is calculated by the counselor or agency in a manner other than the way **you** are calculating it. Consequently you are beyond the cut-off point, and the possibility of any refund, before you know it. Or, you reach the cut-off point and allow it to pass because you are, up to that point, satisfied with their services, and you have been led to believe there is much more to come. Only, there isn't. Once the cut-off point is passed, the career counselor becomes harder and harder to get a hold of.

Clearly this second financial arrangement (as opposed to the hourly) is **to the advantage of the career counselor or agency**, more than it is to the advantage of the job-hunter. There's nothing inherently meritorious about paying someone a whole lot of money before he or she has performed any of the services they say they are going to perform. If you should become increasingly dissatisfied with the counseling or "program" as it progresses, you may be "out" a lot of dough. With no legal recourse. And so, the moral of this tale:

Don't pay any fee that you can't afford to lose.

While you are still doing your information gathering on the three places, find out which of these two financial arrangements the counselor or agency requires. If a contract will be involved, ask for a copy of it, take it home, and show it to a good lawyer.

Having gotten the information **you** want, and therefore having accomplished **your** purpose for this particular visit, you politely thank them for their time and trouble, and depart. You then go on to two other places, and ask the very same questions, please! There ought to be no charges involved for such comparison shopping visits as this, and if they subsequently bill you, inquire politely whether or not a mistake has been made by their accounting department (good thinking). If they persist in billing you, pay a visit to your local friendly Better Business Bureau, and lodge a nice unfriendly complaint against the firm in question. You'd be surprised at how many firms experience **instant repentance** when the Better Business Bureau phones them. They don't want a complaint on their BBB record.

BACK HOME NOW, after visiting the three places you chose for your comparison shopping, you have to decide: a) whether you want none of the three, or b) one of the three and if so, which one.

Look over your notes on all three places. Compare those places. Time for thought, maybe using some others as a sounding board: business friend, consultant friend, placement center, buddy, mate, or anyone whose judgement you trust.

Remember, you DON'T have to choose **any of the three** counselors. If you didn't really care for any of them, listen to your intuition. Choose three new counselors, dust off the notebook, and go out again. It may take a few more hours to find what you want. But remember: the wallet or purse you will be saving is your own.

A Sampler

This Sampler Has Several Sections:

    I. Places Which Counsel Anyone
   II. Help for Women (Many of These Also Serve Men)
  III. Group Support for Those Who Are Unemployed
  IV. Directories of Career Counseling Services in Various Cities/
       States

If you are looking for a counselor in a particular state, check under all four categories, please. Even if a particular resource listed here is not what you are looking for, they may know of other places, not listed here.

The listing of a place here is NOT a recommendation of it. Many of these places are listed at their own request. On the other hand, we never **knowingly** list a place we know to be unhelpful.

If you have had a bad experience with any of them, you will help other readers by letting us know that (our address is in the rear of this book, on the UPDATE form). However, it is **crucial** that you read the preceding section two or three times, **before** you approach any of these sections. Often you could easily have discovered whether a particular counselor is competent or not, simply by asking the right questions. The just response to many a complaint is -- as the Scots would say -- "Ya dinna do your homework."

I. PLACES WHICH COUNSEL ANYONE

ARIZONA

College PLUS Career Connections, 1250 E. Baseline Rd., #104, Tempe, AZ 85283, 602-730-5246. Dr. Warren D. Robb, Director.

Lou Ann S. Dickson, Ph.D., 2131 E. Southern Ave., Tempe, AZ 85282, 602-820-1599.

Harper & Harris Career Consultants, 6101 So. Rural Rd., #128, Tempe, AZ 85283, 602-839-8284. Also at 7207 N. 7th St., Phoenix, AZ 85020, 602-870-0953.

Southwest Institute of Life Management, 11122 E. Gunshot Circle, Tucson, AZ 85749, 602-296-4764. Theodore Donald Risch, Director.

ARKANSAS

Donald McKinney, Ed.D., Career Counselor, Outplacement Center, Cossatot Vocational Technical School, PO Box 746, DeQueen, AR 71832, 501-584-4471.

CALIFORNIA

Judy Kaplan Baron Associates, 737 Pearl St., Suite 208-B, La Jolla, CA 92037, 619-456-1700. Judy Kaplan Baron, Director.

Beverly Brown, M.A., 1932 Overland Ave., #304, Los Angeles, CA 90025, 213-475-2503.

Branham & Associates, 1979 Greengrove St., Orange, CA 92665, 714-637-4694.

Career Development Institute, 690 Market St., Suite 404, San Francisco, CA 94104, 415-982-2636.

Career Development Institute, 425 West 7th, Suite 210C, Hanford, CA 93230, 209-584-2755. Gary F. Goddard, Ph.D.

Career Development Life Planning, 3585 Maple St., Suite 237, Ventura, CA 93003, 805-656-6220. Norma Zuber, M.S.C. & Associates.

Career Dimensions, Box 7402, Stockton, CA 95207, 209-473-8255. Fran Abbott.

Career Planners Personnel Service, 2667 Camino del Rio South, Suite 258, San Diego, CA 92108, 619-299-0455. Richard H. Peerson, Ph.D.

Career Renewal Services, 40 Museum Way, San Francisco, CA 94114, 415-626-2741. Kal Edwards, M.A., Director.

Careerpath Guidance, 106 Thorn St., San Diego, CA 92103, 619-296-1055. Carla Grindle, Licensed Counselor.

Constructive Leisure, Patsy B. Edwards, 511 N. La Cienega Blvd., Los Angeles, CA 90048, 213-652-7389.

Consultants Group (dba Pekras and Associates), 10080 Carroll Canyon Rd., Suite B, San Diego, CA 92131, 619-466-7500 or 549-3200. Philip J. Pekras, Director.

Consultants in Career Development, 2017 Palo Verde Ave., Suite 201B, Long Beach, CA 90815, 213-598-6412. Dean Porter, Senior Partner.

Criket Consultants, 502 Natoma St., PO Box 6191, Folsom, CA 95630, 916-985-3211.

Crystal-Barkley Corp., 29742 Ellendale Dr., Laguna Niguel, CA 92677, 714-495-9649. This is a branch of the John C. Crystal Center of NY. Linda E. Loomis, Associate. Full Life/Work Design Programs, including group workshops and individual consultation.

Cypress College, Career Planning Center, 9200 Valley View St., Cypress, CA 90630, 714-826-2220, Ext. 120.

Margaret L. Eadie, M.A., A.M.E.D., WHAT NEXT Education and Career Consultant, Box 725, Solana Beach, CA 92075, 619-436-1516.

El Chorro Employment Agency, 2040 Broad St., Suite B, San Luis Obispo, CA 93401, 805-544-4858. Progressive job referrals and placements. Periodic career counseling

seminars. Resume preparation. No registration fee. Other fees vary. Monday-Friday, 9 am-5 pm.

Experience Unlimited, Mr. Herman L. Leopold, Coordinator, Employment Development Dept., 1225 4th Ave., Oakland, CA 94606, 415-464-1259/464-0659.

Beverly Neuer Feldman, Ed.D., President of Career Tech Associates, 2656 Aberdeen Ave., Los Angeles, CA 90027, 213-665-7007.

Mary Alice Floyd, M.A., Counselor/ Consultant, 3233 Lucinda Lane, Santa Barbara, CA 93105, 805-687-5462.

G. David Grey & Associates, Imperial Bank Tower, 701 "B" St., Suite 1300, San Diego, CA 92101, 619-239-2992.

Judith Grutter, MS, NCCC, Career Development Consultant, along with J. Ted Vidmar, III, M.D. & Associates, 1499 Huntington Dr., #402, South Pasadena, CA 91030, 818-441-1888.

Arthur M. Hugon, 9432 Gerald Ave., Sepulveda, CA 91343, 818-893-0098.

Life/Career Development, 4035 El Macero Dr., Davis, CA 95616, 916-758-1439. Russell A. Bruch, Director, Career consultant.

Life's Decisions, 2740 Fulton Ave., #114, Sacramento, CA 95821, 916-481-1246. Joan E. Belshin, M.S.

National University Career Center, 4007 Camino Del Rio S., San Diego, CA 92108, 619-563-7250.

New Ways to Work, 149 Ninth St., San Francisco, CA 94103, 415-552-1000. Monday-Friday, 10 am-4 pm. Counseling on negotiating part-time and job-shared positions.

Project J.O.Y. (Job Opportunities for Youth), East Oakland Youth Development Center, 8200 E. 14th St., Oakland, CA 94621, 415-569-8088. Al Auletta, Director.

Marion Bass Stevens, Ph.D., Career & Employment Counseling, 747 Mulberry Lane, Davis, CA 95616, 916-756-0672.

Stoodley & Associates, 15750 Winchester Blvd., #104, Los Gatos, CA 95030, 408-354-2259 and 408-448-0123. Martha Stoodley, M.S., M.F.C.C., President.

Transitions, 171 N. Van Ness, Fresno, CA 93701, 209-233-7250. Margot E. Tepperman, L.C.S.W.

Turning Point Career Center, University YWCA, 2600 Bancroft Way, Berkeley, CA 94704, 415-848-6370, Libby Granett, M.S., Director.

UCLA Extension Advisory Service, 10995 Le Conte Ave., Rm. 114, Los Angeles, CA 90024, 213-206-6201. Monday-Friday, 9 am-5 pm. College sponsored office. Educational and career advising, continuing education courses. No fees.

Paul Zolner, M.S., M.F.C.C., Counseling Consultant, 17341 Irvine Blvd., Suite 109, Tustin, CA 92680, 714-731-7413. Career, educational & personal counseling. First half-hour free consultation.

COLORADO

Career Resource Services, 425 W. Mulberry, Suite 101, Ft. Collins, CO 80521, 303-484-9810. In the Boulder area, contact Rhoney DuQuesne, 303-449-1124.

Colorado Growth Center, Inc., P.O. Box 472, Conifer, CO 80433, 303-831-9578. Art Smith, Life/Work Development Facilitator.

Samuel Kirk and Associates, Central Office, 1418 S. Race, Denver, CO 80210, 303-722-0717.

CONNECTICUT

Accord Consultants, Inc., The Exchange, Suite 305, 270 Farmington Ave., Farmington, CT 06032, 203-674-9654. J. Tod Gerardo, President and Director.

Career-Life Alternatives, 100 Whitney Ave., New Haven, CT 06510, 203-865-7377. Anita Perlman.

Career Services, 94 Rambling Rd., Vernon, CT 06066, 203-871-7832. Jim Cohen, Ph.D., President.

Kathleen Gaughran, 141 Durham Rd., Suite 24, Madison, CT 06443, 203-245-1755.

Gillespie Associates, 9 Berkeley St., Norwalk, CT 06850, 203-838-8464.

Ilise Gold Associates, Career and Life Planning Specialists, 7 Black Birch Rd., Westport, CT 06880, 203-222-9223.

People Management, Inc., 10 Station St., Simsbury, CT 06070, 203-651-3581. Arthur F. Miller, Jr., Chairman.

Regional Counseling Center of Southeastern Connecticut, 76 Federal St., New London, CT 06320, 203-442-4556. Margaret S. Atherton, Director.

John H. Wiedenheft, M.A., Career Development, 38 Barker St., Hartford, CT 06114, 203-527-5523.

DELAWARE

Life/Career Planning, 2413 Brickton Rd., Wilmington, DE 19803, 302-478-7186. Minh-Nhat Tran, Consultant.

DISTRICT OF COLUMBIA

Community Vocational Counseling Service, The George Washington University Counseling Center, 718 21st St. NW, Washington, DC 20052, 202-994-6550 or 944-4860. Robert J. Wilson, Coordinator.

Comptex Associates, Inc., PO Box 6745, Washington, DC 20020, 301-599-9222. Eugene Williams, Sr., Executive Vice President.

FLORIDA

The Career and Personal Counseling Center, Eckerd College, Box 12560, St. Petersburg, FL 33733, 813-867-1166, ext. 356. John R. Sims.

Center for Career Decisions, Atrium Plaza Suite 300, 1515 N. Federal Hwy., Boca Raton, FL 33432, 305-392-4550. Individual/group counseling. Corporate outplacement. Seminars, workshops.

CW resources, 2161 Palm Beach Lakes Blvd., West Palm Beach, FL 33409, 305-689-5009. Toby G. Chabon, M.Ed., N.C.C.C., President. A career and human resources development company.

Ellen O. Jonassen, Ph.D., 1105 S. Ft. Harrison Ave., Clearwater, FL 34616, 813-441-2629.

Life Designs, Inc., 7860 SW 55th Ave. #A, South Miami, FL 33143, 305-665-3212 or 665-9393. Dulce Muccio and Deborah Tyson, co-founders.

Ruth A. Peters, Ph.D., Cypress View Professional Center, 2424 Enterprise Rd., Suite A, Clearwater, FL 34623, 813-797-2512.

Psychological Counseling and Consulting, 4001 W. Newberry Rd., Suite 4-B, Gainesville, FL 32607, 904-371-3082. E.L. Tolbert, Director.

Career Planning Center of Grace United Methodist Church, 458 Ponce de Leon Ave., Atlanta, GA 30308. Mark Canfield, Director.

Career Planning Group, 5262 Walker Rd., Stone Mountain, GA 30088, 404-469-3462. Mark Satterfield, Director.

Career Pursuit, P.O. Box 2313, Decatur, GA 30031-2313, 404-296-1722. Estelle Greene, Career and Management Development Specialist.

Charles W. Cates, Ph.D., 1435 N. Decatur Rd., Atlanta, GA 30306, 404-373-0336.

Judith L. Cole, M.Ed., Lenox Towers, 3390 Peachtree Rd., Atlanta, GA 30326, 404-233-0946.

Educational Information and Referral Service, Lenox Square Professional Concourse, 3393 Peachtree Rd. NE, Atlanta, GA 30326, 404-233-7497. Barbara Buchanan, Executive Director.

ILLINOIS

Abbot Services, 6057 W. Eddy St., Chicago, IL 60634, 312-545-5892. Richard Gans, Career Counselor.

Career Directions, 5005 Newport Dr., Suite 501, Rolling Meadows, IL 60008, 312-870-1290. Peggy Simonsen, Director.

Career Path, 3033 Ogden Ave., Suite 203, Lisle, IL 60532, 312-369-3390. Hours by appt. Donna Sandberg, Counselor.

Career Resources, Inc., 1426 Grant Rd, Northbrook, IL 60062, 312-272-1079.

Career Workshops, 5431 W. Roscoe St., Chicago, IL 60641, 312-282-6859. Patricia Dietze.

David P. Helfand, Ed.D., 250 Ridge, Evanston, IL 60202, 312-328-2787.

Arlene S. Hirsch, M.A., 541 W. Arlington Place, Chicago, IL 60614, 312-528-2859.

Lansky Career Consultants, 676 N. St. Clair #1860, Chicago, IL 60611, 312-642-5738. Individual consultation and workshops. Sliding scale available.

Mark Newman & Associates, Educational & Career Services, 500 Davis St., Suite 600, Evanston, IL 60201, 312-475-1154.

The Professional Career Counselors & Consultants Network (PCCN), 307 N. Michigan #2001, Chicago, IL 60601, 312-332-2760. For $5, PCCN will send you a directory of their members who offer consulting to the public. Jack Chapman, President.

Jane Shuman, Career Management Consultant, 122 Circle Dr., Springfield, IL 62703, 217-529-7220.

INDIANA

Ball State University, Career Services, Muncie, IN 47306, 317-285-5634 or 285-1522. Monday-Friday, 8 am-5 pm.

Career Consultants, 107 N. Pennsylvania St., Suite 404, Indianapolis, IN 46204, 317-639-5601. Mike Kenney, Senior Partner.

Career & Life Transition, 6116 N. Delaware St., Indianapolis, IN 46220, 317-873-6718. Office hours 8:30 am-5 pm, Monday thru Friday. William R. Lesch, President.

John D. King & Associates, Career Counseling and Consulting, 103 N. College, Suite 207, Bloomington, IN 47401, 812-332-3888.

IOWA

Adult Career Change Center, Drake University, Memorial Hall, 26th and University Ave., Des Moines, IA 50311, 515-271-2916.

KENTUCKY

Ronniger Associates, Inc., 1st Trust Centre, 200 S. 5th St., Louisville, KY 40202, 502-583-4115.

LOUISIANA

Career Planning and Assessment Center, Metroplitan College, University of New Orleans, New Orleans, LA 70148, 504-286-7100.

MARYLAND

Careerscope, Inc., Suite 219, Harper's Choice Village Center, 5485 Harper's Farm Rd., Columbia, MD 21044, 301-992-5042/ 596-1866. Ann Sim, Executive Director.

Maryland New Directions, Inc., 12 E. 25th St., Baltimore, MD 21218, 301-235-8800. Marjorie Rosensweig, Director.

Prince George's Community College, Career Assessment and Planning Center, 301 Largo Rd., Largo, MD 20772, 301-322-0886. David C. Borchard, Director.

D. Evan Wallick Associates, 1522 Farlow Ave., Crofton, MD 21114, 301-261-6945. David E. Wallick, National Certified Counselor.

MASSACHUSETTS

Alewife Counseling Associates, 721 R. Pleasant St., Belmont, MA 02178, 617-484-8517. Jane Hynes and John Hamilton. Available evenings and weekends. Initial interview without charge.

Back Bay Resume, 198 Marlborough St., Boston, MA 02116, 617-266-4995. Don Gervich, Ed.D. Career counseling and resume preparation, since 1980.

Career Development Consultant, Ellen J. Wallach, 8 Sherburne Rd., Lexington, MA 02173, 617-862-0997.

Career Directions Inc., 10 Kearney Rd., Needham, MA 02194, 617-449-3336. David Eysmann, Director.

Career Resource Center, Worcester YWCA, 1 Salem Square, Worcester, MA 01608, 617-791-3181. Individual/group counseling, vocational testing, job placement, etc. Fees based on ability to pay. Day and evening hours by appointment.

Center for Career Development & Ministry, 70 Chase St., Newton Centre, MA 02159. Joseph Neville, Associate Director.

Jewish Vocational Services, Workers 55+/ Challenge Program, 11 Hayward Street, North Quincy, MA 02171. This is a nonprofit, nonsectarian agency that specializes in job training, counseling, workshops, and placement, for workers who are over age 55. No fees.

Wynne W. Miller, 785 Centre St., Newton, MA 02158-2599, 617-527-4848. Career counseling oriented toward finding meaning and mission in life; practical, too.

Murray Associates, 555 Washington St., Wellesley, MA 02181, 617-235-8896. Robert Murray, Ed.D., Licensed Psychologist.

New Beginnings Career Center, Assabet Center for Continuing Education, Fitchburg St., Marlborough, MA 01752. Susan Sock, Director, Career Services.

Carl Joseph Schneider, 32 Lincoln Parkway, Somerville, MA 02143, 617-629-2015.

Suit Yourself, 115 Shade St., Lexington, MA 02173, 617-862-6006 or 617-358-4567. Debra Spencer.

MICHIGAN

Career Options, The 511 Bldg., 511 Monroe, Kalamazoo, MI 49007, 616-382-3993.

Career Technologies, 915 N. Sherman, Bay City, MI 48708, 517-892-3999. Karen Thayer, Career Consultant.

Oakland University, Continuum Center for Adult Counseling and Leadership Training, Rochester, MI 48063, 313-370-3033. Personal, educational and career counseling, continuing education courses.

Thibaudeaux Personnel of Grand Rapids, 820 Commerce Bldg., Grand Rapids, MI 49503, 616-459-8396. Donald D. Fink, Ed.D., Director of Career Counseling.

MINNESOTA

Assessment & Vocational Services, Inc., 6135 Kellogg Ave., S., Suite 224, Edina, MN 55424, 612-922-4397. Robert D. Haskin, Director. Career/life planning, counseling.

Career Dynamics, Inc., 8400 Normandale Lake Blvd., Bloomington, MN 55437, 612-921-2378. Joan Strewler, Psychologist.

Leider, Inc., 7101 York Ave. S., Minneapolis, MN 55435, 612-921-3334. Richard J. Leider, Executive & Professional Career Consultant.

MISSOURI

Career Planning and Placement Center, Adult Evening Program, 110 Noyes Hall, University of Missouri, Columbia, MO 65211, 314-882-6803.

NEBRASKA

Career Assessment Center, Central Community College, Hastings Campus, Hastings, NE 68901, 402-461-2456.

Clemm C. Kessler III, Kessler, Kennedy & Associates, Executive Plaza, 6818 Grover St., Omaha, NE 68106, 402-397-9558.

NEW JERSEY

Adult Advisory Services, Kean College of New Jersey, Administration Bldg., Union, NJ 07083, 201-527-2210. Monday-Friday, 9 am-4:30 pm. College sponsored. Educational and career counseling. No registration fee. Other fees vary.

Arista Concepts Career Development Service, 41 Wittmer Ct., PO Box 2436, Princeton, NJ 08543, 609-921-0308. Kera Greene, M.Ed.

Loree Collins, 3 Beechwood Rd., Summit, NJ 07901, 201-273-9219.

Sandra Grundfest, Ed.D., Princeton Professional Park, 601 Ewing St., Suite C-1, Princeton, NJ 08540, 609-921-8401. Career and educational counseling. Job search strategies.

Minsuk, Macklin, Stein & Associates, 14 Washington Rd., Princeton Junction, NJ 08550, 609-275-5800.

W.L. Nikel & Associates, Career Development and Outplacement, 28 Harper Terrace, Cedar Grove, NJ 07009, 201-575-5700. William L. Nikel, M.B.A., Founder.

Pitman Counseling Center, Broadway & Wildwood Ave., Pitman, NJ 08071, 609-589-1050. Betsy McCalla-Wriggins, counselor.

NEW YORK

The John C. Crystal Center, 111 E. 31st St., New York, NY 10016, 212-889-8500. Nella G. Barkley is President of this firm which was founded by the late John Crystal and is based on his unique approach to life/work planning and job-hunting. The center is offering programs in New York and elsewhere in the country. There is also a branch in California: 29742 Ellendale Dr., Laguna Niguel, CA 92677, 714-495-9649. Linda E. Loomis, Associate.

Career Services Center, Long Island University, C.W. Post Campus, Brookville, NY 11548, 516-299-2251. Mince Kohler, Director.

David J. Giber, Ph.D., Career Counselor, 200 East 90th St., New York, NY 10128, 212-996-5365.

Miriam J. Mennin, M.A., National Certified Career Counselor, 33 Andrea Lane, Scarsdale, NY 10583, 914-725-2445, 914-725-5501.

Network Career Resumes, 60 E. 42nd St., Suite 505, New York, NY 10165, 212-687-2411. John Aigner, Counselor.

NORTH CAROLINA

Thomas S. Baldwin, Ph.D., Licensed Practicing Psychologist, 87 S. Elliott Rd., Suite 200, Chapel Hill, NC 27514, 919-929-0496.

Focus, Inc., 211 Six Forks Rd., Suite 203, Raleigh, NC 27609, 919-833-5529..

Joyce Richman & Associates, Ltd., 2911 Shady Lawn Dr., Greensboro, NC 27408, 919-288-1799.

OHIO

Adult Resource Center, The University of Akron, Buckingham Center for Continuing Education, Akron, OH 44325, 216-375-7448. Also has sites at: Akron-Summit County Public Library, 55 S. Main St., Akron, OH.

Career Resources, Third National Bank Bldg., 32 N. Main St., Suite 1245, Dayton, OH 45402, 513-223-8000.

Cuyahoga County Public Library-InfoPLACE (Career, Education & Community Information Services), 5225 Library Lane, Maple Heights, OH 44137-1291, 216-475-2225. Joan Rawlings, Manager; Kathie FitzSimons, Career/Education Consultant; Kathleen Savage, InfoPLACE Librarian. Community information and referral.

J & K Associates, 539J Forest Park Ct., Dayton, OH 45405, 513-274-3630. Pat Kenney, Ph.D., President.

Kahnweiler Associates, Chiquita Center, Suite 1500, 250 E. Fifth St., Cincinnati, OH 45202. They specialize in counseling "the trailing spouse" in dual career couples, where one spouse has been relocated to another section of the country.

New Career, 931 Chelsea Dr., Dover, OH 44622, 216-343-8464. Marshall Karp, M.A., N.C.C., L.P.C., Owner.

Pathfinders, A Division of Special Education, 3497 E. Livingston Ave., Columbus, OH 43227, 614-231-4088. Y. Hayon, Ph. D., Director.

Pyramid, Inc., 1642 Cleveland Ave., NW, Canton, OH 44703, 216-453-3767.

OREGON

CareerMakers, 1336 SW Bertha, Portland, OR 97219, 503-244-1055. Pam Gross, Executive Director.

Joseph A. Dubay, 1012 SW King Ave., Portland, OR 97205, 503-224-3600.

PENNSYLVANIA

Career Management Consultants, Inc., 4349 Linglestown Rd., Harrisburg, PA 17112, 717-657-9668. Louis Persico, Career Consultant.

Options, Inc., 215 S. Broad St., Philadelphia, PA 19107, 215-735-2202. Marcia P. Kleiman, Director.

Priority Two, Rm. 208, Pittsburgh National Bank Bldg., Beaver & Blackburn Rds., Sewickley, PA 15143, 412-741-8368.

David C. Rich, United Ministries in Higher Education, Pennsylvania Commission, 13 Victoria Way, Camp Hill, PA 17011. David C. Rich, Director.

Stepping Stones, Bucks County Community College, Newtown, PA 18940, 215-968-8188. Barbra Bianco, Coordinator.

RHODE ISLAND

Options, Inc., 245 Waterman St., Providence, RI 02906, 401-331-1727. Barbara Van Sciver, President.

SOUTH DAKOTA

Career Concepts, Centennial Square, 2100 S. 7th St., Suite 255, Rapid City, SD 57701, 605-394-5783. Melvin M. Tuggle, Jr., President.

TENNESSEE

Career Resources, 2323 Hillsboro Rd., Suite 300, Nashville, TN 37212, 615-297-0404. Jane C. Hardy, President.

Mid-South Career Development Center, PO Box 120815, Nashville, TN 37212, 615-327-9572. W. Scott Root, President/Counselor.

Secretarial Office Services, 314 N. White St., Athens, TN 37303, 615-745-4513.

TEXAS

Career Action Associates, First Interstate Bank Plaza, Suite 512, 12655 N. Central Expressway, Dallas, TX 75243, 214-392-7337. Rebecca Hayes, Licensed Professional Counselor.

Catalyst Career Consultants, 2520 Longview, Suite 314, Austin, TX 78701, 512-474-7773. Joia Jitahidi, Senior Consultant.

Richard S. Citrin, Ph.D., Psychologist, Iatreia Institute, 1152 Country Club Ln., Ft. Worth, TX 76112, 817-654-9600. Monthly workshops, individual and group counseling, consultation, fees vary.

Creative Careers, 34 Cromwell Dr., San Antonio, TX 78201, 512-735-7287. Jon Patrick Bourg.

East Texas State University at Texarkana, Career Planning & Placement Center, 2600 N. Robison Rd., Texarkana, TX 75501, 214-838-6514. Lila Bowden, Career & Placement Counselor.

Ministry of Counseling and Enrichment, 1333 N. 2nd St., Abilene, TX 79601, 915-675-8131. Mary Stedham, Director.

New Life Institute, Box 1666, Austin, TX 78767, 512-469-9447. Bob Breihan, Director.

Professional Counseling Service, 2103 S. Clear Creek Rd., Killeen, TX 76542, 817-526-7272. Colleen Geehan, CSW, Director, Career Decisions.

San Antonio Psychological Services, 4545 Centerview Dr., Suite 120, San Antonio, TX 78228, 512-737-2039.

UTAH

University of Utah, Center for Adult Learning and Career Change, 1173 Annex Bldg., Salt Lake City, UT 84112, 801-581-3228.

VERMONT

Career Crossroads, 4 High St., Apt. 413, Brattleboro, VT 05301, 802-257-7497.

VIRGINIA

Hollins College, Career Counseling Center, Roanoke, VA 24020, 703-362-6364. Peggy Ann Neumann, Director.

Life Management Services, Inc., 6825
Redmond Dr., McLean, VA 22101, 703-356-
2630. Hal and Marilyn Shook, President
and Vice President.

Psychological Consultants, Inc., 6724
Patterson Ave., Richmond, VA 23226, 804-
288-4125.

Swenholt Associates, Inc., 6308 Crosswoods
Circle, Falls Church, VA 22044, 703-256-
2383. Frankie P. Swenholt, President.

WASHINGTON

**The Individual Development Center, Inc.
(I.D. Center),** 1020 E. John, Seattle, WA
98102, 206-329-0600. Mary Lou Hunt,
N.C.C., President; 8404 27th St. W.,
Tacoma, WA 98466, 206-565-8818.
Ruthann Reim, N.C.C., Director, Tacoma.

WISCONSIN

David Swanson, Career Seminars and
Workshops, Inc., 2300 N. Mayfair Rd.,
Suite 805, Milwaukee, WI 53226, 414-259-
0265.

Making Alternative Plans, Career Counseling for Career Changers, Alverno College,
3401 S. 39th St., Milwaukee, WI 53215,
414-382-6010.

WYOMING

National Education Service Center, P.O.
Box 1279, Riverton, WY 82501-1279, 307-
856-0170.

University of Wyoming, Counseling &
Career Development Center, PO Box 3708,
Laramie, WY 82071, 307-766-2187. Dr. Pat
McGinley.

CANADA

Chaulk & Associates, 425 1st SW, Suite
2603, Calgary, Alberta, T2P 3L8 Canada,
403-269-5456. Wayne Chaulk, Career
Transition Consultant.

Gilmore & Associates, Renaissance Plaza,
150 Bloor St. W., Suite 340, Toronto,
Ontario, M5S 2X9 Canada, 416-926-1944.
Blake Gilmore, Director.

Stevenson Kellogg Ernst & Whinney, 90
Sparks St., 10th Fl., Ottawa, Ontario, K1P
5T8 Canada, 613-238-6512. Kenneth Des
Roches, Principal.

Barbara Teeple, 1002 Knottwood Rd., E.,
Edmonton, Alberta, T6K 3R5, Canada, 403-
463-7759.

YMCA Career Planning & Development, 15
Breadalbane St., Toronto, Ontario, M4Y
2V5 Canada, 416-922-7765 or 922-5027.
Franz Schmidt, General Manager.

FOREIGN

Robert J. Bisdee & Associates, 22 Allenby
Ave., Malvern E., Victoria, Australia 3145,
613-025-4716. Dr. Bob Bisdee, Director.

Centre for WorkLife Counselling, P.O. Box
407, Spit Junction, Australia 2088, 02-969-
4548. Paul Stevens, Director.

Raadgevend Bureau Claessens, Outplace-
ment/Verandering Van Werkkring,
Beneluxlaan 35, 3526 KK UTRECHT,
Holland, 030-886530. Frans Claessens.

N.V. Claessens S.A., Outplacement, Avenue
Louise 479B 54, 1050 Brussels, Belgium, 02
6477590. Marc Embo.

II. HELP FOR WOMEN
(MANY OF THESE ALSO SERVE MEN)

Resource centers for women are springing up all over the country, faster than
we can record them. We are listing here **only a sampling** of same. If you have a
favorite, not listed here, send us the pertinent information - - in format similar to
the next pages. We will then ask them some intelligent questions about their fa-
miliarity with this book, and then we'll list it in the next edition. Don't, however, bother to send us college services which are available only to the students
and alumnae of that college. We don't list places that thus restrict their clientele.
If, inadvertently, we have already listed any such place here that is thus restricted,
please let us know, and we'll gently remove it from the next edition. Incidentally,
the centers which are listed here will know (in all probability) what other centers

or resources there are in your geographical area. Also, try your telephone book's Yellow Pages: "Women's Organizations and Services" or "Vocational Consultants".

In all of this you will remember, won't you, our earlier description (page 313) of all career counseling professionals, as falling into one of three groups: (1) Sincere and skilled; (2) Sincere but inept; (3) Insincere and inept? Well, dear friend, groups or organizations or centers which have been organized specifically to help women job-hunters or career-changers are not -- by that act -- made immune to the above distinctions. Think about it, before you agree to put your vocational life into somebody else's hands. Remember, the numbers game (chapter 2), even if it is expressed in beautifully nonsexist language, is still the numbers game.

RESOURCES FOR WOMEN

ALABAMA

Enterprise State Junior College, Women's Center, Career Development Center, Box 1300, Enterprise, AL 36331, 205-347-7881 or 5431. Monday-Friday, 8 am-4:30 pm.

ARIZONA

University of Arizona, Student Counseling Service, Old Main, Tucson, AZ 85721, 602-626-2316. Monday-Friday, 8 am-noon and 1-5 pm; Tuesday and Wednesday, 5 pm-7 pm. Official college office. Educational and career counseling and personal and marital counseling.

CALIFORNIA

Alumnae Resources, 660 Mission St., Suite 201, San Francisco, CA 94105, 415-546-7220. Emphasis on Liberal Arts graduates. Offers workshops, seminars, individual counseling, and special events. Fees vary. Appointments necessary. Orientation Fridays at noon, free.

Career Planning Center/Business Action Center, 1623 S. La Cienega Blvd., Los Angeles, CA 90035, 213-273-6633. Independent, nonprofit agency. Offers free job board (3,000 listings a month). Wednesday & Thursday, 1 pm-4 pm. Certified career counselor, career assessment, various career workshops, the Annual Women's Employment Options Conference and a vocational library. Men welcome.

Cypress College, Career Planning Center, 9200 Valley View St., Cypress, CA 90630, 714-826-2220, Ext. 221. Monday-Friday, 8 am-4:30 pm. Some evening hours are also available. Official college office. Educational and career counseling. No fees.

Carol March Associates, 2107 Van Ness Ave., Suite 402, San Francisco, CA 94109, 415-775-5588. Individual career counseling, groups and workshops.

Susan W. Miller, M.A., 360 N. Bedford, Suite 219, Beverly Hills, CA 90210, 213-837-7768. Career Counselor, Educational Consultant, private practice. Career counseling for individuals using a structured, action-oriented approach.

Resource Center for Women, 445 Sherman Ave., Palo Alto, CA 94306, 415-324-1710. Monday, Wednesday, Friday, 9 am-5 pm; Tuesday, 9 am-9 pm; Thursday, 11 am-9 pm. Independent, nonprofit agency. Career counseling, Resource library; career workshops and job listings. Fees.

Sacramento Women's Center, Women's Employment Services and Training, 2224 "J" St., Sacramento, CA 95816, 916-441-4207. Receives funding from the Job Training Partnership Act to help low-income women and single parents re-entered the job market. Also, primary resource in Sacramento for women interested in nontraditional employment.

San Jose State University, Re-Entry Advisory Program, Adm. 201, San Jose, CA 95192. Monday-Friday, 9 am-5 pm; Evening appointments by arrangement. Official college program. Educational and career counseling, referral to other services. No fees.

Caroline Voorsanger, Career Counselor for Women, 2000 Broadway, Suite 1108, San Francisco, CA 94115, 415-567-0890. Career counseling, assistance with skills assessment and focusing.

Women at Work, 78 N. Marengo Ave., Pasadena, CA 91101, 818-796-6870. A career and job resource center. Includes workshops and individual counseling. Fees vary.

The Women's Opportunities Center, University of California Extension, P.O. Box AZ, Irvine, CA 92716.

YWCA Center for Career Development, 375 S. Third St., San Jose, CA 95112, 408-295-4011. Patti Wilson, Director

COLORADO

Arapahoe Community College, Career Resource Center, 5900 S. Santa Fe Dr., Littleton, CO 80120, 303-794-1550. Monday-Friday, 8 am-5 pm. Evening appointments are available. Educational, career, and personal counseling, computer based

guidance systems including SIGI, Discover and COCIS; variety of workshops and seminars; job search skills; community resources files; support groups; library; job referral and placement.

Career Development Center, 1650 Washington St., Denver, CO 80203, 303-861-7254. Monday-Friday, 9 am-5 pm; evening services available. Independent nonprofit agency. A comprehensive combination of group and individual sessions for career counseling. Fees vary.

Women's Center, Red Rocks Community College, 12600 W. 6th Ave., Golden, CO 80401, 303-988-6160, ext. 213. Free career planning, resume help, job matching, brown bag lunches. Small fee for workshops, seminars.

Women's Resource Agency, 1011 N. Weber St., #C, Colorado Springs, CO 80903, 303-471-3170. Monday-Friday, 8 am-5 pm.

CONNECTICUT

Fairfield University, Fairfield Adult Career & Educational Services (FACES), North Benson Rd., Julie Hall, Fairfield, CT 06430, 203-255-5411. Monday-Friday, 9 am-4 pm.

Vocational and Academic Counseling for Adults (VOCA), 115 Berrian Rd., Stamford, CT 06905, 203-329-1955. Monday-Friday 9 am-5 pm; weekends and evenings by arrangement.

DELAWARE

The Women's Center, YWCA of New Castle County, 908 King St., Wilmington, DE 19801, 302-658-7161. Monday-Friday, 9 am-5 pm. Other hours by appointment. Career development services, individual counseling, support group, referrals, skills improvement workshops. Nominal fees, scholarships available.

DISTRICT OF COLUMBIA

George Washington University, Continuing Education for Women, 801 22nd St. NW, Suite T409, Washington, DC 20052, 202-994-5762, 994-8164, 994-8165. Monday-Friday, 9 am-5:30 pm. College sponsored. Educational and career counseling, continuing education courses, certificate programs. Fees vary.

FLORIDA

Center for Continuing Education for Women, Valencia Community College North Center, 1010 N. Orlando Ave., Winter Park, FL 32789, 305-628-1976. Monday-Friday, 9 am-5 pm. Educational and career counseling, continuing education courses, personality and vocational testing.

Centre for Women, 305 S. Hyde Park Ave., Tampa, FL 33606, 813-251-8437. Maeve Reddin, Executive Director. The Centre offers job series classes, assessment and counseling, a referral system, Job Club. Registration fee of $25.

Challenge: The Displaced Homemaker, Florida Community College at Jacksonville, 101 W. State St., Rm. 3070, Jacksonville, FL 32202, 904-633-8316. Mimi S. Hull, Program Manager. Program geared specifically to the needs of the displaced homemaker - - support, values clarification, vocational testing, goal setting, etc.

Crossroads, Palm Beach Jr. College, 4200 Congress Ave., Lake Worth, FL 33461, 305-433-5995. Free, on-going program to teach re-entry skills, to build confidence and enhance economic independence. Pat Jablonski, Program Manager.

FACE Learning Center, Inc., 12945 Seminole Blvd., Bldg. II, Suite 8, Largo, FL 34648, 813-585-8155 or 586-1110. Monday-Friday, 9 am-5 pm, and by appointment.

Stetson University Counseling Center, Campus Box 8365, North Woodland Blvd., De Land, FL 32720, 904-734-4121, Ext. 215. Monday-Friday, 8:30 am-4:30 pm.

ILLINOIS

Applied Potential, Box 585, Highland Park, IL 60035, 312-234-2130. Monday-Friday, 9 am-5 pm; evenings and Saturdays by arrangement. Nonprofit educational corporation. Professional counselors. Educational, career, and personal counseling. No registration fee. Other fees vary.

Displaced Homemakers Program, Lincoln Land Community College, Shepherd Rd., Springfield, IL 62708, 217-786-2335. Educational and career counseling, job referral information. No fees.

Harper College Community Counseling Center, Palatine, IL 60067, 312-397-3000. Monday-Thursday, 8:30 am-4:30 pm and 6-10 pm; Friday, 8:30 am-4:30 pm. College sponsored office. Educational and career counseling. No registration fee. Other fees vary.

Jean Davis, Career Counseling, 1405 Elmwood Ave., Evanston, IL 60201, 312-492-1002. Offers career assessment/design, resume and marketing strategies, job interview preparation, individual consultation and workshops.

Midwest Women's Center, 53 W. Jackson Blvd., Suite 1015, Chicago, IL 60604, 312-922-8530. Offers individual counseling, referrals, workshops, job-support groups, apprenticeship and skills training programs. The Center also has an extensive career library. Call for hours and fees.

Moraine Valley Community College, Career Planning and Placement, and Adult Centers, 10900 S. 88th Ave., Palos Hills, IL 60465, 312-974-4300. Monday-Thursday, 9 am-9 pm; Friday 9 am-4:30 pm. Official college office, fees vary.

Northwestern Illinois Career Guidance Center, 1515 S. 4th St., Dekalb, IL 60115, 815-758-7431. Monday-Friday, 8 am-4 pm. John Cassani, Director.

University of Illinois Urbana-Champaign, Office for Women's Resources and Services, 346 Student Services, 610 E. John St., Champaign, IL 61820, 217-333-3137. Monday-Friday, 8 am-5 pm. Official college office. Educational and career counseling. No fees.

INDIANA

Ball State University, Career Services, Muncie, IN 47306, 317-285-5634 and 285-1522. Monday-Friday, 8 am-5 pm.

Fort Wayne Women's Bureau, Inc., 203 W. Wayne St., Fort Wayne, IN 46802, 219-424-7977/426-0023. Peer counseling, Monday-Friday, 10 am-2 pm. Not-for-profit agency. Career counseling, job search skills training, job opportunity book.

Indiana University, Continuing Education for Women, Owen Hall 201, Bloomington, IN 47405, 812-335-0225. Monday-Friday, 8 am-5 pm. Official college office. Educational and career counseling, continuing education courses. Fees vary.

YWCA of St. Joseph County, 802 N. Lafayette Blvd., South Bend, IN 46601, 219-233-9491. Monday-Friday, 8 am-5 pm. Services include: Women's Shelter, Residence, programs for low income women for development of emotional and financial self-sufficiency.

IOWA

Adult Career Change Center, Drake University, 26th and University, Des Moines, IA 50311, 515-271-2916. Monday-Friday, 8 am-4:30 pm, Tuesday 8 am-8 pm. For the greater community. Workshops, information, referral, support services or issues related to career/life planning.

The University of Iowa, Business and Liberal Arts Placement/Career Information Services, IMU, Iowa City, IA 52242, 319-335-3201. Monday-Friday, 8 am-6:30 pm. Career planning and placement assistance, Career Information Center, employer literature, seminars, alumni career services. Small fee for job placement services.

KANSAS

University of Kansas, Adult Life Resource Center, Division of Continuing Education, Continuing Education Bldg., Lawrence, KS 66045, 913-864-4794 or 800-532-6772 (toll free in Kansas). Monday-Friday, 8 am-noon and 1-5 pm. College sponsored. Educational, personal, and career counseling and continuing education. No fee program for displaced homemakers. Other fees vary.

MAINE

The Women's Career Center, Westbrook College, 716 Stevens Ave., Portland, ME 04103, 207-797-7261. Monday-Friday mornings; and by appointment. Independent nonprofit organization. Educational and career counseling, testing and related workshops.

MARYLAND

College of Notre Dame of Maryland, Continuing Education Center, 4701 N. Charles St., Baltimore, MD 21210, 301-435-0100. Monday-Friday, 8:30 am-4:30 pm. Career and educational counseling for adults considering returning to college. Credit courses for adults both daytime and weekends. Fees vary.

Maryland New Directions, Inc., 2517 N. Charles St., Baltimore, MD 21218, 301-235-8800. Monday-Friday, 9 am-5 pm. Offers career counseling, workshops and seminars on employment and life planning issues; resume writing assistance; job referral and information, and programs for special populations.

Goucher College, Goucher Center for Continuing Studies, Towson, Baltimore, MD 21204, 301-337-6200. Monday-Friday, 9 am-4:30 pm. College sponsored. Counseling for adults considering a return to school. Non-credit and credit courses for adults. Referrals for career and volunteer work.

MASSACHUSETTS

Career Resource Center, YWCA, 1 Salem Square, Worcester, MA 01608, 617-791-3181. Monday-Friday, 8:30 am-4:30 pm; evenings by appointment. Fees vary.

Radcliffe Career Services, 77 Brattle St., Cambridge MA 02138. Fee for counseling session. Monday-Friday, 9 am-5 pm, evenings by appointment. Open to general public as well as Harvard and Radcliffe students and alumnae. Fees vary.

Women's Educational & Industrial Union, Career Services, 356 Boylston St., Boston, MA 02116, 617-536-5657. Monday, Tuesday & Friday, 9 am-5 pm; Wednesday, 11 am-6:30 pm; Thursday 9 am-7:30 pm. Independent nonprofit agency. Career counseling, employment advising and referral. Counseling fee is $25.00. Employment advising and referral fees vary.

MICHIGAN

Every Woman's Place, 1706 Peck St., Muskegon, MI 49442, 616-726-4493. Monday-Friday, 9 am-5 pm.

Macomb Community College, Professional and Continuing Education, 14500 Twelve Mile Rd., K-332, Warren, MI 48093, 313-445-7417. Monday-Friday, 8:30 am-5 pm.

Michigan Technological University, Division of Education and Public Services, Youth Programs, Rm. 208 Academic Offices Bldg., Houghton, MI 49931, 906-487-2219. Monday-Friday, 8 am-5 pm. Official College Office. Three one-week Women in Engineering Workshops and over 45 different, one-week Summer Youth Program career exploration sessions. Career education and counseling.

C.S. Mott Community College, Guidance Services and Counseling Division, 1401 E. Court St., Flint, MI 48503, 313-762-0356. Monday-Thursday, 8 am-7 pm; Friday, 8 am-4:30 pm. Health counseling, vocational testing, academic and personal counseling.

University of Michigan, Center for Continuing Education of Women, 350 S. Thayer, Ann Arbor, MI 48104-1608, 313-763-7080.

Western Michigan University, Center for Women's Services, Kalamazoo, MI 49008, 616-383-6097. Monday-Friday, 8 am-5 pm. Evening appointments also available. Official college office. Educational and career counseling. Fees vary.

Women's Resource Center, 252 State St. SE, Grand Rapids, MI 49503. Monday, Tuesday, Thursday, 9 am-5 pm; Wednesday 9 am-8 pm; Friday, 9 am-12 noon. Independent nonprofit agency. Services include personal and career counseling, Displaced Homemaker Program, and employment and training.

MINNESOTA

Chart, 104 Union Plaza, 333 N. Washington Ave., Minneapolis, MN 55401, 612-332-1942. By appointment. Career development and employment services to individuals and organizations. Fees based on sliding fee scale.

Minnesota Women's Center, University of Minnesota, 5 Eddy Hall, Minneapolis, MN 55455, 612-625-2874. Monday-Friday, 8 am-

4:30 pm. Official college office. Informal advising and referral. No fees.

Working Opportunities for Women, 2700 University Ave., #120, St. Paul, MN 55114, 612-647-9961. Monday-Friday, 8:30 am-5 pm. Evening appointments are available. Complete career planning services for women.

MISSISSIPPI

Mississippi State University, Career Services Center, P.O. Box P, Mississippi State, MS 39762, 601-325-3344. Gloria H. Reeves, Director.

MISSOURI

New Directions Center, 806 N. Providence Rd., Columbia, MO 65201, 314-443-2421. Monday-Friday, 9 am-4 pm. Career planning, education referral and job placement center for women. Workshops and individual career counseling.

The Women's Center, University of Missouri, Kansas City, 5204 Rockhill Rd., Kansas City, MO 64110, 816-276-1638. Monday-Friday, 8 am-5 pm. Educational and career counseling, career development workshops, continuing education seminars. Fees vary.

MONTANA

New Horizons, Missoula YWCA, 1130 W. Broadway, Missoula, MT 59802, 406-543-6768. Monday-Friday, 8 am-5 pm. Job counseling, career counseling, job referral, resume preparation. Works with displaced homemakers.

Women's Resource Center, 15 Hamilton Hall, Montana State University, Bozeman, MT 59717, 406-994-3836. Monday-Friday, 9 am-5 pm; (summer hours may vary). Workshops, seminars. Fee varies.

NEW JERSEY

Adult Resource Center, 39 Woodmont Rd., Pine Brook, NJ 07058, 201-575-0855, 335-4420. Monday-Friday, 9 am-4 pm. Evenings by appointment.

Bergen Community College, Division of Community Services, 400 Paramus Rd., Paramus, NJ 07652, 201-447-7150. Monday-Friday, 9 am-5 pm. College sponsored office. Educational and career counseling, adult education courses, continuing professional and career development education. Community counseling is free. Moderate fees for programs.

Caldwell College, Career Development Center, Caldwell, NJ 07006, 201-228-4424, Ext. 307. Monday-Friday, 8:30 am-4:30 pm. College sponsored. Educational and career counseling, limited job referral. Fees vary.

Douglass College, Douglass Advisory Services for Women, Rutgers Women's Center, 132 George St., New Brunswick, NJ 08903, 201-932-9603. Monday-Friday, 9 am-2 pm. Educational and career counseling. Must be a N.J. resident. No fees.

Fairleigh Dickinson University, Career Planning & Placement, 285 Madison Ave., Madison, NJ 07940, 201-593-8945. Monday-Friday, 9 am-5 pm. Official college office, providing career counseling, job listings/referral and placement. Nominal fee for non-Fairleigh Dickinson University community.

Jersey City State College, The Women's Center, 2039 Kennedy Blvd., Jersey City, NJ 07305, 201-547-3189. Monday-Friday, 9 am-4:30 pm. Official college office. Educational and career counseling, library/resource center, public programming. No fees.

Middlesex County College, Community Advisement and Resource Center, 155 Mill Rd., Edison, NJ 08818, 201-906-2550. Monday-Friday, 9 am-5 pm.

Montclair State College, Women's Center, Valley Rd., Upper Montclair, NJ 07043, 201-893-5106. Monday-Friday, 8:30 am-4:30 pm; evenings by appointment. College sponsored office for alumnae only. Educational and career counseling. No fees.

The Professional Roster, 171 Broadmead, Princeton, NJ 08609, 609-921-9561. Monday-Friday, 10 am-1 pm. Independent nonprofit organization. Career counseling, job referral.

Reach, Inc., College of St. Elizabeth, O'Connor Hall, NJ 07961 (mailing address: PO Box 33, Convent Sta., NJ 07961), 201-267-2530. Monday-Friday, 9:30 am-3 pm. Independent nonprofit office. Educational, career counseling, job referral. Fees minimal.

Women's Center, Princeton University, 201 Aaron Burr Hall, Princeton, NJ 08544, 609-452-5565. Monday-Friday, 9 am-5 pm. Consultation, workshops, seminars, library.

YWCA TWIN Career Options Unlimited, 232 E. Front St., Plainfield, NJ 07060, 201-756-3836. Janet M. Korba, Program Director. Provides information on career exploration through informational resources, career interest testing, career counseling, educational and vocational guidance, networking, job referral files and numerous career-oriented workshops. Most of these workshops are offered at minimal or no cost to interested persons in the central New Jersey area.

NEW MEXICO

Young Women's Christian Association, YWCA Career Services Center, 740 San Mateo NE, Albuquerque, NM 87108, 505-266-YWCA. Monday-Friday, 8:30 am-5:30 pm. Career counseling on a group basis. Classes, workshops, support groups, library. Fees on sliding scale: no one turned away for inability to pay.

NEW YORK

Academic Advisory Center for Adults, Turf Ave., Rye, NY 10580, 914-967-1653. Monday-Thursday, 9 am-4 pm, some evenings.

Hofstra University, Counseling Center, 240 Student Center, Hempstead, NY 11550, 516-560-6788. Extensive career and educational testing, job re-entry counseling, job-hunting and interviewing skills, resume preparation. An approved agency of the IACS.

Kingsborough Community College, Office of Career Counseling and Placement, 2001 Oriental Blvd., Rm. C102, Brooklyn, NY 11235, 212-934-5115. Monday-Friday, 8 am-5 pm.

Janice La Rouche Assoc., Workshops for Women, 333 Central Park W., New York, NY 10025, 212-663-0970. Monday-Friday, 9 am-6 pm. Independent private agency. Career strategies counseling. Assertiveness training. No registration fee. Other fees vary.

New Options, 960 Park Ave., New York, NY 10028, 212-535-1444. Monday-Friday, 9 am-5 pm. Evenings by appointment.

Orange County Community College, Office of Community Services, 115 South St., Middletown, NY 10940, 914-343-1121. Monday-Friday, 9 am-5 pm. Official college office. Educational counseling, continuing education courses. Fees vary.

Personnel Sciences Center, 41 E. 42nd St., New York, NY 10017, 212-661-1870. Monday-Friday, 9 am-5 pm. Independent private agency. Educational and career counseling. Fees vary.

Regional Learning Service of Central New York, 405 Oak St., Syracuse, NY 13203, 315-425-5252. Monday-Friday, 8:30 am-5 pm. Independent nonprofit agency. Career and educational counseling. Graduated fee scale.

Ruth Shapiro Associates, 200 E. 30th St., New York, NY 10016, 212-889-4284, 212-679-9858. Monday-Saturday, 9:30 am-6 pm and evenings. By appointment only. Private agency. Career/assertiveness counseling, resume/letter writing. Fees vary.

SUNY at Buffalo, Career Planning Office, 252 Capen Hall, Buffalo, NY 14260, 716-636-2231. Monday-Friday, 8:30 am-5 pm. Official college office. Educational and career counseling, job referral and placement. No fees.

Women's Center for Continuing Education, Syracuse University College, 610 E. Fayette St., Syracuse, NY 13244, 315-423-4116. Phyllis R. Chase, Director. Monday-Friday 9 am-5 pm. Career and educational counseling. No fees.

Women's Career Center, Inc., 14 Franklin St., Temple Bldg., Rochester, NY 14604, 716-325-2274. Monday, Wednesday, Friday, 9 am-5 pm; Tuesday & Thursday, 9 am-8:30 pm. Serving both men and women.

Women's Network of the YWCA, 515 North St., White Plains, NY 10605, 914-949-6227. Annual Networking Conference in October as well as monthly networking second Wednesday of each month.

NORTH CAROLINA

Women's Center of Raleigh, 315 E. Jones St., Raleigh, NC 27601, 919-755-6840. Anne D. Britt, Career Services Coordinator.

OHIO

Resource: Careers, 1258 Euclid Ave., Suite 204, Cleveland, OH 44115, 216-579-1414. For professional development of women with one year of college or more. By appointment only. Fees vary.

University of Akron, Adult Resource Center, Akron, OH 44325, 216-375-7448. Monday-Friday, 8 am-5 pm. Career/life planning, job finding skills, educational guidance. Free individual appointments, minimal fees for workshops.

PENNSYLVANIA

Cedar Crest College, Women's Center, Allentown, PA 18104, 215-437-4471. Monday-Friday, 11 am-7 pm. Educational and career counseling, continuing education courses, career interest testing. Fees vary.

Job Advisory Service, 300 S. Craig St., Pittsburgh, PA 15213, 412-621-0940. Monday-Friday, 9 am-4:30 pm; Saturday, 9 am-1 pm. Independent nonprofit career counseling center. Job counseling, vocational testing, resume writing, workshops. Second career internship program for re-entry women and teachers.

Resume Consultations, Etc., Wynnewood, PA 19096, 215-642-2183. Help with construction of resumes and cover letters, as well as job-networking information.

University of Pennsylvania, Resources for Women, 1208 Blockley Hall/sl, Philadelphia, PA 19014, 215-898-5537. Monday-Friday, 10 am-3 pm. University sponsored, continuing supportive career services, career and resume counseling, workshops, job referral and placement. Fees vary.

Villa Maria College, Counseling Services for Women, 2551 West Lake Rd., Erie, PA 16505, 814-838-1966. Monday-Friday, 9 am-4 pm. Official college office. Educational and career counseling, adult education courses. Variable fees.

SOUTH CAROLINA

Converse College, Office of Career Services, Spartanburg, SC 29301, 803-596-9027. Monday-Friday, 8:15 am-5:00 pm. Free to students and alumnae.

Greenville Technical College, Career Advancement Center, Greenville, SC 29606, 803-239-2964. Monday-Friday, 8:30 am-4:30 pm.

SOUTH DAKOTA

Sioux Falls College, The Center for Women, Clidden Hall, Sioux Falls, SD 57101, 605-331-6697. Educational, personal, and career counseling.

TEXAS

Austin Women's Center, 1700 S. Lamar Blvd., Suite 203, Austin, TX 78704, 512-447-9666. Job listings, job support group, employment workshops and employment counseling. Monday-Friday, 9 am-5 pm; Tuesday, 9 am-8 pm.

Vocational Guidance Service, Inc., 2525 San Jacinto, Houston, TX 77002, 713-659-1800. Monday-Thursday, 8:30 am-7 pm; Friday, 8:30 am-5 pm. Nonprofit organization. Educational and career counseling, job referral and placement. Fees based on sliding scale.

Women's Counseling Service, 1950 W. Gray, Suite 1, Houston, TX 77019, 713-521-9391. Career development. Individual vocational, divorce adjustment, and educational counseling.

Women's Resource Center, YWCA, 4621 Ross Ave., Dallas, TX 75204, 214-821-9595. Monday-Friday, 9 am-5 pm. Vocational testing, individual and group career counseling. Fees vary.

UTAH

The Phoenix Institute, 1800 S. West Temple, Suite 211, Salt Lake City, UT 84115, 801-484-2882. Monday-Friday, 8 am-8 pm. Saturdays by appointment.

VIRGINIA

Mary Baldwin College, Rosemarie Sena Center for Career and Life Planning, Staunton, VA 24401, 703-887-7221. Monday-Friday, 8:30 am-4:30 pm, open Thursday nights until 9 pm. College affiliated office. Educational and career counseling. Fee on individual basis.

Educational Opportunity Center, 7010-M Auburn Ave., Norfolk, VA 23513, 804-855-7468. Monday-Friday, 8 am-5 pm. Nonprofit agency. Educational, career, and financial aid counseling. No fees.

Hollins College, Career Counseling Center, Rose Hill House, Roanoke, VA 24020, 703-362-6364. Monday-Friday, 9 am-4:30 pm.

Old Dominion University, Women's Center, 1521 W. 49th St., Norfolk, VA 23529-0536, 804-440-4109. Monday-Friday, 8 am-5 pm. Call for appointment. Continuing education courses and career counseling.

Re-entry Women's Employment Center, 5501 Backlick Rd., #110, Springfield, VA 22151, 703-750-0633. Monday-Friday, 8:30 am-4:30 pm. Fairfax County Agency. Career planning and job search workshops, counseling, conferences, special programs, information and referral. Career planning workshops for county residents on sliding fee scale; other services for anyone - - free or at minimal cost.

University of Richmond, Women's Resource Center, Richmond, VA 23173, 804-289-8020. Call for appointment.

Virginia Commonwealth University, University Advising Center, Box 2523, 827 W. Franklin St., Rm. 101, Richmond, VA 23284-2523, 804-257-0200. Monday-Thursday, 8 am-7:30 pm; Friday, 8 am-4:30 pm; Saturday, 9 am-1 pm. Marcia F. Zwicker, Director. Official university office. Educational counseling, referral to university career and personal counseling services, continuing education courses.

Woman's Resource Center of Central VA, Inc., Houston Memorial Chapel, Randolph-Macon Woman's College, Box 852, Lynchburg, VA 24503, 804-847-0258. Monday-Friday, 9 am-4:30 pm. Kathryn C. Mays, Executive Director. Specialize in helping displaced homemakers enter/re-enter job market. Career counseling, job search, workshops, support groups. Sliding scale fee.

WASHINGTON

University of Washington, University Extension GH-21, Career/Life Planning, Seattle, WA 98195, 206-543-2300. Monday-Friday, 8 am-4:30 pm. Career counseling, testing, classes, workshops. Fees vary. Evening appointments are available.

III. GROUP-SUPPORT FOR THOSE
WHO ARE UNEMPLOYED

Forty-Plus Clubs. Not a national organization, but a nationwide network of voluntary, autonomous nonprofit clubs, manned by its unemployed members, paying no salaries, supported by initiation fees and monthly dues. Generally speaking (requirements vary from club to club), open only to those who are forty years of age of between $25,000 and $30,000 minimum annual salary previously. The minimum varies from club to club and has been lowered lately, so as not to discriminate against women (who are notoriously underpaid for their talents). The screening procedures vary from club to club, and the process may take up to six weeks. It involves (usually) a personal interview, the checking out of your business references, and an informal meeting with representative active members. Insiders claim at least one-tenth leave without ever finding placement (sometimes due to their own lack of motivation), some try to hang around just for the sense of community (hence stays are often limited to six months, in some locations), and it takes the average successful member up to six months to find placement. While active in the club, members must agree to give typically about sixteen hours a week, or two and one-half days, to club work. Fees and monthly dues vary from club to club. There have been clubs in the following cities: Toronto, Oakland (California), Los Angeles, Chicago, Denver, Honolulu, Philadelphia, Washington, D. C., New York, Cleveland, and Winston-Salem. You will need to check if the club nearest you is still operating. The white pages of your phone book will have their address and phone number (they are all listed under the title of FORTY-PLUS).

Talent Bank Associates, 475 Calkins Rd., Henrietta (near Rochester), NY 14467, 716-334-9676. An organized form of the "Job-Hunters Anonymous" idea. A nonprofit organization comprised of unemployed persons of various professions and skills working together on a volunteer basis to find themselves meaningful, permanent employment. Free of charge. During a recent year, it served 350 people, 79% of whom found long-term employment through this program.

WIN Workshops (Women in Networking), is a six-week seminar limited to fifteen participants. Each group meets from 5:30-8:30, once a week. Geared specifically to women in management who have lost their jobs, expect to lose their jobs or have reached a dead end in their jobs. Contact Emily Koltnow, 730 Fifth Ave., New York, NY 10019, 212-333-8788, for further information and fees.

energy for employment, fourteen job-search groups in the Philadelphia area, providing both emotional and technical support for job-seekers through free weekly meetings. For information about locations, dates, and times, contact: Laura C. Smith, Program Director, energy for employment, 311 S. Juniper St., Suite 1002, Philadelphia, PA 19107, 215-985-1434.

Christian Employment Cooperative. A nonprofit ecumenical Christian effort to meet the needs of the unemployed, by using local congregations to bring together the unemployed, employers, and support groups. For information, contact: Leon Bridges, Executive Director, Christian Employment Cooperative, 465 Boulevard Pl. NE, Suite 210, Atlanta, GA 30308, 404-622-2235.

Career Planning Center of Grace United Methodist Church. On two Saturdays per month, they run one-day workshops (9:30 am - 4 pm). Fee: $25. Exercises must be completed prior to the workshop. For information contact: Mark Canfield, Director, 458 Ponce de Leon Ave., Atlanta, GA 30308, 404-876-2678.

St. Jude's Job Network Club, a nondenominational self-help support group meets every Monday at 7:30 pm at St. Jude's Catholic Church, 7171 Glenridge Dr., Sandy Springs, GA (near northern Atlanta).

Operation Job Search, 2844 South Calhoun St., Fort Wayne, IN 46807, 219-456-3542. A community-wide career assessment program sponsored by the city; the only such program of its kind in the country, at this writing. For all residents of the city of Fort Wayne, who are unemployed or underemployed.

Chicago Career Groups. Meets every other Tuesday evening (at this writing) from 6-8pm at Three Arts Club, 1300 N. Dearborn, Chicago. $20 per session, payable at the door. Reservations are required, call 312-272-1079.

Career Planning and Placement Center, Adult Evening Program, 110 Noyes Hall, University of Missouri, Columbia, MO 65201, 314-882-6803. Tuesday and Thursday, 5-9 pm. Open to the public. Free. Drop-in for research. Schedule individual appointment. Help with goal clarification, resumes, interviews, job-seeking strategies, training opportunities. Job-seeking group.

Career Decisions Job Finder's Club, 2103 S. Clear Creek Rd., Killeen, TX 76542. Every Monday morning from 9-10:30 at the Professional Counseling Service. Registration is $10, payable at the door. Reservations are requested, please call 817-634-2142.

Dublin Library Job Club, 7606 Amador Valley Blvd., Dublin CA. A weekly forum for all career-changers and job-seekers. Sponsored by Modern Career Decisions (Rod Meyer, Executive Director) as a community service. Each meeting focuses on a different subject from Parachute. Meets every Friday at 10 am. Free. 415-846-9071.

Additional groups spring up, monthly, including job clubs and other group activities. Many of these are listed in National Business Employment Weekly, on its pages called "Calendar of Events." Available on newsstands, $3.50 per issue; or, order directly from: National Business Employment Weekly, 420 Lexington Ave., New York, NY 10170. 212-808-6792. Among the listings, you will have to pick and choose **carefully**.

Experience Unlimited.   An organization for unemployed professionals, based in California.   Contact: Mr. Herman J. Leopold, Experience Unlimited Coordinator, Employment Development Dept., 1111 Jackson St., Rm. 1009, Oakland, CA 94607. Mailing address: 1225 4th Ave., Oakland, CA 94606, 415-464-0659/464-1259.

Civic Center Volunteers. Marin County Personnel Office, Administration Bldg., Civic Center, San Rafael, CA 94903, 415-499-6104. Placement in county jobs of volunteer re-entry women, career-experimenters, and students wishing to gain experience. Volunteers sign a contract for each specific job, and receive supervision and evaluation. The purpose of this program is to give work experience in various jobs and provide a place to gain confidence in one's skills, new self-esteem, etc.

IV.   DIRECTORIES OF CAREER COUNSELING SERVICES IN VARIOUS CITIES/STATES

Enterprising souls have for some time now been putting together listings of counselors, agencies, resources, and potential employers for individual cities or metropolitan areas.   While such books, unless they are revised annually, are bound to become outdated rapidly (ah, how well I know) due to places moving, folding, or rising Phoenixlike from their own ashes in a different form, nonetheless these books offer at least a starting place if you are looking for help:

GENERAL

Birnbach, Lisa, *Going to Work: A Unique Guided Tour Through Corporate America*. Villard Books, a division of Random House, Inc., 201 E. 50th St., New York, N.Y. 10022. 1988. Gives an overview of the following cities, with an in-depth coverage of a few major corporations in each: Atlanta, Boston, Chicago, Dallas, Detroit, Los Angeles, Minneapolis — St. Paul, New York City, San Francisco (together with its adjacent "Silicon Valley"), Seattle, and Washington D.C.

Adams, Bob, ed., *The 1988 National Job Bank (4th Edition)*. Bob Adams, Inc., 840 Summer St., Boston, MA 02127. 1987. Information on 10,000 of the nation's largest companies. Very expensive; see if your local library has it.

CALIFORNIA

Sweeney, Patricia; Olmsted, Daniel; Figueira, Hazel; and Marks, Linda, eds., *Looking For Work: A Bay Area Guide to Employment Resources,* New Ways to Work, 149 Ninth St., San Francisco, CA 94103. 1986. An update is in the works.

Fiedler, J. Michael, ed., *The All-New, Second Edition of the San Francisco Bay Area Job Bank,* Bob Adams, Inc., 840 Summer St., Boston, MA 02127. 1985. Note however that the publisher has not updated this book since 1985, and consequently its listings may now be four years out of date.

Beach, Janet L., *How to Get a Job in the San Francisco Bay Area*. Contemporary Books, Inc., 180 North Michigan Ave., Chicago, IL 60601. 1983. An extremely well-done resource guide, describing the nature of the Bay Area, each major industry in that Area, the nature of that industry and key resources, job titles and salary ranges, insiders' advice, key companies or organizations, together with the name of the principal contact therein. Note however that the publisher has not updated this book since 1983, and consequently its listings may now be six years out of date.

Adams, Robert Lang, ed., *The Northern California Job Bank*. Bob Adams, Inc., 840 Summer St., South Boston, MA 02127. 1986. Lists employers, hospitals, universities, government agencies, as well as private employment agencies and services. Note however that the publisher has not updated this book since 1986, and consequently its listings may now be three years out of date.

Camden, Thomas, and Greene, Freda, *How to Get a Job in Los Angeles*. Surrey Books, available (among other places) from B. Dalton, 131 N. La Cienega Blvd., Los Angeles, CA 90048.

California Connections Publication, Box 90396, Long Beach, CA 90809. A directory of public sector employment opportunities.

COLORADO

Faaborg, Barbara and Renault, Susan, *Job Resources for Colorado Women -- Where to Find Good Advice Cheap*. Subar Publications, 2118 Payton Circle, Colorado Springs, CO 80915. 1986.

DISTRICT OF COLUMBIA

Adams, Robert Lang, ed., *The Metropolitan Washington Job Bank*. Bob Adams, Inc., 840 Summer St., South Boston, MA 02127. 1983. Lists employers, hospitals, universities, government agencies, as well as private employment agencies and services. Note however that the publisher has not updated this book since 1983, and consequently its listings may now be six years out of date.

FLORIDA

Fencl, George Jr., and Pritchett, Janie, *The Central Florida Career Guide*. Edge Publishing, P.O. Box 3621, Longwood, FL 32779. 1987. A directory of over 400 employers with contact personnel and projected employment needs, as well as an overview of Central Florida's industry growth trends.

ILLINOIS

Camden, Thomas M. and Schwartz, Susan, *How to Get a Job in Chicago: The Insiders' Guide*. Surrey Books, 500 N. Michigan Ave., Suite 1940, Chicago, IL 60611. 1986.

Adams, Robert Lang, ed., *The Greater Chicago Job Bank*. 4th edition. Bob Adams, Inc., 840 Summer St., South Boston, MA 02127.

MASSACHUSETTS

Boyd, Kathleen, and Ramsauer, Constance Arnold, and Senft, Ruth, *Career Connections: A Guide to Career Planning Services in Massachusetts*. Bob Adams, Inc., 840 Summer St., South Boston, MA 02127. 1983. Note however that the publisher has not updated this book since 1983, and consequently its listings may now be six years out of date.

Adams, Robert Lang, ed., *The Boston Job Bank.* Bob Adams, Inc., 840 Summer St., South Boston, MA 02127. 1987. Lists employers, hospitals, universities, government agencies, as well as private employment agencies and services.

NEW YORK

Camden, Thomas M. and Fleming-Holland, Susan, *How to Get A Job In New York: The Insiders' Guide.* Surrey Books, 500 N. Michigan Ave., Suite 1940, Chicago, IL 60611. 1986.

Adams, Robert Lang, ed., *The Metropolitan New York Job Bank,* Bob Adams, Inc., 840 Summer St., South Boston, MA 02127. 1987. Lists employers, hospitals, universities, government agencies, as well as private agencies and services.

OHIO

Adams, Robert Lang, ed., *The Ohio Job Bank,* Bob Adams, Inc., 840 Summer St., South Boston, MA 02127. 1987.

THE SOUTHWEST

Adams, Robert Lang, ed., *The Southwest Job Bank,* Bob Adams, Inc., 840 Summer St., South Boston, MA 02127. 1983. In addition to primary employer listings, describes those positions with strong hiring outlooks, plus the basics of job-winning, as Adams sees it.

TEXAS

Camden, Thomas M. and Bishop, Nancy, *How to Get a Job in Dallas/Ft. Worth: The Insiders' Guide.* Surrey Books, Inc., 500 N. Michigan Ave., Suite 1940, Chicago, IL 60611. 1984. Note however that the publisher has not updated this book since 1984, and consequently its listings may now be five years out of date.

Jitahidi, Joia, *Making Austin Work.* "Tips to the hidden job market and a guide to Austin's employment resources." Catalyst Publications, Box 15785, Austin, TX 78761.

Appendix D

Religion
and
Job-Hunting:

How to Find Your Mission in Life

Introduction

As I started writing this section on "Religion and Job-Hunting," I toyed at first with the idea of following what might be described as "an all-paths approach" to religion. But, after much thought, I decided not to try that. This, because I have read many other writers who tried, and I felt the approach failed miserably. An "all-paths" approach to religion ends up being a "no-paths" approach, even as a woman or man who tries to please everyone ends up pleasing no one. It is the old story of the "universal" vs. the "particular".

Those of us who do career counseling could predict, ahead of time, that trying to stay universal is not likely to be helpful, in writing about religion. We know well from our own field that truly helpful career counseling depends upon defining the **particularity** or uniqueness of each person we try to help. No employer wants to know only what you have in common with everyone else. He or she wants to know what makes you unique and individual. As I have argued throughout this book, the identification and inventory of your uniqueness or *particularity* is crucial if you are ever to find meaningful work.

This particularity invades and carries over to *everything* a person does; it is not suddenly "jettisonable" when he or she turns to religion. Therefore, when I or anyone else writes about religion I believe we **must** write out of our own particularity -- which *starts*, in my case, with the fact that I write, and think, and breathe as a Christian. So, this article speaks from a Christian perspective. I want you to be forewarned.

I have always been acutely aware, however, that this is a pluralistic society in which we live, and that I owe a great deal of sensitivity to the readers of my books who may have convictions very different from my own. I rub up against these different convictions, daily. By accident and not design it has turned out that the people who work or have worked here in my office with me, over the years, have been predominantly Jewish, along with some non-religious and a smattering of Christians. Furthermore, **Parachute's** more than 3 million readers have included Christians, Jews, members of the Baha'i faith, Seventh-Day Adventists, Mormons, Hindus, Buddhists, Islamics, and believers in 'new age' religions, as well as (of course) secularists, humanists, agnostics, atheists, and many others. Consequently, I have tried to be very courteous toward the feelings of all my readers who come from other persuasions or convictions than my own, *while at the same time* counting on them to translate my Christian thought forms into their own thought forms -- since this ability to thus translate is the indispensable *sine qua non* of anyone who aspires to communicate helpfully with others.

In the Judeo-Christian tradition from which I come, one of the indignant Biblical questions is, "Has God forgotten to be gracious?" The answer was a clear No. I think it is important *for all of us* also to seek the same goal. I have therefore labored to make this section gracious as well as helpful.

R. N. B.

How I Came To Write This

Recently, a woman asked me how you go about finding out what your Mission in life is. She assumed I would know what she was talking about, because of a diagram which appears a number of times in one of my other books, The Three Boxes of Life:

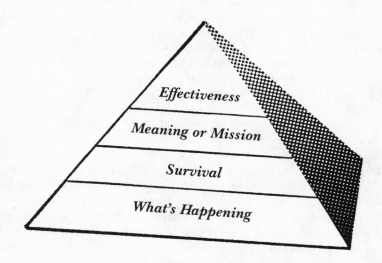

The Issues of the Job Hunt

As this diagram asserts, the question of one's Mission in life arises naturally as a part of many people's job-hunt.

She told me that what she was looking for was not some careful, dispassionate, philosophical answer, where every statement is hedged about with cautions and caveats -- "It may be..." or " It seems to me..." Nor did she want to know why *I thought what I did, or* how *I learned it, or what Scriptures support it. "I want you to just speak with passion and conviction," she said, "out of what you most truly feel and believe. For it is some vision that I want. I am hungry for a vision of what I can be. So, just speak to me of what you most truly feel and believe about our mission in life. I will know how to translate your vision into my own thought forms for my own life, when I reflect afterwards upon what you have said. But I want you to talk about this now with passion and conviction -- please."*

And so, I did. And I will now tell you what I said to her.

The Motive for Finding A Sense of Mission in Life

The motive that drives us to search for A Sense of Mission is our desire for some reassurance of our Uniqueness. We want to feel that we are not just another grain of sand lying on the beach called humanity, unnumbered and lost in the 5 billion mass, but that the Universe -- God -- caused us to be born and put here for some unique reason: to contribute to Life on earth something no one else can contribute in quite the same way. At its very minimum, then, if you search for a sense of Mission you are searching for reassurance that the world is at least a little bit richer for your being here; and a little bit poorer after your going.

Every keen observer of human nature will know what I mean when I say that those who do find some sense of Mission find a very special joy, "which no one can take from them." It is wonderful to feel that beyond eating, sleeping, working, having pleasure and *it may be* marrying, having children, and growing older, you were set here on Earth for some special purpose, *and* that you can gain some idea of what that purpose is.

So, how does one go about this search?

I would emphasize, at the outset, two cautions. First of all, though I will explain the steps that seem to me to be involved in finding one's Mission -- based on the learnings I have accumulated over some sixty years, I want to caution you that these steps are not the only Way -- by any means. Many people have discovered their Mission by taking other paths. And you may, too. But hopefully what I have to say may shed some light upon whatever path you take.

My second caution is simply this: you would be wise not to try to approach this problem of "your Mission in life" as primarily an **intellectual** puzzle -- for the mind, and the mind alone, to solve. To paraphrase Kahlil Gibran, Faith is an oasis in the heart that is not reached merely by the journey of the mind. It is your will and your heart that must be involved in the search as well as your mind. To put it quite simply, it takes the total person to learn one's total Mission.

It also takes the total disciplines of the ages -- not only modern knowledge but also ancient thought, including the wisdom of religion, faith, and the spiritual matters. For, to put it quite bluntly, the question of Mission inevitably leads us to God.

The Main Obstacle in Finding Your Mission in Life: Job-Hunting Compartmentalized from Our Religion or Faith

Mission challenges us to see our job-hunt in relationship to our faith in God, because *Mission* is a religious concept, from beginning to end. It is defined by Webster's as "a continuing task or responsibility that one is destined or fitted to do or specially called upon to undertake," and historically has had two major synonyms: *Calling* and *Vocation.* These, of course, are the same word in two different languages, English and Latin. Regardless of which word is used, it is obvious upon reflection, that a Vocation or Calling implies *Someone who calls,* and that a destiny implies *Someone who determined the destination for us.* Thus, unless one opts for a military or governmental view of the matter, the concept of Mission with relationship to our whole life lands us inevitably in the lap of God, before we have even begun.

There is always the temptation to try to speak of this subject of *Mission* in a secular fashion, without reference to God, as though it might be simply "a purpose you choose for your own life, by identifying your enthusiasms, and then using the clues you find from that exercise to get some purpose you can choose for your life." The language of this temptation is ironic because the substitute word used for "Mission" -- *Enthusiasm* -- is derived from the Greek, 'en theos,' and literally means "God in us."

It is no accident that so many of the leaders in the job-hunting field over the years -- the late John Crystal, Arthur Miller, Ralph Mattson, Tom and Ellie Jackson, Bernard Haldane, Arthur and Marie Kirn, the Pilders have also been people of faith. If you would figure out your Mission in life, you must also be willing to think about God in connection with your job-hunt.

The Secret of Finding Your Mission in Life: Taking It in Stages

The puzzle of figuring out what your Mission in life is, will likely take some time. It is not a *problem* to be solved in a day and a night. It is a *learning process* which has steps to it, much like the process by which we all learned to eat. As a baby we did not tackle adult food right off. As we all recall, there were three stages: first there had to be the mother's milk or bottle, then strained baby foods, and finally -- after teeth and time -- the stuff that grown-ups chew. Three stages -- and the two earlier stages were not to be disparaged. It was all Eating, just different forms of Eating -- appropriate to our development at the time. But each stage had to be mastered, in turn, before the next could be approached.

The Three Stages of Mission: What We Need to Learn

By coincidence, there are usually three stages also to learning what your Mission in life is, and the two earlier stages are likewise not to be disparaged. It is all "Mission" -- just different forms of Mission, appropriate to your development at the time. But each stage has to be mastered, in turn, before the next can be approached. And so, you may say either of two things: You may say that you have *Three Missions in Life.* Or you may say that you have *One Mission in Life, with three parts to it.* But there is a sense in which you must discover what those three parts are, each in turn, before you can fully answer the question, "What is my Mission in life?" Of course, there is another sense in which you never master any of these stages, but are always growing in understanding and mastery of them, throughout your whole life here on Earth.

As it has been impressed on me by observing many people over the years (admittedly through *Christian spectacles*), it appears that the three parts to your Mission here on Earth can be defined generally as follows:

(1) *Your first Mission here on Earth* is one which you share with the rest of the human race, but it is no less your individual Mission for the fact that it is shared: and it is, **to seek out and find, in daily -- even hourly -- communication, the One from whom**

your Mission is derived. *The Missioner before the Mission,* is the rule. In religious language, your Mission here is: *to know God, and enjoy Him forever, and to see His hand in all His works.*

(2) Secondly, once you have begun doing that in an earnest way, *your second Mission here on Earth* is also one which you share with the rest of the human race, but it is no less your individual mission for the fact that it is shared: and that is, **to do what you can, moment by moment, day by day, step by step, to make this world a better place, following the leading and guidance of God's Spirit within you and around you.**

(3) Thirdly, once you have begun doing that in a serious way, *your third Mission here on Earth* is one which is uniquely yours, and that is:

a) **to exercise that Talent which you particularly came to Earth to use -- your greatest gift, which you most delight to use,**
b) **in the place(s) or setting(s) which God has caused to appeal to you the most,**
c) **and for those purposes which God most needs to have done in the world.**

When fleshed out, and spelled out, I think you will find that there you have the definition of your Mission in life. Or, to put it another way, these are the three Missions which you have in life.

The Two Rhythms of the Dance of Mission: Unlearning, Learning, Unlearning, Learning

The distinctive characteristic of these three stages is that in each we are forced to *let go* of some fundamental assumptions which the world has *falsely* taught us, about the nature of our Mission. In other words, throughout this quest and at each stage we find ourselves engaged not merely in a process of *Learning.* We are also engaged in a process of *Un*learning. Thus, we can restate the above three Learnings, in terms of what we also need to *un*learn at each stage:

• We need in the first Stage to *un*learn the idea that our Mission is primarily to keep busy *doing* something (here on Earth), and learn instead that our Mission is first of all to keep busy being something (here on Earth). In Christian language (and others as well), we might say that we were sent here to learn how *to be* sons of God, and daughters of God, before anything else. *"Our Father, who art in heaven ..."*

• In the second stage, "Being" issues into "Doing." At this stage, we need to *un*learn the idea that everything about our Mission must be *unique* to us, and learn instead that some parts of our Mission here on Earth are *shared* by all human beings: e.g., we were all sent here to bring more gratitude, more kindness, more forgiveness, and more love, into the world. We share this Mission because the task is too large to be accomplished by just one individual.

• We need in the third stage to *un*learn the idea that that part of our Mission which is truly unique, and most truly ours, is something Our Creator just *orders* us to do, without any agreement from our spirit, mind, and heart. (On the other hand, neither is it some thing that each of us chooses and then merely asks God to bless.) We need to learn that God so honors our free will, that He has ordained our unique Mission be something which we have some part in choosing.

• In this third stage we need also to *un*learn the idea that our unique Mission must consist of some achievement which all the world will see, -- and learn instead that as the stone does not always know what ripples it has caused in the pond whose surface it impacts, so neither we nor those who watch our life will always know *what we have achieved* by our life and by our Mission. *It may be* that by the grace of God we helped bring about a profound change for the better in the lives of other souls around us, but it also may be that this takes place beyond our sight, or after we have gone on. And we may never know what we have accomplished, until we see Him face-to-face after this life is past.

• Most finally, we need to unlearn the idea that what we have accomplished is our doing, and ours alone. It is God's Spirit breathing in us and through us which helps us to do whatever we do, and so the singular first person pronoun is never appropriate, but only the plural. Not "*I* accomplished this" but "*We* accomplished this, God and I, working together..."

That should give you a general overview. But I would like to add some random comments on my part about each of these three Missions of ours here on Earth.

Some Random Comments About Your First Mission in Life

Your first Mission here on Earth is one which you share with the rest of the human race, but it is no less your individual Mission for the fact that it is shared: and that is, **to seek out and find, in daily -- even hourly -- communication, the One from whom your Mission is derived.** The Missioner before the Mission, is the rule. In religious language, your Mission is: to know God, and enjoy Him for ever, and to see His hand in all His works.

Comment 1: How We Might Think of God

Each of us has to go about this primary Mission according to the tenets of his or her own particular religion. But I will speak what I know out of the context of my own particular faith, and you may perhaps translate and apply it to yours. I will speak as a Christian, who believes (passionately) that Christ is the Way and the Truth and the Life. But I also believe, with St. Peter, "that God shows no partiality, but in every nation any one who fears him and does what is right is acceptable to him." (Acts 10:34-35)

Now, Jesus claimed many unique things about Himself and His Mission; but He also spoke of Himself as the great prototype for us all. He called himself "the Son of Man," and He said, "I assure you that the man who believes in me will do the same things that I have done, yes, and he will do even greater things than these..." (John 14:12)

Emboldened by His identification of us with His life and His Mission, we might want to remember how He spoke about His Life here on Earth. He put it in this context: **"I came from the Father and have come into the world; again, I am leaving the world and going to the Father."** (John 16:28)

If there is a sense in which this is, in even the faintest way, true also of our lives (and I shall say in a moment in what sense I think it is true), then instead of calling our great Creator "God" or "Father" right off, we might begin our approach to the subject of religion by referring to the One Who gave us our Mission and sent us to this planet not as "God" or "Father" but -- *just to help our thinking* -- as: **The One From Whom We Came and The One To Whom We Shall Return**," when this life is done.

If our life here on Earth be at all like Christ's, then this is a true way to think about the One who gave us our Mission. We are not some kind of eternal, pre-existent *being*. We are **creatures**, who once did not exist, and then came into Being, and continue to have our Being, only at the will of our great Creator. But as creatures we are both body and soul; and although we know our body was created in our mother's womb, our soul's origin is a great mystery. Where it came from, at what moment the Lord created it, is something we cannot know. It is not unreasonable to suppose, however, that the great God created our *soul* before it entered our body, and in that sense we did indeed stand before God before we were born; and He is indeed "**The One From Whom We Came and The One To Whom We Shall Return**."

Therefore, before we go searching for "what work was I sent here to do?" we need to establish or in a truer sense *reestablish* -- contact with this "**One From Whom We Came and The One To Whom We Shall Return**." Without this reaching out of the creature to the great Creator, without this reaching out of *the creature with a Mission* to *the One Who Gave Us That Mission*, the question **what is my Mission in life?** is void and null. The *what* is rooted in the *Who*; absent the Personal, one cannot meaningfully discuss The Thing. It is like the adult who cries, "I want to get married," without giving any consideration to *who* it is they want to marry.

Comment 2: How We Might Think of Religion or Faith

In light of this larger view of our creatureliness, we can see that *religion* or *faith* is not a question of whether or not we choose to (*as it is so commonly put*) "have a relationship with God." Looking at our life in a larger context than just our life here on Earth, it becomes apparent that some sort of relationship with God is a given for us, about which we have absolutely no choice. God and we **were and are** related, during the time of our soul's existence before our birth and in the time of our soul's continued existence after our death. The only choice we have is what to do about **The Time In Between**, i.e., what we want the nature of our relationship with God to be during our time here on Earth and how that will affect the *nature* of the relationship, then, after death.

One of the corollaries of all this is that by the very act of being born into a human body, it is an inevitable that we undergo a kind of *amnesia* -- an amnesia which typically embraces not only our nine months in the womb, our baby years, and almost one third of each day (sleeping), but more importantly any memory of our origin or our destiny. We wander on Earth as an amnesia victim. To seek after Faith, therefore, is to seek to climb back out of that amnesia. Religion or faith is **the hard reclaiming of knowledge we once knew as a certainty**.

Comment 3: The First Obstacle to Executing This Mission

This first Mission of ours here on Earth is not the easiest of Missions, simply because it is the first. Indeed, in many ways, it is the most difficult. All can see that our life here on Earth is a very physical life. We eat, we drink, we sleep, we long to be held, and to hold. We inherit a physical body, with very physical appetites, we walk on the physical earth, and we acquire physical possessions. It is the most alluring of temptations, *in our amnesia*, to come up with just a *Physical* interpretation of this life: to think that the Universe is merely interested in the survival of species. Given this interpretation, the story of our individual life could be simply told: we are born, grow up, procreate, and die.

But we are ever recalled to do what we came here to do: that without rejecting the joy of the Physicalness of this life, such as the love of the blue sky and the green grass, we are to reach out beyond all this to **recall** and recover a *Spiritual* interpretation of our life. *Beyond* the physical and *within* the physicalness of this life, to detect a Spirit and a Person from beyond this Earth who is with us and in us -- very real and loving and awesome Presence of the great Creator from whom we came -- and the One to whom we once again shall go.

Comment 4: The Second Obstacle to Executing This Mission

It is one of the conditions of our earthly amnesia and our creatureliness that, sadly enough, some very *human* and very *rebellious* part of us *likes* the idea of living in a world where we can be our own god -- and therefore loves the purely Physical interpretation of life, and finds it *anguish* to relinquish it. Traditional Christian vocabulary calls this "**sin**" and has a lot to say about the difficulty it poses for this first part of our Mission. All who live a thoughtful life know that it is true: our greatest enemy in carrying out this first Mission of ours is indeed *our own* heart and our own rebellion.

Comment 5: Further Thoughts About What Makes Us Special and Unique

As I said earlier, many of us come to this issue of our Mission in life, because we want to feel that we are unique. And what we mean by that, is that we hope to discover some "specialness" intrinsic to us, which is our birthright, and which no one can take from us. What we, however, discover from a thorough exploration of this topic, is that we are indeed special -- but only because God thinks us so. Our specialness and uniqueness reside in Him, and His love, rather than in anything intrinsic to our own *being*. The proper appreciation of this distinction causes our feet to carry us in the end not to the City called Pride, but to the Temple called Gratitude.

What is religion? Religion is the service of God out of grateful love for what God has done for us. The Christian religion, more particularly, is the service of God out of grateful love for what God has done for us in Christ.

Phillips Brooks

Comment 6: The Unconscious Doing of The Work We Came To Do

You may have *already* wrestled with this first part of your Mission here on Earth. You may not have called it that. You may have called it simply "learning to believe in God." But if you ask what your Mission is in life, this one was and is the precondition of all else that you came here to do. Absent this Mission, and it is folly to talk about the rest. So, if you have been seeking faith, or seeking to strengthen your faith, you have -- willy nilly -- already been about *the doing of the Mission you were given*. Born into **This Time In Between**, you have found His hand again, and reclasped it. You are therefore ready to go on with His Spirit to tackle together what you came here to do -- the other parts of your Mission.

Some Random Comments About Your Second Mission in Life

Your second Mission here on Earth is also one which you share with the rest of the human race, but it is no less your individual mission for the fact that it is shared: and that is, **to do what you can moment by moment, day by day, step by step, to make this world a better place -- following the leading and guidance of God's Spirit within you and around you.**

Comment 1: The Uncomfortableness of One Step at a Time

Imagine yourself out walking in your neighborhood one night, and suddenly you find yourself surrounded by such a dense fog, that you have lost your bearings and cannot find your way. Suddenly, a friend appears out of the fog, and asks you to put your hand in theirs, and they will lead you home. And you, not being able to tell where you are going, trustingly follow them, even though you can only see one step at a time. Eventually you arrive safely home, filled with gratitude. But as you reflect upon the experience the next day, you realize how unsettling it was to have to keep walking when you could see only one step at a time, even though you had guidance in which you knew you could trust.

Now I have asked you to imagine all of this, because this is the essence of the second Mission to which *you* are called -- and *I* am called -- in this life. It is all very different than we had imagined. When the question, *"What is your Mission in life?"* is first broached, and we have put our hand in God's, as it were, we imagine that we will be taken up to *some mountaintop,* from which we can see far into the distance. And that we will hear a voice in our ear, saying, "Look, look, see that distant city? That is the goal of your Mission; that is where everything is leading, every step of your way."

But instead of the mountaintop, we find ourself in *the valley* -- wandering often in a fog. And the voice in our ear says something quite different from what we thought we would hear. It says, **"Your**

Mission is to take one step at a time, even when you don't yet see where it all is leading, or what the Grand Plan is, or what your overall Mission in life is. Trust Me; I will lead you."

Comment 2: The Nature of This Step-by-Step Mission

As I said, in every situation you find yourself, you have been sent here to do whatever you can -- moment by moment -- that will bring more gratitude, more kindness, more forgiveness, more honesty, and more love into this world.

There are dozens of such moments every day. Moments when you stand -- as it were -- at a spiritual crossroads, with two ways lying before you. Such moments are typically called "**moments of decision.**" It does not matter what the frame or content of each particular decision is. It all devolves, in the end, into just two roads before you, *every time*. **The one** will lead to *less* gratitude, *less* kindness, *less* forgiveness, *less* honesty, or *less* love in the world. **The other** will lead to *more* gratitude, *more* kindness, *more* forgiveness, *more* honesty, or *more* love in the world. Your Mission, each moment, is to seek to choose the latter spiritual road, rather than the former, *every time*.

Comment 3: Some Examples of This Step-by-Step Mission

I will give a few examples, so that the nature of this part of your Mission may be unmistakably clear.

You are out on the freeway, in your car. Someone has gotten into the wrong lane, to the right of *your* lane, and needs to move over into the lane you are in. You *see* their need to cut in, ahead of you. **Decision time.** In your mind's eye you see two spiritual roads lying before you: the one leading to less kindness in the world (you speed up, to shut this driver out, and don't let them move over), the other leading to more kindness in the world (you let the driver cut in). **Since you know this is part of your Mission, part of the reason why you came to Earth, your calling is clear. You know which road to take, which decision to make.**

You are hard at work at your desk, when suddenly an interruption comes. The phone rings, or someone is at the door. They need something from you, a question of some of your time and attention. **Decision time.** In your mind's eye you see two spiritual roads lying before you: the one leading to less love in the world (you tell them you're just too busy to be bothered), the other leading to more love in the world (you put aside your work, decide that God may have sent this person to you, and say, "Yes, what can I do to help you?"). **Since you know this is part of your Mission, part of the reason why you came to Earth, your calling is clear. You know which road to take, which decision to make.**

Your mate does something that hurts your feelings. **Decision time.** In your mind's eye you see two spiritual roads lying before you: the one leading to less forgiveness in the world (you institute

an icy silence between the two of you, and think of how you can punish them or otherwise get even), the other leading to more forgiveness in the world (you go over and take them in your arms, speak the truth about your hurt feelings, and assure them of your love). **Since you know this is part of your Mission, part of the reason why you came to Earth, your calling is clear. You know which road to take, which decision to make.**

You have not behaved at your most noble, recently. And now you are face-to-face with someone who asks you a question about what happened. **Decision time.** In your mind's eye you see two spiritual roads lying before you: the one leading to less honesty in the world (you lie about what happened, or what you were feeling, because you fear losing their respect or their love), the other leading to more honesty in the world (you tell the truth, together with how you feel about it, in retrospect). **Since you know this is part of your Mission, part of the reason why you came to Earth, your calling is clear. You know which road to take, which decision to make.**

Comment 4: The Spectacle Which Makes the Angels Laugh

It is necessary to explain this part of our Mission in some detail, because so many times you will see people wringing their hands, and saying, "*I want to know what my Mission in life is,*" all the while they are cutting people off on the highway, refusing to give time to people, punishing their mate for having hurt their feelings, and lying about what they did. And it will seem to you that the angels must laugh to see this spectacle. *For these people wringing their hands,* their Mission was right there, on the freeway, in the interruption, in the hurt, and at the confrontation.

Comment 5: The Valley vs. The Mountaintop

At some point in your life your Mission may involve some grand *mountaintop experience,* where you say to yourself, "This, this, is why I came into the world. I know it. I know it." *But until then,* your Mission is here in *the valley,* and the fog, and the little callings moment by moment, day by day. More to the point, it is likely you cannot ever get to your mountaintop Mission unless you have first exercised your stewardship faithfully in the valley.

It is an ancient principle, to which Jesus alluded often, that if you don't use the information the Universe has already given you, you cannot expect it will give you any more. If you aren't being faithful in small things, how can you expect to be given charge over larger things? (Luke 16:10,11,12; 19:11-24) If you aren't trying to bring more gratitude, kindness, forgiveness, honesty, and love into the world each day, you can hardly expect that you will be entrusted with the Mission to help bring peace into the world or anything else large and important. If we do not live out our day by day Mission in the valley, we cannot expect we are yet ready for a larger *mountaintop* Mission.

Comment 6: The Importance of Not Thinking of This Mission As 'Just A Training Camp'

The valley is not just a kind of "training camp." There is in your imagination even now an invisible *spiritual* mountaintop to which you may go, if you wish to see where all this is leading. And what will you see there, in the imagination of your heart, but the goal toward which all this is pointed: **that Earth might be more like heaven. That human's life might be more like God's.** That is the large achievement toward which all our day by day Missions *in the valley* are moving. This is a *large* order, but it is accomplished by faithful attention to the doing of our great Creator's **will** in little things as well as in large. It is much like the building of the pyramids in Egypt, which was accomplished by the dragging of a lot of individual pieces of stone by a lot of individual men.

The valley, the fog, the going step-by-step, is no mere training camp. The goal is real, however large. **"Thy Kingdom come, Thy will be done, on Earth, as it is in heaven."**

Some Random Comments About Your Third Mission in Life

Your third Mission here on Earth is one which is uniquely yours, and that is:

a) **to exercise that Talent which you particularly came to Earth to use -- your greatest gift which you most delight to use**
b) **in those place(s) or setting(s) which God has caused to appeal to you the most,**
c) **and for those purposes which God most needs to have done in the world.**

Comment 1: Our Mission Is Already Written, "in Our Members"

It is customary in trying to identify this part of our Mission, to advise that we should ask God, in prayer, to speak to us -- and **tell us** plainly what our Mission is. We look for a voice in the air, a thought in our head, a dream in the night, a sign in the events of the day, to reveal this thing which is otherwise *(it is said)* completely hidden. Sometimes, from just such answered prayer, people do indeed discover what their Mission is, beyond all doubt and uncertainty.

But having to wait for the voice of God to reveal what our Mission is, is not the truest picture of our situation. St. Paul, in Romans, speaks of a law "written in our members," -- and this phrase has a telling application to the question of **how** God reveals to each of us our unique Mission in life. Read again the definition of our third Mission (above) and you will see: the clear implication of the definition is that God has **already** revealed His will to us concerning our vocation and Mission, by causing it to be "**written in our members.**" We are to begin deciphering our unique Mission by studying our talents and skills, and more particularly which ones (or One) we most rejoice to use.

God actually has written His will *twice* in our members: *first in the talents* which He lodged there, and secondly *in His guidance of our heart*, as to which talent gives us the greatest pleasure from its exercise (**it is usually the one which, when we use it, causes us to lose all sense of time**).

Even as the anthropologist can examine ancient inscriptions, and divine from them the daily life of a long lost people, so we by examining **our talents** and **our heart** can *more often than we dream* divine the Will of the Living God. For true it is, our Mission is not something He **will** reveal; it is something He **has already** revealed. It is not to be found written in the sky; it is to be found written in our members.

Comment 2: Career Counseling: We Need You

Arguably, our first two Missions in life could be learned from religion alone -- without any reference whatsoever to career counseling, the subject of this book. Why then should career counseling claim that this question about our Mission in life is its proper concern, *in any way?*

It is when we come to this third Mission, which hinges so crucially on the question of our Talents, skills, and gifts, that we see the answer. If you've read the body of this book, before turning to this appendix, you know without my even saying it, how much the identification of Talents, gifts, or skills is the province of career counseling. Its expertise, indeed its *raison d'etre*, lies precisely in the identification, classification, and (forgive me) "prioritization" of Talents, skills, and gifts. To put the matter quite simply, career counseling knows how to do this better than any other discipline -- **including** traditional religion. This is not a defect of religion, but the fulfillment of something Jesus promised: "When the Spirit of truth comes, He will guide you into all truth." (John 16:12) Career counseling is part (we may hope) of that promised late-coming truth. It can therefore be of inestimable help to the pilgrim who is trying to figure out what their greatest, and most enjoyable, talent is, as a step toward identifying their unique Mission in life.

If career counseling needs religion as its helpmate in the first two stages of identifying our Mission in life, religion repays the compliment by clearly needing career counseling as **its** helpmate here in the third stage.

And this place where you are in your life right now -- facing the job-hunt and all its anxiety -- is the perfect time to seek the union within your own mind and heart of both career counseling (as in the pages of this book) and your faith in God.

Comment 3: How Our Mission Got Chosen: A Scenario for the Romantic

It is a mystery which we cannot fathom, in this life at least, as to why one of us has this talent, and the other one has that; why God chose to give one gift -- and Mission -- to one person, and a different gift -- and Mission -- to another. Since we do not know, and in some degree cannot know, we are certainly left free to speculate, and imagine.

We may imagine that before we came to Earth, our souls, *our Breath, our Light,* stood before the great Creator and volunteered for this Mission. And God and we, together, chose what that Mission would be and what particular gifts would be needed, which He then agreed to give us, after our birth. Thus, our Mission was not a command given peremptorily by an unloving Creator to a reluctant slave without a vote, but was a task jointly designed by us both, in which as fast as the great Creator said, **"I wish"** our hearts responded, **"Oh, yes."** As mentioned in an earlier Comment, it may be helpful to think of the condition of our becoming human as that we became amnesiac about any consciousness our soul had before birth -- and therefore amnesiac about the nature or manner in which our Mission was designed.

Our searching for our Mission now is therefore a searching to recover the memory of something we ourselves had a part in designing.

I am admittedly a hopeless romantic, so of course I like this picture. If you also are a hopeless romantic, you may like it too. There's also the chance that it just may be true. We will not know until we see Him face to face.

Comment 4: Mission As Intersection

There are all different kinds of voices calling you to all different kinds of work, and the problem is to find out which is the voice of God rather than that of society, say, or the superego, or self-interest. By and large a good rule for finding out is this: the kind of work God usually calls you to is the kind of work (a) that you need most to do and (b) the world most needs to have done. If you really get a kick out of your work, you've presumably met requirement (a), but if your work is writing TV deodorant commercials, the chances are you've missed requirement (b). On the other hand, if your work is being a doctor in a leper colony, you have probably met (b), but if most of the time you're bored and depressed by it, the chances are you haven't only bypassed (a) but probably aren't helping your patients much either. Neither the hair shirt nor the soft birth will do. **The place God calls you to is the place where your deep gladness and the world's deep hunger meet.**

Frederick Buechner
Wishful Thinking — A Theological ABC

Comment 5: Examples of Mission As Intersection

Your unique and individual mission will most likely turn out to be a mission of Love, acted out in one or all of three arenas: either in the Kingdom of the Mind, whose goal is to bring more Truth into the world; or in the Kingdom of the Heart, whose goal is to bring more beauty into the world; or in the Kingdom of the Will, whose goal is to bring more Perfection into the world, through Service.

Here are some examples:

"My mission is, out of the rich reservoir of love which God seems to have given me, to nurture and show love to others -- most particularly to those who are suffering from incurable diseases."

"My mission is to draw maps for people to show them how to get to God."

"My mission is to create the purest foods I can, to help people's bodies not get in the way of their spiritual growth."

"My mission is to make the finest harps I can so that people can hear the voice of God in the wind."

"My mission is to make people laugh, so that the travail of this earthly life doesn't seem quite so hard to them."

"My mission is to help people know the truth, in love, about what is happening out in the world, so that there will be more honesty in the world."

"My mission is to weep with those who weep, so that in my arms they may feel themselves in the arms of that Eternal Love which sent me and which created them."

"My mission is to create beautiful gardens, so that in the lilies of the field people may behold the Beauty of God and be reminded of the Beauty of Holiness."

Comment 6: Life As Long As Your Mission Requires

Knowing that you came to Earth for a reason, and knowing what that Mission is, throws an entirely different light upon your life from now on. You are, generally speaking, delivered from any further fear about how long you have to live. You may settle it in your heart that you are here until God chooses to think that you have accomplished your Mission, or until God has a greater Mission for you in another Realm. You need to be a good steward of what He has given you, while you are here; but you do not need to be an anxious steward or stewardess.

You need to attend to your health, *but you do not need to constantly worry about it.* You need to meditate on your death, *but you do not need to be constantly preoccupied with it.* To paraphrase the glorious words of G. K. Chesterton: **"We now have a strong desire**

for living combined with a strange carelessness about dying. We
desire life like water and yet are ready to drink death like wine."
We know that we are here to do what we came to do, and we
need not worry about anything else.

Final Comment: A Job-Hunt Done Well

If you approach your job-hunt as an opportunity to work on this
issue as well as the issue of how you will keep body and soul together, then hopefully your job-hunt will end with your being able
to say: "Life has deep meaning to me, now. I have discovered
more than my ideal job; I have found my Mission, and the reason
why I am here on Earth."

Appendix E

Questions You Have Asked:

Additional Notes

• Rules for Finding Out in Detail
The Needs or Problems of an Organization

• How Do I Job-Hunt
While I'm Still Employed?

• How Do I Survey a Place
That Is Far Away?

Rules For Finding Out In Detail The Needs
Or Problems Of An Organization

Rule No. 1: If it's a large organization that interests you, you don't need to discover the problems of the whole organization. You only need to discover the problems that are bugging the-person-who-has-the-ultimate-responsibility (or power)-to-hire-you. Conscientious job-hunters always bite off more than they can chew. If they're going to try for a job at the Telephone Company, or IBM or the Federal Government or General Motors or -- like that -- they assume they've got to find out the problems facing that whole organization. **Forget it!** Your task, fortunately, is much more manageable. Find out what problems are bugging, bothering, concerning, perplexing, gnawing at, the-person-who-has-the-power-to-hire-you. This assumes, of course, that you have first **identified** who that person is. Once you have identified her, or him, **find out everything you can about them**. The directories will help. So will the clippings, at your local library. So will any speeches they have given (ask their organization for copies, of same).

If it's a committee of sorts that actually has the responsibility (and therefore the power) to hire you, you will need to figure out who that one individual is (or two) who sways the others. You know, the one whose judgment the others respect. How do you find that out? By using your contacts, of course. Someone will know someone who knows that whole committee, and can tell you who their **real** leader is. It's not necessarily the one who got elected as Chairperson.

Rule No. 2: Don't assume the problems have to be huge, complex and hidden. The problems bothering the-person-who-has-the-power-to-hire-you may be small, simple, and obvious. If the job you are aiming at was previously filled by someone (i.e., the one who, if you get hired, will be referred to as "your predecessor"), the problems that are bothering the-person-who-has-the-power-to-hire-you may be uncovered simply by finding out through your contacts what bugged your prospective boss about your predecessor. Samples:

"They were never to work on time, took long lunch breaks, and were out sick too often"; OR

"They were good at typing, but had lousy skills over the telephone"; OR

"They handled older people well, but just couldn't relate to the young"; OR

"I never could get them to keep me informed about what they were doing"; etc.

Sometimes, it's as simple as that. Don't assume the problems *have to be* huge and complex. In your research you may be thinking to yourself, "Gosh, this firm has a huge public relations problem; I'll have to show them that I could put together a whole crash P.R. program." That's the huge, complex, and hidden problem that you think the-person-who-has-the-power-to-hire-you **ought to be concerned about.** But, in actual fact, what they *are* concerned about is whether (unlike your predecessor) you're going to get to work on time, take assigned lunch breaks, and not be out sick too often. Don't overlook the Small, Simple, and Obvious Problems which bug almost every employer.

Rule No. 3: In most cases, your task is not that of educating your prospective employer, but of trying to read their mind. Now, to be sure, you may have uncovered -- during your research -- some problem that the-person-who-has-the-power-to-hire-you is absolutely unaware of. And you may be convinced that this problem is **so crucial** that for you even to mention it will instantly win you their undying gratitude. Maybe. But don't bet on it. Our files are filled with sad testimonies like the following:
"I met with the VP, Marketing, in a major local bank, on the recommendation of an officer, and discussed with him a program I devised to reach the female segment of his market, which would not require any new services, except education, enlightenment, and encouragement. His comment at the end of the discussion was that the bank president had been after him for three years to develop a program for women, and he wasn't about to do it because the only reason, in his mind, for the president's request was reputation enhancement on the president's part . . . "

Interoffice politics, as in this case, or other considerations may prevent your prospective employer from being at all receptive to Your Bright Idea. In any event, you're not trying to find out what **might** motivate them to hire you. Your research has got to be devoted rather to finding out what **already does** motivate them **when they decide to hire someone for the position you are interested in.** In other words, you are trying to find out What's **Already** Going On In Their Mind. In this sense, your task is more akin to a kind of mindreading than it is to education. (Though **some** people-who-have-the-power-to-hire are **very** open to being educated. You have to decide whether you want to risk testing this.)

Rule No. 4: There are various ways of finding out what's going on in their mind; don't try just one way. We will give a kind of outline, here, of the various ways. (You can use this as a checklist.)

 Analyzing the Organization at a Distance and Making Some Educated Guesses.

1. If the organization is expanding, then they need:

    a. More of what they already have; OR

    b. More of what they already have, but with different style, added skills, or other pluses; OR

    c. Something they don't presently have: a new kind of person, with new skills doing a new function or service.

2. If the organization is continuing as is, then they need:

    a. To replace people who were fired (find out why; what was lacking:); OR

b. To replace people who quit (find out what was prized about them); OR

c. To create a new position. Yes, this happens even in organizations that are not expanding, due to:

  1) Old needs which weren't provided for, earlier, but now must be, even if they have to cut out some other function or position.
  2) Revamping assignments within their present staff.

3. If the organization is reducing its size, staff, or product or service, then they --

a. Have not yet decided which staff to terminate, i.e., which functions to give low priority to (in which case **that** is their problem, and you may be able to help them identify which functions are "core-functions"); OR

b. **Have** decided which functions or staff to terminate (in which case they may need multi-talented people or generalists able to do several jobs, i.e., functions, instead of just one, as formerly).

b
Analyzing the problems of the-person-who-has-the-power to-hire-you by talking to them directly.

It may be that your paths have accidentally crossed (it happens). Perhaps you attend the same church or synagogue. Perhaps you eat at the same restaurant. In any event, if you **do** ever have a chance to talk to her or him, listen carefully to whatever they may say about the place where they work. The greatest problem every employer faces is finding people who will listen and take them seriously. If you listen, you may find this employer discusses their problems -- giving you firmer grounds to which you can relate your skills.

c
Analyzing the problems of the person-who-has-the-power-to-hire-you by talking to their "opposite number" in another organization which is similar (not to say, almost identical) to the one that interests you.

If, for some reason, you cannot approach -- at this time -- the organization that interests you (it's too far away, or you don't want to tip your hand yet, or whatever), what you can do is pick a similar organization (or individual) where you are -- and go find out what kind of problems are on their mind. (If you are interested in working for, say, a senator in another state, you can talk to a senator's staff here where you are, first. The problems are likely to be similar.)

d | *Analyzing the problems of a prospective employer by talking to the person who held the job before you -- OR by talking to their "opposite number" in another similar/identical organization.*

Nobody, absolutely nobody, knows the problems bugging a boss so much as someone who works, or used to work, for them. If they **still** work for them, they may have a huge investment in being discreet (i.e., not as candid as you need). Ex-employees are **not** necessarily any longer under that sort of pressure. Needless to say, if you're trying to get the organization to create a new position, there is no "previous employee." But in some identical or similar organization **which already has this sort of position,** you can still find someone to interview.

e | *Using your contacts/friends/everyone you meet, in order to find someone who:*

1. Knows the organization that interests you, or knows someone who knows;
2. Knows the-person-who-has-the-power-to-hire-you, or knows someone who knows;
3. Knows who their opposite number is in a similar/identical organization;
4. Knows your predecessor, or knows someone who knows;
5. Knows your "opposite number" in another organization, or knows someone who knows.

Supplementary Method: Research in the library, on the organization, or an organization similar to it; research on the-individual-who-has-the-power-to-hire-you, or on their opposite number in another organization, etc. (Ask your friendly librarian or research librarian for help -- tell them what you're trying to find out.)

See also the books listed in on page 123ff.

Rule No. 5: Ultimately, this is a language-translation problem. You're trying to take your language (i.e., a description of your skills), and translate it into their language (i.e., their priorities, their values, their jargon, as these surface within their concerns, problems, etc.). As I emphasized in chapter 6, most of the-people-who-have-the-power-to-hire-you for the position you want **do not** like the word "problems." It reminds them that they are mortal, have hangups, haven't solved something yet, or that they overlooked something, etc. "Smartass" is the word normally reserved for someone who comes in and **shows them up.** (This isn't true of **every** employer or manager, but it's true of altogether too many.) Since you're trying to use **their** language, you should probably speak of "an area you probably are planning to move into" or "a concern of yours" or "a challenge currently facing you" or **anything** except: "By the way, I've uncovered a problem you have." Use the word **problems** in your own head, but don't blurt it out during the interview with your prospective employer, **unless you hear them use it first.**

But in your own private thinking, your goal is to be able to speak in the interview of Your Skills **in terms of The Language** of Their Problems. Here are some examples, in order to bring this all home:

The person who has the power to hire you, was bugged by or concerned about:	You therefore use language which emphasizes that you:
Your predecessor had all the skills, but was too serious about everything.	have all the skills (name them) plus you have a sense of humor.
This place is expanding, and now needs a training program for its employees.	have the skills to do training, and in the area they are concerned about.
All the picayune details they have to attend to, which they would like to shovel off on someone else.	are very good with details and follow-up. (That had better be true, or don't say it.)
Their magazine probably isn't covering all the subjects that it should, but that's just a gnawing feeling, and they've never had time to document it, and decide what areas to move into.	have done a complete survey of its table of contents for the last ten years, can show what they've missed, and have outlined sample articles in those missing areas.

How Do I Job-Hunt While I'm Still Employed?

Many job-hunting books assume that you are unemployed, and hence have complete freedom as to how you allot your time. But what do you do about the job-hunt or career-change, if you are presently holding down a full-time job?

Good question. That is the case in which many find themselves. How many? Well, the government, bless its heart, did a study of job-hunting among employed workers about eight years ago, and discovered that in a typical month -- it was May ten years ago -- 4.2% of all employed workers, or one out of every twenty, went looking for another job sometime during that month. In actual numbers, that represented 3,269,000 people who were job-hunting while still employed. If the same percentage obtains today, it means 4,900,000 are currently employed but job-hunting.

I would like to point out two things about this finding. First of all, it means that one-third of *all* job-hunters are conducting the search while they are still employed.

Secondly, they *must* be successful. There's a lot of movement going on, in the world of work. The *average* nonagricultural firm in this country has to hire -- in a typical year -- as many new people as it has employees. In other words, a firm with three employees will probably have to hire two or three employees each year. A firm with 100 employees will probably have to hire 90 new employees each year. That's on the average. If you want a more detailed breakdown, this is what the study turned up: the average retail firm with say 100 employees may have to hire 136 new people each year; the average firm dealing in services and having say 100 employees may have to hire 111 new employees each year; the average financial institution, 74; the average manufacturing firm, 65; the average transportation or public utilities company, 32; and the average construction company, a whopping 202 new employees for every 100 it currently has.

It is this job-hunting behavior on the part of employed workers which helps to create so many vacancies -- thus increasing *every* job-hunter's chance of success so dramatically.

How do employed job-hunters go about their search? You guessed it: the same way unemployed job-hunters do. According to the government's study, 70% of all employed job-hunters contacted an employer directly. But, back to our original question: how do you find time to do the job-hunt if you are presently holding down a full-time job? We have asked employed job-hunters how they did it, and the sum of their advice to you -- based on their experience -- is:

(1) Determine to keep at it, with every spare hour you can find. Press evenings, weekends, lunch hours and the like, into the service of your job-hunt.

(2) Use evenings and weekends to do the original homework, figuring out what your skills are and what it is you want to do, as well as where you want to do it. Later on in your job-search, use evenings and the weekend also to write thank-you notes, send out letters, and the like.

(3) For the actual calling upon potential employers, if they are in the city where you presently work, press your lunch hours into service. If you "brown-bag it," you will have time to make and keep one appointment, particularly if your intent is to make the interview no longer than twenty minutes -- a good idea, in any case, for the exploratory or information interview. People take lunch hours at all different times: 11:15 a.m., 11:45, 12 noon, 12:30, 1 p.m. While you are on your lunch hour, somebody you want to see hasn't gone to lunch yet, or has just come back. Sometimes you can move your lunch hour -- if the place where you are presently working is flexible about that -- to the 11 a.m.-12 noon time slot.

(4) Press late afternoons into service. Many people you will want to see are on an executive or management level, and they often do not get away from their offices promptly at 5. It is appropriate to estimate how long it will take you to get across town to them, and ask them if they could see you that long after your quitting time, on a particular day.

(5) Press holidays into service. Holidays fall into two classes: those which everyone observes, like Christmas and New Year's Day; and those which some people observe, like Washington's Birthday, etc. In the case of the latter kind of holiday, if you have it off, you will sometimes be able to visit the people you want to see, because they do not have it off.

(6) Press Saturdays into service. Sometimes the people you want to see work on Saturday, or are occasionally willing to set up appointments for Saturday.

(7) Press your sick leave into service. In some organizations, workers accumulate sick leave, and have the right to take it as time off. If that is the case with you, use such days off judiciously, to visit potential employers who interest you.

(8) Press your vacations into service. If you are dead-serious about the importance of your job-hunt or career-change, it is not too great a sacrifice to devote one year's vacation time to your job-hunt. This is especially important if you are trying to secure employment in a distant city. Schedule your vacation in that city, and make arrangements and appointments, by letter and phone, ahead of time.

(9) If you have sufficient savings, the following stratagem may be one you would like to consider in addition to all the above: If you have a whole list of people and places you need to visit, and you require a concentrated period of time in which to do this, and cannot wait until your vacation time, you have the right to ask your present employer if you can have a leave of absence without pay. So long as the time requested is no longer than a week or so, and so long as it is scheduled at the convenience of the employer (i.e., not in the week that they need you the most), this request will often be honored. You can give, as the reason, the simple truth: Personal Business.

Should you feel guilty about job-hunting while you are still employed? Well, sure, if you want to. But there is no need. One-third of all job-hunters are doing the same thing: it is a common practice in our economy. Nothing oddball about it. Moreover, remember these simple truths: Your employer has certain rights, including the right to fire you at any time, for sufficient cause; moreover, they have the right to prepare for this act of firing ahead of time, laying the groundwork, transferring part of your work to other colleagues, etc. You, as employee, likewise have certain rights, including the right to quit at any time, for sufficient cause; moreover, you have the right to prepare for this act of quitting ahead of time, laying the groundwork through interviewing and job-searching.

How Do I Survey a Place
That Is Far Away?

1. *If you are researching a far-away place, set down on paper which information-searches you can do right where you are, and which ones you need others' help with, in the city or place of your choice.*

Your two lists will *probably* come out looking like this:

Searches I Can Do Here	Searches Others Must Do There
A- (in detail:)	
B- (in detail:)	the rest of
C- some detail	C-
D-	D-
E-	E- in detail
F- some	F-

2. *Figure out if there isn't* **some way** *in the near future that you could go visit the city or cities of your choice.*

You may be able to do this even if you are presently employed. Does a vacation fall within the time period you have between now and when you must finally have that job? Could you visit it on vacation? Could you take a summer job there? Go there on leave? Get sent to a convention there? Get appointed to a group or association that meets there? Think it through. You will *have* to go there, finally (in almost all cases) for the actual job interview(s). *If worst comes to worst*, go there a week or so ahead of that interview. Better late than never, to look over the scene in person, and do some on-site research.

3. *For the time being, regard the city or town where you presently are, as a replica of the city or town you are interested in going to (in some respects at least) -- so that some of your research can be done where you are, and then its learnings transferred.*

You recall earlier we discussed the case of a man who loved psychiatry, and plants, and carpentry, and discovered that there was a branch of psychiatry which used plants in the treatment of deeply withdrawn patients. So, our man discovered an occupation where he could use his love of plants and his love of psychiatry together (and presumably use his carpentry to build the planters that would be needed). Suppose you were this man. Having found this out in the place where you live, you could then write to your target city or town to ask, What psychiatric facilities do you have *there*, and which ones -- if any -- use plants in their healing program?

Thus can you conduct your research where you are, and then transfer its learnings to the place where you want to go.

4. *Until you can physically go there, use every resource and contact you have, in order to explore the answers to C, D, and E, on page 369 ff.*

* THE DAILY OR WEEKLY NEWSPAPER THERE.

Almost all papers will mail to subscribers anywhere in the world. So: subscribe, for a six-month period, or a year. You'd be surprised at what you can learn from the paper. Some of the answers to C, D, E and F will appear there. Additionally, from the ads and business news items, you will know which businesses are growing and expanding -- hence, hiring -- in that city.

* THE CHAMBER OF COMMERCE, AND CITY HALL
(OR THE TOWN HALL) THERE.

These are the places whose interest it is (in most cases) to attract newcomers, and to tell them what kinds of businesses there are in town -- as well as some details about them. So: write and ask them, in the beginning, what information they have about the city or town in general. Then later, don't hesitate to write back to them with more specific questions, as your target organizations become clearer in your mind.

* THE LOCAL LIBRARY OR REFERENCE LIBRARIAN,
IF YOUR TARGET CITY/TOWN HAS ONE.

It is perfectly permissible for you to write to the library in your target city, asking for information that may be only there. If the librarian is too busy to answer, then use one of your contacts there to find out. "Bill (or Billie) I need some information that I'm afraid only the library in your town has. Specifically, I need to know about company x." Or whatever.

* YOUR CONTACTS.

Yes, of course, you know people in whatever city or town you're researching. For openers, write to your old high school and get the alumni list for your graduating class. If you went to college, ask for their alumni list also (for your class, at the very least). Subscribe to your college's alumni bulletin for further news, addresses, and hints. If you belong to a church or

synagogue, write to the church or synagogue in your target city, and tell them that you're one of their own and you need some information. "I need to know who can tell me what nonprofit organizations there are in that city, that deal with x." "I need to know how I can find out what corporations in town have departments of mental hygiene." Or, whatever. To find further contacts, ask your family and relatives who *they* know in the target city or town of your choice. You will find, upon patient and persistent exploration, that you know or can contact far more people in that city, who might help you, than you would originally think.

* THE APPROPRIATE STATE, COUNTY, AND LOCAL GOVERNMENT AGENCIES, ASSOCIATIONS, ETC.
Ask your contacts to tell you what that appropriate agency might be, for the field or kinds of organizations (or jobs) that you are interested in.

FOR THAT FARAWAY CITY, SEND YOURSELF

It will ultimately be *essential* for you to visit the geographical area you want to work in -- if it's not where you presently live.

If going into a strange new geographical area is a totally new experience for you, and you have no friends there in your chosen area, just remember there are various ways of meeting people, making friends, and developing contacts rather quickly with people who share some interest or enthusiasm of yours. There are athletic clubs, Y's, churches, charitable and community organizations, where you can present yourself and meet people, from the moment you walk in the doors. You will soon develop many acquaintances, and some beginning friendships, and the place won't seem so lonely after all.

Also, visit or write your high school before you set out for this new town and find out what graduates live in the area that you are going to be visiting for the first time: they are your friends already, because you went to the same school. As I indicated earlier, all of these acquaintances, friends and key individuals have one common name: contacts. Contacts, CONTACTS.

Once you get there, you will want to talk to key individuals *who can suggest other people you might talk to, as you try to find out what organizations interest you.* You will want to define these key individuals in your distant city ahead of time and let them know you are coming. Your list may include: friends, college alumni (if you attended college), high school pals, church or synagogue contacts, Chamber of Commerce executives, city manager, regional planning offices, appropriate county or state offices in your area of interest, the Mayor, and high level management in particular companies that look interesting from what you've read or heard about them.

When you "hit town," you will want to remember the City Directory, the Yellow Pages of your phone book, etc. You *may* want to put a modest-sized advertisement in the paper once you are in your chosen geographical area (or in the place where you currently live, if that is where you intend to do your job-hunting), saying you would like to meet with other people who are following the job-hunting techniques of *What Color Is Your Parachute?* That way you'll form a kind of 'job-hunters anonymous,' where you can mutually support one another in your hunt. With such help, or by yourself, you then set about the process. A job-hunter describes it:

"Suppose I arrived cold in some city, the one place in all the world I want to live -- but with no idea of what that city might hold as a match and challenge for my 'personal-talent bank.' I have an economic survey to make, yes; but I also have an equally or more important personal survey to accomplish. Can this city meet my peculiarly personal needs? To find out, I meet Pastors, bankers, school principals, physicians, dentists, real estate operators, et al. I would be astonished if opportunities were not brought to my attention, together with numerous offers of personal introduction to key principals. All I would be doing is forging links (referrals) in a chain leading to my eventual targets. *The referral is the key.*"

HOW HARD SHOULD I WORK AT THIS?

We kept score with one man's job-hunt. He was researching a distant place. While still at a distance, by means of diligent research he turned up 107 places that seemed interesting to him. Over a period of some time, he sent a total of 297 letters to them. He also made a total of 126 phone calls to that city. When he was finally able to go there in person, he had narrowed the original 107 that looked interesting, down to just 45. He visited all 45, while there. Having done his homework on himself thoroughly and well, -- and having obviously conducted *this* part of his search in an extremely professional manner, he received 35 job offers. When he had finished his survey, he went back to the one job he most wanted -- and accepted it.

No one can argue that you should be dealing with numbers of this magnitude. But this may at least give you some idea of *how hard you may need to work* at this. Certainly, we're not just talking about five letters and two phone calls. We're talking about rolling up your sleeves, and being *very thorough.*

In Memoriam
(continued from page xv)

Inside his heart,
As I saw
From the first time that we met.

That was in Anno Domini
Year 1969.
I had heard of him,
This man with the golden brain,
When I was first doing my research
For the book that would be
Parachute.
Saw his name in a blue and white book
Found at the Presidio
In San Francisco.
A book called then, as it is now,
Who's Hiring Who.
It had ads, in those days;
Saw his ad,
McLean Virginia.
Made a mental note,
The next time I am there,
Be sure to look him up.
He looked like he knew
What he was doing.
Got close to McLean,
Ran out of time,
Decided not to go.
But then a phone call,
A lucky one,
To the author
Of **Who's Hiring Who,**
Who said, "You couldn't have possibly
Gotten me
At a worse time.
I've got a deadline to meet,
And I have no time to talk.
But were I in your shoes,"
(Dick Lathrop said)
"I'd go out to McLean and talk
To a man there named John Crystal."
"I saw his name,
But I haven't time."
"Make it," said he.
So I did.

John Crystal, Diane Piliere, and Dick Bolles

Called at 2:30,
On bended knee,
He could see me at 5,
He said graciously.
We talked until 8,
And I marveled all through
Those hours we talked
At how much he knew.

Well, he was impressed,
As we talked and palavered for hours
That I was a good listener
Or maybe a good farmer,
Able to separate
The wheat from the chaff
In all I had learned
Thus far about the job-hunt.

He was open, direct,
And he held nothing back,
Told me all that he knew
About whatever I asked.
"Writing a book,"
He said,
"To tell the hapless job-hunter
About what's wrong with
The job-hunting system
In this country,
And how to take charge
Of your job-hunt
For yourself?"
He practically rubbed his hands in glee
At the thought that someone
Somewhere
Was willing to listen
To his thoughts about how job-hunting really
Ought to be done,
And was going to put it all in print
Where people could read it
And weep
Before they sowed
New jobs and new careers.

We were kindred souls
And knew it instantly, but
I had to go home,
So across the miles
He began putting every article
He had ever written,
Every clipping
He had ever saved,
Every case history
He had ever studied
About how to improve
The job-hunting "system"
(He always used that word
In quotes,
Or -- when in a merry mood --
Would say, with a smile,
"Our country's job-hunting
Expletive-deleted.")
He put the clippings,
Articles and the case
Histories
Into large manila envelopes
And mailed them off to me
Day after day
Week after week
Three thousand miles away.

It was not the best timing, believe me.
I had already devoured
In book stores
And libraries
Every book that had ever been written
On job-hunting
Or career change
(There were only about eight
At the time;
It was still 1969)
So, naturally
I thought my reading days were done
And the writing time had come.
But I had not counted on meeting
Mister John Curry Crystal:
My reading days
Had only begun.
The stack of materials
Which he sent
Got
Higher

And
Higher
Each day the mailman came. So
My reading got faster,
My learning got greater,
My mastery of the subject got better
As those envelopes kept arriving
From Mr. J.C.C.

Eventually I wrote
The book.
September 15 I began,
November 27th I was done
In the year of Our Lord
1970.
Decided to self-publish the thing,
Handed it to our local copy shop,
In downtown San Francisco.
The number of pages: 169.
"Can you print it,
Bind it,
Put a cover on it?"
I asked.
Why sure, they said,
In just three days.
So December 1st then it was done.
And the first copy went,
By airmail, naturally
To Mister John Curry Crystal
In the city of McLean.

He was mighty pleased,
Yes mighty mighty pleased
At what his clippings
And my pen had wrought.

I gave him copies of the book
And he sent them to everyone
He could think of.
Two thousand copies, easily
Went through our hands
Down to the old P.O.
And this kept up for a year or so
Until one April day, in '72
A Mr. Philip Wood of Ten Speed Press
In Berkeley Californ-eye-ay
Wrote to me across the Bay
To say he'd like to take it
Off my hands,

If I wouldn't mind.
Mind?
Was this an I.Q. test?

November that year it was fait accompli,
John was so glad, he was, to see
The book in print
So when Eye Triple E
(IEEE)
Approached him one year later
About putting his career counseling system
In print, John said he'd do it
Only if
I was to be the writer.
The then Department of Health
Education
And Welfare
Was underwriting the cost,
So they said "Sure," and down I went
To live in old D.C.
For several months.
"Your job,"
They said, "is to turn John's art
Into a science,
If that can be done."

"Well, we'll see,"
Said I.
And took up residence
At the W.E. Upjohn Institute
For Employment Research,
With an office in the building
Where the giants in the field,
Sidney Fine,
And Harold Sheppard
And Harvey Belitsky
Did daily walk those halls.
And every morning I'd study
The files
That John had delivered to me,
And every p.m.
Around 2 or so,
John would drive in from Virginia
With more files, case histories
Of all the people he'd helped
Through the years.
He'd spent an average of 32 hours
Just doing the paperwork
On each of his old clients.

"Art into science!"
I often fumed.
"Just how do you ever
Do that?"

Well, each afternoon
We'd go on outdoors
And sit there at some small cafe
And talk and talk
For hours at a time.
I had my questions
From studying the files
All written out,
Each afternoon,
"Now John, just how did you do this?
Or, "How did you know that?"
And his opening response
Was always the same:
He'd puff on his omnipresent cigarette
(In those past ignorant days)
And say,
"Well, Dick, no one's ever
Asked me that
Before."
It got to be a ritual,
A litany, a joke
Between us,
Day after day:
"Well, Dick, no one's ever asked me that
Before."
"Well, that's fine, John;
But somebody's asking it now."

One night I had to interview John
On a subject most difficult:
'How Do You Survive
After You've Gotten the Job?'
So we went to a little restaurant,
Over in McLean,
And there over a pitcher of sangrias
We talked far into the night,
With me taking notes
On the only thing I had remembered to bring:
The backs of little calling cards,
While we both laughed
'Til the tears rolled down our cheeks
At this spectacle of
Great ideas jotted down
On little calling cards.

I wrote the book, at last:
Where Do I Go
From Here
With My Life?
It was published in '74.
Sidney Fine,
By then our friend,
Wrote the preface to it, while
John and I took credit
As coauthors.

And so it went,
Over all the years
There came no parting
Of the ways.
For, kindred souls are
Kindred souls.
We stayed real close - -
Dinners whenever one of us
Was in town near
To where the other lived.
Workshops taught together,
Walks together
Through pretty parks,
Long talks
On our philosophy
About God and the universe
And man.
And woman.
Phone calls
Once a month
And time together,
Precious time.
Two weeks together last summer
And two weeks together this summer
Just days before his death.

Now he is gone, and
We who knew him weep for our loss, but
This book is his memorial,
My life his testament,
And we believe
That he lives on
In heaven now - -
A place no one has seen.

But I am hopeful that it has
Some heavenly cafe,
And there he sits,

The man with the golden brain,
Asking questions, while God says,
"Well, John,
No one's ever asked me that, before."
After which, of course,
John offers to help
- - If the Lord wouldn't mind - -
With the employment
Of the angels.

John Crystal was born September 18, 1920 in Fort Hamilton, New York, the youngest of three children of Colonel Thomas Crystal and Isabel Crystal. A graduate of Plattsburgh (N.Y.) High School and thence of Columbia University in New York City, with a degree in economics. He served in the intelligence arm of the Army during World War II, serving in North Africa and Italy for three years. After the war he helped set up the Middle East, North African and European operations of Sears, Roebuck and Co., serving as their first manager there. He was subsequently Executive Vice President of William John Mindlin and Company, and he also worked for Warner-Lambert International. He then worked for a brief time for Bernard Haldane Associates, and thence in his own career counseling firm, Shipley and Crystal, in Washington, D.C. He then started Crystal Management Services of McLean, Virginia, during which time he contributed to Parachute *and also coauthored the book* Where Do I Go From Here With My Life? *He subsequently moved to New York City where he and Nella Barkley founded the Crystal-Barkley Corporation and its John C. Crystal Center at 111 East 31st Street in Manhattan, of which he was chairman for a number of years until his death, September 10, 1988, of acute emphysema. He was buried with full military honors at West Point, New York, alongside his father and brother. He is survived by a daughter, Barbara Ann of Annandale, Virginia, a sister, Isabel Merriam, of Bonner Springs, Kansas, and by his beloved fiancee, Diane Piliere, of Montclair, New Jersey. Diane and John had just spent the month of June and part of July in John's beloved Austria, and Switzerland, and half of the month of August out in Bend, Oregon, with me and the participants at our annual two-week workshop, immediately prior to his hospitalization and subsequent death.*

R.N.B.

Author's Notes

As most of you know, this book is revised each year - - substantially.
(It takes us about two months.) This isn't a ploy to sell more books.
I do it because of my desire to make this the most helpful and up-to-
date book that it can possibly be. New and more helpful resources or
ideas for helping the job-hunter or career-changer appear every year.
Also in my annual two-week workshop in Bend, Oregon, I discover
(with my colleague Daniel Porot) clearer and clearer ways of explaining old techniques. Also, each year I get better tools for doing the
revisions: this year the whole book got put on computer disk (I work
on a Macintosh Plus) so I was able to rewrite and rearrange the entire
book for greater clarity (an endless task). I am deeply grateful to
every job-hunter or career-changer who has written to express how
much this book changed their life, and to tell me which particular
ideas, thoughts, or parts of the book they found particularly helpful.
That ensures that in my annual revisions I don't accidentally eliminate
an idea which readers found useful or inspiring.

This year, necessity dictated I also lay out a more helpful job-
hunting "map" that more job-hunters could understand and use, so I
created a new "map" which is Appendix A this year - - although parts
of it are also to be found in chapters 4 and 5. For those counselors
familiar with (and enamored of) the old "map," I'm sorry but I received
enough letters from readers to convince me it had to be changed
and improved. This 1989 one has all the parts of the old but it works
much better; as usual, it will **ultimately** be available as a separate
instrument from Ten Speed Press. For the foreseeable future, the
"old" map will still be available from them.

Last year's Appendix on "Finding One's Mission in Life" is in the
book again this year, because so many readers asked to have it remain
in. I am still working on future Appendices related to "Personal Computers and Job-Hunting" and "Job-Hunting and the Handicapped,"
though I'm not going to say when they will appear. In due time.
For me at least, writing is like baking a cake. It's done when it's done.

And now my usual, but nonetheless heartfelt, annual litany of
thanks: the major clerical work on this revision, particularly the
Appendices, was done again this year by Erica Chambré. As I say
each year, I literally could not have accomplished this revision without
her. She is my right hand, having first started working for me fourteen
years ago, and by now she knows my mind in all things.

As for the book after it leaves my hands, I want to express for
the umpteenth time my great debt of gratitude and affection for
Bev Anderson, who has done the layout of this book (and all my
other works) year after year, since it first came out in '72. She is

not only a genius, but a delight to work with. I want also to acknowledge Haru Watanabe, who typesets the six chapters of this book - -
and does it with diligence and great faithfulness. My thanks also to
Carl Haeberle and Laura at The Mac Studio for their excellent work
on the Appendices.

Behind the scenes, my deep gratitude as always to Phil Wood, my
publisher and - - in these later years - - friend. I would give my books
to no other. I appreciate all the help that his associate, George Young,
and Jackie Wan give each year in helping this book get done and get
done right.

I thank all those leaders in this field of career development or
job-hunting, who have shared with me their wisdom, their ideas and
most of all their friendship over the years: Daniel Porot, Sidney Fine,
Peter Drucker, Arthur Miller, Dick Lathrop, Tom and Ellie Jackson,
John Holland, Bob Wegmann, Howard Figler, Carol Christen, and
above all, the late John Crystal.

I would like also to publicly acknowledge the Lord God, our
Great Creator, as the One who has given me the talents and the
inspiration to write this book - - and the will to revise it yearly. Indeed,
He has given me whatever gifts and compassion I possess. My thanks
to my dear Aunt, Sister Esther Mary, now in her eighties, who has
taught me so much about this - - from my youth up. And finally,
I want to thank my wife, Carol, for all her encouragement and love
over the years. As all who know her will attest, she is a wonderful
woman, I am most blessed to be her husband, and the lucky thing is,
I know it.

R.N.B.
P. O. Box 379
Walnut Creek, CA 94597

October 14, 1989

A Grammar Footnote

I want to explain why singular verbs are used throughout this book with the apparently
plural pronouns "they" or "them" or "their." Casey Miller and Kate Swift, authors of
the classic *The Handbook of Nonsexist Writing* suggested this approach. In their book,
and in their correspondence with me, they contended that the pronoun "they" once
was treated as both plural and singular in the English language, just as "you" was and is;
but with respect to "them" this usage changed at a time in English history when
agreement *in number* became more important than agreement *in gender*. Faced today
with such common artifices as s/he, or he/she, they argue that it is time now to bring
back the earlier usage of "they," because given the sexist consciousness of most writers

and readers these days, agreement in gender is now more important than agreement in number. They further argue that this return to an earlier usage has already become quite common out on the street -- witness a sign by the ocean which reads "Anyone using this beach after 5 p.m. does so at their own risk." So, this is what I have done. I offer this explanation because I have gotten my share of letters from grammarians who, when they see "they" used with a singular verb, dash off scolding letters to authors -- that say, "If you want to be a writer, start by cleaning up your grammar!"

As for my commas, which invariably offend unemployed English teachers so much that they write me to apply for a job as my editor -- in order to save unnecessary correspondence I guess I'd better also explain these. The commas are all deliberately used according to my own rules -- rather than according to the rules of historic grammar (which I do know). My own rules are: write conversationally, and put in a comma *wherever I would normally stop for a breath, were I speaking the same line.*

INDEX

Update for 1990

To: PARACHUTE
        P.O. Box 379
        Walnut Creek, CA 94597

☐   I think that the information in the '89 edition needs to be
        changed, in your next revision, regarding (or, the following
        resource should be added):

_____

_____

_____

_____

_____

☐   I cannot find the following resource, listed on page _____ :

_____

_____

_____

_____

_____

Name _____

Address _____

_____

(Please submit this before June 1, 1989. Thank you.)

Other Books by Richard N. Bolles

THE THREE BOXES OF LIFE
And How To Get Out Of Them

"Parachute" has reshaped the way people think about jobs and how to find them. *The Three Boxes of Life* calls for as much change in the way we think about school, work, and retirement.
" . . . a rich and rewarding guidebook that provides literally hundreds of resources and opportunities for growth."—*Library Journal.* "Why aren't learning, working, and playing, lifelong—simultaneous—activities rather than boxes or blocks of times as we traditionally have been taught they must be?"—*American School Board Journal.* " . . . truly a monumental work which provides a wealth of information."—*Journal of College Placement.* " . . . an eloquent plea for the restructuring of our work lives."—*Career Planning and Adult Development Newsletter.*

Contains hundreds of resources, exercises, charts, illustrations and the complete *Beginning Quick Job-Hunting Map.* 6 x 9 inches, 480 pages, $9.95 paper. $14.95 cloth

WHERE DO I GO FROM HERE WITH MY LIFE?
by John C. Crystal and Richard N. Bolles

Here is *the workbook* for the self-motivated individual, student, professional or anyone who has an interest in a systematic approach to job-hunting and career mobility, bringing together two of the leading people in the field. "A master work in career literature." *Washington Star-News.* 9 x 7 inches, 272 pages, $9.95 paper

THE NEW QUICK JOB-HUNTING MAP
Advanced Version

A practical book of exercises designed to give job seekers detailed help in analyzing their skills, finding the right career field, and knowing how to find job openings and get hired. This is a 48-page version, 8½ x 11 inches, of the exercises printed in this book, $1.95 paper.

THE QUICK JOB-HUNTING MAP FOR BEGINNERS
Offers special help to new job seekers and others looking for their first jobs. 8½ x 11 inches, 32 pages, $1.25 paper

TEA LEAVES:
A New Look At Resumes

Richard Bolles describes how well resumes work, or don't work, and why. Also what you can do about it. 6 x 9 inches, 24 pages, $.50

Available at your local book store, or when ordering direct from the publisher please include $.75 additional per clothbound copy for postage and handling, or $.50 additional per paperback copy for postage and handling.

1👁 TEN SPEED PRESS • Box 7123, Berkeley, California 94707
